Modern Family

Modern Family

The Untold Oral History of One of Television's Groundbreaking Sitcoms

Marc Freeman

ST. MARTIN'S
PRESS
NEW YORK

First published in the United States by St. Martin's Press,
an imprint of St. Martin's Publishing Group

MODERN FAMILY. Copyright © 2020 by Marc Freeman. Foreword copyright © 2020
by Christopher Lloyd. All rights reserved. Printed in the United States of America. For
information, address St. Martin's Publishing Group, 120 Broadway, New York, NY 10271.

www.stmartins.com

Photographs on page 491 courtesy of the author

Designed by Steven Seighman

The Library of Congress Cataloging-in-Publication Data is available upon request.

ISBN 978-1-250-26003-1 (hardcover)
ISBN 978-1-250-26004-8 (ebook)

Our books may be purchased in bulk for promotional, educational, or business use. Please
contact your local bookseller or the Macmillan Corporate and Premium Sales Department at
1-800-221-7945, extension 5442, or by email at MacmillanSpecialMarkets@macmillan.com.

First Edition: 2020

10 9 8 7 6 5 4 3 2 1

Contents

Foreword

My thoughts often go back to August 2009. The pilot has been shot and the series has been ordered, but apart from a relative handful of studio, network, and advertising people, no one in America has a clue what *Modern Family* is.

Which means that we are showing up to work at the barn that is stage 5 on the Fox Studio lot, and we are, eighty or so of us, making episodes of a thing that isn't really a thing yet.

But there is an unmistakable suspicion that what we are making may be . . . well, we would never have used the word *good* or *special* or any other terms to tempt the itchy fingers of the lightning bolt–wielding comedy gods. But it did feel promising.

How else to describe the sensation of discovering that Sofía Vergara isn't just beautiful but is a first-rate clown? Or that Ed O'Neill can do more with a raised eyebrow than most actors can do with a soliloquy? Or that Julie Bowen and Ty Burrell, both consummate professionals, are reducing each other to a demonstrably unprofessional level of laughter mid-take on a daily basis? Or that Eric Stonestreet's rubbery face is making us marvel five different ways in five consecutive takes, forcing his scene partner Jesse Tyler Ferguson to counterpunch in five different, equally inventive ways?

And it's not just that our actors are showing a resourcefulness we had no clue they possessed. The chemistry within each couple is palpable (and this is a thing you simply can't gauge until you see your actors in scenes together . . . you can hope, but you can't know). Yes, it is by design that we have a more buttoned-up spouse and a more combustible one in each couple, but who knew these twosomes would seem so real? The actors make us understand why these people would be with each other—would be good together. This Gloria WOULD choose this Jay. This Claire WOULD find this Phil irresistible.

Across from stage 5, where this happy experiment is playing out, another is happening in a different barn. This is where our writers gather and where we have stumbled into a highly effective and Marquis de Sade–worthy process premised upon the idea that this show is only going to be good if it feels real to people, so we are all going to have to unburden ourselves of our most embarrassing personal stories, because that is the grist our comedy mill seems to need.

Now revealing an embarrassing personal anecdote to a roomful of comedy writers is, on the survival instincts scale, right up there with rubbing yourself with salmon and lying down outside a cave full of hibernating bears. But so it is that Danny Zuker tells us of his gallstones attack and his wife's changing into a sexy outfit before the hunky EMTs arrive. And Brad Walsh tells us of his doomed ice dancing partnership with his sister. Dan O'Shannon's father once canceled Christmas. Bill Wrubel went out with a woman on Halloween but wasn't sure if it was a date or just a fun Halloween night out, so he wore a Spider-Man costume under his clothes. These and other inglorious tales all become the basis for episodes.

Six weeks pass like this. The stories are coming easily in barn 1, though not without plenty of averted eyes at the lunch table. (Did I really reveal that, at thirteen, I practiced mouth-to-mouth resuscitation on my sister in a lifeguard training class . . . that's pretty damn close to admitting I made out with my sister, both of us wearing goddamned bathing suits!) And in barn 2, the actors and directors and cinematographers and costumers and gaffers and set-dressers—everyone—are showing a dedication to detail that is the hallmark of professionalism, or at least the hallmark of don't-let-me-be-the-one-to-screw-it-upism.

And thus we arrive at our premiere night, September 23, 2009.

We gather, those eighty or so of us, at a Mexican restaurant, and we watch our show as America watches it for the first time, our secret a secret no more. And I remember two things best from that night. One, that life was about to be very different for all of us. And two, that there is no better feeling than being on a team where your teammates make you better.

Ten years have passed since that time—250 episodes, marvelous additions to our wondrous cast, a parade of the best comedy writers in Hollywood all submitting to our cheek-reddening process. It's been a dreamy journey. We've seen our child actors become adults (they were always brilliant—now they're just older, with houses). We continue to find stunning skills among our cast. Julie playing Claire's inability to confront the topic of death without smiling? . . . Ed playing both remorse and boundless love walking his son down the aisle . . . Ty, who makes us cry with laughter every week, making us cry the even better way learning that his daughter is no longer a virgin . . . And Sofía speaking Russian, Jesse fighting off a pigeon, Eric going to pieces at the choice Sophie had to make. The list goes on . . .

In those earliest days, we'd have only occasional guests come to our set. Once we premiered, this number grew, to the point where, in the final seasons, we'd commonly have thirty or forty visitors, in their own gallery, observing as we made our show in that same barn we'd started out in. And the comment most often heard was, "You all look like you're having such a great time." Well, it's important to note here that we are entertainment professionals, people steeped in the black arts of make-believe, who know how to put on appearances for an audience.

It's also important to note that those people were right; we were having a great time. Every day. It was a joy to be part of that family.

—*Christopher Lloyd*

Family Tree

DeDe Pritchett

Jay Pritchett

Stella Pritchett

Joe Pritchett

Cameron Tucker

Mitchell Pritchett

Claire Dunphy

Lily Tucker-
Pritchett
&
Rexford Tucker-
Pritchett

Dylan Marshall

Haley Dunphy

Poppy Marshall
&
George Marshall

Gloria
Delgado-Pritchett

Manny Delgado

Javier Delgado

Phil Dunphy

Alex Dunphy

Luke Dunphy

Modern Family

Introduction
The Long Goodbye

As *Modern Family's* final season cycles down toward its inevitable conclusion, I detect a certain nostalgia and melancholy pervading stage 5 on the 20th Century Fox Studios lot. In a few months, the cast will exit stage left for the very last time. The crew they've come to love for the past eleven years will swoop in and strike the sets. The Michelangelo mural with Mitch and Cam in place of God and Adam will get painted over. The zebra chairs and leather sofa in Gloria and Jay's household reupholstered or placed into storage. The two-story Dunphy set, a rarity for TV soundstages, broken down and recycled for use in other productions.

You can't help but feel a certain romanticism in the change of seasons. The loss of fallen leaves soon to be replaced by new growth, a full bloom. For the hundred-plus people that make *Modern Family,* that doesn't make letting go any easier, however.

"I'm of the mind-set that I know the end is coming, but I don't want to think about it, because I get upset," concedes Sofía Vergara (Gloria Delgado-Pritchett). Jesse Tyler Ferguson (Mitchell Pritchett) tries to take it all in. "I want to be very present in each and every moment, because this is a once-in-a-lifetime thing."

Flashback to ten years ago, August 29, 2010, at the Nokia Theatre in downtown LA: The Television Academy's Sixty-Second Primetime Emmy Awards. *Modern Family,* its first time out of the gate, has received six nominations, including Outstanding Comedy Series, which it will win that night, then rinse and repeat for the next four years. At that moment, however, cast and crew have no idea what the future holds for them—the accolades; the fans like Steven Spielberg, shout-outs of praise from both presidential candidates in a bitterly contested election season (President Obama and then candidate Mitt Romney); the mobs of followers they encounter in Australia, the appearances on *Oprah* and *Ellen*. They just try to take in the evening's sensory overload of glamour surrounding them.

Who could have ever expected this? Not Ty Burrell (Phil Dunphy), a self-described "guy with his life on his shoulders, carrying all his worldly possessions back to New York after getting crushed by Hollywood." Not Eric Stonestreet (Cameron "Cam" Tucker), whose longest TV role to date had lasted all of eight days. Not Julie Bowen, expecting to be fired at the table read, before the pilot, after airing, perhaps even today.

In little more than a year, this ensemble cast had skyrocketed from Ed O'Neill and the no-names (sounds like a Motown band, fitting since Ed used to front a rhythm and blues band in Ohio) to industry darlings comparing notes about Leno's and Letterman's greenrooms. Tom Hanks suddenly approaches them: Tom goddamned Hanks. He gives the *Modern Family* contingency the once-over. "Hello, you talented sons of bitches."

Today, I'm watching those talented sons of bitches film a scene for Emmy-winning writer/director Elaine Ko's script "The Prescott." The episode marks the return of Stephen Merchant, reprising his role as bath butler extraordinaire Leslie Higgins. I see that Merchant has had the entire cast sign his script, a personal memento that clearly brings with it some meaning for him.

Ed O'Neill literally moseys past me now. Cameras must be ready to roll; otherwise, O'Neill wouldn't be there. He doesn't like idle time. "Ed would like to shoot the rehearsal and go home immediately," says Bowen. As series cocreator Steve Levitan points out, "An Ed impression on set is him tapping his watch and looking around, like, 'Why aren't we done?'" O'Neill wouldn't disagree with their assessments. He'd double down on it. "He wants to get home to grill some meat," says Bowen.

When he does have downtime on set, he holds court with anyone interested in a good yarn. Today, I hear anecdotes about David Mamet, *Married with Children*, Brazilian jujitsu, Kirk Douglas, the NFL's Pittsburgh Steelers, Ohio deejay Booker Bell, the film *Shane*, his best friend in school, and a few past regrets—all in between a camera reset. O'Neill could entertain a wall. Stonestreet wants to bottle that folksy demeanor. "My idea for Ed, when this is all over, is to do a podcast called *Burning It Down with Ed O'Neill,* where Ed says, 'I'm never working in this business again, and now I can tell all the stories about all the people that I've worked with,' because he's got great frickin' stories."

All week, I've heard everything labeled as "the last" of something. The last October shoot. The last staff pumpkin-carving contest. The last travel episode, to Paris (Ireland fell through), a fine French adieu courtesy of executive producer Jeff Morton, who handles such logistics. "The Last Thanksgiving" episode, already in the can. "The Last Christmas," ready for production next week. The last holiday party, in which everyone will wear matching onesies and receive their annual holiday ornament courtesy of Nolan Gould (Luke Dunphy), a tradition he started the first year as a ten-year-old cherub. "It's cool because each one has a photo of the cast taken that year. You can see the evolution of us."

Gould, his best buddy in the world, Ariel Winter (Alex Dunphy), who plays his older sister, and Rico Rodriguez, who plays Vergara's son, Manny Delgado, have grown up with one another before our eyes. I can't imagine going through my awkward teen years on-camera. Right now, they sit in director's chairs, a stone's throw away from the Dunphy den. Meanwhile, onstage, Courtney Cox and David Beckham—guest stars this week—rehearse a scene with Merchant. Originally, someone else had been slated to play Cox's role, but that actress had pulled out at the last second, causing short-term chaos. "We'd never had anyone just cancel like that on us before, and it was especially frustrating because we'd already jumped through a lot of hoops to accommodate her schedule," said Ko. Emmy-winning casting director Jeff Greenberg quickly whipped up a list of names and then pulled Courtney Cox out of a hat. Try to see if you could do that yourself. With all the plotlines so closely interconnected, Ko had to spend last weekend rewriting the story.

Cocreator Chris Lloyd comes over to bend it like Beckham, actually to bend Beckham's ear. "The Prescott" episode belongs to Lloyd. The other cocreator, Levitan, owns the stage next week. For all intents and purposes, they run two separate shows, not that audiences ever notice. Over the course of close to thirty years, their relationship has evolved from peers to friends to partners to personae non gratae. Daddy and Daddy have divorced, but have a shared custody arrangement for their creation.

Their children, however, remain thick as thieves. Like the cast and crew of many long-term shows, they'll claim to be family. That happens when you end up hanging out on set with coworkers more than you do your own kin. Unlike many casts and crews, however, they really act like one: the good, bad, happy, sad—all of it. "It's odd. I can't tell you how many times we say, 'I love you,'" admits assistant prop master Steve Miller. "You don't say that at your job. The whole crew is doing that. It's crazy how much you hear that."

Sharing such an experience as this breaks down any façade of best behavior. People can be sweet, moody, or act spoiled. They may bark, even bite at times. Emotions can heat up. Things can get tense. But it always passes. "This is literally the only way I can describe it," says Ferguson. "I've known Eric longer than I've known my husband. We're playing a married couple, and it's a very intimate thing. The only way to have a healthy relationship is to get through conflict together. I think that's what makes relationships stronger. It's no different for Julie and me or Ed and me. That's a testament to how much we care about each other."

That caring extends from the showrunners down to the vice chancellor of coffee and burritos, as writers' assistant Matt Plonsker likes to refer to himself. "On most shows, you're forced to be with one another and become an oddball family," points out associate producer Andrew Brooks. "On our show, we spend time with each other voluntarily, outside of time on set, which I think is super rare."

Brooks recently flew to Kansas with Stonestreet to watch Stonestreet's beloved NFL Kansas City Chiefs play a home game at Arrowhead Stadium. Stonestreet has season tickets to Los Angeles Kings hockey games, located right by the glass, that he gives to crew members. Associate producer Rachael Field has practically been adopted by Bowen and now produces projects with her. Winter takes crew members to escape rooms, her current obsession. Burrell and Gould take a TV father–TV son vacation practically every summer.

Ask cast and crew some of their favorite memories and they won't point to a particular episode or scene. They'll call out playing craps together after filming in Vegas; country dancing after a day's work in Jackson Hole, Wyoming; dressing up to watch Floyd Mayweather take Conor McGregor down on the big screen in a private room at the Hard Rock in Lake Tahoe. They had an entire island to themselves in Australia, to hang out for no other reason than hanging out. "In the nighttime, we would come together for dinners and drinks. It's super fun to be thrust together in a hotel," says Vergara. "We all make the effort to do things like that. 'Let's all come down and meet at this time.'"

Sometimes, it can be small moments. "We understand we all have the silliest jobs," says Bowen. She has a running inside joke with on-set dresser Josh Elliott and a few other crew members. When any of them—such as Elliott, for example—has to fluff a pillow on the couch or do some inane task, they'll mutter near the other, "I went to college." That's to point out that, as Bowen puts it, "this is the most bizarre way to spend your time, and it's really fun and silly."

Elliott knows Vergara isn't a morning person. He also knows she loves Hot Tamales, not to mention cake. One morning, he put some Hot Tamales in a bowl. Vergara came in a little cranky, recalls Elliott. "I had the bowl over on Jay's and Gloria's counter. I shook it so it made a little bit of noise, like when you shake the Friskies box and your cat comes running. She came over and took some Hot Tamales and gave me a smile like, 'You know me.'"

Leslie Merlin, a guiding light who makes sure everyone is where they need to be and that everything gets done, had the entire cast tape messages for her proposal video to her wife. "Ed gave me the dad talk," she shares. "'Are you sure? How do you know you're sure? Tell me the reasons why.' I don't have a father. He knew that."

Merlin broke her arm on set once. (Side note: She hurts herself a lot.) Cast and crew chipped in to pay. *Get the bucket* has become a set catchphrase. "It means anytime we hear Leslie's stumbled, we get the bucket to raise money for her repairs," says Burrell.

Back on set, "The Prescott" has a lot of moving parts. As a director, Ko must keep track of all the converging storylines being filmed out of sequence, of course, adding to her challenge. Plus, they filmed earlier in downtown LA at a high-rise luxury apartment building catering to people with enough money to not have to ask about cost. On another stage rests a seventeen-foot-tall monstrosity of a waterslide trucked over in chunks from Texas. Through the wonder of Hollywood, they will shoot most of the slide onstage with a blue screen, which they will marry to a mini slide they built and connected to the luxury apartment's pool. One day, Vergara slides five feet into the pool; the next, she finds herself at the top of the slide onstage with Merchant. All this complexity will mean twelve- to fourteen-hour days, common with other shows but not here. Because of the fast-paced mockumentary style they use, people often get home around lunchtime, making the show the envy of the industry. Furthermore, each family only shoots for part of the week. Half days, a few days a week? Do the math. Impressive, but not this week. No wonder cast and crew apologize over and over to me for the inconvenience. For them, this schedule must be Armageddon. They keep telling me I picked the wrong week to come. I personally think one man's apocalypse can be another's paradise, but I play along for appearances.

I'm watching a family created from a family created to entertain families and general audiences. Although I've contributed next to nothing here, they've made a point of including me in their adventure. They've made me feel like I belong. I think I get the whole life-affirming-experience vibe here. How the show and everyone made it to this point tells a story about persistence, creativity, collaboration, struggle, disappointment, disagreements, and, in the end, triumph and accomplishment. Like all good stories, this one, with reruns that will live on in posterity, starts at the beginning.

The Alliance

Cocreators Levitan and Lloyd followed very divergent paths to reach the same crossroads.

STEVE LEVITAN (*cocreator*): I was a TV reporter and morning anchorman in Madison, Wisconsin. I decided that wasn't the career for me, so I started to work in advertising in Chicago. I knew that I wanted to write TV.

CHRIS LLOYD (*cocreator*): I got out of Yale and spent two years in New York toiling at some onerous temp jobs, basically stewing in self-loathing over not really doing anything with my life. The desire to make that stewing stop finally outweighed my fear over failing in an industry in which my father was a big success,* so I moved to LA and gave writing a try . . . and mostly failed at first, but at least I was confronting the beast.

LEVITAN (*cocreator*): I started to write scripts on my own, but it's really hard, a million miles away. It didn't seem like a real career. Then when I was doing a TV campaign for Miller Beer, I came out to LA and

---

* Lloyd's dad was legendary sitcom writer David Lloyd (1934–2009), who worked on *The Mary Tyler Moore Show, The Bob Newhart Show, Taxi, Cheers,* and *Frasier.* Lloyd wrote what many consider to be one of the greatest sitcom scripts ever, "Chuckles Bites the Dust" for *The Mary Tyler Moore Show.* When he passed away during *Modern Family*'s first season, his son paid tribute with a title card containing Chuckles's famous salutation and catchphrase: "A little song, a little dance, a little seltzer down your pants."

started to meet people in the business. I was told I needed to move here, so I did.

LLOYD (cocreator): Various terrible scripts came out of me, but they were getting a little bit better, and it was a pleasure to actually be attempting to write.

LEVITAN (cocreator): I took a job doing movie trailers and TV commercials for Disney and Touchstone Pictures. I showed my scripts around like crazy. One landed in a pile of freelance submissions for *Wings* [1990–1997]. Two guys there, Bill Diamond and Mike Saltzman, liked a *Cheers* script I'd written. I was invited to come in and pitch.

LLOYD (cocreator): Eventually, I sent one to Witt/Thomas/Harris.* They offered me a job as a writer's intern for *Golden Girls* [1985–1992], which meant for $350 a week, I could sit with the writers but get paid like a PA. When the show got renewed for the back nine the first season, they needed writers and asked me to write a script. I chewed my fingernails to the elbows. When I turned the script in, it wasn't great, but good enough that they offered me a four-year contract, so I signed it.

Levitan went to Paramount Studios and met with Wings *creators David Angell, Peter Casey, and David Lee. Lloyd, a writer and producer there for several years by then, attended the meeting as well.*

LEVITAN (cocreator): I pitched some ideas. They liked one and gave me a chance to write a freelance script. It was a very daunting process since I'd never done it before. Chris was always a quiet force in the room. He's not a big, boisterous personality, but when he talks, people listen because he's very smart and very funny. We became friends.

LLOYD (cocreator): He was a smart and funny writer. We worked together

---

* TV producers Paul Junger Witt, Tony Thomas, and Susan Harris. Together, they made *Soap* (1977–1981), *Benson* (1979–1986), *The Golden Girls* (1985–1992), and more.

a year on *Wings,* and then I left to go do *Frasier* [1993–2004]. We remained colleagues and friends outside of that.

They reunited during Frasier's *second year, where Lloyd and Joe Keenan served as showrunners. Levitan joined the staff through the end of the third season, at which time his own show,* Just Shoot Me *(1997–2003), made the prime-time lineup.*

LEVITAN (*cocreator*): Neither of us was married in the beginning. We finally both did and had kids. They were approximately the same age. Our families hung out. Our wives got along well. Chris and I used to go on trips together. We went with NBC to the Sydney, Australia, Olympics in 2000.

Right around then, Levitan got offered a deal by 20th Century Fox Studios and left Just Shoot Me. *He created what he calls "a bunch of shows that went on the air for a year and then went off."*

LEVITAN (*cocreator*): I decided to take a break because I felt like I was hitting my head against the wall a little bit. I was getting paid a lot of money, and I wasn't creating hit shows and it was bugging me. I knew I needed something to shake it up, because it just wasn't working.

Levitan and his agent, Jay Sures, talked about Levitan creating a writing/producing entity in which he could create original content but also help other writers develop their pilots and get them on the air.
Meanwhile, Lloyd, having left Frasier *after its seventh year, produced a short-running series with Keenan—Bram and Alice (2002). He and Keenan then returned to* Frasier *for its final year in 2004, followed by* Out of Practice *(2005), starring Henry Winkler as a couples' counselor. It also only lasted one season, at which point Lloyd's contract with Paramount expired.*

LLOYD (*cocreator*): I'd been there seventeen years. During that era, the sitcom world had become a much smaller one. There was a lot of wondering about if the form had run its course.

JASON WINER (*director / executive producer*): There was a sitcom recession. Cable comedies were growing more successful. Younger people especially wanted to lean into their comedy and not be spoon-fed. Broadcast TV had tried to respond to that trend but hadn't been doing it that well.

STEPHEN MCPHERSON (*ABC Entertainment president*): I think there were a lot of efforts on network TV that weren't good or successful, and so people got a little gun-shy. Frankly, there had been so many sitcoms that there wasn't as much talent working in them. Somebody would have three good minutes at the U.S. Comedy Arts Festival in Aspen and they'd get a deal. And then they'd do a show and it would be God-awful because there was nothing there.

LEVITAN (*cocreator*): Chris and I felt like we needed to do something to shake it up. So, during lunch one day, I started floating out there the idea of teaming up. It was a little weird because when you're friends, you don't want to say, "Hey, do you want to team up?" and have the other person say, "No."

LLOYD (*cocreator*): It was more of an overture. Steve had an idea of what us forming a partnership could be. He said, "Hey, we're both at liberty at the same time. What would you think about forming a company where we could supervise other less experienced writers and bring our experience to bear? Get a few shows going and be a mini-company?"

LEVITAN (*cocreator*): We were the right people at the right time for each other. A deal came together relatively quickly at Fox. They were very nice and had always been supportive. And so we started our little company, the two of us and a few assistants.

LLOYD (*cocreator*): Ultimately, we found ourselves saying we might take these writers' ideas and end up writing them ourselves, so why don't we just start from scratch on something?

They landed on an idea about a veteran newscaster who returns to his Pittsburgh roots and forms a love-hate relationship with his coanchor. They had one name in mind to star: Kelsey Grammer.

LEVITAN (*cocreator*): We sort of felt that it was dependent on Kelsey doing it, so Chris and I went up to Kelsey's house and pitched him the show. He seemed enthusiastic, but guarded, so we were in waiting mode. I wanted to buy a Mercedes S-Class at the time. It was too expensive, though, and I didn't want to splurge on it. But I said, "If Kelsey does this show, maybe I could buy this car." Then one day, Chris calls me up and says, "Well, I guess you can buy your S-Class, because Kelsey's in." Then Patty [Patricia Heaton] joined in, and suddenly there was a lot of heat behind the show. Chris had worked with Ty Burrell on *Out of Practice* and was really singing his praises, so we wrote a part for him. Then Josh Gad fell into place and Fred Willard. It was a dream cast.

Back to You *premiered on the Fox Network in 2007.*

LLOYD (*cocreator*): It was fairly traditional. It certainly wasn't the first show set in a newsroom with an antagonistic love-hate relationship between a man and woman.

LEVITAN (*cocreator*): It was a little more broad than I personally wanted it to be. I'm not blaming Chris or anything like that. I was just yearning for something that felt real.

From early on, the showrunners butted heads with Fox Television executives. The relationship quickly soured.

LLOYD (*cocreator*): The show, I think, was funny. A lot of people thought it was funny. But it was the age of arrogance at Fox Television, where executives thought they knew how to make any show work even though the people who were issuing ultimatums had no experience writing or producing anything.

LEVITAN (*cocreator*): I have a big problem with most broadcast network marketing for comedies. You can imagine that poster of everybody standing there with a funny look on their face. It always looks ridiculous. I remember driving into work one day and seeing a giant billboard at the front of Fox studios with Kelsey and Patricia, tangled up in a mic cord. The copy read "The news hits the fan." I was so horrified by that. I called the network president and said, "What is that? What does that even mean?" He's like, "Don't you get it? That's the same saying as 'The shit hits the fan,' but we put 'news' in instead." I go, "Yeah, I grasp the concept of what you were going for. But why? Why is that smart at all?"

The show had a lot of hype behind its premiere, but unfortunately not the ratings. Many shows struggled that season, though, in large part due to the hundred-day Writers' Strike (November 2007–February 2008). The strike brought Hollywood production to a standstill, destroying any momentum shows had. When Hollywood finally got back to work, Fox executives believed they knew how to best revive the show's flailing ratings.

LLOYD (*cocreator*): The best executives to me are the ones who say, "I think I'm going to trust the people who've given their entire lives to figuring out problems from a writer's standpoint as opposed to my knee-jerk ideas about how something should happen." They had a dumbass head of the network who wasn't one of those people. He decided he knew better than the writers how to write. He decided there were certain things the show needed to do to be a success. Steve and I both said, "We think those are terrible ideas."

LEVITAN (*cocreator*): I agree with Chris. I didn't like the way that was handled at all. He asked us to change one of the actors out [Lily Jackson replaced Laura Marano as Grammer and Heaton's ten-year-old daughter]. We didn't think that was necessary. It wasn't going to fix anything. And of course, it didn't. It was terrible for Laura, and we felt terrible. But at the end of the day, we felt like we're going to get canceled if we don't.

LLOYD (*cocreator*): At a certain point, they said the answer to our show was to add Nicole Richie to the cast because probably somebody had watched her do something that made them laugh the night before. It was at that point we said, "If you guys don't know to trust the people who've made it their life's work to think about stories and characters and make good shows, then we have no real interest in being in business with you."

The Fox geniuses at that point got a very high and mighty attitude and said, "Well, then, we'll cancel your show," which they proceeded to do.

JOSH GAD (*Kenneth Ploufe*): We thought it was going to run forever. It got canceled the week of my wedding.

FRED WILLARD (*Frank Dunphy*): In fact, we all went to his wedding on the day we found out. It was tough.

LEVITAN (*cocreator*): Sometimes you cancel a show because the cast doesn't have chemistry or the show's not funny. But we had all the pieces in place. It was a matter of continuing to hone and find our exact tone. If we'd gone to CBS, it would still be on the air. But it's hard for me to stay mad about it because otherwise *Modern Family* never would have happened.

That doesn't mean the story had an entirely happy ending for Levitan.

LEVITAN (*cocreator*): I never did buy that car.

Levitan and Lloyd, with one year remaining on their Fox deal, owed the studio one more script. To take their minds off what Lloyd refers to as "the wound-licking over the early demise of Back to You," *they focused their efforts in a different direction.*

LLOYD (*cocreator*): I had read a first-person article by a music critic for the *New Yorker*,* who had made a nice life for himself living with Asperger's. He was on his own, working as an esteemed professional, but funny things would happen to him where he would not pick up social cues. It seemed like an interesting character that hadn't been dealt with on television.

LEVITAN (*cocreator*): Josh Gad was going to play someone with Asperger's who's part of a family.

---

* Tim Page, "Parallel Play," *New Yorker*, August 13, 2007, accessed October 20, 2019, https://www.newyorker.com/magazine/2007/08/20/parallel-play.

GAD (*Kenneth Ploufe*): It was a very loose idea with me as a screwup and my dad. They were thinking Ed O'Neill for my dad. We went to pitch CBS, and it was a complete disaster. We left thinking, "Okay, that's not going to happen anytime soon."

LEVITAN (*cocreator*): I think they were scared that the subject matter might look like we're making fun of Asperger's, which we absolutely weren't.

LLOYD (*cocreator*): We then thought about writing something a little bit more personal.

LEVITAN (*cocreator*): We used to come in all the time and talk about our families. What did you do this weekend, parenting things, or arguments we'd gotten in with our spouses. We realized that those were some of the funniest things we were talking about. We looked around the TV landscape and saw there currently weren't many family shows. I think *Everybody Loves Raymond* [1996—2005] was the last really good one. So we saw an opportunity there.

WINER (*director / executive producer*): At the time, I believe the only family comedy on broadcast TV was *According to Jim*. They were out of vogue.

SAMIE KIM FALVEY (*ABC Entertainment head of comedy*): It was a decidedly uncool thing, at that moment, to put out there in the world. It wasn't something that people were looking for.

PAUL CORRIGAN (*writer / executive producer*): Snark was ruling the roost. I'm sure world events had some say in that, like 9/11 or things like that.

LLOYD (*cocreator*): There was this prevailing sentiment that comedy had to be cutting edge in the sense that it was take-no-prisoners. They're going to make fun of everybody and all the sacred cows. It was very cynical, without any real human emotion behind it. The opposite of that was introducing emotion to a story. That was uncool and old-fashioned. So it was risky for us to say we're going to have plenty of laughs but we're also going to explore some emotion, even if the cool kids are going to laugh at us for doing so.

LEVITAN (*cocreator*): Chris and I both loved shows like *Cheers* that can have a monster laugh and then sneak up on you with a very poignant moment that really gets to you. Then that moment's broken up with another giant laugh. That to us has always been the high-water mark in TV comedy.

LLOYD (*cocreator*): At the end of the day, there's no surprise in insult comedy, nothing touching you or making you feel a range of emotions besides feeling slightly outraged or titillated by something extreme you've observed. That's a narrow range to work within. Once you add back in surprise, laughter, crying, or identifying with situations and characters, that's a far broader experience.

LEVITAN (*cocreator*): Chris and I like our shows to be about something and not just going for the pure laugh of it all.

LLOYD (*cocreator*): We were pushing ourselves to be a less traditional family comedy. That led us to a more sprawling approach to telling the story of different families. We stumbled into all of that.

> *They found the perfect vehicle for their vision within a mockumentary.*

First Days

Radio productions like Orson Welles's The War of the Worlds serve as precursors to TV mockumentaries in their real presentation of fiction. On television, mockumentaries can be traced back to TV specials such as the political satire Pat Paulsen for President *(1968), sketches on* Monty Python's Flying Circus *(1969–1974), and Albert Brooks's short films on* Saturday Night Live *(1975–). In 1995, Showtime launched the first mockumentary series, the long-forgotten* Sherman Oaks, *which told the over-the-top escapades of a fictitious wealthy plastic surgeon and his network of friends, family, and patients.*

Most people, however, credit Stephen Merchant (a future guest star on Modern Family*) and Ricky Gervais for popularizing the mockumentary sitcom with their breakout BBC series,* The Office *(2001–2003).*

STEPHEN MERCHANT (*Leslie Higgins*): *The Office* began as a little exercise. I was a trainee at the BBC and had a camera crew for a day. Instead of shooting other trainees in a real mini-documentary, I wanted to do a fake one. At the time in England, there were a lot of documentaries about very ordinary places like call centers or driving schools. We were slightly imitating that.

Merchant and Gervais incorporated common documentary visual cues—camera-facing interviews, herky-jerky camerawork, peekaboo cinematography—to capture life at the Slough branch of the fictional Wernham Hogg Paper Company.

MERCHANT (*Leslie Higgins*): Because it's documentary style, you don't have to hit your marks as accurately. The camera can readjust, punch in for emphasis, and all these other useful tricks. It ends up becoming the best of both worlds, because you have all the freedom of a classic shooting style but also the looseness and speed of the documentary style.

LEVITAN (*cocreator*): I credit everything back to *Spinal Tap* [1984] and *The Office*. It's a wonderful form for comedy, a quick and efficient way to get what the character is thinking without having to work in clunky dialogue which nobody would ever say.

LLOYD (*cocreator*): It's a tried-and-true form of expression. There are plays written by Aristophanes and Euripides where the action stops and the character steps to the edge of the stage and brings the audience in. Thornton Wilder wrote plays in the '20s where there would suddenly be a pool of light on the side of the stage and the character would step into it and tell you what he or she was feeling or what you needed to know to move the play forward.

LEVITAN (*cocreator*): (*jokingly*) I don't find those as funny as *Spinal Tap*.

The NBC version of The Office *(2005–2013) Americanized the British series, becoming the network's Thursday night 9:00 p.m. anchor. Its success prompted NBC to launch a second work mockumentary,* Parks and Recreation *(2009–2015), in the time slot in front of it.*

In addition to camerawork, mockumentaries differ from traditional multi-cam sitcoms in production. The latter has the luxury of rewriting and rehearsal time over the course of a week, culminating in filming with three to four cameras in front of a live audience. Mockumentary production resembles more that of a film, much less rewrite and rehearsal time, with fewer cameras, filming over multiple days, without the feedback of studio audience laughter. Switching styles can be intimidating.

LLOYD (*cocreator*): I was leery of the form because I had done nothing but multi-cams in my entire career and happily so.

LEVITAN (*cocreator*): I did *Greg the Bunny* [2002] and *Oliver Beene* [2003–2004], which were single-camera shows. And I had done this low-budget mockumentary pilot called *FootHooker* about an American rock band that was big in Asia but completely dead in the U.S. I really enjoyed that form. It brought a natural grit to the whole tone of things. When we started talking about a family show, the notion came up of doing it like a reality show, making it feel like you're looking into somebody's life.

LLOYD (*cocreator*): There's a lot of precedent for direct-to-camera communication. Once I started immersing myself in that and seeing the benefits to it, I got more comfortable with the idea.

Unlike current mockumentaries that focus on a public workplace, Levitan and Lloyd took the pioneering step of bringing the format to the home front.

LLOYD (*cocreator*): We thought, what we're exploring here are the complexities of family and all the feelings that get stirred up in dealing with lots of unspoken stuff among family members. This is a way for characters to express themselves to us in ways they might be uncomfortable doing to each other.

DAN O'SHANNON (*writer / executive producer*): It enabled us to cram a lot of material into twenty minutes. Instead of trying to bury exposition in a scene where characters talk to each other and happen to set up the story, we put Phil on a couch and he says to the camera, "There's a party Saturday night."

DANNY ZUKER (*writer / executive producer*): I don't think you can have as many speaking roles on our show unless they did that. You'd have to take a few extra lines of dialogue to make that exposition seem natural, and we don't have a few lines of dialogue to spare.

Levitan and Lloyd also reimagined the family sitcom template by focusing on multiple families instead of the expected one.

LLOYD (*cocreator*): There's no traditional family anymore. We could have chosen five or six to get at a more perfect depiction of all the different shapes and sizes of American families today. Once we hit on three, that seemed like a broad enough approach to explore different types, but not so broad that we couldn't service all these characters on a week-to-week basis.

They agreed to set it in LA because they knew all about raising kids there. The challenge became finding the common thread that tied all the families together.

LEVITAN (*cocreator*): There were all sorts of ideas being thrown around. For a while, it was three families in a cul-de-sac.

LLOYD (*cocreator*): We looked at telling parallel family stories that might be linked thematically, dealing with a particular child-rearing issue or theme each week.

LEVITAN (*cocreator*): The construct of the show would be to hit everybody. In the beginning, we weren't too worried about hitting everybody equally, but it ended up that way.

LLOYD (*cocreator*): The linchpin was when we decided to make them all part of the same family.

LEVITAN (cocreator): What we loved about *Frasier* was adult siblings. There's a lot of that in *Wings*, too. That's always a very powerful area for stories, because there's so much history.

ED O'NEILL (*Jay Pritchett*): The idea that it was three families, separate, but related. That's the thing I noticed when I read the pilot. This show had legs. They could go with one family one week, another the next, and another the next. You could mix and match and do so many things for diversity and interest.

LLOYD (*cocreator*): We came to the idea that it might be really fun in the pilot to imagine these families as unrelated. We're depicting American family life and then at the end, we find out they're joined as part of this one larger family.

Next came defining each of the three families.

LEVITAN (cocreator): We tried three siblings. One of them was single for a while.

LLOYD (*cocreator*): She preceded the gay couple. She was raising a child on her own. It was a viable idea. There are plenty of single-parent families out there.

LEVITAN (cocreator): But I'm glad we didn't do that. It's hard to do dating stories on a show that's supposed to be family friendly. That's when we decided to have a gay sibling raising a kid with his partner. You can't do a show called *Modern Family* and not have one of the newest kinds of families there is. When we landed on that, I remember thinking, "Well, there goes the middle of the country."

LLOYD (*cocreator*): We bounced between two schools of thought. One was, there goes the middle of the country. The other was if we're going to have a gay couple, let's have two funny actors in a believable relationship going through a lot of the same parenting issues that straight couples go through. We always liked how in many ways they were the most traditional of the families, like a TV couple from the 1950s. It might make them more relatable to less open-minded people. I can't say we predicted that, but that's what wound up happening.

The third sibling idea ultimately returned to the womb. In its place, the show's creators discovered a different dynamic, a generational one, that offered unlimited potential for family conflict.

LEVITAN (*cocreator*): One of my friends suggested, "What about one of the parents?" It immediately clicked. I called Chris and said, "What about this?" And he immediately said, "Yeah, that's good. That's really good."

LLOYD (*cocreator*): Suddenly we went, "This really feels like a series because there are all these dynamics to explore."

LEVITAN (*cocreator*): Then we said, "Let's give the dad a young wife and new kid. Here he thought he was going to marry this hot young woman and be happy, but she comes with baggage that makes him have to readdress all the things he did wrong with his first family."

LLOYD (*cocreator*): We thought it would be fun if Jay had an ethnic wife who's a little bit of a mystery to the family members. It wasn't just to get diversity into the show. It was more to make the family dynamics messier.

LEVITAN (*cocreator*): For a little while, Jay's wife was African American. What changed that was Sofía Vergara being brought to our attention.

GAD (*Kenneth Ploufe*): I remember going to their office and seeing a picture of Sofía. They said this hilarious young lady has a deal with ABC. They were developing a character around her and had some ideas for other characters.

Initially, they made Gloria a bikini bartender.

LEVITAN (*cocreator*): There was a joke that Jay met Gloria at the pool party he threw when his divorce from DeDe [Shelley Long] became final, which I thought was funny.

LLOYD (*cocreator*): It always seemed to me a little too cliché that she was there just to wear a bikini and that that would be enough for Jay. We were gravitating more toward Gloria being a bit more substantial.

LEVITAN (*cocreator*): We really thought it was important that you not think that she's a bimbo. If Gloria had been a bikini bartender that Jay met and married, you wouldn't like her nearly as much. We wanted her to be tougher than that and savvier. She's a very unique character. She's not a character you can say, "Oh, that reminds me of Diane Chambers or Lucille Ball."

They revisited their Asperger's character for her son.

LLOYD (*cocreator*): Steve liked the idea of making Manny Asperger-y, but it didn't seem right to me.

LEVITAN (*cocreator*): A good friend of mine's kid has Asperger's. He cracks me up to no end. I thought that would be an interesting thing for Jay to deal with. I was actually a really big proponent of that for a while. Chris was resistant, however, so we kept digging.

An unconventional eccentricity of one of Lloyd's children sparked Levitan's imagination.

LEVITAN (*cocreator*): Chris has a really funny, quirky family. His son used to walk around the house, as I recall, in a velvet smoking jacket.

LLOYD (*cocreator*): Yeah, he still has it. He might have more than one. My son's always been a little bit of a dandy.

LEVITAN (*cocreator*): We thought, let's embrace that dynamic of Jay's son being a little bit more mature, for his age, a little bit quirkier than the average kid. We said he's a ten-year-old Antonio Banderas.

Lloyd found his version of Manny's voice outside of his home in the pages of the novel The Brief Wondrous Life of Oscar Wao.

LLOYD (*cocreator*): It's about this hopeless romantic who doesn't have the tools necessary to succeed in the world of romance, but remains a dreamer, believer, and romantic. He had an idea that he was going to attract beautiful older women by dint of his heart and soul. The audience would look at that and go, "You're setting yourself up for disappointment because that's not the way the world works." Once we started writing in that direction, it seemed like the right choice.

They struggled with Pritchett's career path.

O'NEILL (*Jay Pritchett*): In the pilot, they never said what I did, but I was a blue-collar guy. I think I went to Steve at some point and asked, "Why am

I wearing these stupid clothes? I can play this other kind of guy." I played the governor of Pennsylvania on *West Wing* [1999–2006]. I said, "It isn't a problem for me to play somebody with some money and a position, which is what I think you guys want out of the part." Then they changed it.

CLINT MCCRAY (*script coordinator*): I think initially he was a stereo king. He sold car stereos and window tinting.

LEVITAN (*cocreator*): It was loosely based on Al & Ed's Autosound. They do all that car stuff. It was something where he had multiple businesses. It was a blue-collar thing that turned into a pretty good moneymaking venture.

LLOYD (*cocreator*): But then car stereos stopped being a going thing. We knew we wanted some household item that didn't have a lot of grandeur to it. Somehow we gravitated toward closets and blinds. Whether they actually go together in the world, I don't know, but it opened a rich vein of comedy in that Jay, then Claire, and others take the world of closets so seriously.

O'NEILL (*Jay Pritchett*): I became the guy who has the upscale closet business, which I really liked much better than a guy under a car.

They knew using children could prove problematic, yet many of their story ideas involved parenting. That meant the children needed to be more than window dressing or topics of conversation.

JEFF MORTON (*executive producer*): Our show was about three families, and kids were a huge part of it.

Not sitcom children, though, as in strikingly articulate, precocious stereotypes defined by brainless, repetitive catchphrases like "What you talkin' about, Willis?" or "You got it, dude."

MORTON (*executive producer*): In a lot of sitcoms, you try and hide the kids. You bring them in for a certain amount of time and try not to give them too much.

LEVITAN (*cocreator*): If you remember *Everybody Loves Raymond,* and this is not a criticism at all, but what they would do is the kids would come in, run up to their room, and were gone. They were there to remind the audience that these people were parents, and that was about it.

Levitan and Lloyd ended up with almost as many children parts as they did adult ones.

LLOYD (*cocreator*): It's hard for me to imagine what the series would have been like if Phil and Claire were talking about off-screen kids. Those kids' problems were the drivers behind half of our episodes.

The third family, the Dunphys—Claire, Jay's daughter; her husband, Phil; their children, Haley, Alex, and Luke—proved to be the most mainstream of the three families.

LEVITAN (*cocreator*): The Dunphy family was very, very loosely based on my family and the fact that I had two daughters and then a son. Their names are similar, but we changed the dynamics, of course, to make it more clear. For example, my daughters are not like Haley and Alex. Haley's shallow and popular with boys, and Alex is smart and serious and not the most popular girl in school.

Lloyd's inspiration came from a different source, a point of contention he has with Levitan—definitely not the first or last between them.

LLOYD (*cocreator*): The show was based on our imagination. The only passing similarity was that there was a husband and wife, not a unique characteristic, and three kids in the same order as his kids. I think that he liked the idea that it was based on his family and wouldn't qualify it. That rubbed me the wrong way. People would say they ran into these kids out in public and they'd say, "*Modern Family* is based on our friends from school." My kids would hear that and they'd ask, "Is that true?" If it was based upon his family, then I would have been thinking about his family while I was writing the pilot alongside of him. And I was not. I was thinking of what was going to make these characters funny.

Origins aside, the showrunners next took to naming everyone.

LLOYD (*cocreator*): Often in pilot writing, it becomes handy to quickly attach a name to a character so you can stop saying "the dad" or "the mom."

Character names can be as defining as any character trait. The inspiration for names in Modern Family *came from many different sources.*

LEVITAN (*cocreator*): I think the idea for Jay's name came from my agent, Jay Sures. I think what we liked about it was we thought Gloria would call him "Yay" a lot, and that made us laugh. And of course she never did. But we thought that was funny.

LLOYD (*cocreator*): Manny may have been influenced by Sofía's own son, Manolo.

LEVITAN (*cocreator*): There's a real estate agent in Malibu whose last name is Pritchett.

LLOYD (*cocreator*): Cameron was named after an actor/director friend, Cameron Watson.

LEVITAN (*cocreator*): My college roommate's last name was Tucker. That had a nice country feel to it, which was part of Cam's character.

LLOYD (*cocreator*): Cameron's real-life partner is named Steve, so we jettisoned that for obvious reasons and landed on Mitchell because it sounded somewhat uptight.

LEVITAN (*cocreator*): Lily was originally something else, but it seemed like a pretty name for an Asian baby, and there was a good joke in the pilot where Phil says, "Isn't that going to be hard for her to say?"

Neither remembers the origin of Phil, but they do recall where his middle name, Humphrey, came from.

LLOYD (*cocreator*): We had a writer whose boyfriend was named Humphrey, and Humphrey Dunphy seemed irresistible.

While Levitan doesn't take credit for Claire, he recalls a Claire in high school and always liked the name. The Dunphy surname comes from local news anchor Jerry Dunphy, who also incidentally served as inspiration for news anchor Ted Baxter from The Mary Tyler Moore Show.

LEVITAN (*cocreator*): Somehow we stumbled on that one. There's something happy about it.

As for the Dunphy children . . .

LEVITAN (*cocreator*): Luke is named after my son's best friend at the time [named after DeDe's father in the show]. It had a nice strong feel to it.

For the Dunphy daughters, Levitan borrowed from his own life.

LEVITAN (*cocreator*): My oldest is Hannah, so that's Haley. My middle one is Ally, but her real name is Alexa. We call her Ally, and that's Alex.

LLOYD (*cocreator*): Steve came in one day and had named the characters. He passed this off as something that made it easier to proceed since we had working names for everybody. I found it pretty cheeky that he had obviously named the kids after his own kids and cheekier still that he never particularly acknowledged that he had done so until now. It might have made sense if he'd written the pilot on his own. I didn't make an issue out of it because there were other people in the cast and obviously the show isn't reducible to character names. It's weird, however, to decide you're going to name characters in a show you're writing with someone else after your own kids. You're supposed to be collaborating with someone, not trying to put something past him.

The showrunners, despite their different perspectives, managed to focus on the more important task at hand—completing their pilot pitch. To do that required answering one fundamental question about the documentary: Why this family? They found the answer from the documentarian himself.

LEVITAN (*cocreator*): A Dutch documentary filmmaker.

LLOYD (*cocreator*): Geert Floortje. We liked that his name was impossible to pronounce.

LEVITAN (*cocreator*): When Geert was a kid, he'd been a foreign exchange student from Holland who came to America and lived with the Pritchett family for a semester. He had a major crush on Claire. And Mitchell had a major crush on him.

LLOYD (*cocreator*): After a year, he moved back to Holland and became a filmmaker. But he always stayed in touch with what he referred to as "my American family." That family eventually branched out to form new families. He thought that would make a cool documentary.

So did the creators. Borrowing a page from Floortje's vision, they named their pilot My American Family. *Now they needed a network that wanted to share that family with the rest of the world.*

Written in the Stars

Norman Lear. Ryan Murphy. Shonda Rhimes. Chuck Lorre. Some of TV's most successful television producers developed television pilots that never made it on air. Levitan and Lloyd encountered their own share of disappointments, too. Modern Family felt different, however, like the type of project that creative people spend a lifetime trying to conceive.

In 2008, the major broadcast networks—ABC, NBC, CBS, and Fox—still retained the overwhelming majority of television viewers. Levitan and Lloyd pitched their idea to all of them, save one: Fox. They wanted nothing to do with them ever again.

MCPHERSON (*ABC Entertainment president*): No network lineup was particularly a powerhouse. CBS was pretty strong with dramas. NBC was the strongest on the comedy front, but there weren't a lot of great half-hour comedies being done. We were certainly struggling on that front at ABC.

FALVEY (*ABC Entertainment head of comedy*): Our only returning comedy was *According to Jim*. We wanted to focus on what ABC does well and how we could possibly reach a broader audience in the comedy space.

Workplace sitcoms like the American version of The Office, Parks and Recreation, *and* 30 Rock *(2006–2013) ruled NBC's airwaves. CBS gravitated more toward relationship comedies like* Two and a Half Men *(2003–2015),* The Big Bang Theory *(2007–2019), and* How I Met Your Mother *(2005–2014). ABC looked to add to that.*

FALVEY (*ABC Entertainment head of comedy*): We really turned our sights toward family comedies. Part of it was feeling that the contemporary modern American family wasn't being represented on TV. I knew that firsthand because I hadn't grown up like those families I saw on TV. We thought it was a way to bring older and younger people together. It made a lot of sense.

Levitan and Lloyd went to CBS first.

LLOYD (*cocreator*): CBS hadn't done any single-camera comedies up to that point, but they made a decent offer and put a clock on it [a limited-time offer].

LEVITAN (*cocreator*): NBC really liked it, but they had *The Office* and were coming out with *Parks and Recreation*. That's two mockumentary shows. They said they can't have a third. They told us if we didn't do it mockumentary style, they'd like it. We thought, "No, we want to keep this."

From the beginning, they believed that ABC afforded them the best opportunity, leading them to meet with that network last, with other opportunities in hand if they had any, which they did.

LEVITAN (*cocreator*): They had a great tradition of family shows and they had needs. Stephen [McPherson] was also a friend. And very importantly, ABC had a holding deal with Sofía Vergara, so if we wanted her, it had to be ABC.

ABC Entertainment president Steve McPherson feared going in what the competition had to offer.

MCPHERSON (*ABC Entertainment president*): I knew that those guys were in high demand, so I always assumed there were other people courting them.

LLOYD (*cocreator*): ABC almost didn't happen.

LEVITAN (*cocreator*): Stephen had to drive to a company retreat in Ojai or something.

LLOYD (*cocreator*): They were going to pass on it because Stephen didn't think he'd be able to hear the pitch in time.

LEVITAN (*cocreator*): It just didn't feel like a CBS show to us, though.

Levitan's agent and copresident of United Talent Agency, Jay Sures, helped arrange a last-second breakfast meeting between Lloyd, Levitan, McPherson, Falvey, and other ABC executives at his Brentwood home.

LEVITAN (*cocreator*): We sat down and took them through everything. It was interesting, in a really good way, that we were sitting there in someone's living room, in a family home, talking about this show. It felt very right.

Levitan, an avowed technology geek, effectively put his talents to work, using a laptop for his pitch. While common today, it proved less so back then. That would pay dividends soon enough.

LEVITAN (*cocreator*): We knew we wanted to lay it out in a way that it was a surprise that they were all in one family, because that's going to be the big twist of the pilot. It would be hard to do if you're explaining how one thing leads to another and they're trying to keep things straight. At the time, I enjoyed playing around with Keynote [a presentation app], which was fairly new to me back then. It was nice to have a reason to play with it.

FALVEY (*ABC Entertainment head of comedy*): It was pretty brilliant. It showed the characters within the three different families.

Their presentation included slides with prototypes for each family member.

LEVITAN (*cocreator*): That became a thing of mine after having pitched so many pilot scripts through the years. I always thought it would be smart to do your dream casting, give a visual to the reader, and have it in a place where they can easily flip back to it if they get confused. It gives them clarity so nothing gets in the way of the comedy.

MCPHERSON (*ABC Entertainment president*): They plugged in actors that made sense, even if they weren't available. Some of them were absolute possibilities, people we had deals with, like Sofía, that were looking for work. And some of them were people that were great placeholders for the kind of actor they wanted in that role.

LLOYD (*cocreator*): We felt it was going to be easier for them to get the idea if we attempted to tell a story about the American family. What is the American family anymore? It used to be a very traditional family, but what is it today? We kept popping back and forth among the various stories.

MCPHERSON (*ABC Entertainment president*): They very smartly constructed the pitch the way the pilot was written.

FALVEY (*ABC Entertainment head of comedy*): It was definitely one of the bigger casts that had been on TV in a comedy for a while.

LLOYD (*cocreator*): At a certain point, we said the story we're following for the gay family is that they've adopted this daughter, but because one of the dads has a troubled relationship with his family, he hasn't admitted to them yet that he's done this. His mate, who's always encouraging him to be a more complete and relaxed person emotionally, is encouraging him to let his family know because it's too big a thing to hold back. And so a night is scheduled where they're going to announce it to the family and then the family shows up. Truly, although it seems so predictable now, every time we pitched it at the networks, they were like, "What? They're all the same family?" It was the clincher moment.

MCPHERSON (*ABC Entertainment president*): It was brilliant. It was not only very smart but incredibly enticing and such a great sales piece. It's one of the better pitches I've ever heard as a TV executive.

FALVEY (*ABC Entertainment head of comedy*): You're like, "Wow." So much of that was a pre–*This Is Us;* this cool reveal in the pitch.

MCPHERSON (*ABC Entertainment president*): The pilot touched on things that were sensitive but did it in a way that was effective, funny, and meaningful. It managed to walk the perfect line between having a real backbone of meaning: relatable family life and comedy.

LEVITAN (*cocreator*): Stephen immediately sparked to it. He said, "What kind of stories would you tell?" We started pulling out some funny little notions of stories, including one that we ended up using in the pilot, where Phil has to shoot Luke with a BB gun.

MCPHERSON (*ABC Entertainment president*): Steve said that he had punished his son the same way Phil punishes Luke in terms of shooting him with a BB gun if he ever shot his sisters. It was politically incorrect, but so relatable and real.

LEVITAN (*cocreator*): All of a sudden, it occurred to me, "I have the video on my computer." So I go, "Wait, hold on a second." I showed him the clip and told him Phil will do that with Luke. He immediately said, "I want it. Let's do it."

MCPHERSON (*ABC Entertainment president*): I wanted a family show that reinvented ABC's tradition of family shows. This fit the bill perfectly. I was just concerned I wouldn't get the deal, so I said, "We have to have this." We agreed to make the pilot and attach a penalty if we don't go to series.

FALVEY (*ABC Entertainment head of comedy*): One of the things that really drew me in was this idea of a contemporary American family that we have been longing and searching for and knowing that the magic of the show would be that different people would see themselves in different families. Therefore, it would bring in lots of different types of people and families.

While the idea sounded great, it remained just that—an idea.

LLOYD (*cocreator*): We hadn't written the script yet. It was all theoretical.

Diamond in the Rough

"My American Family" Pilot Story Pitch 9-16-08
Levitan and Lloyd presented the following pilot pitch to McPherson as an outline for the first episode.

After a brief introduction from Dutch
Filmmaker Geert Floortje, we meet
three families through three intercut
stories:

Traditional family:

A very simple story in which Haley,
the oldest daughter, announces at
breakfast that she's having a boy over
for the first time and all she wants
is for no one to embarrass her. Phil
(the self-proclaimed "cool dad") takes
this in stride because he knows he can
intimidate the boy. Claire, secretly
thrown because this is the first stage
of her kids slipping away, pretends
to be okay with it and cautions the
rest of the family not to embarrass
Haley. Later, after Phil's attempts to
intimidate the boy have embarrassingly

failed, Claire sees Haley and the boy
lounging on Haley's bed, but again
pretends to take it all in stride. She
invites Haley and the boy to join the
family in going out for ice cream.
When Haley and the boy decide at the
last minute to go get coffee instead
of ice cream, Claire freaks out and
makes a scene, telling all the kids
at Starbucks to "Put down your coffee
and cell phones and go be kids! You're
fifteen, who the hell are you talking
to?!!!" Haley is mortified.

The general storyline involving Haley and Dylan made it to the pilot, tying into Claire's personal journey and mortal fear of her daughter making the same youthful mistakes and indiscretions she had. As appetizing as Starbucks and ice cream sound, it never developed as part of the story's third act.

Older husband, young wife:

Jay, as usual wearing clothes that are
too young for him, has an idea for how
to spend the day with Sofía, his young
wife, that doesn't include her young
son, Manny. Sofía says Manny's father
is picking him up at five to take him to
a ball game—they can have some alone
time then. Sofía lets Jay know that the
toilet is clogged. Jay suggests calling
a plumber. Sofía says that's a waste of
money; besides, it's a chance for Jay to
teach Manny how to be self-sufficient.
Manny and Jay clearly want no part of
this arrangement.

In the bathroom they plunge away,
getting nowhere. Sofía brings in a
closet auger to help clear the clog.
After Jay figures out how to use it, he
pulls out the source of the clog: his
favorite do-rag. He looks at Manny.
Manny denies flushing Jay's do-rag down
the toilet, making some veiled old man
jokes in the process. Sofía defends
Manny, saying he would never do such a
thing.

It's 6:15, and Manny is still waiting by
the curb with his baseball mitt—his dad
hasn't shown up. Finally his dad calls,
saying he can't make it for some lame
reason. Manny is clearly disappointed.
Jay takes this in (this gets resolved
later).

At this point, they hadn't named Gloria yet, so they used Vergara's first name instead. The character, as outlined here, plays a rather
passive role. Levitan and Lloyd ultimately gave her much more to do
in the pilot, enough to hint at character layers to peel for seasons to
come. Jay's fashion story survived as a minor plotline in support of the
age difference conflict between him and Gloria.

The story of Manny, his capricious dad, and Jay got tabled
and then revisited in the sitcom's second episode, "The Bicycle
Thief."

McPherson nixed the toilet bit entirely. Ironically, that story came
from Levitan's real life. Sometimes truth can be too gross and unrelatable. "One of my son's friends basically crapped in his pants and was
so embarrassed he tried to flush it down the toilet, completely clogging
it," recalls Levitan. "Also, apparently after bad shows, Letterman used

to flush his ties down the toilet, which I learned while working on The Larry Sanders Show."

Two gay men and a baby:

This story starts on an airplane where Mitchell and Cameron bring their new baby daughter home from Vietnam for the very first time. Everyone ogles the baby until they realize that she is being adopted by a gay couple—which clearly weirds a few people out. They stop at the grocery store, where Mitchell reads the riot act to someone who says, "A baby with two Twinkies, that's just wrong." He is sheepish after Cam points out the baby squishing two Hostess Twinkies all over herself behind them. When this new family arrives home, Mitchell is upset to find a mural that Cameron had painted in the baby's room while they were gone. The mural is a heavenly cloud scene, but for some reason, the muralist painted Cameron and Mitchell peeking out from behind a cloud with angelic wings—making them look like fairies. Meanwhile, the baby won't stop crying, and Mitchell is convinced it's because the baby wants a woman. Adding to their pressure, Mitchell's family is coming over tonight.

In the pilot, the airplane interior and grocery store scenes blend into one airplane scene. Mitchell's fear that the baby needs a mother distracts from the larger, more relatable plotline of Lily's adoption and introduction to the family. The muralist idea, from Lloyd's own life, remained in the story.

The Three Stories Converge . . .

. . . when Claire, Phil, and the kids and Jay, Sofía, and Manny show up at Mitchell and Cam's condo, revealing to the audience that Jay is actually Mitchell's father and that Claire is his sister. We quickly get a sense of family tension (i.e., Jay is not entirely comfortable with Mitchell's lifestyle; Claire doesn't approve of her father's young wife; Phil finds it hard not to stare at his wife's father's young wife; Haley is not talking to her mother).

Cameron makes a grand entrance with the baby, and everyone goes crazy for her.

Finally, off to the side, Mitchell confides in Claire that he's terrified this sweet, gorgeous little baby, whom he already loves so much, will grow up to be ashamed of him and Cam. Claire glances over at her daughter, then at her father dressed way too young, and says, "Oh, honey, don't be ridiculous. She's a daughter, and you're a parent. Of course she'll be ashamed of you." Claire says something about the difficulty of raising children, which Jay overhears.

As everyone tries to get their turn
with the baby, Jay notices Manny
sitting alone. He approaches and makes
some sort of gesture like, "Maybe we
could go to a ball game sometime."

On that sweet sentiment, in voice-
over, Geert Floortje delivers a quirky,
yet poignant summary of the American
family.

Mitchell confiding his fears to Claire of Lily being ashamed of him
and Cam suggests that Mitchell fears the impact of his sexual orientation. Throughout the entire run of the series, Cam and Mitchell never
question who they are.

Jay and Manny's sweet ending takes the edge off Jay and narrows
the potential for more conflict. Thus, it had to go. Geert's destiny
reached an even more tragic conclusion.

Not in My House

The transition from pilot pitch to pilot script brings with it constant discovery. Plot devices, backstory, and narrative float in and out. New characters rise while early favorites fall out of favor. The first such casualty in their script became the visionary documentarian himself, Geert Floortje.

LLOYD (*cocreator*): The note that came down early on from the executive echelon and studio was that they thought the one thing we should do is expand the character of the documentarian. This is what will make our show stand out, and it's the one thing we eliminated.

LEVITAN (*cocreator*): The first draft had a funny little opening and closing with Geert. I think you heard him asking questions in the interviews, but it risked becoming an appendage that you had to serve every week.

LLOYD (*cocreator*): We were going to wind up having to break the fourth wall all the time.

LEVITAN (*cocreator*): We realized it lifts right out and you don't miss it for a second. So we lost it very early. When we turned in our draft, the network was like, "What happened to that? We really liked that idea." We had to convince everyone that it was better without it.

They also concluded that Geert's personal documentary, his life's work, needed to go, too.

LLOYD (*cocreator*): We started asking a lot of questions like "Are these people really dealing with cameras in their house all the time? How are these intimate moments ever possible when they've got these cameras in their face?"

LEVITAN (*cocreator*): There would be times when you'd want to show a scene, for example, of a couple having a conversation in bed or something happening in the bathroom. The characters wouldn't let a cameraman be in the bathroom with them.

MERCHANT (*Leslie Higgins*): In a real documentary, there's no possible way this could exist. Who on earth would let you film in the bath?

LEVITAN (*cocreator*): Jay wouldn't have allowed a camera crew in his house. I don't think that Claire would think that's a good thing for her kids. We started to realize that if these were the kind of people who allowed their kids to be filmed growing up for some movie or TV show, we wouldn't like them as much, and I wanted to like them.

ZUKER (*writer / executive producer*): David Brent and Michael Scott probably would have been better off in their lives if that camera wasn't there, because it made them worse people. They always were performing for it, especially Brent. He viewed it as his star-making turn.

TY BURRELL (*Phil Dunphy*): Most mockumentaries are based more on character and awkwardness. We use hard jokes, old-fashioned multi-cam jokes, but in that mockumentary style. I think that has actually helped. People are sick of multi-cam because they see the punchline coming. This is a way where you can disguise it and still feel it in real time.

LEVITAN (*cocreator*): I would sometimes say to the actors, "Treat the joke like a bag of drugs. The cops are chasing you. You just have to crack open the door and drop them out the side of the car and keep driving. Don't stop and say, 'I'm going to do a joke here.' Just throw it away in performance."

ZUKER (*writer / executive producer*): I was an advocate for making the documentary. In fact, I had a pitch, had we done that, which I still love, but it would have been wrong for the show. We introduce a family member who never signed the release. And we pixelate and alter his face and voice. And throughout the series, we never really see who he is.

> *In the first season, writers and directors tried to remain true to the idea of a documentary crew, even though they understood that they didn't exist, only choosing shots where a crew could conceivably have room enough to shoot.*

WINER (*director / executive producer*): What was great in the early going was we really adhered to it. If the camera was following one of our characters up to a door, we wouldn't shoot them from inside the room because there wouldn't be a camera crew waiting inside.

GAIL MANCUSO (*director*): The documentarian shouldn't be ahead of where the family is, like preset in a scene. You're supposed to be following the family wherever they're at.

MERCHANT (*Leslie Higgins*): Ricky [Gervais] and I were always trying to be scrupulous about what seemingly might have been caught on-camera by a documentary team. I remember asking Greg Daniels [creator of the American version of *The Office*] about it. Isn't that going to hamper you when you're into your third or fourth season? He smartly observed that by that time, it will just be a shooting convention. People will forget that it's supposed to be a documentary. That's what happened. And so my feeling is by the time *Modern Family* came along, it was emulating that to some degree.

WINER (*director / executive producer*): It added to the very real and different feel of the show when it debuted. But once it became a hit, it became less important that the show distinguish itself visually from the rest of TV.

O'SHANNON (*writer / executive producer*): Finally at one point—it might not have been until the start of the second season—Steve said, "You know what? There is no documentary. This is just a style of storytelling." We went, "Okay," and didn't worry where a documentarian would stand.

LEVITAN (*cocreator*): There hasn't been one bit of blowback from the audience. Not one word. I don't think people care.

MERCHANT (*Leslie Higgins*): I remember talking to someone on the *Modern Family* set who said to me, "What I love about our show is it's got a completely unique visual style. It's like a documentary with these talking heads." And she was completely oblivious to my involvement with *The Office* and was taking great pride in the distinctive style of the show. I said, "Oh, it is very unique."

The final major casualty of the pilot became the series name, My American Family. *With Geert gone, "My" didn't refer to anyone.*

MORTON (*executive producer*): To me, it was one of our lucky breaks. *My American Family* is a more cumbersome title. *Modern Family* is much better. It's two words, quick and direct. *Modern*'s a good word, too.

LEVITAN (*cocreator*): Chris didn't love *Modern Family*. He said it says it too clearly and blatantly. It might as well say *Family*. I liked *Modern Family*. There was *Modern Love,* that Albert Brooks film. I thought it said it, so I kept pitching it over and over again. It seemed right.

LLOYD (*cocreator*): It was always on our list of titles but seemed a little basic, like we ought to be able to do better than that, but then as often happens with character names, you start referring to it that way and then it becomes the name of the show. I still don't think it's an exciting name, but it gets the job done.

Family Portrait

Having established the family tree, Levitan and Lloyd now needed to flesh out the family members—as individuals, part of a nuclear family and members of an extended one.

In the Dunphy family household live Phil and Claire and their children, in descending order, Haley, Alex, and Luke.

The husband

LLOYD (*cocreator*): Phil's like a dog that might chase a butterfly or not; might roll over on his side and enjoy the sun.

BURRELL (*Phil Dunphy*): I know people like Phil. There's one who I thought about in particular, who has this for-better-or-worse quality; not very introspective but very smart. He's lived a life of hard work and hard play, and that's about it. And he seems about the happiest person I've known.

ZUKER (*writer / executive producer*): I think Phil's somebody who loves his family and people. He's so enthusiastic about anything he's doing to the point that he's the perfect father.

The wife

LEVITAN (*cocreator*): Claire's a thinker. That's one of the reasons that she and Phil are such a good dynamic. She overthinks things, and Phil tends to underthink them.

O'SHANNON (*writer / executive producer*): Rather than simply being a naysayer, which is pretty one-dimensional, Claire recognizes this trait in herself and struggles with it. Compounding the struggle is the fact that Phil is always coming up with spontaneous ideas, many of which *need* to be shut down. The same is true with her competitiveness and need to be right. It's Claire's inner battles, the deals she makes with herself, the self-judgment when she fails, that make her a more layered character.

JULIE BOWEN (*Claire Dunphy*): There's that scene in the pilot where we're scheduling shooting Luke with the BB gun. That scene meant the most to me because it was the one time we realized Claire's on board with all of it. She's not just a finger-wagger. She's as odd as the rest of this bunch.

The marriage

O'SHANNON (*writer / executive producer*): I imagine Phil and Claire in the middle of the night. Phil can sleep like a baby as long as he knows his family's safe. Claire, meanwhile, is wide awake going over something she said at a party ten years ago and beating herself up for it.

ZUKER (*writer / executive producer*): I think Claire knows that Phil has made her a better person, kept wonder alive in her life when she could potentially descend into the cynicism of her Pritchett upbringing. His enthusiasm for the little things is infectious. It can be exhausting sometimes, too, but the net result is fantastic to her.

O'SHANNON (*writer / executive producer*): It was important that Claire and Phil love each other and enjoy each other's company. Once in a script,

Phil said something dumb or inadvertently insulting. She was supposed to say she wanted a "Phil-vorce." Julie didn't want to say it, and in retrospect, she was right.

Parenting

LLOYD (*cocreator*): I think when many of us have kids, there's a trust those kids have that you can exploit in a funny way, which is reverting to being a little bit of a dope around them and they're not going to reject you. They're going to like it. So you can, a little bit, rediscover your childhood. You dance, put on a stupid hat, do an impression, or tell a story around your kids in a way you'd maybe be too self-conscious to do around your adult friends. It's freeing. I think that's what makes Phil a very winning parent. Of course, 90 percent of the credit for that goes to Ty, because he can go to extremes in his goofiness but also make it believable and, when called upon, be so real and heartbreaking.

MANCUSO (*director*): One of my favorite things is when Phil has these great fathering moments. In "White Christmas" [season 7], Andy and Haley are in the closet (literally) having this affair when Andy's fiancée, Beth, comes over as a surprise. Phil sits down Andy and tells him to get his act together. "If it's a fling, it's over. You understand me? And if it's something real, then you stay honest with Beth. It's time to step up and be a man." Those moments with Phil are really special.

LEVITAN (*cocreator*): We did a thing where Haley had to write a college entrance essay about having to overcome difficulties in her life. She got a terrible grade on it and blamed her mom, saying she made everything so easy for her. Claire says she's right and wants to show her something that happened to her once to show she could really relate to it. She takes Haley out to the woods and leaves her there, shouting out the car window, "Now you have something to write about." I really thought that was delightful because in this day and age, with kids so needy and entitled, it was her doing something that the audience probably really liked, even though it was such a mean thing to do.

In the Pritchett-Tucker household reside Mitchell, Claire's brother; his partner for the past five years, Cam; and their adopted daughter, Lily.

The husband

LLOYD (*cocreator*): Mitchell's a little repressed, an uptight guy who's a bit too smart for his own good. He took his closeted homosexuality and channeled that into being a high achiever. He went to an Ivy League school but still had a lot of stuff to work out emotionally.

ELAINE KO (*writer / executive producer*): He's definitely repressed, and a bit guarded, but a lot of that's magnified because he's always next to Cam. I love Mitch's neuroses—they make him a fun character to write. I find discomfort funny.

JESSE TYLER FERGUSON (*Mitchell Pritchett*): I think he's a wonderful balance for someone like Cam. He needs that person that's going to push him to let go and live spontaneously. He fights against that at times, which is part of the beauty of their relationship.

The husband

ERIC STONESTREET (*Cameron "Cam" Tucker*): I wanted Cam to be someone that celebrates people, so when he doesn't celebrate someone, we can all get on board that we don't like that person.

CORRIGAN (*writer / executive producer*): What Eric did with Cam was he really created this big, flamboyant, and somehow grounded character.

Lloyd (*cocreator*): My wife leads a very robust social life and doesn't always let me know. The extreme example of that was literally coming home and having a valet hand me a ticket as my car pulls up. We had that with Cam, feeling like he's incapable of not helping people in need. And while it makes Mitchell a little crazy that his house is going to be so unpredictable, how mad can he get, because what Cam is doing isn't selfish?

The marriage

BILL WRUBEL (*writer / executive producer*): Chris always made a point of reminding us that Cam and Mitch were homebodies. I think it was really important to him and Steve. These guys were in a committed relationship with a baby. They're doing simple things like trying to figure out what to give their kid for breakfast or give a good birthday party. That normalizes them as a couple.

LEVITAN (*cocreator*): A lot of people have a lot of preconceived notions about who gay people are. So the number-one thing is to show that this couple wants what most people want. They want to be good parents, they want to have a good relationship between them.

FERGUSON (*Mitchell Pritchett*): I once got in trouble for calling them the new Bert and Ernie, but I do feel that there's that yin and yang with them. I think you need that balance. You need the salty piece to go with the sweet. You need the acidity to go with the oil. I feel like they're a really beautiful balance for one another.

In the Pritchett home dwell Jay, the father of Mitchell and Claire, his fiery young Colombian wife, Gloria, and Manny, her young son from her first marriage.

The husband

WRUBEL (*writer / executive producer*): I always thought Jay's the protagonist of this series. This show is about this old white man's world that's changing all around him. His one son's gay with an adopted kid, and his daughter's married to this unconventional guy. It's like him having to tolerate a new world.

LEVITAN (*cocreator*): But also how that changing world's forced to deal with a generation that's not changing as fast as they are.

O'NEILL (*Jay Pritchett*): Before we started shooting, I was thinking, "It's Sofía and me, who's going to believe this?" Then I thought, "I don't even know what it's like to be my age." I always knew what it was like to be twenty, thirty, thirty-five. There was nothing really out of bounds. You could go out and pick up women. It may not be admirable, but it's okay. But at my age, going into this thing, sixty, I didn't even know what's appropriate in terms of men and women. What am I allowed to or supposed to do? I thought, "Play that insecurity, that doubt. Play it like you feel."

The wife

LEVITAN (*cocreator*): Where we often go wrong in this business is taking a woman who looks like Sofía and turning her into a sexy character. We took Gloria and turned her into a fiercely protective mother who loves her husband not for his money but because he's a good man who'll be a good influence on her son.

LLOYD (*cocreator*): The thing that made Gloria work, and a lot of that comes from Sofía, is that she's extremely loyal to family. She would throw everything aside to make sure she was there for Manny's recital at school. Once we saw that side of her character, we thought, "Oh, we can forgive any of what might seem extreme emotions or slight shallowness because she has values that are much greater than that."

SOFÍA VERGARA (*Gloria Delgado-Pritchett*): Sometimes I hear people say Gloria's stereotyping Latin women. I come from Colombia. The women there are very involved in everything that's happening in the family. They dress sexy. I wanted to put all those realistic things in the character. This is how they are. You can't tell me I'm stereotyping them. I know them. I know this woman. This woman is me.

The marriage

LEVITAN (*cocreator*): We played around with the idea of her as a gold digger in an episode, but it was to play with the idea that many people would look at them and say to Jay, "Oh, you must be rich." Over and over and over again, we make sure you never get the sense that she's with him for his money. What she's there for is because he's the opposite of her ex-husband. He's a good man, honest, and dependable, and he'll be a good influence for her son.

LLOYD (*cocreator*): Gloria pressuring Jay to be a better man was an important part of that character. She's not just an appendage for him but someone who challenges him. Maybe he didn't quite know what he was signing up for when he got together with her, but we like seeing her push him to be better.

O'NEILL (*Jay Pritchett*): Sofía and I said it probably started with Gloria's need to provide security for her and her son. This is an older man, but he seems a nice enough guy. He has a good business. He's generous, funny. And then it eventually became love.

The parents

Jay, a meat-and-potatoes man with traditional values, struggles to understand Manny, a stargazing romanticist who believes magical thinking can make dreams come true.

LLOYD (*cocreator*): Manny wears puffy sleeves and writes poetry. He has lots of moods. All of the stuff that Jay's dad said to him growing up is never going to apply to this kid, so he's going to be a challenge for Jay.

O'NEILL (*Jay Pritchett*): Jay's never going to be Manny's father. He's got a father. But he's something. It's one of those interesting things to play because Manny's father occasionally visits and Jay has to take a step back. But he's always going to be there for the kid no matter what. I take that from my father. He was a tough guy, a steelworker and truck driver. Someone asked me not long ago, "Did your father ever tell you he loved you?" I said, "No." And he said, "That's too bad." I said, "He didn't have to. I knew he did." That's the truth, the truest thing I could say. I knew he would do anything for me. That's what I take into that with Manny. It's about making sure he's going to be okay.

Phil and Jay

As for the extended family, certain relationships stand out, such as Jay and Phil's. Jay loves football. Phil loves cheerleading. Jay can handle silence. Phil must anxiously fill the void. Jay keeps his emotions at bay. Phil wears his on his sleeve, pants, socks, shoes, and face. Jay has a daughter. Phil got that daughter pregnant accidentally and out of wedlock. He feels he must constantly make up for that.

LLOYD (*cocreator*): That Phil-Jay dynamic makes a lot of us squirm because we've been through relationships with our father-in-law that doesn't quite approve of us. I think it goes directly to fathers and sons. You always feel like a little bit of a schlub around your father, like you're always being seen at your worst. We explored that with Phil wanting to go fly Jay's model airplane with him. Jay may or may not have intentionally flown the plane into Phil. Claire seizes on that. She asks him, "Have you ever told him that you like him or love him?"

BURRELL (*Phil Dunphy*): That episode has one of Ed's and my favorite scenes where Phil comes in and tries to make some connection with Jay. That scene really sets the tone for their whole relationship. I always feel like it's double Dutch in jump rope, where Phil's waiting for just the right moment to come in and he's constantly getting tangled with the rope and Jay. That scene in particular is trying to feel it out and getting it wrong and getting it wrong and getting it wrong. I think that he really truly admires Jay and wants to be liked by him. He thinks that Jay's cool. Phil's the type of person who would think Jay's closet innovations are remarkable. It's just magical what he's done with closets.

O'NEILL (*Jay Pritchett*): When I was a teenager, my best friend had older brothers. They were athletes, nice, but a little bit arrogant. One evening, I came over early to get my friend. He was busy doing something with his mother. Meanwhile, his younger sister was getting ready for one of her first dates. The father and brothers were watching a football game. This poor fucking kid who was taking their sister out gets let in by the mother. The dad and brother don't even get up. They're watching the game. She says she'll tell her daughter he's here. They don't say, "Sit down." They don't say anything to him. They're watching the game. I look at him and he's dying, standing there dying. It went on for ten minutes and then finally she came down. The kid was never so happy to get out of a place with that kind of tension. I never told Ty this, but I think of that sometimes when I play a scene with him. That kind of silence without any expression whatsoever. There's nothing for him.*

Jay, Claire, and Mitchell

Jay has a lot to make up for with the children from his first marriage, Claire and Mitchell.

FERGUSON (*Mitchell Pritchett*): Mitchell has a very complex relationship with his dad, which I am so attached to as a story point. I think it's so important to tell those stories about parents not immediately accepting their children, not tied up in neat bows. I love the messiness of the relationship.

O'NEILL (*Jay Pritchett*): Jay wasn't the best parent in the world. He was working a lot, trying to establish a business. He wasn't home a lot. He ran around and drank a bit. His son and daughter got a short shrift in terms of Daddy. And now he's married a beautiful younger girl, and they resent that a bit.

---

* In season 2's "Dance Dance Revelation," Jay apologizes and tells Phil, "You've got to stop taking that stuff personally. I'm like that with everybody. I'm tough. I don't like to take guff." He even admits sometimes he thinks the boys would be better off being like Phil. The feeling lasts all of thirty seconds.

Claire carries with her a grudge for the childhood she feels Jay never gave her. Like many of us, she includes her dad as part of her life while also passive-aggressively expressing past resentments. Jay takes it all, because he loves his daughter and carries the burden of the mistakes he made as her father.

O'NEILL (*Jay Pritchett*): The idea that I kind of screwed Claire up is always an ongoing scene. I'm always trying to get out from under that. Like "Was this really my fault, and if it is, isn't it time to get over this?" which is maddening for her and frustrating for me.

LLOYD (*cocreator*): Claire knew early on that a way to get Jay's attention and affection was to be the son he never had. I think that Jay welcomed that, but also saw a tenacity and rebelliousness in her. That push-pull carries on into adulthood. She's a little bit of a daddy's girl but would resent the implications of that. Those scenes when they let down their hair and show vulnerability toward each other, and in so doing, show what they still need from each other, were always my favorites. When their company was subsumed by the other company run by those younger guys and Jay confessed to her he didn't want to be a mascot, the old guy in the office to tell stories, and she told him in her own way he was feared and revered and shouldn't worry about that—I liked that scene quite a bit.

As for her brother, Claire summarizes her feelings in her toast at his wedding:

INT. RECEPTION AREA

We're mid-ceremony. Claire is giving her toast.

> CLAIRE
> I was his big sister. His big brother.
> His nemesis. His protector. His best
> friend. I was his first partner—and I
> loved every minute of it.

Mitch opens up in an interview from another episode, recalling how he and Claire, as kids, used to be ice-skating partners.

MITCHELL INTERVIEW

> MITCHELL
> Yes, my sister and I were actually a
> very good team.
> We were called "fire and nice." I was
> "fire," 'cause of the red hair, and
> Claire was "nice," because it was
> ironic and she wasn't.

Phil and Gloria

Phil and Gloria fleetingly meet in the pilot.

INT. MITCHELL AND CAMERON'S DUPLEX—DAY

They all ad-lib greetings. Claire and Gloria
exchange an awkward hug.

> PHIL
> Hi, Gloria. Wow, that's a beautiful
> dress.

> GLORIA:
> Ay, thank you, Pheel.

> PHIL
> (hearing "feel")
> Oh, okay (feeling her dress). Ooh,
> it's—

                    CLAIRE
            (slapping his hand away)
    That's how she says *Phil*. Not *feel*.
    Phil.

VERGARA (*Gloria Delgado-Pritchett*): When you're in the middle of a scene and everybody's holding the laughs, you know it's something that's going to work.

WINER (*director / executive producer*): That scene is an exchange of two lines and a couplet. Yet that interaction establishes a comedic dynamic that set those three characters for the entire series. Phil's flummoxed by Gloria's passion, sensuality, and being. Claire finds it funny and ridiculous. She's constantly running interference for the ways that Phil gets himself in trouble tripping over Gloria.

BURRELL (*Phil Dunphy*): That has a lot to do with Phil the talking dog because that was the only way to make that not feel lascivious. He's a person without impulse control. He sees something shiny and beautiful and reacts without thinking.

   Eleven individual characters intricately woven together in countless conflicting ways. The complexity of family brought to life onscreen. But would audiences care?

LLOYD (*cocreator*): I can honestly tell you when we finished writing it, I said to some of my old *Frasier* writer friends at a party, "I think the writing makes me laugh, but I'd sell it to you for $10 because I don't see any future for this show." And that was about six months before we premiered. But with every layer we got into after that, seeing actors come in, then seeing them together and then on film, there was a growing level of belief. The final piece was when we were watching the first assembly. I thought, "I don't want to jinx this, but I think this might be great."

The Wow Factor

Modern Family's original cast called for ten talking parts alongside one baby. Emmy-winning casting director Jeff Greenberg, an industry veteran with more than twenty years' experience working on iconic shows such as Cheers, Wings, *and* Frasier, *inherited the daunting task.*

JEFF GREENBERG (*casting director*): *Ten roles is big for a half-hour show. But because the script was so good and I was so excited about it, I didn't feel overwhelmed. I was super charged to dive into it.*

Greenberg had the rare luxury of working with a script that came with visual prototypes for each character, plus he knew both showrunners very well.

GREENBERG (*casting director*): *We talked about look, type, and a lot of the specifics for what makes a character unique. We'd always talk about age range. It's never the actual age of the actor; it's what the actor plays. Then I went and made a couple of lists for each part.*

Greenberg created character breakdowns for all the parts, which he posted online.

GREENBERG (*casting director*): *We use Breakdown Express.**

---

* Breakdown Express is an online component of Breakdown Services, the primary casting distributor of information about casting for casting directors, talent

It's a description of the character in terms of age, look, and context of how we use them. That gets distributed online to all the agents and managers in show business. They then submit clients who they feel are appropriate. For a series regular, you get well over 1,000 submissions.

Modern Family, for example, received approximately 1,400 submissions for Claire and Phil each. Mitch, Cam, and Haley garnered roughly 900–1,000 submissions; Jay, 500. The specificity of Manny's age, ethnicity, and character led to that part receiving the smallest number of submissions, yet even that role ended up with around 200.

Oftentimes, because casting directors want certain types, actors audition alongside the same people time and time again.

Greenberg always tries to be supportive, knowing what the process feels like from the other end, having been an aspiring actor himself once. In reality, very qualified people don't always land roles.

STONESTREET (*Cam Tucker*): *I always point out that it isn't like you suck. They don't think you're necessarily right for the part or what they're looking for right now.*

ALLEN HOOPER (*casting associate*): *Ashley Jensen tested at the studio for Claire. You have somebody that's brilliant like Ashley, phenomenal on* Extras. *You think it's a gimme that an actor'll book anything they audition for because of how great you see them in one thing. But in addition to how damn good they are, it's how the role fits the actor that finally decides it.*

---

representatives, and actors. According to its website, Breakdown Express coordinates the release of casting information, submissions from talent representatives, and online auditions. It releases more than 43,000 projects per year throughout North America and maintains a database of over 845,000 actors. Breakdown Services, Ltd., https://breakdownservices.com/.

BOWEN (*Claire Dunphy*): *You know how many shows are on that I auditioned for and didn't get? You get used to it. It's a bummer, but you get used to it. It's part of the gig.*

Actors tend to judge their auditions harshly.

HOOPER (*casting associate*): *Every actor thinks they've done worse than we do, unless they're delusional. They're so involved in the character that they don't see it as we do. There's a blog post Jeff and I saw from a lady who read for a guest spot on season 4. Her audition went so badly that she quit acting. We're reading it thinking, "We don't remember this at all." I looked at my notes. They read, "Fine. A little over the top." She thought she was so God-awful that she quit.*

After the producers get a look at the casting director's options, they pare down the list of potentials to a select few, who then work their way to studio and network auditions.

GREENBERG (*casting director*): *It's a mandate that the studio and network want choices. Three is ideal. Two's usually fine. Sometimes you can bring up to five. You go to the studio first so they can whittle it down to their top two or three. Quite often, they want context. You go in with your favorite person and you want to show them someone else really good, too, so that the people making the final call can judge why your person is better. They like to be a part of making decisions.*

It used to be that actors would read in the network president's office while staring at pictures of the executive's family and paperweights on their desk. That method eventually got replaced by stages with theater seating or couches.

FALVEY (*ABC Entertainment head of comedy*): *If I'm being really fair about it, the casting process can be flawed. At the time, you would bring actors in to audition in front of you, which doesn't make* *a lot of sense, but there wasn't much use of technology then as there is now. Inevitably what would end up happening is someone wouldn't audition well, but they were a great actor or vice versa. If you've ever watched a show and thought, "How does that person keep getting cast in stuff?" that's probably why.*

Modern Family casting somehow avoided all that. Casting came through a combination of determination, demonstration, and dramatization, resulting in the absolute best choices for each role.

LEVITAN (*cocreator*): *I can look back and think of all the things that could have, might have, or should have gone wrong, and somehow magically they all came together in this one moment when we needed them. It's a miracle.*

That miracle began with the casting of Ed O'Neill.

Tough Love

Jay Pritchett—sixties, successful businessman, divorced. Recently married Gloria; struggles to stay "young" for her.

It's going to come down to Jay, in any kind of crisis in the family, whatever it might be. Whatever it is, it will go through me.

—ED O'NEILL

Ed O'Neill has had a long and distinguished career appearing on Broadway, television, and in movies. Most people, however, remember him as Al Bundy, from the long-running Fox sitcom Married with Children.

O'NEILL (*Jay Pritchett*): I enjoyed *Married with Children.* I had my problems with some of the shows, but when it was funny, it would make me laugh out loud, so I was proud of it. It was obvious to me, however, that it wasn't the kind of show that was going to win any awards or be the critics' darling. Some people thought it was a bit gross and dysfunctional in a way they found more than offensive.

Because the show did not deal in subtleties, neither did the comedy or performances.

O'NEILL (*Jay Pritchett*): My character drove the show. It sometimes necessitated over-the-top frenetic acting, where you're really pushing the comedy.

Sometimes you push it too far. But you don't know until you get there, you know?

When the series ended its run, O'Neill gravitated away from sitcoms to prominent roles in one-hour television dramas, such as The Big Apple (2001), Dragnet (2003–2004), David Milch's John from Cincinnati (2007), and The West Wing (1999–2006).

By 2008, after almost three decades of acting, the sixty-three-year-old thespian had nothing left to prove to Hollywood. While he still relished performing, he didn't have to work, an enviable position for any actor. As a result, he didn't find Modern Family *as much as Levitan and Lloyd found him.*

LLOYD (*cocreator*): Ed was enjoying his semiretirement, working when he felt like it. He had a house in Hawaii. He basically let his agents know he wasn't in the market for another series at this stage in his life.

O'NEILL (*Jay Pritchett*): My manager called and asked if I'd take a meeting with Chris Lloyd and Steve Levitan. I said, "They do sitcoms, right?" He said, "Yeah." I said, "I don't want to do any more sitcoms." He told me they hadn't written anything yet. It was a "courtesy meeting." I said, "I don't like that sort of thing. If I go in there and have no intention of doing it, it feels insulting." He said, "Trust me. Go in and talk to them. It's good to know them. They do things." So I went to their offices on the Fox lot. And the first thing I tell them is, "I'm not interested in a sitcom, guys. I did eleven years on *Married with Children,* and that's enough."

LLOYD (*cocreator*): Then he started telling stories about Youngstown, Ohio [his hometown], or some off-Broadway theater thing he'd done or being on a private plane with Al Pacino. You can't say a word that doesn't trigger a story from him. I thought, "I could hang with this guy all day."

O'NEILL (*Jay Pritchett*): They came at me from a bit of a different angle. They said, "Your show had a live audience, with four cameras. This is two cameras, and we're going to shoot it like a movie with no audience." Some-how, they must have found out I don't like live audiences. The reason for that was I had a theater background. A lot of actors that come from the theater think they're going to like studio audiences, but it's really not a live theater audience. They're sitting behind cameras, looking at monitors. Of-tentimes, they laugh at inappropriate times and blow the timing of a joke. It's an annoyance. I told them that doing it as a movie was a plus for me, but I still don't want to do a half hour. So they ended the meeting by asking if I'd read their script after they wrote it. And I said of course, I'd be happy to. About a year later, I get a package in the mail. I looked and saw their names on a script and thought this must be that pilot they wrote.

LLOYD (*cocreator*): He read the script almost under protest. We let him know that based upon that previous meeting, we had a good feeling about him.

O'NEILL (*Jay Pritchett*): I read it. And then I read it again. And I thought, "Oh shit, this is good." So I called my manager and said, "I think I'm going to have to do this." And he said, "It's not an offer. They're out to Craig T. Nelson."

GREENBERG (*casting director*): When there's an offer on the table, you can't offer it to two people.

LEVITAN (*cocreator*): We'd met with Craig T., and he was very nice. And we'd met with Ed, and he was very nice. We had a tough decision to make. We went to the network and said, "Listen, we're a little stuck on this. We can go either way. We think they're both amazing actors. Do you have a strong point of view on it?"

GREENBERG (*casting director*): It was fifty-fifty, so they had Steve McPherson toss a coin and make the call. He said to go with Craig T. Nelson.

LEVITAN (*cocreator*): What came back to us later was that because Craig T. was on the cover page of our script, that they leaned toward him.

O'NEILL (*Jay Pritchett*): In a way, I was relieved, because I thought, "I don't have to make a hard decision."

LLOYD (*cocreator*): Craig T. seemed to like and understand the character. We had an idea it would go well, but we kept thinking about Ed for some reason. Does he fit a little bit better with some of the other elements we have in mind? We were in negotiation with Craig T., however, and there was no unwinding that.

LEVITAN (*cocreator*): Then Craig T. countered rather aggressively.

GREENBERG (*casting director*): He wanted star money, and it wasn't a star show. It's an ensemble show. I understand from his agent that he regretted his decision. I'm not surprised.

LEVITAN (*cocreator*): And we started to hear some rumblings that maybe he was a bit difficult on set. Then he made this quote bashing people on food stamps and welfare for taking from the government.* That scared us, frankly. There was a lack of self-awareness there and compassion that worried us. Meanwhile, all we kept hearing is that Ed O'Neill is the nicest person on the planet. We decided to pull the offer and go to Ed.

LLOYD (*cocreator*): You hear things about people and you take them with a grain of salt. If you've worked in Hollywood long enough, there's negatives and positives said about anyone. What we had was a firsthand indication that Ed was going to be a blast to work with. I think that played a much bigger role than anything that had been insinuated about Craig T. Honestly, I can't tell you Craig T. wouldn't have been great in the role. He's a really funny actor and would have brought a different quality.

LEVITAN (*cocreator*): Craig T. would have been fantastic in the role.

---

* The quote he made was: *"I've been on food stamps and welfare. Anybody helped me out? No, no, they gave me hope. And they gave me encouragement and they gave me a vision that came from my education."*

GREENBERG (*casting director*): I think he and Ed possess the right qualities for the role of Jay; a certain guy's guy; older, still attractive, funny; came up the hard way. But Ed is Ed. He's so sublime in the part that it's hard to think anyone would be better.

LEVITAN (*cocreator*): He's a wonderful dramatic actor who doesn't like drama. He doesn't tolerate people acting out. He doesn't want to hear your bullshit. I've always said that's a wonderful number one to have on your call sheet. Somebody who helps set a tone like that.

LLOYD (*cocreator*): He's very warm and funny with a natural storytelling ability. He imbues the character with this charm. And you can't do better than that.

They went back to O'Neill. The ball fell in his court.

O'NEILL (*Jay Pritchett*): My agent called and said, "They couldn't make the deal with Craig. They're back to you." I said make the deal. He said, "They're not paying your quote." I said make the deal. It's a hit show. He said, "But you're not the star." I said, "I know that. I like that about it. It's an ensemble. It's more interesting to me." We made the deal.

GREENBERG (*casting director*): Ed was willing to take less money than he would normally take knowing if the show was successful, he'd make it in the back end, which he certainly has and then some.

FALVEY (*ABC Entertainment head of comedy*): At first, you're living with the idea of Craig and how amazing he is. Then this other idea comes in and feels smart in a different way. It struck me as not being an obvious choice, but made so much sense when I heard it. I remember driving on the freeway and thinking, "Oh my God. That's a brilliant idea." Reinventing Ed O'Neill was so smart.

GREENBERG (*casting director*): Ed has said for years that when he was on *Married with Children*, everyone would say, "Great job," and "Congratulations, you're on a hit." But he said this show validated him in a way that he never got before. People whose opinion he really cares about, in terms of the work, have let him know how much they appreciate what he does. It's a combination of an artistic and commercial success. I don't think a day goes by that he doesn't appreciate it.

O'NEILL (*Jay Pritchett*): *Married with Children* was a great job. I loved and appreciated it greatly. But I never got a whole lot from my acting peers. I've always felt that you get a job like this, you're very lucky. When it started to play out as it did, all that recognition that we got early on, other actors who would appreciate it, guest stars who were dying to do it, that was all new to me. I love that about it and how much people like the show. If you're doing that thing, you want that pat on the shoulder, you know?

LLOYD (*cocreator*): He's said to me countless times, "Chris, this is the best job I've ever had. I would have done it for free. Don't tell my agent, but I would have taken this job for free."

Coal Digger

Gloria—thirties, Hispanic, beautiful, strong, quick-tempered. Protective mother. Divorced six years ago.

I wanted Gloria to be Latin. I wanted her to be how I remember the women in Colombia, like my mom and aunt. They're very loud, very passionate, and stick their nose in everybody's business because they care.

— Sofía Vergara

When Sofía Vergara relocated from Colombia to Miami, Florida, in 1998, she had her young son, Manolo, and little else. Almost five years later, she made her first appearance on an American sitcom. It would be another seven working in short-term sitcoms and independent films before she got to show off her comedic talents and unique melding of languages as Gloria Delgado-Pritchett.

VERGARA (Gloria Delgado-Pritchett): In 2002, I did an episode of *My Wife and Kids,* which is where I met Damon Wayans.

MCPHERSON (ABC Entertainment president): Damon became interested in producing something for her. They did a pilot together with Joey Lawrence called *I Married Sophia.* That was the first time that I met her.

In the 2004 pilot, Lawrence played a once-successful New Yorker strapped for cash who marries a foreign woman in need of a green card. When an INS agent grows suspicious, the fake couple, along with her seven-year-old son, end up cohabitating. Vergara didn't like the finished product.

VERGARA (*Gloria Delgado-Pritchett*): It started as one kind of script and then the network stepped in. By the time we shot it, it had become something different. It didn't test high.

The pilot didn't get picked up by the network.

MCPHERSON (*ABC Entertainment president*): We loved her, though. I thought she was such an amazing talent, special and unique, so we made a holding deal with her.

GREENBERG (*casting director*): A holding deal's when a studio or network pays an actor a chunk of change to have exclusive services, usually for a year, in regard to their projects.

As part of that deal, Vergara guest-starred on another Wayans-produced ABC series, Rodney (2004–2006), starring stand-up comedian Rodney Carrington. Meanwhile, McPherson continued looking for more substantial parts for her.

VERGARA (*Gloria Delgado-Pritchett*): I shot a pilot called *Hot Properties*. That show lasted half a season.

ANDY GORDON (*writer / executive producer*): She was hysterical. From table read to run-through to live audience shows, she made everything funnier. I found myself pitching jokes for her character more than anyone else, because she always made me look good.

McPherson extended Vergara's holding deal a second year.

VERGARA (*Gloria Delgado-Pritchett*): Stephen was always a big believer in me. He kept saying he was going to find something amazing for me.

After a while, though, I was like, "I'm done. Let me see if there's something somewhere else."

And then he extended her deal a third year. During that time, Gordon brought her to the attention of Levitan and Lloyd.

GORDON (*writer / executive producer*): I was helping Steve and Chris on the pilot for *Back to You*. They had an actress playing a Hispanic weather girl that they were concerned about. She wasn't landing jokes. I told them they had to read Sofía for the part, that she would destroy it.

LEVITAN (*cocreator*): He said, "If you're looking for somebody, she's really gorgeous and really funny. She knows how to land a joke."

But Back to You *aired on the Fox Network and Vergara still had that holding deal at ABC.*

GORDON (*writer / executive producer*): Ultimately, Steve and Chris did make a change. Unfortunately, it was with another actress who also couldn't keep up with the comedy talent on set. Every time she blew a joke, I'd say, "You should've hired Sofía."

LEVITAN (*cocreator*): We remembered that while we were writing the *Modern Family* pilot.

In 2007, McPherson attached Vergara to a mid-season replacement show from David Letterman's Worldwide Pants production company, The Knights of Prosperity. *The series, starring Donal Logue, followed blue-collar misfits in New York City who rob celebrities.*

MCPHERSON (*ABC Entertainment president*): It was originally supposed to be called *Let's Rob Mick Jagger*, but we couldn't get the rights to say that.

Jagger did, however, serve as executive producer for the pilot episode, in which the characters actually do attempt to rob him (Jagger never appeared on the show).

VERGARA (*Gloria Delgado-Pritchett*): I had to move to New York with my son to do it. It was a lot of hard work because there were six people in the cast and we were all in every scene. But it was amazing.

The series lasted thirteen episodes. ABC didn't pick it up for the fall.

VERGARA (*Gloria Delgado-Pritchett*): After that, I went back to Stephen and pleaded, "Let me go. Let me go. I can find something else."

GREENBERG (*casting director*): ABC's holding deal with Sofía was four years old by then. They really believed in her, so they kept reupping it.

VERGARA (*Gloria Delgado-Pritchett*): Stephen was like, "No, I'm going to find you something." And then he did: *Modern Family*.

MCPHERSON (*ABC Entertainment president*): It was absolutely perfect for her.

LLOYD (*cocreator*): Gloria has an extroverted personality, a freeness with emotions. She screams and yells. When Larry David talks about writing his character on *Curb Your Enthusiasm*, he says, "I'm not really like that guy, but I wish I could be more often in life, the guy that has the guts to say stuff all the time." I think we all feel that way, that we all have that desire to be a little bit more like Gloria.

LEVITAN (*cocreator*): We got tapes on Sofía, which is what you did back then. We could tell that she had something going on there.

The showrunners wanted to meet her, to get a sense of how she might fit within their vision of the Gloria character. She came to visit their offices.

LEVITAN (*cocreator*): She has a presence about her. She's so charming and winning, but she didn't have the same confidence then that she has now, because she was still relatively unknown. We immediately knew she was the right person.

LLOYD (*cocreator*): She's extremely loud and extremely vivacious. The loudness can be very off-putting in some people. For some reason, every time Sofía does something loud, it's 27 percent funnier.

GREENBERG (*casting director*): Sofía is Sofía. She's very much her character. I've seen her out in the world. The waves part for her. Had I not had so much to do with the other parts, I might have tried to come up with a list of actresses just in case, but to this day I couldn't think of someone as perfect for that part as Sofía.

Although keenly interested in the part, she waited until she got the offer and read the final script.

GREENBERG (*casting director*): It wasn't a foregone conclusion.

VERGARA (*Gloria Delgado-Pritchett*): When I read the part, I was a little worried. This woman was supposed to be an immigrant, superhot, who marries this older guy. Ed is twenty years older than me. At the beginning, I thought, "Oh my God, I think people are going to hate this character because she's the typical fucking gold digger." The moment I met Ed, though, I thought that this could totally work. I could make this woman be in love with this guy and I don't think anyone's going to write that it's unbelievable. And since the first episode aired, I don't think anyone has.

Kids These Days

Manny—eleven, Gloria's son and Jay's stepson. Old soul, sensitive, passionate, a young romantic.

What makes Manny unique is he doesn't really care what other people think. He's always just been himself. A passionate old soul and a mama's boy.

—RICO RODRIGUEZ

By 2009, eleven-year-old Rico Rodriguez from College Station, Texas, had been employed as a working actor for almost five years on a wide spectrum of TV shows, including Nickelodeon's iCarly *(2007–2012) and Ryan Murphy's* Nip/Tuck *(2003–2010), playing the role of "the kid." Then one day, the kid's agent passed along a pilot script to him for the role of Manuel Alberto Javier Alejandro Delgado, a.k.a. Manny.*

LLOYD (cocreator): The objective with Manny was to make him a mystery to Jay. Jay's got this beautiful, sexy wife, but there was a little asterisk, and that asterisk was Manny. He comes with the bargain, and he's not going to be easy for Jay. She's devoted to her son, but even to her, he's a bit of a mystery. She wonders, "How did I get a poet for a son, someone who feels all the weight of the world all the time?" It was this fun character to write, but good luck casting it.

GREENBERG (*casting director*): I knew it would be one of the most difficult roles to cast, which it was. I knew from the early days that they were talking about Sofía, so I was looking at Hispanic boys between the ages of eight and thirteen. I read a total of 198 Mannys. Only 8 were good enough to bring to the producers.

LLOYD (*cocreator*): Jeff did a great job. He brought in a range of kids. Oftentimes, kids at that age are as cute as can be. They've done cereal commercials and know how to smile so that you can see every single one of their teeth. But they're not so adept at playing things like forlornness, which is what Manny had.

RICO RODRIGUEZ (*Manny Delgado*): I remember going in and reading Manny like this player, someone opposite of what he is now. Jeff said, "Rico, that was good, but for Manny, think of him as Antonio Banderas in a ten-year-old kid's body: suave, passionate, very articulate with his words." And I was like, "What does the voice of *Puss in Boots* have to do with this kid?"

Rodriguez made it to callbacks.

RODRIGUEZ (*Manny Delgado*): I did what Jeff wanted me to do. After the audition, he said, "Yes, exactly. That was really good. Thank you for taking direction." That felt awesome. And then I didn't hear back for a month. I figured I must have not gotten it, which is okay. I'd go to the next one and fight. The next thing you know, my manager gets an email saying they want to see me again, but this time for a producer's session. I was like, "They want me back?" I was so excited.

LLOYD (*cocreator*): He certainly isn't one of these polished Hollywood kids that knows how to give you a firm handshake and tell you a funny story that his mother coached him to tell you in the car ride over. He's a raw, interesting kid. We loved him from the start. He was virtually unknown, but he had a somber quality that was funny. And he was very warm in the auditions.

Rodriguez worked his way up the audition ladder to the network test.

RODRIGUEZ (*Manny Delgado*): That was probably the most nervous I've ever been in an audition. They had two other kids who were going up for Manny. They were different. One spoke fluent Spanish. I don't know how to speak Spanish. I thought, "They want me here for a reason. Because I'm a little different."

LEVITAN (*cocreator*): There was another kid who was more conventionally cute, but there was this quality Rico had that he looked like he would drive Jay a little crazier, and that appealed to us. He's a quirky kid. If he's too cute, he disappears a little bit. That's where you get into kids that look like they're on a Disney show. It's not as interesting or as fun.

RODRIGUEZ (*Manny Delgado*): I walked in. It's one chair on a stage, like a little mini-auditorium, with a big spotlight on it. Behind the big spotlight is Jeff. I look around and think, "This is a big room for just me and him." And then I look up and there's probably thirty people—it looked like fifty to me, and they're looking at me—all these big cheeses from Fox and ABC. It made me even more nervous, but I work best under pressure. So I kicked it into a new gear.

LLOYD (*cocreator*): There was one bit where he had to go running. He went running clear across the room. He was so genuine that he didn't realize you could pretend to run or take one step. I thought that's very dear.

RODRIGUEZ (*Manny Delgado*): Manny gets out of the car and runs off to pick flowers for Brenda Feldman. So I jumped out of my chair and ran across the stage like a madman because that's what the scene told me to do. Everyone got a nice little chuckle out of that. Why is this kid running? I only need him to say the lines. They clapped and laughed at what I was saying. I thought, "Okay, that's good. At least they're not frowning."

LEVITAN (*cocreator*): He had that quality, that weird, offbeat element. It was a different way to go.

RODRIGUEZ (*Manny Delgado*): We're on the freeway on our way home and my agent, Diane, calls my mom, who puts it over the speaker. She says, "So, Rico, how'd it go?" I told her I thought I did well. Usually the sign of a good audition for me is when it's like a blur. They laughed. "Well, Rico," she said. "I think you did really good because you got the role." I was in shock. I called my dad immediately. He was ecstatic. I didn't call my sister yet because we were heading home. Me, being the jokester that I am, decided to prank her and tell her I didn't get it. So when I got home, I put water near my eyes so it looked like I was crying. When I entered my apartment, she was like, "Rico, how'd it go?" I turned on the acting chops a little bit and said, "You know, Raini, I think I did horrible because they said they didn't like me and I didn't get it." She said she was so sorry. She was consoling me, making sure I'm okay, giving me a nice pep talk about doing good the next time. And I said, "Raini, you know the crazy part about it?" She asked, "What?" I go, "The crazy part is I actually got it."

He almost lost it, however, after the pilot.

LEVITAN (cocreator): Our one concern was that he was a little hard to understand. When we shot the pilot, we were always searching for the takes where we could really understand him.

MORTON (executive producer): They had ideas to make him a Don Juan character, and so he needed some verbal dexterity. I spoke to his mom after the pilot and said, "We love Rico, but one of the things you need to do in these next few months is get him some diction lessons."

RODRIGUEZ (Manny Delgado): Steve and Chris told me, "If you can't get it fixed, we're going to have to go another way." I didn't want this opportunity to fall because I didn't do something right. So I went back to my acting class and told my acting teacher, Helen. And so for half a year, I was in classes. During a scene, she'd stop me and say, "Rico, I can't understand a word you're saying." I'd start again, and she'd go, "I still can't hear you." And then slowly but surely, it fixed the problem. When we went to the first episode, Jeff, Steve, Chris, and Jason said they were really impressed and happy because they love me and didn't want to have to find a new Manny. Obviously it benefited me.

The kid had made it to the big time.

I Don't Know How She Does It

Claire Dunphy—late thirties, uptight suburban mom, tries to make every day special for her kids; needs control.

I don't think it's as simple as her needing control. I think Claire feels misunderstood a lot because she voices her opinions quickly. She's misunderstood. She's just misunderstood.

—JULIE BOWEN

Someone within every household has to keep the trains running on time. Within the Dunphy family, Claire fills that role, along with the duties of conductor, dispatcher, brake operator, railcar loader, and occasional passenger. Casting such a complex character tasked Greenberg with finding an actress who could balance a commanding presence with comedic chops.

LLOYD (*cocreator*): We were looking for a funny actress. I'd always been a fan of Kristen Johnston.

MORTON (*executive producer*): Phil would have been a whole different character if she'd done it.

FALVEY (*ABC Entertainment head of comedy*): Can you imagine what that would have looked like?

GREENBERG (*casting director*): We were on our way to test her, but she took another role in the *AbFab* [*Absolutely Fabulous*] series, which quickly died. She wasn't right for Claire anyway.

> *Many other well-known names came up in conversation, all of whom took a pass.*

GREENBERG (*casting director*): We made early overtures to Lisa Kudrow. I found out after the fact that Lisa's agents never brought it to her, which is a big no-no, as they didn't think she'd want to do another ensemble show.

FALVEY (*ABC Entertainment head of comedy*): I wanted Leah Remini to read for it, but she was "offer only." I tried and tried and tried, but couldn't get her agent to get her to read.

GREENBERG (*casting director*): We wanted to read her to see if she could lose her New York accent, because Claire was distinctly from California. She agreed to read but first wanted to meet with us.

HOOPER (*casting associate*): She came in and sat down with Steve and Chris.

GREENBERG (*casting director*): Afterward, she changed her mind and refused to read. It was a sign to us she couldn't lose the accent. Steve also had an informal chat with Debra Messing, asking if she'd be interested, and she wasn't. She commented later that she regretted it. We read a lot of other great comedy ladies, the best of comedy. Rachel Harris auditioned for us and was great. We wanted to test her, but she passed. I think she was newly single and didn't want to play a mother of teenagers.

HOOPER (*casting associate*): I would imagine that was true for a number of the people that passed.

GREENBERG (*casting director*): We mentioned her name to Steve McPherson, and he said he loved her and that we could offer it to her, so we did, and she still said no.

LEVITAN (*cocreator*): If you think about some of the other actresses we were considering for that role, it's amazing because it would have not only changed Claire, but it would have changed Phil and Mitchell. It was all interdependent.

A revolving door of potential Claires entered and exited, 212 actresses in all.

GREENBERG (*casting director*): I pre-read 105 and then read 107 with the producers. I was out of comic actresses to bring in, within the age range, and it was on my shoulders. We didn't have anyone. There were these two actresses, but they weren't available because they were very pregnant. One was Kimberly Williams-Paisley, who lives in Nashville and wasn't interested in flying in. The other was Julie Bowen. Julie's body of work was an asset because she'd done such great stuff over the years and the network loved her.

BOWEN (*Claire Dunphy*): Stephen McPherson gave me a shot before anybody did. I think he made my first holding deal as an actor.

MCPHERSON (*ABC Entertainment president*): We were very familiar with Julie's work, and I knew her a little outside of that. She's kind of like that everywoman, that all-American wife.

MORTON (*executive producer*): I'd done a show, *Jake in Progress*, with John Stamos. At the end of our first season, we got Julie to do a four-episode arc. She was a breath of fresh air. So when they said they were having trouble finding Claire, I told them about my *Jake in Progress* experience with Julie.

Pregnancy didn't stop Bowen from drudging through pilot season.

BOWEN (*Claire Dunphy*): Pilot season's brutal. It's like you're an automaton. I was out auditioning all the time. Whoever was going to see my pregnant ass, I was going to go in. Some of them you love. There was one that year in which I auditioned with Romany Malco. I knew we had a great audition and that I wasn't getting it because I was pregnant.

GREENBERG (*casting director*): I didn't ask Steve and Chris if I could bring in a pregnant actress, because they might have said no, so I brought her in.

LEVITAN (*cocreator*): She walked in very pregnant.

BOWEN (*Claire Dunphy*): I had a meeting in Chris's office, which I hated. Just have me read. You get to this point in your career where you're not supposed to be reading for things. I didn't care. I wanted to work.

WINER (*director / executive producer*): I think Julie would have been a slam dunk for Claire if it weren't so daunting that she was seven months pregnant. Given the fact that the Dunphys were scripted to have three kids and there were no plans to give them babies, we'd have to cover it up, and that would be a challenge.

BOWEN (*Claire Dunphy*): Every time I went in, they'd sit there and look at my stomach. I was so huge I think they believed that I must be giving birth any minute. I dress like a boy, too. My sisters say it's the Derelicte collection from *Zoolander*. They must have thought, "Who is this rumpled collection of clothing that just rolled through?"

> While testing for Modern Family, *Bowen got called in to test for a multi-cam pilot also at ABC, referred to only as "untitled Tad Quill comedy pilot" (Tad Quill was the producer). That show's premise revolved around two couples: new parents and recent empty nesters.*

BOWEN (*Claire Dunphy*): The female lead was pregnant. Of course, if I could have picked a job, it would have been *Modern Family,* but I didn't get to pick. I had to audition.

LLOYD (*cocreator*): From our side of things, we responded to not just how funny she was but how real she was. Her physicality, her reactions, made her seem real in a smaller way.

GREENBERG (*casting director*): The Claire auditions were never hilarious, because Claire's the sane one, but Julie definitely found this tightly wound version of it. She saw the humor where many actresses didn't. She really understood something about this woman and connected with her.

WRUBEL (*writer / executive producer*): The trap with Claire is she was, as writers would say, Dr. No. She'd be like, "No, Phil. No, Phil. No, Phil." The trick was making her the grounding force in that household, but also somebody who could enjoy her husband's antics.

LLOYD (*cocreator*): Julie projects tremendous intelligence and strength, which we wanted in that character. Phil's going to be a little bit of a man-child, and you get the sense that Claire is the commander of this slightly unseaworthy ship that is this family. So she has to project strength that doesn't go over the edge into being unlikable. She found a way to take the onus off of that.

Bowen's auditions for both parts went well. In such situations, the actor places their preferred choice in first position, committing them to that project should an offer come in. Bowen put Modern Family *first. Meanwhile, Levitan and Lloyd continued to struggle with the pregnancy issue.*

LEVITAN (*cocreator*): We were looking at her, thinking, "Is there any way we can make this work? Can we shoot this pilot and not have the world see she's pregnant, or could we possibly delay the shooting of this pilot?"

BOWEN (*Claire Dunphy*): It wasn't until a couple of visits and auditions that somebody said, "When is the baby due?" and I said, "Baby? No, no, no. There's two of them, and they're not coming until May." At that point, I saw what I thought in my mind was the dramatic eye rolling and their sighing, "Forget it." That was not the reality, I'm sure, but it was in my head. I went home and sobbed because I was never going to get this job. So I took myself out of first position for *Modern Family* and put myself in first position for the other pilot, because I thought I had a better shot of actually getting it.

Bowen did indeed read the room completely wrong.

LEVITAN (*cocreator*): Chris and I came to the conclusion that if successful, this is a seven- to ten-year decision we're making. We shouldn't make it based on one pilot week. We should play for the long haul here and not worry so much about the pilot.

A few days before the studio test for the other series, Bowen found out that Modern Family *actually wanted her.*

BOWEN (*Claire Dunphy*): I didn't know that I actually had a shot at it. I thought, "Oh no, I've done the wrong thing." If the other show hires me, I have to go to that show. Legally, I didn't have a choice. I was really mortified and disappointed because I'd done this to myself, taken myself out of the running.

GREENBERG (*casting director*): At that point, we tested Constance Zimmer, who we liked as well.

HOOPER (*casting associate*): She tested at the studio with Ashley Jensen and Natasha Henstridge. Only Constance went on to network.

BOWEN (*Claire Dunphy*): Constance is a friend of mine who's incredibly talented and wonderful. That to me is very intimidating, because Constance is one of the most talented actresses I know.

Bowen went to plead her case before ABC's head of casting.

BOWEN (*Claire Dunphy*): Both shows were on the same network. I said, "Can't you tell the other show not to hire me and then let *Modern Family* hire me?" and she said, "No, we can't." I was watching my life slip away in front of me. I did *Ed* [2000–2004] in the early 2000s, where I was in second position. I got hired on a different pilot. They ended up recasting *Ed* and coming back to me, which I'm so grateful for, because that was a wonderful four years. But I didn't think I'd be lucky enough to have that happen twice.

Luck had nothing to do with her earning the part. Getting the right person in her corner did.

MCPHERSON (*ABC Entertainment president*): I made the change. *Modern Family* was a much more promising pilot, so I went with strength.

With Claire cast, Greenberg needed to match Bowen in a believable relationship with an endearing goofball man-child.

MCPHERSON (*ABC Entertainment president*): Steve and Chris were very focused on the pairing. It wasn't "We got one half of it, let's add it in." It was always a discussion of "Okay, we have this person, do they pair up well with that person?" Those couples are obviously integral to the DNA of the thing, so there was a lot of discussion about, if it's Julie, then who becomes her husband? What's the right match?

Levitan and Lloyd knew who they wanted for the role of Phil Dunphy from the get-go, which of course meant that the road to getting there would present countless roadblocks that almost blew up the whole project.

Phil on Wire

Phil Dunphy—late thirties, real estate agent, upbeat, goofy, thinks he's cooler than he is.

I don't think that Phil is dumb. I've just always thought of him as blissfully uncomplicated.

—Ty Burrell

Ty Burrell's long, arduous journey from unknown character actor to head of the Dunphy household began as it does for many actors—constantly and chronically unemployed. A play here, a guest spot on Law & Order *there, a movie every few years—not nearly enough to pay the bills. He diligently tried to book commercials but never landed a single one. If not for his supportive wife, Holly, unhappily toiling away in a giant bank in New York City, they would never have been able to rub two quarters together to pay the rent in their Astoria, Queens, apartment.*

His fortunes finally began to change, however, on a West Coast trip in 2005, at a casting session for Lloyd's CBS series Out of Practice.

LLOYD (cocreator): I'd seen Ty in a Dennis Quaid movie [*In Good Company*] about office politics. He had this crazy pageboy haircut, with this deadpan, no-affect delivery. He was a hilarious character with a smallish role, but he jumped off the screen. And then literally four days later, David Rubin, our casting director, brought him in.

BURRELL (*Phil Dunphy*): I stayed in town for pilot season, the classic transient actor coming to LA, looking for work. I had no experience with sitcoms at all.

LLOYD (*cocreator*): Ty was a knock-around New York stage actor. He was thirty-six, offbeat. That scares studios and networks because they get leery of anyone approaching forty who hasn't made their mark yet.

> *Burrell tested for the role of Oliver Barnes, sleazy plastic surgeon son of series lead, Ben Barnes (Henry Winkler). He zipped past producer auditions, graduating to the final round with the studio and network.*

BURRELL (*Phil Dunphy*): Chris likes to tell the story of me bringing my bags to the screen test because I was staying later than I could afford in LA. He saw me packing my stuff, getting ready to go back to New York, and thought, "That poor sap."

LLOYD (*cocreator*): He'd hired a taxi and then got past the first stage of the process, which was the studio test. Paramount liked him, but it was going to be two hours until we could get over to CBS, where they were going to hear him read. I saw him run out to the taxi and ask the guy, "Could you wait? I might need you to drive me to CBS." It broke my heart because I thought, "This guy has no money at all. And he's telling a taxi to wait for two hours." As much as I loved him, I thought, "CBS is never giving him this part." And then he got the part, which shows you how much I know.

> *When* Back to You *first got picked up by Fox, Lloyd brought Burrell back into the fold, playing the role of field reporter and anchor wannabe Gary Crezyzewski.*

BURRELL (*Phil Dunphy*): I was a cad who was somewhat closer to Phil in a lot of ways. I think Steve, Chris, and I spent enough time around each other off-screen that my dopey but well-intended side may have come out.

When it came time to write the Modern Family *pilot, the creators framed Phil specifically with Burrell in mind.*

LEVITAN (*cocreator*): We wrote Phil for Ty because there's something about the fact that this guy is unrelentingly nice, never stops trying, and is a big kid. All of that applies to Ty.

LLOYD (*cocreator*): We knew him to be an extremely inventive and funny actor who hadn't been properly exploited yet by Hollywood. We thought, "This guy is waiting to be a star."

BURRELL (*Phil Dunphy*): They said, "We have this pilot we wrote and this part with you in mind." I've been in that situation enough to know that doesn't mean you have the part, that ultimately a network and studio have to sign off. But it still doesn't save you from emotionally going there.

GREENBERG (*casting director*): Steve and Chris thought it was a slam dunk. He's the guy.

Getting Fox Studios and ABC on board with their vision proved easier said than ultimately done. While Fox Studios signed on, ABC proved to be an impenetrable barrier.

WINER (*director / executive producer*): So often, a network's perspective of an actor is colored by its most recent experience with them. Ty had done a pilot for ABC the year before, a multi-cam that didn't come out well (*Fourplay* by *Will and Grace* creators Max Mutchnick and David Kohan).

GREENBERG (*casting director*): It was bad. Everyone was bad in it, and yet there were some good people in the cast.

LEVITAN (*cocreator*): Ty played a character who was, by definition, the dull guy. Ty, of course, played it authentically, and consequently the network thought that he was dull.

BURRELL (*Phil Dunphy*): The whole point of the character was he basically had no emotion. He was super dry and immovable in a lot of ways. Stephen's [McPherson] interpretation of it was I was an incredibly boring actor.

MCPHERSON (*ABC Entertainment president*): That was my only knowledge of the guy. Not the résumé you're looking for. When my head of casting came to me and said, "They really want Ty Burrell," I said, "You mean the guy in that God-awful pilot we did?" and they were like, "Yeah, that's the guy." I thought, "Oh man, how can I do that? It makes no sense."

LLOYD (*cocreator*): They said they didn't remember him being that funny, to which we said, "Well, the part wasn't funny. He was the straight man to someone else meant to be funny."

BURRELL (*Phil Dunphy*): That previous character didn't serve me well. I remember seeing Stephen and one of his assistants at a party the night after the *Modern Family* pilot aired, and this semi-drunk assistant was like, "Who knew you were good?"

LEVITAN (*cocreator*): They were very resistant to him. They thought they could find someone flashier and better.

GREENBERG (*casting director*): We offered Phil to Matt LeBlanc. We liked his big-kid quality. He passed.

    Many others took a pass on auditioning, including Rob Huebel, Brendan Fehr, Joel McHale, Thomas Lennon, and Stranger Things' *sheriff, David Harbour.*

GREENBERG (*casting director*): We brought in actors because we had to, but they were placeholders. It was Ty.

Levitan and Lloyd managed to convince the network to bring Burrell in for a screen test in front of ABC executives.

BURRELL (*Phil Dunphy*): They call it a screen test, but there's nothing about it that's on-screen. You're actually doing a live performance for people in this little theater, which is absolutely no way to determine who's going to be the right person for a show that takes place on a television screen.

WINER (*director / executive producer*): It's not designed for live performances. The room absorbs sound. You don't hear any echo. You only hear your own voice in your head. It feels like you're dying because you can't hear the laughter coming back to you. How anyone ever got cast for a TV show is a miracle.

MCPHERSON (*ABC Entertainment president*): He's right. It's not wired for sound. It's completely awkward. They basically stand up there in front of a big TV screen and do the lines cold with no set or anything.

LEVITAN (*cocreator*): Stand-up comedians tended to do better because they're used to walking in and making people laugh. You're putting on a show for somebody, and that's not the role. That's not the job. It was a silly exercise that's been largely done away with now.

CLAUDIA LYON (*VP of casting at ABC*): The funniest thing about the room was when actors were done, they had to walk back up a ramp and out the door. It was the slowest closing door in the world. You'd be sitting in the room, with everybody holding their breath, waiting fifteen seconds for the door to close.

HOOPER (*casting associate*): I'd try and grab the door and help it along, but it had a really strong self-closing device that went at its own speed.

Within this Chorus Line *audition setting, Burrell took his first network test. It didn't go well.*

GREENBERG (*casting director*): They said, "No, we're not fans." We were dumbfounded because we were his biggest fans on earth.

BURRELL (*Phil Dunphy*): From my perspective, my audition was too broad. I was nervous. It was a tight, stagy performance, which I take full responsibility for. I wouldn't have given me that part either.

MCPHERSON (*ABC Entertainment president*): His audition was not good, and he already had a strike unfairly against him coming in, so it would have been a miracle if in that awkward space he had been able to prove anything to us.

LLOYD (*cocreator*): The job of being a network president is not an easy one. I think Stephen's style is to be decisive. "This is how I see it, and I've got to go with what I see." Having said that, I think he was respectful of us. Had other people brought him the same project with an actor he felt wasn't right for the role, he probably would have said, "Guys, I've made up my mind." He didn't do that with us. He said, "I respect you guys. I will keep him in the mix, but I'll ask you to keep looking for other people."

GREENBERG (*casting director*): When they said no, we had to find other guys again, while we worked with Ty some more.

MORTON (*executive producer*): I'd done a short-lived series with Rob Corddry, who I thought was great, so I emailed Rob and introduced him to Steve to see if they wanted to pursue that. Rob turned the opportunity down. He told me years later, "Well, I guess that wasn't my best decision."

Through persistence and patience, they managed to get a second audition for Burrell.

GREENBERG (*casting director*): We brought Ty back along with other actors, and once again he was rejected. They all were rejected. We had to keep looking. It was so frustrating for us because we knew if he got the job, he'd be one of the home run hitters on the show, which has proved to be true.

BURRELL (*Phil Dunphy*): The second audition I thought went better, but it obviously wasn't good enough. I failed to convey the best aspects of the script. They didn't think I was very good, and my self-loathing agreed with them.

LEVITAN (*cocreator*): They were resistant to the point where they were like, "Look, we don't want him in this role." We had to at least explore other actors, and we did. We read a lot of really good actors. With all due respect to those actors, we almost made a gigantic mistake in casting some of them. We knew Ty was right.

GREENBERG (*casting director*): We were told by ABC, "We don't want to see Ty anymore; please don't bring him back," which was devastating to us because he was our guy. But we were stuck. We auditioned a lot of guys, a total of 232 in eleven weeks. In the meanwhile, Ty was passing up other opportunities because he wanted the role very much, but he also wanted a job. So he was very gracious to stick with us. We tried to be as gracious as we could to him, because we appreciated him so much for hanging in with us.

WINER (*director / executive producer*): Steve and Chris understood that it didn't behoove them to twist the network's arm and say, "This is our guy." The network had to be excited by the choice, or else it wasn't going to work long term. So they kept going back to the drawing board. They weren't despondent. They didn't get frustrated. They never went, "Screw these guys." They kept going back saying, "This isn't how the network sees the character. Maybe the material isn't giving the right impression." And they kept revising it.

LEVITAN (*cocreator*): We weren't happy with any of the choices. They didn't feel right, so we came up with the idea of doing a screen test, which was unusual back then, but now is very common.

LLOYD (*cocreator*): We said, "Let's shoot a scene with him and one with another actor," who was our other choice. One of them we shot at Steve's backyard and one at mine.

BURRELL (*Phil Dunphy*): My agent and wife both advised me that I was being disrespected by ABC. They said, "Forget it. Let it go. You don't need to be doing this." My wife, being an amazing person, was trying to protect me from going in and having my feelings crushed for a fifth time.

MORTON (*executive producer*): We decided to try out our mockumentary shooting style, so we got a couple of camera guys and a crew of about five. We went to Steve's house to shoot Ty's screen test with Sarah Hyland and another kid who was testing for Luke.

BURRELL (*Phil Dunphy*): That's really where I owe them, because they went way beyond to film it. They knew that the script needed to be filmed but also that I needed every bit of help that I could get after stinking up a couple of screen tests.

LEVITAN (*cocreator*): One scene was Phil and Haley talking together. Another was an interview scene with Phil and then Phil dancing to *High School Musical*. Then there was the scene where Phil's shooting Luke in the backyard.

Lloyd and Levitan had Winer work one-on-one with Burrell to give him pointers and a better feel for how to play the role.

BURRELL (*Phil Dunphy*): Jason did such an amazing job of helping me to relax, which I was not, going into something in which I had already been told I'm terrible at, that there's no way I'm going to get this part.

WINER (*director / executive producer*): Ty was so brilliant at playing the silences—the pained moments between really distinguished him. I could understand how those moments couldn't shine through in the live tests with the network, but once we were filming it, the comedy of that awkwardness played like gangbusters.

MORTON (*executive producer*): A few days later, we went to Chris's backyard and shot the same thing.

GREENBERG (*casting director*): We did a screen test with Steven Weber, who we love. We did *Wings* with him, and he's amazing. He was a great choice, too.

MORTON (*executive producer*): We used a girl who didn't get the Haley part. Nolan Gould played Luke.

NOLAN GOULD (*Luke Dunphy*): It was very cool and exciting for me to see what filming a scene might actually be like with people who could potentially be my TV father and TV sister. When I booked *Modern Family* and met Ty, my new TV dad, it was weird, because in my ten-year-old mind, I had pictured the other guy as my TV dad. I felt for a second like I was cheating with a new TV family.

GREENBERG (*casting director*): Tony Hale also came in live to audition. Tony wasn't really right for the part, but we had to bring in other choices in service of trying to get Ty hired. And yet, if they weren't going to hire Ty, we wanted someone else good and funny.

WINER (*director / executive producer*): They loved Tony comedically as an actor and were trying to get him in the show—first as a potential Cam, but after they cast Eric, they tried him as Phil.

With the first day on set rapidly approaching, an editor worked through the weekend, converting the backyard footage into a presentation.

MORTON (*executive producer*): We were on deadline and had to go to the network to see Stephen and get the last parts cast. Our editor was behind schedule, and so I said I'd run them over to ABC. I drove like crazy from Fox and delivered the tapes. They brought them into a conference room. I had to use the bathroom, and by the time I came back out, I heard people laughing hysterically in the room.

LYON (*VP of casting at ABC*): It was like looking at magic happen. It was so funny, the way the words and jokes landed. It felt right immediately.

FALVEY (*ABC Entertainment head of comedy*): If you saw that tape, I defy anybody not to laugh. It was really one of the funniest things I'd ever seen. Jason shot it brilliantly. They were so smart about it.

MCPHERSON (*ABC Entertainment president*): To be honest, it literally changed the process at ABC when I was there. We started putting people on film much more because it proved our process was incredibly flawed. Thank God those guys pushed through.

> It took a total of twelve weeks for Burrell to land the role written for him.

WINER (*director / executive producer*): They were able to see exactly why Ty was so funny in the drier style of the show. Laughter in a situation like that is democratic. That's what won him the role.

MCPHERSON (*ABC Entertainment president*): Once I saw it on film, I knew I was wrong, and I believe that's when I said to them, "I'm wrong and you're right."

GREENBERG (*casting director*): I don't ever remember a network executive saying aloud in a roomful of people, "I was wrong." But he did because he saw how brilliant Ty was and what the show was going to be. And he became the biggest cheerleader you could want and dream of for your show.

LLOYD (*cocreator*): I will go one further and say after we shot the pilot and he looked at it, he said, "Boy, you guys were right. I'm really glad you talked me into this one." That was not a politically safe thing for him to say because the show could have crashed and burned. The traditional network executive thing to do would be to wait until it was on TV. If it was a success, then you call the producers and tell them they were right. He didn't wait, and I credit him for that.

LEVITAN (*cocreator*): Most guys want to be proven right. Stephen was above that, and I've always appreciated that.

MCPHERSON (*ABC Entertainment president*): It's really a lesson in you can't judge an actor by the work he's done for a project. You have to look at the project and ask, "Was it a good project? Did he have good material?" The previous pilot he did was terrible. It was the exact opposite with Chris and Steve, who are unbelievably talented. They saw his talent, wrote to it, and he was incredible.

The Future Dunphys

I will tell you that casting those kids set the bar for the casting of all kids to come on ABC. I don't know what happened before I got there, but from when I was there, the bar was set.

—CLAUDIA LYON

You can't have offspring resembling their parents if the parents don't exist. Because casting Phil and Claire came down to the wire, so, too, did choosing the Dunphy children. To give a sense of the timing, Bowen and Burrell won their roles on February 25 and 26, respectively. The entire cast met for the first time five days later on March 3. The final selections quickly fell into place within days.

LLOYD (*cocreator*): The kids? Forget about it. We were never going to find those kids. I'd worked with Jeff a long time on *Frasier* and we didn't do a lot of kid casting, so I was like, "I hope you know this world, because I don't." Sure enough, he brought us a great range of kids.

GREENBERG (*casting director*): Steve and Chris had to have options. We had to find the best ones and then fit pieces of that puzzle.

Haley—sixteen, social, fashion-conscious, rebellious, has a wild streak

She's like a fairy. Haley Dunphy is Tinker Bell; she can only have one feeling at a time.

—SARAH HYLAND

Most eighteen-year-old actresses have yet to make a mark in the industry. By that age, the multitalented Sarah Hyland, she of the soulful big eyes straight out of a Margaret Keane painting, had already been steadily working for fourteen years.

GREENBERG (*casting director*): Sarah will tell you that she doesn't remember a time when she wasn't in show business, starting at four years old playing Howard Stern's daughter in *Private Parts*.

LLOYD (*cocreator*): She was a veteran. She'd been in musicals, plays, and movies, but she has an incredibly innocent, sweet quality, too.

As a teen, she also went through what she describes as her "awkward phase," when hormones kick in, faces break out, and the body changes form.

SARAH HYLAND (*Haley Dunphy*): They don't want your face super close-up on a film or TV screen then. That's when you go to theater, because you're far away and they can't tell what you look like. That's what happened to me.

Hyland had recently graduated high school in New York, carrying a nearly 4.0 GPA. She could probably have had her choice of which college to attend, if she hadn't accidentally missed the application deadlines.

HYLAND (*Haley Dunphy*): I was working on *Lipstick Jungle* [2008–2009] and doing workshops of the musicals *Next to Normal* and *Shrek*.

Then in November of 2008, three months into its first season, Lipstick Jungle *got canceled, changing Hyland's career path.*

HYLAND (*Haley Dunphy*): As soon as I found that out, I decided I'm moving to LA. I'm not doing another pilot season in New York because the excuse is always, "We're going with a local hire. We don't want to pay to move you out here."

BOWEN (*Claire Dunphy*): I have no idea what it's like to be on your own at an age where you might be making decisions that you might regret or that could change your life. I never had to do that. I would hate to think of the choices I would have made in those shoes.

HYLAND (*Haley Dunphy*): Everyone always says that, but I don't see the ballsiness of it. I was just trying to not share a room with my brother anymore. I'm a very independent creature. I live by my work, and as long as I'm working, then I'm good.

*Hyland knew people in Los Angeles, like childhood friend and fellow actress Andrea Bowen, and had her Coogan Account to lean on while getting her through pilot season.**

HYLAND (*Haley Dunphy*): I told myself if I didn't book something in two months that I would go back to New York, go to college, and rethink life. *Modern Family* was maybe my fourth audition that year for pilot season.

---

* The Coogan Account is part of the Coogan Law (1939), a California state law named after Jackie Coogan (1914–1984), one of the first child actor stars. When Coogan turned twenty-one, he learned his parents had spent all of his earnings. The law ensures that wages earned by minors in the entertainment industry belong to them and not their parents. "Coogan Law," SAG-AFTRA, accessed December 15, 2019, https://www.sagaftra.org/membership-benefits/young-performers/coogan-law.

What ended up as the type of role actors would kill for began as a second choice for Hyland.

HYLAND (*Haley Dunphy*): I'd auditioned for this pilot, *Limelight.* It was basically *Fame* about kids in college. My character was a musical theater major, in love with gay men. It was everything that I was as a teenager, so I really, really wanted it. And when I didn't book it, I was heartbroken. Meanwhile, my agent at William Morris submitted me for *Modern Family,* but because I was eighteen, they passed. Her assistant at the time, who's now my agent, called Jeff Greenberg's office and said, "You really, really need to see her. She doesn't look like she's eighteen." And they said, "Fine, bring her in."

Although a comedic part, Hyland had almost no comedy experience at the time.

HYLAND (*Haley Dunphy*): I was always a rape victim, a murderer, an orphan, or a girl who's too ugly and can't lose her virginity, so she cries about it all the time.

Greenberg pre-read a total of 185 Haleys. He sent 16 onto producers.

GREENBERG (*casting director*): I remember Sarah's first audition being quite confident. Probably some of that self-assurance was because she was eighteen playing fifteen, but also because she's so theatrically experienced.

HOOPER (*casting associate*): She was one of the few and only actresses we read that were older and able to truly play the age we wanted them to play.

LEVITAN (*cocreator*): She's this tiny little thing and all heart. She wears it on her sleeve. Her emotions burst through those giant eyes.

GREENBERG (*casting director*): She had a real feel for the material. I didn't have to give her notes. She knew what she was doing.

Her only real surprise involved Lloyd, absent from her audition that day. She mistook the name for being Christopher Lloyd the actor, a common issue Lloyd encounters.

HYLAND (*Haley Dunphy*): I thought that I was going to meet Doc from *Back to the Future.* I was so upset he wasn't there. I thought, "Hopefully I get this and get to meet him at some point."

Hyland sailed through auditions, making it to the final two. Before her final network audition, however, she received an odd request.

HYLAND (*Haley Dunphy*): They said one of the actors screen-testing for Phil can't be there on the actual day. So will you go to Steve Levitan's house? They're putting something on tape there. I said, "Of course." Even though this is technically not my screen test, it felt like it basically is. Griffin, Steve's youngest son, came down with all of his Nerf guns and BB guns and stuff. I don't know if he was bringing them down for the scene because that was one of the ones we were doing.

Waiting at her dreaded final network audition, she saw Bowen preparing for her final test against Constance Zimmer and Amy Yasbeck from Wings. *Finally, she got brought onstage, the same dreaded one that gave other cast members nightmares.*

HYLAND (*Haley Dunphy*): I couldn't really see anybody and couldn't hear a damn thing. So I assumed that they didn't find anything funny at all, which is the greatest feeling when you're auditioning for comedy.

LLOYD (*cocreator*): She did a thing that's extremely difficult for kids and adults alike, which is she found a way to portray a slightly dim bulb but not in a clichéd way.

Hyland tested against Skyler Samuels, who would go on to star in The Nine Lives of Chloe *and* The Gifted.

HYLAND (*Haley Dunphy*): I thought I was going to see a lot more Haleys, but it was down to me and a fourteen-year-old blonde. In my experience, it always goes to the blonde. I was feeling a bit defeated at that point. Being the girl with brown curly hair, it never tends to work out in my favor.

It did, for her and for Samuels.

HOOPER (*casting associate*): I always bring up Skyler because fairly soon after *Modern Family*, she was the lead in *The Nine Lives of Chloe* on ABC Family. She was the title character in a show that was waiting for her because she didn't get *Modern Family*.

HYLAND (*Haley Dunphy*): Steve told me, after we left, they went into the network and said, "One is fourteen years old. One is eighteen years old, which one's which?" And they all said obviously I was the fourteen-year-old. And when he told them, they thought it was amazing. I don't know if my talent had anything to do with me actually booking the role. It might have just been the fact that I looked very young.

Alex—thirteen, female, smart, cynical, insightful for her age

She's extremely intelligent, extremely loyal, unpredictable, kind of savage, and forever evolving.

—ARIEL WINTER

Ariel Winter Workman didn't have Hyland's fourteen years of acting experience when she auditioned to be Alex Dunphy. Then again, as an eleven-year-old, how could she? She did, however, have a healthy list of credentials under her belt, including numerous voice-overs for animated characters. Nothing truly stood out, however, until she did a dramatic multi-episode arc on ER's final season, playing the daughter

of a mother dying of cancer, which Greenberg had seen. That became
her golden ticket for auditioning for Modern Family.

ARIEL WINTER (*Alex Dunphy*): The whole audition process was quite long for me. I think I did seven auditions. My first time, I went in at the very end of the day to see Jeff Greenberg. I read with Jeff, and he said, "Can you wait a second?" He brought in Allen [Hooper]. I read it again and went about my day.

GREENBERG (*casting director*): I was surprised at how adept she was at comedy.

WINTER (*Alex Dunphy*): A lot of the other actors had backgrounds in comedy, and I really didn't. So it was a little scary for me because it was unknown territory. I had auditioned for things like everyone does, but I had never done a show like that.

GREENBERG (*casting director*): The audition scene had her helping Claire bake a cake. For her callback, I asked her to mime making the cake and stirring the batter.

WINER (*director / executive producer*): It's an acting school trick. You give them a prop or something to do so that their lines come off as natural and thrown away. Ariel was so gifted with that. She mimed her secondary focus.

GREENBERG (*casting director*): She brought the scene to life, mixing the frosting, pulling things off shelves, dealing with the ingredients. And she's skillfully doing that at age eleven! It's not usually a great idea to do too much of that in an audition, as it can be a bit stagey and distracting, but this was the exception to the rule, as she really made it work to her advantage.

WINER (*director / executive producer*): It was weirdly distracting, but also virtuoso.

Winter made it to the network test. As she sat in the waiting room, she spied Rodriguez, whom she had worked with before on a movie, and Gould, along with another potential Alex, who seemed as if she had connections with some of the decision-makers. She had no idea what waited for her behind the door leading onto the stage. No one had prepared her for the cold and sterile environment with that damn lone spotlight.

WINTER (*Alex Dunphy*): The room was totally dark. Looking out, I couldn't see people's faces, but I knew it was a big room filled with executives. I did the scene, and not one person laughed. I was mortified. I was sobbing because I thought that I'd ruined it. I left that room thinking, "Oh my God, it's destroyed. I got this far. Nobody laughed. I did a horrible job."

According to Winter, she learned later that network executives supposedly don't laugh on purpose to see what kids do under pressure.

WINTER (*Alex Dunphy*): The whole thing is savage because nobody really wants to work with kid actors. I get it. Sometimes it's hard, but it's a lot of pressure. What I did under pressure in there was good, but when I left I was freaking out.

GREENBERG (*casting director*): Steve McPherson thought her audition was indeed a bit too theatrical, but she made it work and aced the audition; she threw away all of the jokes easily, at the same time possessing Alex's special brand of smarts and cynical confidence.

LLOYD (*cocreator*): Ariel had a seriousness about her, a world-weariness about her, which we really liked.

WINTER (*Alex Dunphy*): Thirty minutes later, they called and said they were booking me. I was not even home yet. It was an amazing feeling. It really was.

GREENBERG (*casting director*): I auditioned 95 Alexes and was thrilled with the sous-chef with whom we ended up.

Luke—ten, immature, simple, not the brightest bulb

Luke has become a very good representation of the quintessential American teenage boy: focused on chasing girls and not caring about grades.

—NOLAN GOULD

Like most kids, ten-year-old Nolan Gould liked acting, but most of all loved being a rough-and-tumble boy. Off-screen, the MENSA member exhibited intelligence beyond his years, which he balanced with his penchant for injuring himself.

Whereas you would think getting an audition for a hot pilot script would excite a young actor, Gould felt anything but. They had booked his audition not just on a Saturday but on Valentine's Day.

GOULD (*Luke Dunphy*): I'd been eating candy all day that my mom had given me. I didn't want to audition. Acting's an adult world, and I wanted to be a kid. But I went in and read the script in a way that was very hokey and over the top, imagining that there was a laugh track behind every sentence.

GREENBERG (*casting director*): He had no experience. He hadn't done comedy before. The comedy stuff he was watching was probably that multi-cam Disney stuff that has its own specific style. Single cam is way more subtle. He didn't know the style. I gave him the note to relax, be himself, and really talk to me. You don't have to project beyond me sitting three feet away. He took the note beautifully.

GOULD (*Luke Dunphy*): I'm really lucky that Jeff is such an amazing guy and worked with me, which is something that's rare for a casting director to do. To take that time was really special.

More than eighty boys had been invited to pre-read with Greenberg. Out of that group, Greenberg brought ten little cherubs to the next round.

GOULD (*Luke Dunphy*): I came in for a callback with Steve and Chris. I was super intimidated by them. I didn't know who they were by reputation, but they looked like "those guys." I think they were wearing suits, which is weird because to this day I've only ever seen them in suits at awards shows.

LLOYD (*cocreator*): We had to believe that this kid was really enamored with his dad and was figuring things out at a slower rate than other people but he was going to figure them out eventually. When we did those screen tests where Nolan had to get shot, he was really funny with "you hit my bone." Like he could talk very frankly with his dad, but you knew he was going to come back for more with Phil. There was something very endearing about him. Set against his two older sisters, he was someone that would be fun to see tortured by them all the time. He had a trusting quality that we liked.

MORTON (*executive producer*): When Nolan was a little kid, he was cute, slightly overweight, and so funny. There's a clip in the *Stripes* trailer where Bill Murray walks off the plane. He made you laugh even when you didn't know what he was doing. Nolan reminded me of that. Something about him made you laugh.

Gould impressed the suits, working his way up the ladder to the network test. Similar to Hyland, the producers requested him to help with the filmed screen tests for the Phil finalists. He ended up at Lloyd's.

GOULD (*Luke Dunphy*): To this day, I'm still amazed by that house. It's the coolest thing I've ever seen. I grew up far outside in Phoenix City, Alabama. It's a very small suburban town on the outskirts of Fort Benning, which is where my dad was stationed. When I did the audition, I'd lived in LA for five years already, way out in Santa Clarita, so to be invited to this big producer's house . . . I was blown away. He had a game room with an arcade. I thought, "This is the life. This is why you work, so you can have an arcade machine."

A few days later, he found himself in front of the network executives without the arcade. His sides included a scene written for the audition that never made it on air.

GOULD (*Luke Dunphy*): It was a conversation between him and Phil. That idea of Luke being innocent and Phil being a giant man-child that's popped up a lot.

He found out he got the part on his way back from that final test.

GOULD (*Luke Dunphy*): It was one of the craziest weeks of my life. It was nonstop running around, learning lines, and being stressed out. By that point, I was glad to have it over. I was really happy, but I needed sleep.

After a long, drawn-out, but hardly uncommon process, casting for the Dunphys had concluded. Lloyd and Levitan had found their family.

GREENBERG (*casting director*): They really looked like a family. That's a very challenging part of casting sometimes, making a family look like a family. I was very proud of the way they looked and related to each other. The kids not only rose to the occasion, but they kept getting better and better. It was like a miracle, all of them.

LLOYD (*cocreator*): You try and squint and close one eye to see if they'd be like a family, but you don't really know it until you shoot the scene and say, "Is America going to buy these people as a family?" And they did.

Best Men, Part 1

Mitchell—mid- to late thirties, gay, environmental lawyer, emotionally restrained, worrier.

No one wants to watch characters who aren't flawed. I think Mitch's flaws are not only hilarious but really moving.
                                        —JESSE TYLER FERGUSON

Jesse Tyler Ferguson started out in the world of theater, quickly succeeding on and off Broadway as a singer, dancer, and actor. As a renaissance man, however, he wanted to test out other venues, maybe make a little money while at it, so he could better support his stage aspirations. So he shuffled off to Hollywood to look for work in television. While he found some success, by 2008, he found himself longing for the bright lights of his adopted New York home.

FERGUSON (*Mitchell Pritchett*): I was planning on moving back to do a play. It was right after the Writers' Strike had ended, and I was burned out on LA.

While not a household name, his talents had been noticed.

LLOYD (*cocreator*): He'd done a couple of series and was on everybody's "watch this guy" list.

Ferguson, however, felt like anything but a hot commodity. His most recent effort, the highly anticipated CBS sitcom directed by TV legend James Burrows, The Class, had fizzled out after a mere nineteen episodes. Not surprisingly, the Broadway veteran took the news hard, resigning himself to the fact that maybe his time on television had ended before it ever really began.

FERGUSON (*Mitchell Pritchett*): You're never put on the hot show of the season. Then it happened and the show didn't work, so I was like, "Okay, that was my opportunity." I think optically for me, I knew it was a huge deal to be on that show, and I did make a name for myself in small circles, but it didn't feel especially big because the show got canceled.

LEVITAN (*cocreator*): I'd seen him on *The Class*, but I became a fan watching him in the play *The 25th Annual Putnam County Spelling Bee*.

For decades, Greenberg had immersed himself in New York theater. He knew many brilliant New York theater actors like Ferguson who hadn't been afforded the opportunity to make it on television.

GREENBERG (*casting director*): I really tried to cull from the New York stage great actors who were not known on TV. One of the reasons I was hired on *Cheers* is that they fired the casting director for bringing in too many familiar TV faces. When I started on that show, the first part I had to cast was Cliff Claven's mother, and the first picture I pulled out was Frances Sternhagen's.

Greenberg knew Ferguson's work all too well on stage and television.

GREENBERG (*casting director*): When I was putting together the lists for Cam and Mitchell, there were a handful of actors that I thought could be right for both, and he was one of them.

FERGUSON (*Mitchell Pritchett*): I saw the script and loved it. I thought it was very smart, beautifully written. I was really attached to the character of Mitchell. Then I looked at the appointment sheet I got from my agent and saw I was meant to read for Cam.

GREENBERG (*casting director*): That's because I thought it'd be the more difficult part to cast.

FERGUSON (*Mitchell Pritchett*): I asked if I could read for Mitchell. They told me that they really wanted me to read for Cam. So I went into that first audition in front of Chris, Steve, and Jeff and read Cam as I would have read Mitch. Steve stopped me halfway through the audition.

LEVITAN (*cocreator*): Seeing that read, I could easily see him as Mitchell. He was really relieved. He said, "Oh, thank God, because that's the part I really want."

FERGUSON (*Mitchell Pritchett*): He asked me to go out into the hallway, look at the Mitch sides, and then come back in. I really wanted to nail it and didn't feel comfortable going out and looking at new material, so I said I'd rather come back another day, which I think is a gamble for an actor because there's always someone in the wings waiting to take your job.

GREENBERG (*casting director*): He came back three days later and gave the perfect Mitchell audition.

LLOYD (*cocreator*): He had a really interesting neurotic comic energy to him, an uptight guy who's a little bit too smart for his own good. He was very funny at showing that bottled-up-ness. We thought, "This guy is great."

FERGUSON (*Mitchell Pritchett*): I find people who take themselves super serious to be hilarious, which I think Mitch does. I also really embrace the moments where he lets himself go. I find him to be a wildly intelligent, smart, and sometimes too-serious guy.

With the producers on board, Ferguson graduated to the studio audition.

GREENBERG (*casting director*): Jesse was already a studio favorite because he'd done a short-lived series there called *Do Not Disturb*. Dana Walden [cochairman of 20th Century Fox Television] loved him. The other two people who tested were Matt Oberg, who has guest-starred on our show since, and Mo Rocca. We flew Matt out from New York. Mo tested by tape but got cut by the studio, so we only took Jesse and Matt to the network.

FERGUSON (*Mitchell Pritchett*): Ironically, Ty was also testing that day. He likes to remind me how calm I was. I'm typically a set of nerves when it comes to auditioning. But I felt a strange Zen-like quality that day. I loved and wanted the part. At the same time, I had other opportunities in New York and didn't feel like I needed it for a paycheck.

BURRELL (*Phil Dunphy*): He wasn't nervous, and I was terrified as I always am in every screen test. I was facing a corner, mumbling my lines to myself like a schizophrenic. Jesse came over and tapped me on my shoulder. In a very happy-go-lucky way, he says, "Hey, we both know Josh Gad." He didn't have a care in the world.

Ferguson crushed the second audition, as he did the third and final one for the network.

GREENBERG (*casting director*): Jesse's really a skilled comic actor. What can I say? When it works, it works. But we felt we hadn't found our Cam yet, so we had to keep looking.

LLOYD (*cocreator*): The question became: Who's going to be a good counterpart to Jesse? Some of it we refined in the writing; Mitchell's a little repressed, so let's go the other way with Cam. Let him be all about heart, emotion, and expressiveness. Be who you are. That will be a good complement to Mitchell, a funny prod, constantly trying to get Mitchell out of the shell that he's lived in his whole life.

Cam would turn out to be the most difficult role to cast of all.

Best Men, Part 2

Cameron—midthirties, gay, free with emotions, lives in the moment, surprisingly strong.

I never looked at Cam as gay. I never really thought that that was an important thing for me to be playing because it was already there. We're two men in a relationship.

—ERIC STONESTREET

As simple and straightforward as Ferguson's casting proved to be, Eric Stonestreet's, in contrast, resembled that of Sisyphus, pushing a rock up one side of a mountain to land the role of Cam, coming back down the other without it, and then starting the arduous process all over again.

STONESTREET (Cam Tucker): When I moved from Chicago to LA, I called it playing in the big sandbox. I wanted to see if there was an opportunity for me to find success. I had a reel of commercials that I'd done and quickly got an agent. I met a very important commercial director named Joe Pytka who took a liking to me. He's one of those guys who once you're in his group, he keeps rehiring you. I shot sixty commercials with him in which I was painted every color of the spectrum: blue and red for Coors Light, green for Xerox, you name it. It was the dawn of fat guys painted on TV being the height of hilarity, which helped me to purchase my own home. Then at some point, I said, "Okay, I'm not going to do that any-more. I'm good on that stuff." So I focused on auditioning for pilots and TV shows when they'd come along. Just like every actor, I didn't get most of them. But I always felt like I was making a good impression in the room.

GREENBERG (*casting director*): Eric had been auditioning for me for well over a decade. I brought him in for many things but never hired him. He actually tested on another series Steve did called *Say Uncle*.

STONESTREET (*Cam Tucker*): Steve has no memory of ever meeting me, hardly unique in this business. It wasn't that long before *Modern Family* that I had a meaningful conversation with an actor friend of mine, Marshall Bell. I told him that I'd never tethered myself to being rich or famous. What I was going for was having a meaningful part, feeling like I was a collaborator on something versus just walking in, nailing my six lines, and leaving. I was in a low valley that all actors get in, which is, "Why am I doing this? Am I ever going to have an opportunity to find a success that I think I'm capable of and want?" Marshall asked, "What else would you do?"

MCPHERSON (*ABC Entertainment president*): Eric told me later if he wasn't cast in something that season, he was going to go home and open a butcher shop.

STONESTREET (*Cam Tucker*): Most guys want to cook out on the week-ends, but they don't know what they should cook or how they should cook it. I think it'd be fun to find an old retired butcher and have a really cool meat market, you know, *Stonestreet Meats*. Marshall talked me out of it. He said I'm too deep in the business. I was on the carousel, and something was going to click for me at some point.

GREENBERG (*casting director*): We read 228 Cams over eleven weeks. I brought in a lot of ethnic choices. One of the actors who tested was Kevin Daniels, who has recurred over the years as Longinus, their African American friend who's very tall and funny.

Other actors included funny, lesser-known talents, such as Frank Caliendo, Kevin Bernston, Todd Louiso, and Jim Rash.

WINER (*director / executive producer*): Josh Gad auditioned for Cam before I officially came on board. Steve and Chris wanted to develop something for him, as he was so clearly a burgeoning star.

FERGUSON (*Mitch Pritchett*): He made his Broadway debut in the same show as me. And so they knew we liked each other and they put us in the same room together for a chemistry read. I don't think it fully clicked. They were trying to figure out who Cam was, and Josh's version of Cam wasn't what they wanted.

WINER (*director / executive producer*): He then withdrew himself from consideration to do this crazy musical that he'd workshopped: *Book of Mormon.*

Stonestreet learned about the role of Cam in a roundabout way rather than through normal channels.

STONESTREET (*Cam Tucker*): My group of friends, we always help each other with auditions. So one day, I got a phone call from my friend Matt Corboy, who said he was auditioning for a show and would I help him with his material?

MATT CORBOY (*actor*): I said, "Hey, buddy, I got a series regular audition for a new pilot called *My American Family*. It's for this gay character, Cameron Tucker." He said, "Come on over." So that afternoon, we sat in his two big red leather chairs, and he helped me work on the audition. Then I went in and auditioned for Jeff Greenberg. A couple of days later, I called Eric up and said, "Hey, buddy, I got called back. Can I come over again?" So, we sat in his two big red leather chairs again and worked on it. Then I went in and read for the producers. I got the word that I wasn't going any further on the project. Eric called me up and said he couldn't stop thinking about that audition.

STONESTREET (*Cam Tucker*): I called my manager and said, "I want to audition for this." He figured I meant for Phil. I said I wanted Cam, that I thought I would crush that part. And so he called, but no one would see me. He made call after call after call to make them see me.

LLOYD (*cocreator*): Eric had a hard time getting an audition. He said it was a struggle. That happens. You have certain ideas about who would be good and who wouldn't, and we're always surprised.

STONESTREET (*Cam Tucker*): I don't think they really knew what Cam looked like, but when I walked in the room, I don't think they thought, "Wow, that's Cam."

GREENBERG (*casting director*): The prototype for Mitchell had been Andy Richter, who's a big guy, but he wasn't interested in it. So they were thinking big guy for one of the parts. It wasn't a necessity, but they were open to it.

STONESTREET (*Cam Tucker*): There's a scene in the pilot when Mitchell and I walk into Lily's room to see the mural that Andre has done for them. Cam gasps and says, "Oh my God, do you love it?" That reminded me of my mom making Christmas cookies and asking, "Well, do you love it?" That was my little portal into the character. With my limited acting experience and teaching, I knew the world of opposites worked. And with my physicality and size, I thought impersonating my mom might work.

LEVITAN (*cocreator*): Eric carries himself a certain way, very down to earth, a man's man. He's a midwestern farm boy who's got a tough-guy way of carrying himself. When he transforms into Cam, it's a whole different way of walking, holding his arm, holding his head up. I think Cam holds his head up much higher than Eric does.

CORBOY (*actor*): I was floored at how much funnier he made the words on the page, certainly much funnier than I did. I'd have to stop when we were reading because I was laughing so hard at the choices he was making. And then he read for Jeff.

GREENBERG (*casting director*): He figured it out. On a dime, he can switch to Cam. He doesn't need prep. He puts his mother in his head and becomes Cam. It's technique. That's a real skill. He found his way in and gave the best audition of anyone who read for that part.

STONESTREET (*Cam Tucker*): Jeff passed me on to the producers. I did the audition, and they passed. "It's not going any further." That's the term they always use. So that was the end of it. I was like, "Okay, I've been down this road many times." I knew the show was going to be something special, which made it hard.

LEVITAN (*cocreator*): Eric came in and killed it. He was very precise and professional. Just the way he carried himself into that room. He was genuinely funny right off the bat. And I think our reaction was, "That was really funny." But boy, that's not how we'd envisioned Cam, for whatever reason.

LLOYD (*cocreator*): We may have been going off the type of actor we had in mind, which was a Tony Hale kind of character.

LEVITAN (*cocreator*): You have a vision of what a character should be, but you have to roll with it a little bit. Sometimes. I see this in pilots, you roll so much that the character changes, and suddenly you've messed up a very important dynamic because the casting's wrong.

> *While the prolonged search for Cam continued, Winer came on board as the pilot's director and collaborator.*

WINER (*director / executive producer*): Chris and Steve encouraged me to familiarize myself with who they'd seen so far. There was a folder of people they liked but weren't so sure about. Eric was in that file. I knew Eric from ImprovOlympic in Chicago. I knew how funny he was, having seen him improvise onstage. I thought maybe he would pop in a second read.

STONESTREET (*Cam Tucker*): I remember reading that Jason was going to direct the pilot and thinking, "Okay, this is good," because Jason knows me and has seen me perform. I might have an ally in the room now.

LEVITAN (*cocreator*): If Jason said some positive things about Eric, I don't know that that made the difference, but God bless him for weighing in. It's always good to hear positive things that someone's funny in other situations.

LLOYD (*cocreator*): We went about reading another forty people for the role and then said, "Let's bring Eric back in." I've been through enough pilots where I've learned to be open-minded and see if someone makes you laugh. That's a rare thing. The trick is to adjust your thinking, and that is precisely what happened with Eric. He was really funny.

LEVITAN (*cocreator*): We were always very cognizant that we had to be flexible but, at the same time, true to what we envision these characters to be.

LLOYD (*cocreator*): I remember the story of the casting of Sam Malone on *Cheers*. They'd envisioned him as a Stanley Kowalski–type brute who'd been a football player. He was all animal urge and not very thoughtful, the complete opposite of Diane Chambers. They were trying to cast him, and then one day, Ted Danson walked in. He's about 160 pounds and six foot four, no one's idea of a brutal ex-football player, but somehow, he made it work, and they wound up adjusting the character.*

GREENBERG (*casting director*): Steve and Chris were a little concerned with if you'd buy Jesse and Eric as a couple. I don't know whether this is a humble brag or not, but one of the prototypes for Mitchell and Cam is me and my husband, Lars. We've been together for a very long time and are longtime friends of Steve and Chris. They didn't want the gay guys in the show to be these West Hollywood clones with six packs and model-like looks. They wanted them to look like real guys who were on the geekier side, which I guess Lars and I are.

LEVITAN (*cocreator*): I always say we didn't want Mitch and Cam to be fit or fabulous. That was *Will and Grace*. They had done that and done it really

---

* They made Sam Malone a retired baseball pitcher instead, a much better fit for Danson's stature.

well. We wanted to show a different gay relationship. It certainly reflected the people that we knew in our lives. Jeff and Lars fit that bill.

They asked Stonestreet to come back in for another read.

STONESTREET (*Cam Tucker*): They told me they wanted me clean shaven. Normally, I don't like shaving for anybody because I don't want to ever look too desperate. I never dress the part or anything like that. Somebody gave me advice at the beginning of my career. They said, "You're playing the role of actor. You don't have time to jump through a bunch of hoops for people and put on a chef's costume because they want you to. You've got other auditions. You're a professional actor." I always liked that. For this audition, however, I went to Ralph Lauren in a Macy's near my house. I told the lady there, "Hey, will you help me pick out an outfit? I have this audition tomorrow. And this is the character." She gave me a pair of shoes, a pair of blue navy pants, a lavender shirt, and a gray zip-up cardigan. I told her if I get the part I'm going to come back and thank her for helping me pick this outfit out. [He left her a note.] So I strapped that outfit on, got clean, shaved, went in, and did the part the exact same way and again they passed. Now I was pissed because I'd spent money. I was like, "This is bullshit." But I was still willing to let it go. I did the best I could. A few days later, I got a call saying they'd changed their minds and that they wanted to put me in the room with Jesse. So I had a weekend to get ready to go in and test for 20th Century Fox.

Stonestreet tested with two other actors, Jim Rash and Kevin Bernston, who would later appear as Raymond, ex-boyfriend of Mitch and Cam's friend Jamarcus.

STONESTREET (*Cam Tucker*): I could hear other people going in and hearing laughs and stuff.

Stonestreet managed to maintain his focus. He got a much more positive reaction this time.

WINER (*director / executive producer*): When someone's in the zone, connecting to the material, it generates a kind of laughter that's unmistakable, and that was definitely Eric.

CORBOY (*actor*): Jason described it that when Eric left, everyone in the room was silent because they'd just witnessed the most amazing audition for Cameron they'd seen. And then Jason says, "Well, I think we know who's going to play Cameron." He still had to go to the network to make it formal, but by then everyone knew how funny he was, and it was a foregone conclusion.

The next day, he tested for ABC executives with Jesse in tow again.

STONESTREET (*Cam Tucker*): I never really involved my parents in Kansas in anything unless it was big, but I called them the night before and told them I was testing for a show and to send positive vibes and get prayers going.

FERGUSON (*Mitchell Pritchett*): Everyone saw the same thing. There was something really special about Eric. He was bringing this really flamboyant character to life, but it was very rooted in reality. It came from a very organic place, and I think that was really evident.

GREENBERG (*casting director*): It's an actor's trick. If it's grounded, you can get away with a lot more.

FERGUSON (*Mitchell Pritchett*): Auditions in general are really stressful, and he was handling the stress in a way that most people weren't. He did get a little nervous once we got into the room.

STONESTREET (*Cam Tucker*): I pushed it a little bit because I didn't get a laugh that I was supposed to get.

FERGUSON (*Mitchell Pritchett*): And in response to that, he overcompensated and did a really super gay Z snap after a line, which also fell flat.

STONESTREET (*Cam Tucker*): Jesse loves reminding me I did a *Z* snap, which was uncharacteristic of what I was doing with the character. I was like, "Oh shit. Where did that come from? Why did I do that?"

FERGUSON (*Mitchell Pritchett*): And so in my head, I thought, "Oh no, he's bombing this. He's getting nervous and overthinking this." Even Eric will admit that was a moment in which he thought he'd blown it. At least he's admitted that to me.

STONESTREET (*Cam Tucker*): I'd been successful and gotten my laughs all throughout the process, three other auditions. When I didn't get that laugh, I fell back on, "They wouldn't have me here if they didn't think I was good enough. Go back to what got me here in the first place." But the truth is, man, it was so scary.

HOOPER (*casting associate*): There's this long hallway that goes from the screening room to the lobby area where the actors are waiting. My job is to walk out with the actor and then get the next one. Eric, as he was walking out, was wondering if he had done the best work, if there were moments he could have hit that didn't go the way he had hoped. I thought he'd done a great job.

Stonestreet had been here before. He knew the drill for pilot season. Actors do it every year until they get a series. Then they hope that series gets picked up by the network and lasts. Most times it doesn't, placing them back in the hunt again.

STONESTREET (*Cam Tucker*): I lived in Valley Village at the time. It was about a twelve-minute drive home. It was raining. I pulled into my driveway, and my manager called and said, "Eric, you know, there's good days and bad days, and I know you've had your fair share of bad days, and this happens to not be one of them. You got the part, bro." Jason later indicated to me that when it came time to decide if I was the right guy for the part, that Stephen McPherson stood up and said, "Funny is funny, and that guy is fucking funny. Hire him."

In anticipation of playing their new roles as a happy couple, Ferguson and Stonestreet decided to meet up outside the studio and spend some time together bonding.

STONESTREET (*Cam Tucker*): I was talking to my dad as I was getting onto the freeway, saying, "Well, I'm going to go meet my TV boyfriend." My dad said, "Well, that's something I thought I'd never hear."

FERGUSON (*Mitchell Pritchett*): It was a coffee date at a café near my house in Silver Lake. We were getting to know each other on a human level.

STONESTREET (*Cam Tucker*): I didn't have anyone significant in my life at the time, and I don't know that he did.

FERGUSON (*Mitchell Pritchett*): There were people in the coffee shop with balloons and roses. One of us checked our phone, and we realized it was February 14, Valentine's Day.

STONESTREET (*Cam Tucker*): It was a really sweet moment. We didn't really know each other, but we were thinking, "This has to mean something good."

FERGUSON (*Mitchell Pritchett*): What I was really drawn to about Eric was he'd been working in this business for a long time, but he had never really broken through with an opportunity like the role of Cam. He seemed so grateful and humbled by it. He didn't seem like so many actors I meet that have this false sense of importance.

STONESTREET (*Cam Tucker*): All of us have had a different version of struggle to get to where we are. And when all of a sudden you're now "important," you have the choice to play the role of their version of who they think you are or to stay true to yourself.

GREENBERG (*casting director*): Eric rose to the occasion. He was waiting for the right part at the right time. That was obviously it. We really struck gold with finding that guy.

CORBOY (*actor*): I will never forget during the pilot, Eric and I were sitting together. [Corboy appears in the pilot as Josh, described by him as "douche soccer dad who hits on Gloria."] Jeff walked right up to Eric, and he was almost in tears, and said, "I am so proud of you. You fought for this part, to get this audition, and then you were so funny that you kicked the door down to get this part and you did it." And now, ten years later, we can't imagine that part not being Eric Stonestreet. It moved me that Jeff gave enough of a shit to say, "We're so proud of you." It warmed my heart. The little guy won.

Great Expectations

On March 3, 2009, Modern Family's ensemble cast assembled for the first time for a pre-table read inside Building 1 (known today as the Steven Bochco Building) on the Fox lot. A pre-table read provides an informal rehearsal before the all-important network table read, where network executives deliver notes and verdicts, which at times can include recasting.

HYLAND (*Haley Dunphy*): I pulled up in my car blasting Lil Wayne or something like that and saw Ariel in this almost all-purple outfit. I had looked her up online and thought, "Oh my gosh, we look so much alike."

RODRIGUEZ (*Manny Delgado*): I felt excited. This was something I always wanted to do, and now it was happening! I was nine years old thinking, "Wow! Look at this table! Look at all the chairs and all the food and soda you can drink. What? I can drink those?"

Settling into the room, cast members took a look around at the sea of mostly unrecognizable faces, their new adopted television family. In addition to the excitement of the experience, a sense of familiar dread, well known to actors, pulsed through the room.

BOWEN (*Claire Dunphy*): I was sweating bullets. I hate table reads. I've been fired after a table read before.

BURRELL (*Phil Dunphy*): I've been fired at every part of the process. You're so expendable. You can be in the pilot, even in the first episode, and still be replaced. It's such a weird business.

Everyone knew O'Neill, considered the "get" actor and perhaps the securest performer in his new role due to his iconic role as Al Bundy.

FERGUSON (*Mitchell Pritchett*): I was very intimidated by Ed. I'd been watching him on television for many, many years. I'm meeting this guy who's a celebrity that I admire, yet at the same time, he's going to be playing my father. I had to really talk myself into talking to him a lot and getting to know him.

O'Neill's notoriety didn't extend to everyone, however.

RODRIGUEZ (*Manny Delgado*): My dad was telling me who my TV parents were and said, "And your dad is"—and took a pause—"Ed O'Neill." I looked at him and said, "Who's that?" And he goes, "Al Bundy." I said, "I have no idea who you're talking about." Then he showed me a picture, and I said, "Doesn't ring a bell at all."

First impressions remain etched in cast members' minds.

FERGUSON (*Mitchell Pritchett*): I remember Sofía hugging everyone in the room and my being shocked because Sarah was talking about living with her boyfriend. She looked to me to be sixteen years old.

HYLAND (*Haley Dunphy*): I was very excited to meet Jesse because I loved him in *The 25th Annual Putnam County Spelling Bee*. I was also really excited to meet Julie Bowen because I was a massive fan of *Ed,* and she had the same last name as one of my childhood best friends [actress Andrea Bowen].

STONESTREET (*Cam Tucker*): I knew Ty from *Black Hawk Down,* and a zombie movie he was in [*Dawn of the Dead*] and *Out of Practice.* He was this journeyman actor. I didn't know him as playing this kind of character necessarily.

BOWEN (*Claire Dunphy*): Steve had sold Ty so hard to me. "He's so talented. He's so great. We'd looked at everybody, and this was the guy." I thought, "Why are you telling me how great Ty is?" Nobody needed to sell me on this job. I'd be lucky to work with a monkey on this script.

BURRELL (*Phil Dunphy*): I'm sure she was unintimidated after being around me for sixty seconds and seeing me in all my beta glory.

VERGARA (*Gloria Delgado-Pritchett*): Julie was sitting down at the table. She was perfect from the boobs up. Then she got up, and I saw that she was fucking seven and a half months pregnant. I was like, "Holy shit, she's going to give birth right now."

O'Neill found himself staring out into a sea of anonymity.

O'NEILL (*Jay Pritchett*): I didn't know anyone. I think I had seen Julie on *Boston Legal* once when I was channel surfing. I'd never seen Sofía, didn't know Ty, Eric, Jesse, and certainly didn't know the kids.

The awkwardness of introductions led to bumbling chatter.

WINTER (*Alex Dunphy*): I said super awkward things thinking they were cool. I said something really strange about giving birth to Julie. I know Jesse and Julie heard it. I think they remember it to this day.

BURRELL (*Phil Dunphy*): I asked Nolan if he was named after Nolan Ryan. He rolled his eyes at me like it was the one hundredth time he was answering that question. I could sense him thinking, "Old dumb man, please leave me alone."

GOULD (*Luke Dunphy*): In truth, I was named after someone who was named after Nolan Ryan. I called my TV parents "Mr. Burrell" and "Mrs. Bowen," trying to be super respectful. They let me know then and there to stop calling them Mr. and Mrs. Everyone here was going to be equals. We weren't just going to be coworkers, we were going to be friends. That meant a lot to me. That was really cool.

No reaction quite matched the one toward Vergara.

STONESTREET (Cam Tucker): I saw Sofía walk in and thought, "Holy cow, she's a really pretty, pretty woman."

O'NEILL (Jay Pritchett): When I first saw her, I thought, "This makes perfect sense. Nobody's going to believe us." In fact, I think some people still don't.

BOWEN (Claire Dunphy): I couldn't believe how pulled together and gorgeous she was. You don't think someone is going to be that sexy and beautiful and also be smart and funny. I figured she'd be tough or trashy to undercut all that gorgeousness, but no, she doubled down.

STONESTREET (Cam Tucker): I had a moment with Ty where I nudged him underneath the table. I was like, "Oh my gosh, she's beautiful. I'm going to have to work really hard not to stare at her."

BURRELL (Phil Dunphy): I knew Eric was playing Cam and assumed he was gay. But after hearing that, I was like, "Okay, so, he's very straight."

Levitan and Lloyd handpicked a small circle of friends for their audience, including the pilot's production department heads and writing peers like Shawn Ryan, creator of the critically acclaimed FX series The Shield.

SHAWN RYAN (creator of The Shield): Steve, Chris, and I worked in the same building. As a drama writer, I really admired the comedy work they did, and I think they were intrigued by the drama work I did. So one day, somebody comes to my office and says Chris and Steve are doing a private read-through of their pilot. Would I be interested in coming? Anything to avoid doing real work. So I said, "Of course."

The cast eventually sat down to business, reading the script straight through in real time.

O'NEILL (Jay Pritchett): I started listening to everyone, watching them. I thought, "Jesus Christ, they're all good. This is amazing."

LLOYD (*cocreator*): It was revelatory, because it was the first time we'd seen or heard their voices side by side. What do Julie and Ty sound like as a married couple? How do Ed and Sofía sound?

LEVITAN (*cocreator*): You're praying they all find chemistry together.

LLOYD (*cocreator*): I think it was the first relaxation where we knew we made the right decisions in casting. They were all great.

LEVITAN (*cocreator*): That's 100 percent true. You believed that Jesse and Julie could be brother and sister and could have come from Ed. You believed the Dunphy kids could have come from Julie and Ty. Ed and Sofía worked because they're so different. It all worked.

MORTON (*executive producer*): Sofía reads her first entrance, and all I could think was, "My God, we've got Lucille Ball with Desi Arnaz's voice."

VERGARA (*Gloria Delgado-Pritchett*): I was worried about playing the character the right way. I was thinking, "How should she be? Was she supposed to be shy or really out there?"

BURRELL (*Phil Dunphy*): She crushed the table read. She has such a natural feel. I thought, "She didn't get this part just because she's pretty. She got this part because she's hilarious."

MORTON (*executive producer*): The kids were a big revelation, too. It was amazing to see how good they were at that age.

WINTER (*Alex Dunphy*): I'm type A, so for me, I wanted to get everything perfect.

FERGUSON (*Mitchell Pritchett*): It's always a wild card when you're working with kids. These kids felt very real. They had their shit together, more than any of the adults.

Levitan and Lloyd couldn't have been more thrilled with the results. Before they disassembled, production wheeled in a surprise cake for Bowen, in honor of her birthday that day. They quickly learned not everybody welcomes such recognition.

FERGUSON (*Mitchell Pritchett*): She didn't want to celebrate it. We all wished her a happy birthday, and she basically fell into herself. That hasn't changed. She still hates her birthday.

BOWEN (*Claire Dunphy*): They started singing "Happy Birthday." I was mortified. I was really, really, really anxious. I wanted to get out of that room as fast as I could because I was sure the longer I lingered, the more chance they would give me the ax.

As the cast made their way outside, Levitan coerced everyone to pose for an impromptu cast photo.

The producers then retreated to Lloyd's office with a small group of writer friends to polish the script.

RYAN (*creator of* The Shield): Steve asked me, "What did you think?" I said, "When you get invited to these things, you spend a lot of time thinking about what you're going to say that's going to sound complimentary when you didn't think the thing was so great. I have to tell you in complete honesty, this thing is fucking great. I don't have anything to tell you about how to improve it. I really think you have something here."

Levitan, Lloyd, and assembled writers worked through the script, scene by scene, joke by joke, tweaking content in places they felt needed punching up.

LLOYD (*cocreator*): Some really nice elements went in at that point, like Jay's voice-over at the end, which you find out is actually Manny's poem to the girl he likes. It was a nice little touch we discovered.

RYAN (*creator of* The Shield): The one scene occupying the most conversation was Mitch and Cam on the plane bringing Lily home. That conversation must have been at least an hour long.

In Levitan's notes from the meeting, he details the debate:

> *Mitchell is very strong and confident around everyone but his family. Or, in the airplane scene, would it be better if Cameron wants to give the speech and Mitchell wants him to let it go? Maybe we should reverse their roles?*

LLOYD (*cocreator*): There was a conversation about how militant or strident we wanted Mitchell to seem straight off the bat because you're meeting this character. It seemed a tiny bit risky to see him get up and address an airplane full of people in a wrap-yourself-in-the-pride-flag way. That isn't who Mitchell really is. He's a little bit more tremulous than that.

LEVITAN (*cocreator*): You're defining them in that very first scene. You're learning so much about who they are. If we're shooting that scene today, there's a chance Cam's the one making that speech and Mitchell might be the one saying, "Keep it down." Back then, it felt right. I could still make a case for it because Mitchell is a lawyer.

LLOYD (*cocreator*): That scene is tricky because it's really just introducing these characters, but it doesn't really launch the story. The story is Cam putting pressure on Mitchell to finally introduce Lily to the family. And I think we really underscored that part of the story in the rewrite.

Interestingly, Mitchell didn't start off as an attorney. They landed on that during rewrites, moving him out of a dentist's chair and into a lawyer's one instead. Working through such minutiae can help refine characters and discover new areas to explore.

LLOYD (*cocreator*): A dentist seemed a profession for someone who was a little cloistered, a little emotionally withheld. He could disappear into people's mouths, but maybe not engage in life that much. But then you start asking questions like, if we're going to go to his workplace, is a dentist's office as exciting as another profession might be? We gravitated to lawyer because we thought that might give him stories that we could bring home and talk about.

They discussed the potential reaction to Mitchell's and Cam's sexuality.

LEVITAN (cocreator): One of our friends, who's gay and a very good writer, was very worried about Mitchell and Cam. He thought we had too much of them, that America hates gay people. And this is a gay man talking. We thought, "They're going to have to learn to love them." That's the bit.

ABRAHAM HIGGINBOTHAM (writer / executive producer): He was a strange presence that day, to be perfectly honest. I think he felt like a lot of people felt, that you'd better put that gay couple in the background a little bit more or no one's going to watch. I believe those were his words. I think he was more of that old-school thinking, nervous about it at the time.

They gave Jay a harder edge. When Munny fails at wooing a girl, Jay initially provided paternal encouragement.

```
             ORIGINAL SCENE


INT. MALL—DAY

Gloria hugs Manny.

                   MANNY
         I gave her my heart and she gave me a
         pretzel dog.
                   (then)
         That was pretty stupid of me, wasn't it?

                   JAY
         You know what, Manny, no it wasn't
         stupid. It was fantastic. You took
```

a big swing, and I respect the hell
out of that. C'mon, let's go get some
lunch. Anywhere you want to go.

Jay took a different approach in the rewrite.

REVISED SCENE

<u>INT. MALL—DAY</u>

Gloria hugs Manny.

                    MANNY
          I gave her my heart and she gave
          me a picture of me as an old-time
          sheriff.

Manny holds up a picture of himself, sad, but
with a Photoshopped mustache, cowboy hat, and
old-timey background.

                    MANNY
          That was pretty stupid of me, wasn't
          it?

He looks to both of them.

                    GLORIA
          No, mi amor, it was brave.
                    (looks to Jay)
          Right, Jay? Brave.

                    JAY
          Well, you'll know better next time.
          Come on, let's get a pretzel.

LLOYD (*cocreator*): We like that Jay's struggling. He doesn't think it's entirely right for a ten-year-old to be writing a poem to a girl who's way over his station in life because he's a little bit old-school. He's going to tell the kid, his stepson, "I don't know if that's the smartest thing you did. Let's learn from this mistake," as opposed to telling him, "You're going to be fine." It was a conscious decision to rough him up a little bit. I think a bit of that came from spending time with Ed. He's a very bighearted guy. He can say harsh things, but he has a little Irish twinkle in his eye and you forgive him. We wondered, "Is this going to make the character unlikable?" Once we had Ed doing it, we went, "No, that's totally likable because it's totally believable as to what that guy would do, and it leaves us room to explore as we move forward."

In Levitan's notes, he highlighted fleshing out Claire's motivation for helicopter-parenting Haley:

> Claire was wild growing up. She dated bad boys and did many stupid things. She's a bit surprised she's alive and wants to keep her kids from making the same mistakes she did.
>
> At sixteen (or fifteen) she had sex in her bedroom, while her parents were home, by blocking the door with her feet.
>
> Possible replacement of Alex beat: "Mom, how old were you when you first had sex?" Interview: "Fifteen." Back to scene: "Your father and I got married when I was twenty-two" (or something like that).

BIANCA CHAN (*writers' assistant*): They were discussing how to make Claire's character more likable and relatable. They thought she was a little too uptight with Haley and wanted to give her some underneath motivation for why she was that way.

WINER (*director / executive producer*): Julie would be the first to admit she had some wild days as a teenager and in her twenties. They borrowed that as a backstory for the pilot and series to give Claire anxiety about who she was, especially as it related to Haley.

Another debate involved whether Claire mirrored too much the stereotypical sitcom wife who shakes her head at the crazy antics of her larger-than-life mate. One scene in particular, in the Dunphy kitchen, caused a lot of debate: punishing Luke for shooting Alex with his BB gun.

HIGGINBOTHAM (*writer / executive producer*): There was concern that Claire was too finger-waggy. We thought, "Why couldn't she be the parent who said, 'You promised you were going to shoot him, now shoot him'?" I thought it was a funnier attitude if she was the one saying to take him into the yard. That was something that came from watching my sister and parents.

LEVITAN (*cocreator*): Phil wanted to be the fun, cool dad that everybody likes, and she was the disciplinarian. That was a nice breakthrough for the characters.

```
                ORIGINAL SCENE


        LUKE
They're just plastic BBs. It was an
accident.


        CLAIRE
        (to Phil)
What did I tell you would happen if
you bought him a gun?


        PHIL
        (to Luke)
What did I tell you would happen if
you shot any animal or any person?


        LUKE
That you would shoot me.
```

                    PHIL
That's right! Come on. Let's go.

He starts for the backyard.

                    CLAIRE
Are you insane, you're going to shoot
him?!
He's got a birthday party. He can't
show up with a big hideous welt. You
can shoot him later. He'll be home at
two.

                    ALEX
Does anyone care about my hideous
welt?

Levitan's notes reflect the change in character.

*Claire insists that Phil shoot Luke because that was the
deal they made. Phil really doesn't want to go through
with it. Later, after shooting him, Luke says, "I thought
you were my friend!" Phil (upset): "I am your friend!"*

They revised the scene this way:

                  REVISED SCENE

                    LUKE
They're only plastic BBs. It was an
accident.

                    CLAIRE
                  (to Phil)
What did I tell you would happen if
you got him a gun? Deal with this.

                         PHIL
                    (to Luke)
          Buddy, uncool.

                         CLAIRE
          That's it? That's—No, the agreement was,
          if he shoots someone, you shoot him.

                         PHIL
          We were serious about that?

                         CLAIRE
          Yes, we were and now you have to
          follow through.

                         LUKE
                    (crying)
          I'm so sorry.

                         CLAIRE
          Liar.

          Luke drops his crying instantly.

                         CLAIRE
          Go.

Lloyd (cocreator): Phil's this guy who so loves his kids and likes being kid-like around them that he was more comfortable with issuing a threat and not following through with it. And Claire, perhaps with a little Jay in her, says this will be lawlessness if we issue threats and don't follow through. We have to follow through. It made for a funnier scene where Phil has to go out there to do it and he's struggling. He almost feels he's getting shot himself doing this. Then he backs off because he couldn't shoot Luke and then shoots him accidentally and then Dylan comes out and Phil shoots him accidentally and then shoots himself. Shooting Dylan was something we improvised. Phil shooting himself was something we thought we would try, and Ty's one of the great physical comedians so he made that funny.

Levitan and Lloyd kept rewriting right up until the all-important network table read, held at a large event room at ABC Studios in Burbank. Here, a pack of show-me network and studio executives, each with their own ideas of how to make a successful series, listened in.

HYLAND (*Haley Dunphy*): I was really excited to be on that Disney lot with the animation building because I'm a big Disney fan.

BURRELL (*Phil Dunphy*): We were airing on ABC, so I assumed we were filming at ABC. I rented an apartment within walking distance. I very cockily sauntered in and let everyone know I was able to walk to work while they had to drive. Then somebody informed me that we were filming the pilot at Fox and that I basically had an hour-plus commute ahead of me. About midway through that season, I had to get out of my lease.

MORTON (*executive producer*): I had developed a kidney stone that day, and as we were about to start, I got a terrible attack and could barely function, but I didn't want to leave the room, because I wanted to see what was going to happen. So I went to the back. The only comfort I could get was lying down and propping my head up.

LEVITAN (*cocreator*): He was like a dog under the porch. I felt terrible for him.

The room response echoed the success of the pre–table read, albeit with a larger and louder audience for a script already creating buzz around town.

MCPHERSON (*ABC Entertainment president*): It took on this energy. The energy itself felt like another character in the show. Each actor so funny in their own way. It's hard to have that many people in a pilot and have you care about all of them.

LYON (*VP of casting at ABC*): When everyone elevates the role of each other, when everything is clicking into place, you notice.

Burrell had to overcome his angst over seeing McPherson in the audience.

BURRELL (*Phil Dunphy*): It was incredibly intimidating for me because I knew I was doing this in front of someone who didn't like me as an actor.

MCPHERSON (*ABC Entertainment president*): He lit up that table read. People were crying, laughing. His interviews were hilariously funny, but he did it in such a lovable way. You fell in love with that dad immediately. I laughed about it afterward with Ty and apologized over and over.

FALVEY (*ABC Entertainment head of comedy*): I was looking at how the kids were really holding their own. That's an intimidating space, and there are a lot of adults and heavy hitters. The kids hung in there.

GOULD (*Luke Dunphy*): It was nonstop laughter. People were on the edge of their seats. At this point, it started to dawn on me that *Modern Family* was going to be something different. I had heard stories from people on other TV shows on how difficult it is to get a show off the ground. There are so many roadblocks. And *Modern Family* was flying by all of them.

The network had very few notes to share—more music (which they ignored) and perhaps a modified tone.

Lloyd (*cocreator*): They were concerned about where the comedy was coming from. They wanted something more absurd like that *Family Guy* style of "Remember the time we were all gathered and a kangaroo came running through our kitchen?" and then we cut to the scene of the kangaroo running through the kitchen. They were kind of urging us more toward that. They were entitled to their uneasiness. Once the show premiered, all of that relaxed very quickly.

Given a stamp of approval, the producers could now move on to the next big step: filming the pilot.

Pilot

Levitan, Lloyd, and Winer shot the Modern Family *pilot over the course of one long week in the spring of 2009.*

IWONA SAPIENZA (*script supervisor / director*): It was like working on any other pilot. You never really know where you're going with it. You're hoping for the best, but ultimately, only one out of a million gets picked up.

STONESTREET (*Cam Tucker*): I remember listening to everyone in the makeup trailer talking about what would have happened had they not got this part. Julie was still in second position on a pilot. Sofía had a holding deal. Ed's rich as fuck and had a pot roast in the Crock-Pot and a bottle of red wine ready. He didn't care. Jesse was workshopping *Elf* on Broadway. I'm standing in the background thinking, "Wow, I had a Lowe's [home improvement store] callback next week."

Without a template in place, cast and crew spent long days trying to find the show's essence.

BURRELL (*Phil Dunphy*): Jason's a perfectionist in a great way. We did stuff over and over again and improvised a lot until we felt like we'd exhausted everything.

BOWEN (*Claire Dunphy*): We tried different things to find out who these people were and how they related to each other. I had to figure out why Claire loves this guy.

VERGARA (*Gloria Delgado-Pritchett*): I was thinking about Gloria. I was worried how that character is going to work. How's she supposed to dress? How's she supposed to talk? You're concentrating on everything.

FERGUSON (*Mitchell Pritchett*): There was talk of maybe having me shave for the pilot. I got very nervous about that because I know they test these things in front of random audiences. I thought if someone sees me looking too young and says something, it's going to get stuck in the ear of the producers and they're going to recast me.

The greatest logistical challenge in filming the pilot concerned camouflaging Bowen's ever-expanding womb.

BOWEN (*Claire Dunphy*): My face was pregnant. I had tons of hair and looked like I got lip injections because I was so puffy. And I had these enormous boobs that were terrifying. I read online, before I made my "No Google" rule, about how I clearly had plastic surgery. What? Those were painful cow udders.

Bowen discovered the perfect smoke screen within the Dunphy household.

BOWEN (*Claire Dunphy*): I said, "Nolan, you have be the baby blocker."

GOULD (LUKE DUNPHY): My head and shoulders were at the perfect height to stand in front of Julie's pregnant belly. That became my job for the entire pilot and all photo shoots. I'm still referred to this day as "the baby blocker."

In scenes where Claire found herself without her son, the director and producers got more creative.

WINER (*director / executive producer*): I constantly changed the way I covered her up. I used slightly offset camera angles and activity. They became a trademark of her character and the show.

LEVITAN (*cocreator*): We put a bunch of props in front of her—laundry, cereal boxes, pillows, whatever we could think of.

WINER (*director / executive producer*): We measured the height of the kitchen island. We put her in low shoes or no shoes and then set the camera at a slightly lower angle than it would otherwise be. That hid enough of her belly behind the counter. The one shot I was most worried about was the interviews. It was Julie who grabbed a pillow and said she could use this.

BOWEN (*Claire Dunphy*): There's a scene where I'm coming up the stairs with a laundry basket, yelling Haley's name because she's alone in her bedroom with Dylan [Reid Ewing]. In my mind, we shot it four hundred times. In reality, it was probably eight. But with a lot of babies in me, it was a challenge to walk into that room saying Haley's name instead of gasping it. When they asked if I could do one more, I said, "Of course I can." And then my brain went, "Can you? You're massive. These are not normal circumstances. You can't roll over in bed. You can only eat standing up. This isn't easy."

The baby blocker's first scene proved difficult as well.

INT. DUNPHY HOUSE—STAIRWAY—DAY

Luke has his head stuck between the railings. Phil rubs baby oil on the railings and on Luke's head.

              PHIL
    Buddy, why do you keep getting stuck
    like this?

              LUKE
    I thought I could get out this time.

              ALEX
        (as she crosses past)
    I'm just gonna say it: he needs to be
    checked by a specialist.

GOULD (*Luke Dunphy*): I was embarrassed because they were putting a ridiculous amount of Vaseline on my hair and face, trying to shove me into this banister and then pull me out. I was like, "All right, this is how I'm starting my career on this show." I really didn't understand that this was for the sake of comedy.

BURRELL (*Phil Dunphy*): It's a tricky thing about comedy, where you look terrible. You have to learn that it's beneficial for the scene and joke. When you're first starting out, you mainly think you look terrible.

GOULD (*Luke Dunphy*): Ty was aware that I wasn't particularly comfortable. When we were done with the scene, he said, "Can we give it up to Nolan for being a trooper on this?" and led a round of applause. Ty's done that multiple times with everybody when he knows we're doing something we don't particularly want to be doing, but know it's good for the show. He's literally the best human being ever.

```
                    AIRPLANE SCENE


Boarding passengers file down the aisle passing
Mitchell, who holds on his lap an Asian baby,
Lily. Cameron enters with a large carry-on and a
bag of goodies. The passengers look away and flip
uncomfortably through their magazines. Mitchell
notes this.


                    MITCHELL
          You saw that, right? Everybody
          fawning over Lily, and then you walk
          on and suddenly it's all,
               (picking up magazine)
          "Ooh, Sky Mall. I've got to buy a
          motorized tie rack."
                    (then)
          All right, I'm giving the speech.
```

CAMERON

You are not giving the speech. We're
going to be stuck with these people
for the next five hours.

MITCHELL

You're right, you're right. Okay. I'm
sorry.

PASSENGER #3
(amused)
Look at that baby with those cream
puffs.

MITCHELL

Okay, excuse me, but this baby would
have grown up in a crowded orphanage
if it weren't for us "cream puffs"—
(standing up)—and you know what? To
all of you who judge, hear this—

CAMERON

Mitchell!

MITCHELL

—love knows no race, creed, or gender,
and shame on you small-minded,
ignorant few—

CAMERON

Mitchell! She's got the cream puffs.

Cameron points out that Lily has grabbed a
cream puff out of his bag of goodies and is
squishing it.

                    MITCHELL
        Oh.

Cameron stands.

                    CAMERON
        We would like to pay for everyone's
        headsets.

STONESTREET (*Cam Tucker*): It was originally a grocery store where a lady was buying a bunch of cat food. Somebody in line called us Twinkies. They changed Twinkies to cream puffs.

LEVITAN (*cocreator*): They made us change it because of a product-advertising sales note.

STONESTREET (*Cam Tucker*): I got the biggest laugh every time when I said, "We would like to pay for your cat food." After, we turned it into, "We would like to pay for your headsets."

RYAN CASE (*director/editor*): That whole scene to me is the cream puff scene. We had to bring Eric back in and have him ADR [Automated Dialogue Replacement] "It's the cream puff" because he mouthed it and we wondered, "Could people look at it and know it's a cream puff? Does the joke even work if we can't tell what it is?" It was so you could understand the whole joke.

WINER (*director / executive producer*): Steve and I had an argument with the scene. I wanted to sneak a view of their private conversation between the crack in the seats because that's where I felt a cameraman accompanying them would be. They wouldn't have this conversation if the camera was literally on their faces. Steve was envisioning it, I think, more conventionally covered for comedy purposes, more clearly a shot of their faces. I was arguing where the camera should be, and ultimately that's where it was.

SAPIENZA (*script supervisor / director*): The biggest thing Jason said to me was, "Please keep me honest when cameras are rolling so we're always getting two actors looking at each other when they're talking." We were shooting on the airplane. We had a camera at the front and back of the plane. I went up to David Hemmings [the pilot's director of photography] and said, "Our eyelines are crossing." When Mitch is talking to a woman in the row next to him, they were both looking in the same direction. Everyone pooh-poohed me about it and said they'd work it out in editing. The last day of shooting, we reshot the scene.

FERGUSON (*Mitchell Pritchett*): We ended up having to erect half an airplane in front of the house that we were shooting at for Mitch and Cam. It was wild for everyone.

Within the show's first five minutes, before the main title, viewers meet the three families through interviews and scenes.

After the title sequence, Levitan and Lloyd start playing with the interview format, creating jokes in editing by contrasting Phil's bragging to the camera with having nothing to boast about in reality.

```
                    PHIL INTERVIEW

                         PHIL
          I'm the cool dad. That's my thing.
          I'm hip. I surf the web, I text:
          LOL—Laugh out loud, OMG—Oh my God,
          WTF—Why the face . . .  You know, I
          know all the dances from High School
          Musical.

Flashback to Phil demonstrating a dance from
High School Musical as his horrified kids, along
with a couple of their friends, look on.
```

BURRELL (*Phil Dunphy*): I did a bunch of dances I thought would be most awkward for a middle-aged white guy. Crumping was one. I basically spent a couple of days on YouTube.

LLOYD (*cocreator*): The kids being so mortified that Dad's dancing again. It gave us, in fifteen seconds, pretty good insight into who this character was. Alan Tudyk came up with that WTF joke in an audition. We thought it was funny, but it was a little tricky to say, "Hey, we can't offer you the part, but could we steal that really funny improvised line?" He was very gracious about it and said of course.

```
INT. DUNPHY HOUSE—DAY


Phil and Claire head to the kitchen as Alex
appears in the doorway, holding her arm. Luke
enters carrying an air-soft gun.


                    ALEX
          Luke just shot me!


                    LUKE
          I didn't mean to.


                    CLAIRE
                (to Alex)
          Are you okay?


                    ALEX
          No, the little bitch shot me.
```

WINTER (*Alex Dunphy*): I just thought that was hilarious being a kid. People laughed and it was affirming. I was thinking, "At least I'm doing a good job. Cool."

LEVITAN (*cocreator*): At first they said you can't have kids swearing like that, and I said, "That's exactly why we need to have that joke in there, to send a strong signal that this is not the same show you've seen a hundred times."

Burrell improvised a recurring joke that ran the course of the first season and series. It involved a broken tread on the staircase.

WINER (*director / executive producer*): He would trip on the same step every time up and down the stair and say, "Gotta fix that step." That was a combination of his brilliant comedic improv mind and his incredible physical comedy skills. The fact that he always trips on a step that he can never quite remember to fix is quintessential Phil as expressed by Ty.

SAMEER GARDEZI (*staff writer*): He had such perfect timing on that. Every time he walked up the stairs, the exact same step, the exact same cadence.

BURRELL (*Phil Dunphy*): Every time we were near the stairs, we would find a way to get it in there. It got more and more fun for us to find a way to shoehorn it into scenes it had no intention of being in. It felt like the most fun mission to figure out a way to put it in, including dramatic scenes.

LLOYD (*cocreator*): In the first season finale, Claire's trying to get a family portrait together and wants everybody lined up on the stairs. She realizes Phil had never fixed the stair that he had promised her he'd fix. Then she tries to fix it herself and makes it worse. All that from one of the throwaway bits in the pilot.

A small moment, but big visual joke, came from Lloyd's experiences.

INT. LILY'S ROOM—DAY

Cameron looks at the wall above the changing table where a mural has been painted. It is a heavenly scene, full of clouds. Emerging from one cloud are Cameron and Mitchell painted like angels with wings.

                    CAMERON
          (gasping)
Oh my God, do you love it?

                    MITCHELL
What the hell is it?

                    CAMERON
I had Andre do it while we were gone.

                    MITCHELL
Is that us with wings?

                    CAMERON
We're floating above her, always there
to protect her.

                    MITCHELL
Oh, that's reassuring, right, Lily?
Yes, we tore you away from everything
you know, but don't worry, things are
normal here. Your dads are floating
fairies.

LLOYD (*cocreator*): I have a gay friend who does that in people's houses—he frescoes up their ceilings. I thought, "Man, that's a specialized field. You need to live in a particular part of the world to have any demand for that service." So I thought that could be one of their friends, and how would that apply in their lives? It seemed like an over-the-top fun Cam thing to do.

It got embellished by Richard Berg, the show's production designer.

RICHARD BERG (*production designer*): To me, it sounded like Michelangelo's image of God and Adam in the Sistine Chapel, where they're reaching out to touch each other. I pitched it to Steve and Chris, and they said,

"Go with it." I turned it over to a scenic artist who worked on the Fox lot. He did a rough painting of it, and then we went right onto the wall after that.

FERGUSON (*Mitchell Pritchett*): The house that we shot in was in this butch guy's house. We ended up taking over his bedroom to use as Lily's room. We painted it completely pink and put a mural of two men as angels in his bedroom. Obviously they restored his house the way it was, but I like the idea that underneath paint somewhere, in this guy's house, still is that layer of pink paint with that mural on it.

The entire episode culminates in the big reveal to the audience in Mitchell and Cam's living room: all three separate families belong to the same one. The moment hit home with an immense emotional impact for audiences.

MUSIC CUE: LION KING "CIRCLE OF LIFE"

Everybody turns. Cameron enters holding Lily. In time to the music, he dramatically raises her toward the heavens. They all look at one another, mystified.

                MITCHELL
We adopted a baby. Her name is Lily.

                CAMERON
Exciting!

                MITCHELL
Just turn it off.

                CAMERON
I can't turn it off, it's who I am—

                MITCHELL
The music.

MCPHERSON (*ABC Entertainment president*): We weren't sure we were going to be able to get *The Lion King* rights.

FERGUSON (*Mitchell Pritchett*): There was talk about maybe doing another version with some other song. We didn't do it, because it had to be the song.

MCPHERSON (*ABC Entertainment president*): We had to go to Elton John to clear the music. It was absurd because it was Disney and we owned it, but that's the way rights worked.

LLOYD (*cocreator*): I was a little worried about "Circle of Life" because it seemed so extreme. Is this going to play as over the top, or are we in for a penny and a pound with Cam and his way of introducing the child? Once we shot it, whatever concerns I had went away because it was really funny, and Eric was so funny with it.

STONESTREET (*Cam Tucker*): For Lily's introduction, I asked Marissa Borsetto, our first wardrobe designer, for something with a Vietnamese feeling. I said Cam's a performer, and he'd definitely have brought a souvenir back from Vietnam. Marissa came up with a kimono.

FERGUSON (*Mitchell Pritchett*): It was a very over-the-top moment, but we found the tone of the whole series in that moment. It was so big, but we all played it so truthfully. I think that's what made it funny. We weren't playing for laughs, and in turn, it's hilarious. It was all rooted in truth, and I think that's what we have carried through with the show.

WINER (*director / executive producer*): I think what we may have been pushing for in that moment is emotional truth as it relates to the character in spite of the fact that the character's doing something somewhat ridiculous. That's a tough thing to try and find. And I think Eric nailed it.

STONESTREET (*Cam Tucker*): I viewed my walk out there as the most important thing my character has ever done. I was carrying the crown jewels. The intention in my face, the intention in my walk, is very specific. I was really trying my best to make eye contact with every person in the room, trying to have a meaningful look. Look at what I'm doing. This is happening now. Here it is. I wanted to give it this overemphasis of importance and let the humor come from that.

GOULD (*Luke Dunphy*): Eric's performance was so utterly ridiculous. You might see me crack a smile because I was trying so hard not to laugh.

Mitchell's plight about telling his family about Lily may anchor the episode, but Jay's reaction after being such a gruff curmudgeon throughout drives home the truth and emotion of the moment.

ZUKER (*writer / executive producer*): These are subtle humiliations that make up a life. When he sees this baby. Ed is such a brilliant actor. Everything, all the regret of all the shit he had said is in there. Watching that softening's fantastic.

LLOYD (*cocreator*): We probably shot that scene for thirty minutes. In one of them, we asked Ed to give us a private moment that shows his confusion and feeling a little lost. Ed's so great. He knew exactly how to process that. We looked at it and said, "We have to use that because it's him being so touched and flustered and not sure what is going on, but it also gives him a turn to embrace this whole thing at the end." It's certainly one of the most memorable moments from the pilot.

LEVITAN (*cocreator*): For a while, we had a scene at the end where some people went into Lily's room and then everyone else heard them over the baby monitor. It was where some things got resolved, but it felt too logical. By having this moment where Jay accepts this baby, we had everything we needed right there.

At the end of the episode, playing under the credit roll, Levitan and Lloyd added a tag in which Phil and Luke play basketball on a trampoline.

CASE (*director/editor*): One of the great things about *Modern Family* is that the end credits run over a fun joke. It's a comedic bit for thirty seconds, related to the episode, but not super important.

WINER (*director / executive producer*): The idea occurred to us while in the backyard of the Dunphy house. That trampoline was a bit of character-inspired set dressing, like of course Phil's the kind of father that would have a trampoline back there.

LLOYD (*cocreator*): We thought, "Let's shoot something and see what comes of it." So, we slid a basketball hoop next to a trampoline and sent Ty and Luke in there. Ty's game for anything, and Nolan's the same. We said, "Start playing basketball."

GOULD (*Luke Dunphy*): I thought this was going to be awesome. I can't believe I'm getting paid to play basketball on a trampoline. I'm going to hit some really cool dunks and stuff. I'm going to impress everyone on set.

WINER (*director / executive producer*): What he didn't know was we'd whispered to Ty that the basic comedic premise was, what if Phil's so competitive he won't let Luke score?

LLOYD (*cocreator*): We told him, "Go to town on him as though you're playing your older brother instead of your ten-year-old son."

BURRELL (*Phil Dunphy*): That was the idea. Phil was going to dominate Luke. I had no idea Nolan was unprepared for that.

LLOYD (*cocreator*): He slapped the ball into the next yard.

BURRELL (*Phil Dunphy*): I was having a blast. It was so fun and exhausting. It was clearly harder for Nolan.

GOULD (*Luke Dunphy*): No matter what I did there was this big strong hand blocking my shot. I kind of got upset with Ty. I'm trying to impress everyone, not thinking that it's a scripted TV show and you can't be whoever you want to be and that what happens to your character is not a reflection of you.

BURRELL (*Phil Dunphy*): What a terrible moment for him to have this new grown-up he's working with apparently trying to show him up in front of a bunch of people.

GOULD (*Luke Dunphy*): Wanting to dunk and having it constantly denied. I've never felt so small in my life.

BURRELL (*Phil Dunphy*): If I had known then, I would have begged for his forgiveness.

> *For their production logo, the show's final shot, Levitan and Lloyd used a spinning album with the names Levitan and Lloyd and pictures of their kids on the center label.*

LEVITAN (*cocreator*): You couldn't tell which name was first. It seemed pretty clever.

When shooting wrapped, the cast gathered for a party. No one knew what came next. This could either be the first or last step of something. Rodriguez didn't want the moment to be lost.

RODRIGUEZ (*Manny Delgado*): When I would wrap previous jobs, I'd give certificates to all of the crew and cast. Like "Best Director" and write their name and then sign mine. That's what I did on the pilot. I gave them all certificates. I said, "It was great working with you." I wanted to make sure they knew that I appreciated them and liked working with them. All the cast and crew were so nice to me. In my head, it was something I could give them as a token of my appreciation for making this experience a great one.

> *After editing and finishing, the producers had a completed product ready. The power then shifted to audiences and their reactions.*

The Verdict

Every spring in New York, television's major broadcast networks host upfronts, a dog and pony presentation in which ebullient network executives reveal their fall prime-time schedule to advertising buyers. Based on the response, the networks then pre-sell advertising for the upcoming year, commonly referred to as upfront advertising sales. In 2009, ABC's presentation took place at Lincoln Center.

SAPIENZA (*script supervisor / director*): I had a friend who helps put together skits for upfronts. There was a day when she couldn't work, so she called to see if I was available. I went in. All of a sudden, Ed shows up. I said, "If you're here, that means *Modern Family*'s getting picked up." He said, "I guess." A day or two later, I emailed Jeff [Morton] and wrote, "I guess this is good news?" He wrote me back, "Yes, I'll be seeing you in the future."

The overwhelmingly positive response to Modern Family *in test screenings led ABC to take the extraordinary step of announcing the show and its thirteen-episode pickup weeks before upfronts (along with its new one-hour sci-fi drama,* Flash Forward*).*

Bowen remembers all too well how she heard the news.

BOWEN (*Claire Dunphy*): It was May 7. I know this because I was lying on a gurney in a hospital, between contractions, when Steve called to tell me. I hadn't yet gone into the delivery room. I said that was great, and then all of a sudden, I had this massive contraction. I said, "I have to go!" He asked, "What are you doing?" I said, "Giving birth!"

McPherson had decided to gamble big on his fall schedule by offering up a completely new Wednesday night of programming: four sitcoms and one drama (Hank, The Middle, Modern Family, Cougar Town, *and the one-hour drama* Eastwick). Modern Family, *at the nine o'clock hour, would serve as the night's anchor. That made drumming up enthusiasm for the show at upfronts extra important.*

MCPHERSON (*ABC Entertainment president*): We were really focused on how to present *Modern Family* and make the show work on our schedule given that we didn't have a hit comedy like *Seinfeld* to put it behind. I felt that a trailer would undercut the entire pilot because you'll reveal that these people are one family. Because I thought their original pitch was so wonderful and well constructed, I took the bold step of airing the entire pilot.

FALVEY (*ABC Entertainment head of comedy*): I was told I needed to get a version of the show ready for upfronts. I was so confused by that. We were incredibly proud of the pilot, but that's a tough audience who's seen a lot and have an Impress Me sign written on their foreheads.

LEVITAN (*cocreator*): I was glad the network had that kind of confidence in us. But the last time that it had been done, it didn't go very well.

Hardly anyone ever airs a full episode at upfronts. They don't want to risk poor word of mouth dooming a series before it ever even airs. NBC had made that fatal mistake in 2004 with Joey, *in which Matt LeBlanc reprised his seminal* Friends *role of Joey Tribbiani. What seemed like a slam-dunk concept became dead man walking after its upfronts screening. That show staggered through two seasons before mercifully being taken out of its misery.*

Levitan also worried about the space.

LEVITAN (*cocreator*): A room can take on a life of its own. The sound could be bad. People may want to get to a party or get antsy. You never know how things will play out.

Instead of waiting to hear secondhand about the reaction to the preview, Levitan jetted to New York to be there live. He invited the cast to accompany him. Burrell and Hyland happened to be in town and joined him.

BURRELL (*Phil Dunphy*): I had just wrapped my work on this film, *Morning Glory*, at 2:00 p.m. Steve called and said, "If you can, get here by 3:00 p.m." I jumped in a cab, still pretty much in makeup, and zipped over. I walked up to the big doors at the back of the auditorium, literally as the doors closed behind me. Stephen [McPherson] was up on stage saying, "We're going to show you the entirety of this pilot. Ladies and gentlemen, this is *Modern Family*."

MCPHERSON (*ABC Entertainment president*): It was a full house plus a private cable feed to people in other places like Chicago and LA. There were probably five to ten thousand people total.

FALVEY (*ABC Entertainment head of comedy*): I remember vividly, all of Avery Fisher Hall going dark while they pulled down the screen, and thinking, "I'm not going to breathe for the next twenty-two minutes."

Within the first twenty-two seconds, McPherson knew he had made the right move.

BURRELL (*Phil Dunphy*): I stood in the dark in that doorway and watched people go crazy. I was blown away. So many laughs were missed because people were laughing over setups. I had never seen anything work like that, ever.

FALVEY (*ABC Entertainment head of comedy*): Immediate, uproarious laughter that went on and on. People laughed so hard they were missing the next three jokes.

LEVITAN (*cocreator*): It built and built and built until finally, *The Lion King* moment, which got a really big applause. Ty, Sarah, and I, we all kept looking at each other, tapping each other like, "Wow, this is really working."

BURRELL (*Phil Dunphy*): You try not to get your hopes up, but we knew leaving that the pilot was special. It's hard to know if a pilot can sustain that, but it really was the beginning of feeling like we have something here.

MORTON (*executive producer*): By the time they left, we were already gold with advertisers. I remember being back at upfronts a few years later and they were still remembering it. "Nothing compared to that time . . ."

LEVITAN (*cocreator*): I think Sarah and Ty walked in rather anonymously and walked out surrounded by well-wishers. I did my best to look like I was with them.

HYLAND (*Haley Dunphy*): It felt like a Broadway show, where you exit the stage door and people are outside with their playbills for you to sign. I didn't take it in, the sense of, "I'm a star now." In my naive eighteen-year-old brain, I thought they liked us because they'd just seen us.

FERGUSON (*Mitchell Pritchett*): I come from the world of theater. To have a whole group of people in a room laughing at the same thing—that's what it means to have success. That probably was the moment when we realized we're at least going to do well the first year. It felt like all the cards were stacked in our favor.

ABC advertisers old and new wasted no time in lining up.

HYLAND (*Haley Dunphy*): I had done a national Olive Garden commercial right before I moved to LA. They told me it was going to start airing in a month or two. I really could have used that money then. Standing outside the theater, these people came up to me and said, "Sarah, we're from Olive Garden. We've been meaning to send you an email that your commercial's going to start soon." I knew they were only picking it up because I'm on

Modern Family. And then of course it started airing like on every *Modern Family* commercial break. It was on TMZ, showing me slurping noodles with that "brown chicken, brown cow" music behind it. I don't get easily embarrassed, but that was of course Murphy's law. I made money from it, though, so I guess it was good.

Variety *summed up the event this way: "Using its upfront presentation to maximum advantage, ABC showcased one of the best comedy pilots to come down the pike in a long time."* The onus for success now fell on sales and marketing and word of mouth.*

KYLE WEBER (*associate producer*): I was at some random party talking with a woman, and she asked what I did and I said, "I'm working on this pilot, *Modern Family*." And she responded, "Oh my God, I love that!" She'd seen a cut and I was like, "Really?" The way she responded to it stuck with me. She wasn't saying it was good. She kept talking about how it was amazing. That kept happening. People kept talking about it like it was the best thing ever.

Marketing teams and creative talent tend to make for bad bed partners. In one camp, you have the showrunners, who—ninety-nine times out of one hundred—believe that the less you reveal, the more audiences will tune in. In the other corner, you have executives wearing their business caps, who believe you attract bigger audiences by revealing surprises ahead of time. In their minds, that creates "must-see television."

LLOYD (*cocreator*): Network marketing departments almost always say, "What's the funniest moment or biggest surprise of a show? That's what we have to use in the promo." To which the creative people always say, "But by revealing that, you're going to destroy the thing that you're supposed to be promoting." We fought this battle on *Frasier* a million times, to the point where we would refuse to give them episodes. One time, we literally deliv-

---

* Brian Lowry, "Upfront Presentation Scorecard: ABC's 'Family' Value," *Variety*, May 19, 2009, accessed October 25, 2019, https://variety.com/2009/voices/opinion/upfront-presentation-scorecard-abc-family-shines-5505/.

ered it to the network three days before it was to air because I was so sure they were going to give away several big surprises.* It wound up working.

LEVITAN (*cocreator*): We put a lot of effort into hiding the ball about the family. We thought that it was a really great moment for the audience to experience. Then ABC came to us and said, "We want to do something you're going to hate, which is reveal that this whole family is one family." We said, "Absolutely not."

LLOYD (*cocreator*): Yeah, we had a violent dislike for it. It was the thing that made people sit up in their chairs and clap when we presented the idea to them. I said, "Do you remember your reaction to this? Why would we want to deny the biggest audience the same reaction?"

LEVITAN (*cocreator*): They told us to keep an open mind and read the research.

MORTON (*executive producer*): The research showed that more people would likely watch and continue to watch if they knew the characters were related beforehand. Ruining the surprise seemed counterintuitive to me.

LEVITAN (*cocreator*): It was overwhelming. It was so overwhelming that while we were certainly still hesitant, we ultimately had to give in because we wanted the show to succeed.

WINER (*director / executive producer*): What I've come to realize after doing a number of shows and seeing how they were marketed is that marketing doesn't land. People don't absorb the details of what they're watch-

---

* In the episode "Merry Christmas, Mrs. Moskowitz," Frasier pretends to be Jewish for his Jewish girlfriend because her mother's visiting and isn't keen on her marrying outside of the faith. Simultaneously, Niles takes on a role in a Christmas pageant to make inroads with Daphne. In the midst of Frasier's charade, Niles enters Frasier's apartment dressed as Jesus. According to Lloyd, it resulted in one of the series' most prolonged studio audience laughs. Knowing the network would want to use Niles as Jesus in the promo, Lloyd didn't give them access to the episode, which won the Emmy for writing that year.

ing. I think the audience experienced the surprise all over again in spite of the fact that marketing blew it for them.

LLOYD (*cocreator*): You don't win every network battle. We got a huge rating, which I'm sure they took to be proof that they were right. But I could also make the argument those same number of people would have watched and had an even better experience had they not been told about that big surprise. But it's a moot point now because lots of people watched and continued watching, and that was the goal.

WINER (*director / executive producer*): My opinion has evolved over the years. At the time, I was with everyone in believing it was a travesty. Looking back and seeing that the show was a hit out of the gate, I think the network could say they were right to do what they did, that there was something satisfying seeing the family together in the marketing.

Dedicating more than 50 percent of his fall marketing budget to one show paid off and then some.* Some purists, however, the few who got to witness the pilot pre-marketing, stuck to a different opinion.

RYAN (*creator of* The Shield): I remember being floored when I saw it. I felt bad for the people being presold that they're part of the same family, because I thought it was such a cool twist.

ZUKER (*writer / executive producer*): It was such a satisfying, surprising moment that you don't get in network sitcoms. I felt bad for the audience that they would never know that particular experience. It felt like we were screwing them over a little bit. I still contend it was a bad idea. Had they not done that, I don't think the show would have been any less of a hit.

The cast and writers congregated in a variety of scenarios to watch the pilot before it premiered.

---

* Lacey Rose, "'Modern Family' Grows Up," *Hollywood Reporter,* September 18, 2012, accessed October 27, 2019, https://www.hollywoodreporter.com/news/modern -family-grows-up-370587.

JEFFREY RICHMAN (*writer / executive producer*): I couldn't do the first season, because I had a contract on another show. Chris showed me the pilot on a computer in New York, and I couldn't believe it. I had read the script and felt it was really good, but I had no idea the execution would be like that.

BRAD WALSH (*writer / executive producer*): I thought, "This is so subtle, good, and well made. This is not going to be on TV for very long at all."

O'NEILL (*Jay Pritchett*): I went by myself to the studio. They put me in a room. I watched it alone, and then I had them play it again. I watched it twice because I was so impressed with it. I was convinced that it was a hit. I thought, "If we don't fuck it up, it's going to be a great show."

STONESTREET (*Cam Tucker*): We were on Ventura Boulevard, in Encino, on our way to Versailles [a local Cuban restaurant]. I had my best friend in the car and a coworker of his with me. My phone rings. It was an unavailable number. So I answered it. The voice on the other end goes, "Eric." I said, "Yes?" He said, "Ed O'Neill." Everyone's looking at me. I'm giving them the "don't say anything" sign. And I said, "Hey, Ed, what's going on?" He says, "Eric, I just saw the pilot. It's fantastic. You're fantastic. Everyone's great." And I said, "That's awesome." And he goes, "Eric, listen to me. If this show doesn't go ten years, I don't know what the fuck I'm doing in this business." I said, "Well, Ed, I'm going with you on this one, because I haven't been in the business like that." He said, "We're going to get to know each other very well."

O'SHANNON (*writer / executive producer*): I was impressed that they had crammed so much material into twenty minutes, but at the same time gave it these moments to breathe. It's a bit of a magic trick really.

Cast members, still with no idea about the level with which America would rally around their show, shared the moment with friends and family.

HYLAND (*Haley Dunphy*): They sent me a DVD. I went over to my guy friend's house, Ryan Pinkston [*Punk'd*], where we would all hang out. To this day, he still tells this story of how he remembers eighteen-year-old Sarah saying, "I've got this pilot." He thought you don't ever want to see someone's pilot for the first time in front of them. Like, what if it's bad? I was excited because I wanted to see their reaction. And then he watches it and was like, "Fuck, this is amazing. How do I get on the show?"

FERGUSON (*Mitchell Pritchett*): When you're an actor asking your friends, "Can I show you that pilot that I did?" everyone's thinking, "Oh God." No one wants to sit through that. But everyone I showed it to looked at me and said, "This is going to be a big deal." It was that affirmation from my friends and other actors who have been through that process that made me think this is different.

STONESTREET (*Cam Tucker*): I took the pilot home to Kansas, and my parents had a barbecue at their house. I told them to invite as many people as they wanted to watch the pilot, and they did—like sixty people. We did two screenings. One group went down to my parents' bedroom, and then the next group went down. I watched where they laughed, where they didn't laugh. I thought, "Holy shit." I remember sending an email to Steve and Chris: *I can report from the breadbasket that we're funny.*

Most of the cast assembled on the show's premiere night, September 23, 2009, to celebrate the pilot's airing and the beginning of an exciting new chapter in their lives. Modern Family *premiered that night to 12.7 million viewers, the highest network numbers of the night.**

RODRIGUEZ (*Manny Delgado*): I was at this pizza parlor called Mr. Gatti's in my hometown of College Station in Texas. We threw a big premiere party. I had a little autograph session where people could come out to support a local celebrity who was on TV. The place had four big theater screens that usually had cartoons playing. But they synced them that night to ABC, and all four screens played the pilot. I remember watching the first

---

* Adam Bryant, "ABC's Comedy Numbers Are No Laughing Matter," *TV Guide*, September 24, 2009, accessed October 24, 2019, https://www.tvguide.com/news/ratings-abcs-comedy-1010156/.

scene and then all the names popped up, and when it got to me, everyone was cheering. It took my breath away. I was ten and seeing myself on TV. My family was proud of me. No matter where the show went from here, I had this.

Now they only had to put together twenty-three more episodes of the same or better quality in the next eight to nine months to make it to the end of the season and lock up a second one.

Unplugged

When networks air pilots for test groups, they show everything except the show's theme song and title. On a practical level, these bits add cost to a show that may never reach air. More importantly, however, preview audiences hate them.

> **WINER (*director / executive producer*)**: *They've actually discovered test audiences judge the title quite harshly. It hasn't been normalized for them through advertising.*

Therefore, filming a title sequence takes on special significance to a cast.

> **BURRELL (*Phil Dunphy*)**: *We're filming this because it's going to be on the air. It sounds ridiculous, but it's hard to believe sometimes when you've spent as much time unemployed as we all have and done as many auditions, literally thousands, as we have, that you're filming title credits. You're pinching yourself, at least I was.*

For *Modern Family*'s title sequence, executive producer Morton turned to Shine Studio. Shine has designed titles and graphics for many TV shows and feature films, including *The Goldbergs, Fresh off the Boat, Pitch Perfect,* and *La La Land.*

> **MICHAEL RILEY (*creative director at Shine Studio*)**: *Jeff said he liked the idea of doing something with frames, but he wasn't really specific about what that should be.*

LEVITAN (*cocreator*): *There was an HP commercial at the time where they did these cool things with frames where the image would become a frame. I thought that was really cool. I think that family photos and frames are very family-ish.*

A 2009 half-hour comedy ran twenty-four minutes (today it's closer to twenty-two). Because of such time limitations, the producers wanted to keep the title sequence concise.

LLOYD (*cocreator*): *Honestly, we thought we're doing a series where we have to service eleven characters. We'd probably rather have those extra twenty seconds to start our storytelling.*

Shine pitched a handful of ideas revolving around the interconnection of families.

RILEY (*creative director*): *When I talk at design schools, I bring* Modern Family. *It's where the only good idea in our presentation was the one we ended up doing. We had one storyboard that was a timeline of families. We started with imagery of cavemen and Neanderthals and then went through history with different families. We had another with a 3-D blue house. As you moved around the house, in each window we found different family members. Then you pulled back and the house became a box that contained the typography that said* Modern Family. *We had a concept that was a family tree with leaves falling. We pull back and it said* Modern Family *in the middle of an engraved tree. We had a paper cutout of a family that looked like the Dunphy family. Then it closed up. When it opened again, it was a silhouette of the entire family. Think about that. It's saying the Dunphys are at the center of the family. I think it's a terrible idea. We presented a montage of overlapping family frames and one in which we animated the characters using '60s-style animation. That's because in* Back to You, *Steve and Chris did an animated character-driven title sequence. We thought that might be appealing to them.*

The producers opted for the family frames. Then they figured out how to use them.

RILEY (*creative director*): *I think our original storyboard had a smooth transition into the main title and then out of it, but they ultimately decided that they'd like a moment of silence. Steve wanted to have something that started off really energetic with a beat over the cold opening so that when you got into the main title, you were on this ride. The beginning of act 1 is a new chapter, so let's have a moment of clarity.*

FERGUSON (*Mitchell Pritchett*): *Now, when we get to that place where we know something's going to be in the freeze-frame of that opening, sometimes as a cast we'll sing it.*

Winer came up with the idea to have each family pose in front of their home.

WINER (*director / executive producer*): *I wanted to shoot exteriors because so much of the show is shot inside. I thought it's a nice opportunity to remind everyone what the exterior of each environment looks like and to associate each family with their house.*

The houses reside in different locations in LA, including Cheviot Hills and Brentwood. A tight shooting schedule led to a guerrilla filmmaking style.

RILEY (*creative director*): *Jeff [Morton] would call a few hours before and say, "Hey, I think we're going to get a window to go shoot at Mitch and Cam's house. Could you please be there at 11:15?" So we'd show up and be the first ones there and wonder, "Are we in the right place?" Then a truck would speed over. They'd roll the dolly off the back and in fifteen minutes they'd have the camera up and hair and makeup there. Then Mitch and Cam would come in a car. We literally had twenty minutes to get the shot. Every house was the same way.*

Each family takes a beat to settle themselves when on-camera.

RILEY (*creative director*): *Jason said he thought it would be funny for the actors to be primping. He wanted to add a little energy and get the moment of capturing a Sears family portrait moment where everyone's trying to make themselves look good. So he'd yell, "Primping! Primping! Primping!" and then "Photo!" and everyone would get into position and look at the camera.*

The last exterior, at the Pritchetts', cuts to the final shot: the entire family situated together over a white background. In the center, Winter and Hyland hold a frame containing each family shot, one inside the other. They flip the frame over to reveal the *Modern Family* logo inside.

RILEY (*creative director*): *I didn't want to cut to a logo. I thought there was value in having those kids flip to it. You have to do something interesting to reveal the mark.*

WINTER (*Alex Dunphy*): *It was cool to be the one that got to flip the frame. It's still cool. I was a little stressed out about the green screen situation. There's nothing in the frame. What if it's lopsided? Am I going to flip it a weird way? What if I get fired based off this frame? Actors being extremely dramatic. That's something we occasionally do.*

HYLAND (*Haley Dunphy*): *I feel like they had Ariel and I flip it a lot. And it's like the wrong angle. We were at that time very different heights. That made it harder than it should have been.*

BURRELL (*Phil Dunphy*): *I felt stressed out for the kids because they were really little at the time, and they were being asked to flip that thing on time in the right spot. Meanwhile, seven-year-olds are driving tractors on farms all over America, but still for some reason, I was feeling stressed for them.*

GOULD (*Luke Dunphy*): *Over the years, we've had to go back and re-create that because the kids have aged so much. I get a little anxiety when we have to redo it. It takes so long. It's genuinely stressful. One time, I got slapped with the frame by Ariel.*

WINTER (*Alex Dunphy*): *Nolan did get whacked. It was mildly entertaining.*

Riley chose a *Modern Family* title graphic that only uses lowercase letters.

RILEY (*creative director*): *That was a thing with a lot of typography back then. Making the first letter a capital suggested an importance to those two words that typographically gave the voice of the font some gravitas that seemed inappropriate. To me,* modern family *seems like part of a pull quote from an article about a modern family rather than this is* the *modern family.*

Next came the theme music, courtesy of musician and composer Gabriel Mann, whom Winer knew from some of his early directing experiences.

GABRIEL MANN (*musician/composer*): *It was challenging because you really want to make a statement in a short amount of time. You used to have all the time in the world and could tell a story like* Gilligan's Island. *Now it's not like that anymore. I've done some at three, five, and seven seconds. They're like a miniature statement. In retrospect, twelve seconds was a luxury.*

Two camps formed over the type of music to use.

MORTON (*executive producer*): *I wanted to use a piece from composer Dan Licht, who had scored many things for me over the years.*

LLOYD (*cocreator*): *I wanted something punchy and short. I like the* Will and Grace *theme. It's very bouncy music and seems energetic. The challenge is to get it all into eight to twelve seconds.*

MANN (*musician/composer*): *Jason said, "Why don't you make something that's like a big band?" So I went to the studio and went for it. I had a great trumpet player and teacher, Tom Marino. I* played the piano. Once we got closer to the real thing, I used a drummer and bass player. I did the vocals. A traditional shout chorus in an old-school big band has all the guys in the band doing some "hey" or "yeah" or whatever they do. I divided the music by the frame of the different families. There's four phrases and an ending. It was very interconnected. It beats you over the head with the energy and fun.

MORTON (*executive producer*): *Dan's had a more memorable theme. Gabriel's was all big energy. The reactions split equally among the decision-makers. Ultimately, we couldn't really break the tie, so we had Stephen [McPherson] weigh in. He chose Gabriel's because he liked its in-your-face energy.*

Not everybody agreed with the decision, although they accepted it.

LEVITAN (*cocreator*): *I never loved the main title song, to tell you the truth. I wanted one that maybe had a little bit more warmth to it. It's nothing against Gabriel because many people loved it. It didn't feel like our show to me, but it is after all these years.*

MANN (*musician/composer*): *Steve came over to the studio, and I did dozens of versions of a more heartwarming direction with many different iterations like the heartwarming cues at the end of the show I do, these acoustic and bass organic instrumentations. At some point, I think he gave up because everyone else was sold on the other thing.*

LEVITAN (*cocreator*): *Music is so mercurial. Sometimes a theme hits you with, "Wow, that's amazing." The first time I heard the* Mad Men *theme, I thought. "That's great." That's what I was looking for. At the end of the day, you have to land on something, and this was by far the best thing we had.*

MORTON (*executive producer*): *Gabriel did a great job. It was the right decision. I'm a movie music and big TV theme fan. I get swayed by that type of thing. My late father-in-law was a big-time trumpet* player who played in MGM musicals. He was involved with some of the great Hollywood music. I remember him saying that he went to a scoring session for Jaws. When John Williams had them do the ba-dum, ba-dum on a musical level, it was very simple. All the musicians quietly laughed. Forty-five years later, it's one of the most iconic pieces in movie history. The Modern Family theme goes hand in hand with the show.

Under Pressure

Reviewers almost universally anointed Modern Family *as the freshest and funniest sitcom of the season.*

The best new half-hour of funny television in a season rife with half-hours of funny television.

—The New York Times[*]

Smart, nimble and best of all, funny, while actually making a point about the evolving nature of what constitutes "family."

—Variety[†]

Long on heart, brimming with great characters, smartly cast, expertly written and funny from start to finish, "Family" is the obvious choice for best new fall comedy—and possibly best series.

—The Hollywood Reporter[‡]

---

[*] Ginia Bellafante, "'I'm the Cool Dad' and Other Debatable Dispatches from the Home Front," *New York Times*, September 22, 2009, accessed November 1, 2019, https://www.nytimes.com/2009/09/23/arts/television/23modern.html.

[†] Brian Lowry, "Modern Family," *Variety*, September 20, 2009, accessed November 1, 2019, https://variety.com/2009/tv/reviews/modern-family-1200476044/.

[‡] Barry Garron, "Modern Family Season 1: TV Review," *Hollywood Reporter*,

Modern Family *is immediately recognizable as the best new sitcom of the fall in part because it's not recognizable as any other sort of sitcom.*

—ENTERTAINMENT WEEKLY*

America is sorely in need of a new laugh-out-loud comedy, and we think **Modern Family** *is it.*

—TV GUIDE†

With great success, however, come great expectations. To deliver on the pilot's promise, Levitan and Lloyd assembled an all-star lineup of television comedy writers, veterans from shows such as Cheers, Frasier, Newhart, Will and Grace, and Roseanne, all fortuitously available because of a perfect storm of circumstances starting with the networks' decision to produce fewer sitcoms.

LLOYD (*cocreator*): Not that long before *Modern Family,* NBC had programmed fourteen comedies. Now they were down to five. There were a lot of very experienced writers and a dearth of jobs.

Additionally, many writers hadn't fully recovered from the sting of the 2007–2008 strike. Countless talented scribes—drama, comedy, cable, and late-night—had been unemployed for months on end. That can break anyone in spirit and solvency.

September 22, 2009, accessed November 1, 2019, https://www.hollywoodreporter.com/review/modern-family-season-1-tv-93562.

* Ken Tucker, "Modern Family," *Entertainment Weekly,* updated October 9, 2009, accessed November 1, 2019, https://ew.com/article/2009/10/09/modern-family/.

† Mickey O'Connor, "Fall TV: TVGuide.com's Editors' Picks," *TV Guide,* September 1, 2009, accessed November 24, 2019, https://www.tvguide.com/news/fall-tv-tvguide-1009366/.

ZUKER (*writer / executive producer*): I went almost an entire year without a paycheck with three kids and a house that I realized after the strike I couldn't afford. I had friends who had to sell their home.

Lastly, Levitan and Lloyd had written a laugh-out-loud script generating industry buzz. That left them in the driver's seat in a buyer's market for talent.

LLOYD (*cocreator*): We found some of our favorite writers from previous shows we'd worked on: Corrigan, Walsh, Zuker, Wrubel, and O'Shannon. We were blessed to have an extremely talented group.

WALSH (*writer / executive producer*): Except for me and Paul [Corrigan], they were all people who had run shows. It was a room you couldn't normally afford. But after the strike, these people were suddenly available. It was basically a room of the designated hitters from other staffs.

WRUBEL (*writer / executive producer*): I was under a deal at ABC and had just quit *Ugly Betty*. I read the pilot script, which I liked. Then I watched the pilot. Ninety-nine percent of the time, it gets worse. This got better. I thought it was incredible, the best pilot I'd ever seen. This is the kind of series that if you get on, you start going to awards shows.

ZUKER (*writer / executive producer*): After watching it for exactly seven minutes, before all the great twists and turns, all I could think about was, "I will do sexual favors for anybody on this staff to get on this show, or not do sexual favors; whatever they want."

O'SHANNON (*writer / executive producer*): I watched the pilot in awe—there were so many avenues for comedy: human behavior, physical bits, silly wordplay, supersmart structure. Even if they hadn't hired me, I'd have started showing up and pitching until they forcibly ejected me from the lot.

Whereas most sitcoms typically include two storylines per episode, a major A and minor B, Modern Family's *template of generating three*

A storylines placed a huge amount of pressure on writers to create air-worthy content week in and week out. These stories needed to stand independently of one another, while also thematically converging at the end.

O'SHANNON (*writer / executive producer*): We were bending over backward to make episodes in which all three have stories that had some kind of thematic link. There were times we'd have two stories that shared a strong theme, and one that wouldn't quite fit. If we had one of those wrap-ups at the end, we'd have to write the voice-over broadly enough to touch on all three stories, creating the illusion that they were all connected. But sometimes it was a little tenuous.

LEVITAN (*cocreator*): In a perfect world, you establish a theme for an episode and break stories to serve that theme. Sometimes, however, someone pitches something hilarious and that perfect world flies out the window.

WALSH (*writer / executive producer*): Chris and Steve were very focused on making sure that at least one of the stories had heart and was "about something." When we would break stories, we would make a little heart symbol on the cards next to whichever story we thought had the most gravitas to make sure each episode had that element.

LEVITAN (*cocreator*): It was okay if that "heart" moment was subtle. We just wanted the audience to feel something at some point in every episode.

ZUKER (*writer / executive producer*): We wanted those emotional moments to come organically out of a funny story. A lot of times in early drafts, we were thinking about this big emotional ending. Sometimes, though, we didn't earn it or we saw it coming from a mile away. We definitely learned, in those first six episodes, what's emotional and what's cloying.

For story ideas, Levitan and Lloyd encouraged writers to mine their pasts and monitor the present, turning the writers' room into confessional therapy.

WALSH (*writer / executive producer*): We broke episodes 2 through 6 together, all of us in the same room. That was a lot of sharing funny, embarrassing stories about our families, with Chris and Steve at opposite ends of the table, curating our anecdotes into what became the show. Then at some point in preproduction, because we had so much to do and enough people, we started breaking up into two rooms.

The first script submitted, "Run for Your Wife" by Corrigan and Walsh, focused on the first day of school in two households and Mitchell and Cam overreacting to Lily bumping her head. The script went through the wringer at the network. In summary, it didn't wow them.

LLOYD (*cocreator*): ABC said it was a little flat in places, which was a tone-deaf thing to say. It was them being nervous Nellies because they didn't really know what the show was and hadn't seen numbers yet.

O'SHANNON (*writer / executive producer*): I believe we could have handed in any episode after the pilot and they would have thought the same thing. The pilot was so amazing. No script could live up to it.

Corrigan and Walsh never forgot the network's reaction, self-deprecatingly labeling it "the flat 101."

LLOYD (*cocreator*): They had been a little bit stung, and justifiably so, by what the network said, so they decided to hang that tag on themselves as many times as they could.

WALSH (*writer / executive producer*): Chris delighted in assigning us the "flat 301" or "flat 401" episode or whatever episode it happened to be.

Levitan and Lloyd knew better than to bite the network hand feeding them, unless that hand belonged to the Fox network. There they could be sharks. With ABC and McPherson, however, they felt they'd found a collaborative partner. Being as such, they chose their battles carefully. One concerned overzealous network executives directly contacting writers. Levitan and Lloyd both stepped in to quickly put the kibosh on that.

WALSH (*writer / executive producer*): At some point, Paul and I got a call from the network. Forty-five minutes later, we came out of our office and Steve wanted to know where we'd been. We said we were talking to the network and that they had a bunch of notes on the cut. I started to read them. Steve said something like, "It's a good episode, it's done." He contacted them and asked them to please submit their notes in written form. Then he said, "Hey, guys, let's go for a walk. The phone's about to ring, and I don't want to be around."

WRUBEL (*writer / executive producer*): I got a call from a network exec as I was driving home on a Friday about my script. I called Chris, and he said, "That's not okay." He basically told them, "Any notes you have go through me. Don't bother the writers individually." That always meant a lot to me. The writers were protected from network interference.

Meanwhile, cast and crew had reassembled at their new home, stage 5. The outside world remained oblivious to the efforts taking place inside. Working within a "no-audience zone," production lacked a reactive compass to guide them. This made jittery network executives grow even more so by the day.

LLOYD (*cocreator*): We were shooting episodes and making ourselves laugh, but at that point, it's still only eighty people on a soundstage.

CORRIGAN (*writer / executive producer*): We would have screenings for the whole crew in one of the theaters on the lot. I think that really helped build a sense of camaraderie around what we were doing because they often don't get to see episodes until they air.

STEVE MILLER (*assistant prop master*): Those early days were sunshine and lollipops. We were all thrilled and happy to be going to work. I literally could not wait to get up, because we were doing really good work. It was new and fresh to us, and we would just laugh.

In thinking, rethinking, and overthinking their strategy, network executives decided to switch the order of episodes 2 through 6. "Run for Your Wife" got bumped from flat 102 to flat 106, replacing it with "The Bicycle Thief," written by Wrubel.

LEVITAN (*cocreator*): I think *"Run for Your Wife" is* an excellent episode. It has one of my favorite moments with Claire, where she's sitting and reading a book, trying to ignore Phil, who's bored because the kids have gone back to school. It was so still and quiet, and so real to me.

CORRIGAN (*writer / executive producer*): I'm guessing for the network it was about what can you promote? A big splashy promo that says, "This week, Claire reads," isn't an easy sell.

MCPHERSON (*ABC Entertainment president*): Honestly, I think networks tend to overthink these types of decisions. Strategically, you get many new viewers the second week, so you try and make that episode a good one to introduce people to the show who may not have seen the pilot. Jimmy Burrows used to say to me, "Do the pilot over and over again the first season."

McPherson employed Burrows's strategy, lumping a number of episodes together that had similar emotional wrap-ups at the end.

WRUBEL (*writer / executive producer*): "*The Bicycle Thief*" had simple stories and a nice bit of emotion between Jay and Manny at the end. I don't think it was the strongest of the first six, but the network—for whatever reason—thought it seemed like the most similar in tone to the pilot.

ZUKER (*writer / executive producer*): Manny sitting on the curb with Jay in his Mickey Mouse ears because his dad's not coming. That was a beautiful moment.

WRUBEL (*writer / executive producer*): Rather than burying Manny's father, Jay makes up a lie to cover where his dad is, and then he and Gloria take Manny to Disneyland. That to me is an example of an attempt to humanize Jay without being sappy. For all of his bluster, there was sensitivity underneath him that he didn't give away often, but was there when necessary.

LEVITAN (*cocreator*): Truly one of my favorite scenes ever. Jay not only saves the day for Manny, but he makes Manny think his real dad is the hero. To me, it's a great example of defining a character by his actions. You see that and you know why Gloria married Jay.

The network continued pressing the panic button, asking for reshoots for the first three episodes.

MILLER (*assistant prop master*): Those first four to five weeks, as we were shooting, we were always going back and reshooting stuff. In a week we would shoot two to three scenes from different episodes or an added interview.

MORTON (*executive producer*): We joke we're still doing reshoots. It was lateral moves. They were worrying to death, and their fears were unfounded. The only improvement for all that trouble was the end of "Coal Digger."

In "Coal Digger," Gloria learns of Claire's distrust of her, revealed when Luke lets it slip that his mom had called Gloria a "coal digger," which everyone else recognizes as a mispronunciation of "gold digger."

ZUKER (*writer / executive producer*): If your dad brought Sofía home after the wedding, that would cause some strife in your family.

In the original ending, Claire apologizes, and they resolve their problems. The network wanted something bigger.

WRUBEL (*writer / executive producer*): We were watching a cut and kicking it around, and Steve pitched something about pushing each other in a pool. Then we went off and wrote it. It was a good piece of problem-solving by Steve that could tie everything together.

FINAL ENDING

<u>INT. JAY AND GLORIA'S HOUSE—DEN</u>

Jay, Cameron, Mitchell, Phil, and Alex are watching the game. Haley's nearby on her cell phone. Luke and Manny are playing pool. As Gloria and Claire cross through:

                    JAY
     Hey, you guys work that out?

                    CLAIRE
     Almost. Gloria just wants me to jump
     in the pool.

Jay resumes watching the game with interest.

                    PHIL
     What?

<u>EXT. JAY AND GLORIA'S HOUSE—BACKYARD—MOMENTS LATER</u>

Claire and Gloria exit the house and head toward the pool, followed by the family.

                    LUKE
     This is so awesome.

                    HALEY
     I know. Mom does not look good wet.

                          JAY
           Gloria, is this really necessary?

Claire is at the edge of the pool.

                         CLAIRE
           No, no, Dad, it's okay. I'm doing
           this to prove just how sorry I am to
           Gloria. It's the least I can do. Here
           I go.

She crouches down to jump.

                         CLAIRE
                (to Gloria)
           You're seriously not going to stop me?

                         GLORIA
           Why would I stop you?

                         CLAIRE
           Because I think just by standing
           here, I've more than demonstrated
           that I'm willing to—Oh, hell.

Claire jumps in. Everyone claps and
cheers. Claire surfaces and swims over to
Gloria.

                         CLAIRE
           Are you happy?

                         GLORIA
           Yes, I forgive you.

Claire reaches up a hand to Gloria.

                        CLAIRE
          Okay, give me a hand.

Gloria starts to reach for her. Jay stops
her.

                        JAY
          Aw, that's the oldest trick in the book.
          She's going to pull you in there.
                    (beat)
          And that's my job.

Jay pushes Gloria in the pool.

                        PHIL
                  (to his kids)
          This is funny, but this is also a
          teaching moment. Think about . . .

Jay pushes him in the pool and turns to
face the group. Luke and Manny charge at
Jay. They both hit him simultaneously and
all three topple into the pool.

                        MITCHELL
          What?

Mitchell grabs Alex and jumps in with her.

                        HALEY
                  (into phone)
          You're not going to believe this.

Back on Haley, we WIDEN to reveal that
Cameron is next to her.

                    CAMERON
          Cannonball!

As Cameron runs for the pool and jumps in,
we . . .

                    FADE OUT

O'NEILL (*Jay Pritchett*): The pool was such a wonderful release of tension. We shot many takes right up to that final point. And then we let loose. The joy of the release and the family coming together in that way I think was something people really liked.

LEVITAN (*cocreator*): It was more visceral than logical, just like the *Lion King* moment in the pilot. Sometimes that's all you need.

> *The constant network meddling, combined with a desire to impress their bosses and peers, took its toll with the writers, leading to pervasive insecurity, self-doubt, and a lot of self-imposed stress.*

ZUKER (*writer / executive producer*): We all break the stories together so we all feel invested in each other's stories, but when you're writing that first draft and turning it in, it's scary. Do I have these voices? Can I match that pilot? It felt very high pressure. I was absolutely terrified writing "En Garde" [his first script]. There were honestly moments in that first season where I didn't want to be there.

CORRIGAN (*writer / executive producer*): For the first couple of years, there was something we liked to call *Modern Family* syndrome. A lot of writers were taken down by it.

WALSH (*writer / executive producer*): Two of us ended up in the emergency room with gastrointestinal problems, and there was an EMT up here at some point for a panic attack.

ZUKER (*writer / executive producer*): I wound up in the hospital with a stomach issue. I'm not saying they're linked, but they probably were linked.

Yet in going through the war together, they bonded as siblings, supportive and lovingly competitive.

HIGGINBOTHAM (*writer / executive producer*): I don't think there was competition in the sense you wanted to win over someone. That was not the vibe in that room. But did people delight in getting to a joke first? Yes. Would we laugh out loud and say you hated someone for pitching something before I thought of it? Absolutely. That's the dynamic. You're playing. You want to be the one doing it well and not the one having a shitty day or week.

WRUBEL (*writer / executive producer*): That's very astute. It was competitive in that you want to do your best. I always found that it was better than collegial; we were friends. We worked really hard, liked each other, and really wanted to do a good show. Everyone was talented. You wanted to make them laugh and have them say that was a great idea. That felt good.

CORRIGAN (*writer / executive producer*): I think Abraham's right. Friendly competition is the way to describe it. Part of it is, and I think this comes from having a staff of a lot of experienced people, if someone else pitches a joke that gets you out of a scene and moving on, you're that much closer to going home. We all appreciated that.

LLOYD (*cocreator*): Comedy is a defense. The part that you don't hear about very often is the insecure part underneath it or the need to be accepted, of which everybody has in spades. I think that's what you're hearing. But it's that sensitivity, that insecurity that makes them capable of writing the emotional part of the show. If you just hired a bunch of clowns that came in and pitched a bunch of jokes, laughed, burped, and were competitive with one another but weren't insecure, we probably would never tell stories that made people cry. And those are the best stories we tell.

Much as comedians live for audience laughs, so, too, do comedy writers. Lacking a studio audience, they found theirs in social media.

While the show aired on the East Coast, the writers would turn to social media to gauge audience reaction to episodes in real time. They called it "Google Mirth."

LEVITAN (*cocreator*): Viewers commented as the jokes were happening. It was such an amazingly unique experience as a TV writer to hear your audience react and to see which jokes, moments, and characters they love.

O'SHANNON (*writer / executive producer*): Often, they'd quote favorite lines, and I'd be secretly anxious, waiting for one of mine to come up. I wonder if the other writers felt like that. They must have.

LEVITAN (*cocreator*): They did.

The mirth extended out into the real world as well.

LLOYD (*cocreator*): I can remember in the first season being at restaurants and hearing people talk about this new show that they were watching. I would obnoxiously hush the people at my table so I could listen to what they were saying.

*The network's reaction, after the show's premiere, told them everything they needed to know. After airing a mere three episodes, ABC picked up the sitcom for the entire season.**

Surviving those first episodes united cast, crew, and writers. It also brought to everyone's attention the showrunners' different tastes.

O'SHANNON (*writer / executive producer*): Chris and Steve hadn't landed on the system of dividing up episodes as cleanly yet. So if Chris was out of the room, Steve might work on a story with us and send a writer off on an outline. Then when the writer came back, Steve would be gone

---

* Natalie Abrams, "ABC Picks Up *Cougar Town, Modern Family* and *The Middle*," *TV Guide,* October 8, 2009, accessed October 24, 2019, https://www.tvguide.com/news/abc-cougar-modern-1010661/.

From left: Steve Levitan, Christopher Lloyd, and the legendary sitcom director James Burrows on the set of their first cocreated sitcom, *Back to You* (2005–2006). *(Courtesy of Andy Gordon)*

Characters:

The Dunphy Family

Claire
Late 30s, uptight suburban mom, tries to make everyday special for her kids, needs control.

Phil
Late 30s, real estate agent, upbeat, goofy, thinks he's cooler than he is.

Haley
16, social, fashion-conscious, rebellious, has a wild streak.

Alex
13, smart, cynical, insightful for her age.

Luke
10, immature, simple, not the brightest bulb.

The Pritchett - Delgado Family

Jay
60s, successful businessman, divorced. Recently married Gloria, struggles to stay "young" for her.

Gloria
30s, hispanic, beautiful, strong, quick-tempered. Protective mother. Divorced six years ago.

Manny
12ish, Gloria's son - Jay's stepson. Old soul, sensitive, passionate, a young romantic.

Mitchell & Cameron's Family

Mitchell
Mid-to-late 30's, dentist, gay, emotionally-restrained, worrier.

Cameron
Mid-30's, gay, free with emotions, lives in the moment, surprisingly strong.

Lily
Baby girl, adopted from Vietnam.

Prototypes for *Modern Family*'s characters, taken from the original pilot script. The images are a combination of celebrities, internet faces, and Steve Levitan's children. Only Sofía Vergara and Ty Burrell made it off the page and on to the screen.

Stage 5 on the 20th Century Fox Studio lot in Century City, which *Modern Family* has called home for the past eleven years. *(Courtesy of Larsen & Talbert Photography)*

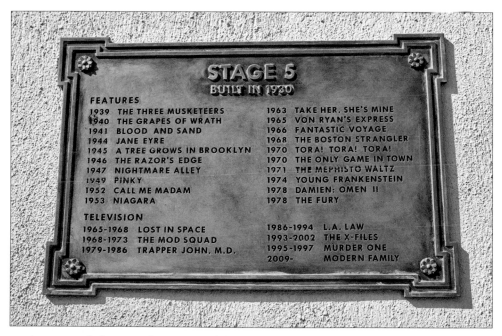

An engraved plaque on the exterior of the stage commemorates all the productions, past and present, that have filmed inside its walls. *(Courtesy of Larsen & Talbert Photography)*

The first picture of the entire cast taken after the pre–table read, March 3, 2009. *(Courtesy of Steve Levitan)*

From left: Jesse Tyler Ferguson, Ty Burrell, and Eric Stonestreet goof off with a fake baby Lily at the show's first photo shoot, taken while filming the pilot. *(Courtesy of Eric Stonestreet)*

The full cast at the show's first photo shoot, conducted directly after filming Manny's soccer game. Notice Nolan Gould performing his duties as Julie Bowen's baby blocker. *(Courtesy of Eric Stonestreet)*

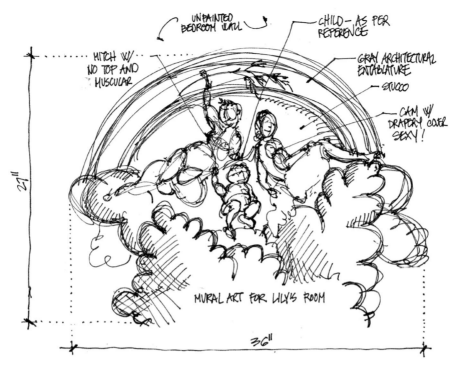

UNPAINTED BEDROOM WALL

CHILD — AS PER REFERENCE

MITCH W/ NO TOP AND MUSCULAR

GRAY ARCHITECTURAL ENTABLATURE

STUCCO

CAM W/ DRAPERY COVER SEXY!

27"

36"

MURAL ART FOR LILY'S ROOM

Production designer Richard Berg's original sketch for the Michelangelo mural with Mitchell and Cam in place of God and Adam in Lily's bedroom. *(Courtesy of Richard Berg)*

Lily's finished bedroom, with the finished Michelangelo mural as painted by Mitchell and Cam's friend Longinus. *(Courtesy of Claire Bennett)*

The Dunphy kitchen, built to match the one used in a real Pacific Palisades home in the pilot. *(Courtesy of Claire Bennett)*

The Dunphy staircase leading to the second floor, filled with family pictures taken for the show and from the actors' real lives. *(Courtesy of Larsen & Talbert Photography)*

The Pritchett kitchen, with Gloria's fashion stamp of fiery red walls and zebra chairs. The rafters above provide a perspective of the vertical reach of the set. *(Courtesy of Larsen & Talbert Photography)*

The Pritchett-Tucker household basked in night light with archways to define the space and create depth. *(Courtesy of Larsen & Talbert Photography)*

Sofía Vergara leaving the Dunphy house with a box of "knicker-knackers, snicker-snacks." *(Courtesy of Steve Levitan)*

From left: Rico Rodriguez and Aubrey Anderson-Emmons eye each other on set. *(Courtesy of Jesse Tyler Ferguson)*

The writers discovered a rich vein for comedy with Jay's business, Pritchett's Closets & Blinds. Here, Julie Bowen waits to shoot a scene in the Closets & Blinds conference room, which in real life was the writers' conference room. *(Courtesy of Andy Gordon)*

Luke, ready to serve the Godfather, in season 4's "Fulgencio." *(Courtesy of Steve Levitan)*

A holiday tradition: the annual Nolan Gould ornament with cast photo. *(Courtesy of Larsen & Talbert Photography)*

Eric Stonestreet's scrapbook reveals the portrait of the artist as a young clown. *(Courtesy of Larsen & Talbert Photography)*

So I married a clown: Cam and Mitchell, the early years. *(Courtesy of Jason Winer)*

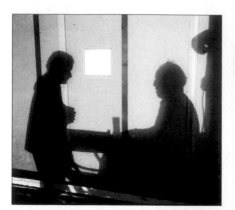

Writer Christy Stratton and Stella break the fourth wall. *(Courtesy of Andy Gordon)*

(above) Two silhouettes of creativity: cocreator Christopher Lloyd *(left)* and writer/executive producer Danny Zuker plot their next storyline. *(Courtesy of Steve Miller)*

Ed O'Neill on the Fox lot, heading for his trailer or looking for a nice T-bone to barbecue for dinner. *(Courtesy of Andy Gordon)*

Lights! Camera! Burrell! *(Courtesy of Andy Gordon)*

Sarah Hyland as the tooth fairy we all wish we had as kids (from season 4's "Career Day"). *(Courtesy of Steve Levitan)*

(above) Nolan Gould and Ariel Winter, friends at first sight. *(Courtesy of Steve Levitan)*

Mud on white: a family portrait from season 1's aptly titled finale, "Family Portrait." *(Courtesy of Marc Freeman)*

From left: Jesse Tyler Ferguson, Eric Stonestreet, Sofía Vergara, and Ed O'Neill chill in the Pritchett-Tucker living room. *(Courtesy of Steve Levitan)*

A spider sits down beside Prince Harry in season 10's Halloween episode, "Good Grief." *(Courtesy of Jesse Tyler Ferguson)*

The show's production designer makes a concerted effort to keep the sets alive, such as by adding subtle touches like newly arrived mail. *(Courtesy of Larsen & Talbert Photography)*

Eric Stonestreet, the self-described drum-playing, pig-raising, football-playing clown, shows off his inner Keith Moon. *(Courtesy of Andy Gordon)*

Phil on a wire. Don't try this at home, unless you have the physical comedic skills of Ty Burrell. *(Courtesy of Steve Levitan)*

This Old Wagon: this is one of the ways that the show films car scenes—four cameras on a hood mount capturing footage inside of a car. *(Courtesy of William Munro)*

The *Modern Family* cross-shooting technique mastered by director of photography James "Baggs" Bagdonas *(background)*. Two cameras catch all the action, just out of each other's line of sight, without having to be reset or having the scene relit. *(Courtesy of Larsen & Talbert Photography)*

Jesse Tyler Ferguson and Eric Stonestreet play Candid Camera at a table read. *(Courtesy of Andy Gordon)*

(above) Destiny thy name is Aubrey. Anderson-Emmons (left) playing in the park with the Hiller twins, who played Lily before her. This photo helped Anderson-Emmons land the part of Lily. (Courtesy of Amy Anderson-Emmons)

(right) Lloyd and Little Orphan Ferguson talk shop during the filming of season 7's "Double Click." (Courtesy of Jesse Tyler Ferguson)

Phil's book of Zen with statements for living a full Phil life, from season 4's "Schooled." (Courtesy of Larsen & Talbert Photography)

PHIL'S-OSOPHY

PHIL DUNPHY

When life gives you lemonade, make lemons. Life will be all like, "What?!"

Start each day as if you've already messed it up and have been given a second chance.

(*above*) From left: Barkley, Jay's dog butler, who creeped out Gloria in season 1's "Not in My House." Barkley was subsequently retired from the show, living out his days in the writers' room as a gum server. Rebarka, Barkley's female counterpart, featured in season 5's "Las Vegas," also was retired to the show's prop room, where she maintains a dust-free environment. (*Courtesy of Larsen & Talbert Photography*)

(*below*) The view from video village, two cameras and a full cast. (*Courtesy of Andy Gordon*)

and Chris would rework the entire story. Then the writer would come back with a whole new outline and Steve would say, "What happened to the story I pitched?" And so on. The writers would spin around and try to make these two different people happy when it was impossible. It drove people crazy that first season.

GARDEZI (*staff writer*): The saying in television is that in dysfunction comes a genius. And part of it probably was a little bit true. I think that there were so many chaotic things going on within the room dynamic and outside the room dynamic.

MCCRAY (*script coordinator*): The problems were there, but we made it through the first season. It was going into the second season that things really fell apart.

Fizbo

Initially, the newly hired writing staff only had the pilot script as their north star: twenty-two minutes that broadly introduced eleven family members. As they mined the recesses of their hearts, minds, and memories, they also reached out to their closest collaborators, the cast themselves, inviting them up into the writers' room for a series of luncheons to chitchat about how they perceived their characters.

O'SHANNON (*writer / executive producer*): When you first write a pilot, it's nothing but words on a page. The authors have a definition of each character in their heads. But as soon as the actors come along, breathe life into it, and make it 3-D, they're going to bring their own stuff, their own quirks and strengths. You have to be open to letting the character on the page merge with the one coming out of the actor.

WINER (*director / executive producer*): It can be very helpful to hear the actors give their own takes on their characters. What were they thinking when shooting the pilot? What was the backstory they invented or the future that they projected? Great ideas can come out of those assumptions.

LLOYD (*cocreator*): I think some of the actors felt a little threatened by that, like, "Don't start pulling things out of my life because I'm not the same as my character."

BURRELL (*Phil Dunphy*): The only stories I had were us being a childless couple and/or unrelatable things like being an actor in New York trying to carve out a life for myself. So I don't think they took a lot from me.

BOWEN (*Claire Dunphy*): I don't think I have the confidence in my own abilities as an actor to introduce real parts of myself.

LLOYD (*cocreator*): Julie mentioned a love of organizing things like the Container Store. That became a Claire trait.

BOWEN (*Claire Dunphy*): Right. In the way that some people talk about sex, I talk about my Brother P-Touch, the king of labelers. Any house I go to—like my sister's house, a vacation house, or my in-laws' house—when you open a closet, you'll notice my obsessive labeling of everything within an inch of its life.

LLOYD (*cocreator*): Ed once tried out for the Pittsburgh Steelers and is a pretty good jazz singer. We had him sing karaoke once. That was a fun thing to discover about the character.

O'Neill also has a black belt in Brazilian jujitsu, having learned the martial arts from the legendary practitioners the Gracie family.

O'NEILL (*Jay Pritchett*): The old man would enter his sons in tournaments. If they lost, he'd give them five dollars and if they won they'd get two. The idea being you learn more when you lose. If you win, you get the two because you don't need it. You won.

He showed off some of his skills in the season 1 episode "Game Changer," where he tries to teach Mitchell how to fight. In demonstrating on Mitchell "the sleeper hold," he ends up causing him to pass out.

O'Neill also loved to interject his Youngstown, Ohio, roots into stories.

O'NEILL (*Jay Pritchett*): Jay was a huge fan of this guy named Booker Bell, a deejay who used to do gags on the radio. Jay's over the moon when he meets him. There was an old friend of mine named Boots Bell. He was a great deejay out of Youngstown, Ohio, station WHOT. Everybody that saw the episode in the Cleveland-Youngstown area knew who we were talking about.

LEVITAN (*cocreator*): Sofía had her son very young and raised him under, at times, trying circumstances, often the two of them alone. She was a fiercely protective mom the entire time. They remain very close to this day. And that's what resonated with Gloria and Manny.

CORRIGAN (*writer / executive producer*): Somebody asked Sofía if, growing up, she was always the prettiest girl. Everyone expected her to say, "No, of course not. I had my awkward stage." But her response was, "Yes, I was always the prettiest."

FERGUSON (*Mitchell Pritchett*): I shared my relationship with my dad, which is great now. He's so supportive of me. But he had a very hard time navigating my being gay. He would conveniently forget, years after I came out. Like he would ask me if I had a girlfriend, and I would say, "Dad, oh my God, we've been over this. I don't have a girlfriend. I'm gay." And he'd say, "Oh yeah. Your mother mentioned something about that." He was really resistant to the information. They basically put that idea into Ed's character, being very resistant, which I really admire.

No one could compare, however, to the overall life experiences of Stonestreet.

STONESTREET (*Cam Tucker*): I always thought, "If I get the part, I have enough of a diverse background that they're going to want to mine some of it." I was the drum-playing, pig-raising, football-playing clown that wanted to be a marine and prison guard.

Out of Stonestreet's self-proclaimed string of descriptive adjectives, one immediately stood out: clown. Stonestreet first innocently dropped word about his made-up character, Fizbo the clown, during a lunchtime conversation while shooting the pilot.

STONESTREET (*Cam Tucker*): Chris Lloyd overheard me talking and said, "Did you say you used to be a clown?" And I said, "Yeah." And he said, "I assume there's pictures of this?" And I said, "Oh God, yeah. Lots of pictures."

LEVITAN (*cocreator*): As soon as we heard that, we said, "We're definitely doing that, and it's going to absolutely drive Mitch crazy, because he hates it."

Clowning around might sound like fun and games to some, but to clowns, their craft represents an art form, the soul of entertainment and joy. In other words, Stephen King won't be giving any commencement speeches at a clowning college in this lifetime.

WINER (*director / executive producer*): They take the history of clowning very seriously. There are specific clowning styles when you go to clown college. Fizbo was an Auguste clown.

STONESTREET (*Cam Tucker*): By definition, an Auguste clown causes trouble due to his unintentional childlike nature. Some call Augustes idiotic, but most think of the character as an innocent buffoon causing trouble that others have to fix.

Somewhat fittingly then, the introduction of Fizbo left behind a trail of real-life mayhem. That began during one of the aforementioned writers' room luncheons.

WALSH (*writer / executive producer*): Eric was going on and on about the art of clowning and how important it was to him. The entire time, Jesse was eating a salad, barely containing an eye roll, suffering through the story of his costar's love of clowning.

STONESTREET (*Cam Tucker*): I then brought in an article that was written about me in the fifth grade, about how I wanted to go off and join the circus someday and entertain people and perform. I showed them that to get the juices flowing.

LEVITAN (*cocreator*): I still have a Fizbo business card he gave me from when he was a kid.

WALSH (*writer / executive producer*): Eric also brought by a scrapbook full of pictures of him as a clown as a young boy, next to a pig. It was crazy.

CORRIGAN (*writer / executive producer*): We actually used some of those pieces in the Fizbo episode.

After the initial story breakdown, Corrigan and Walsh took on Fizbo. What should have been an exciting writing challenge quickly spun out of control into a nightmare.

O'SHANNON (*writer / executive producer*): "Fizbo" was the one where it came to a head, where things really became untenable with Chris and Steve.

MCCRAY (*script coordinator*): "Fizbo" was a horrible experience for everybody because Chris and Steve had such different visions of what they thought the story should be.

No matter what they did, Corrigan and Walsh couldn't lock down a draft.

WALSH: (*writer / executive producer*): It wasn't clear why we were struggling. So I was taking it personally. I remember being into my second scotch at home, telling my wife, "I'm finally on *Seinfeld,* and I'm blowing it."

The tension reached the point of impacting production.

WALSH: (*writer / executive producer*): You would get notes on an outline from one of them and address those notes. Then, like a fool, you'd bring those addressed notes to the other showrunner. It wouldn't be to their liking or taste, so they'd give you a new direction. You'd go execute that direction, and then, showing a great inability to learn, you'd bring the second revision to the original showrunner who now is looking at you like,

"What the hell is going on?" These guys weren't on the same page. You had two separate tastes that you were trying to simultaneously address.

WRUBEL (*writer / executive producer*): It was that. It was becoming clear they had different approaches to storytelling. And it was obvious that they couldn't both rewrite episodes.

WALSH (*writer / executive producer*): We kept writing a different ending to please alternating showrunners. We were confused why we weren't hitting the target. In hindsight, it's because the target kept changing. Paul and I were in the office all weekend, pulling our hair out, trying to figure out how to simultaneously please both of them.

ZUKER (*writer / executive producer*): We were asked to choose. What happened to us as tiebreakers, you knew that when you opined on an idea you were necessarily going against a person that could fire you. You were creating a negative impression with one of them. I'm not saying they're vindictive, because they weren't. They have skin in the game. You're stuck in the middle. My experience as a child of divorce was as helpful as any writing experience I had to survive on that show.

CORRIGAN (*writer / executive producer*): What we came up with was the version that's on the screen. But I think, personally, Chris stopped giving notes at some point because I think he saw what was going on. We ran out of time, and we had to have a table read and start shooting.

WRUBEL (*writer / executive producer*): Chris threw his hands up, and it became a Steve episode.

LLOYD (*cocreator*): "Fizbo" was probably the one where we said, "This isn't going to be good for our staff."

WRUBEL (*writer / executive producer*): Splitting work up would be best.

The actors—in their trailers or onstage—stayed an arm's length away from the writers' soap opera. They often didn't have a clue about that week's script until given the first draft prior to a table read. Stone-street clearly had no idea what the writers had in store for him when he received episode 7.

STONESTREET (*Cam Tucker*): It was raining outside. I went to my truck in the parking lot. I called my parents and said, "You are not going to believe this. Are you sitting down for the title of the next episode we're going to shoot?" They said they were. I said, "It's called 'Fizbo.'" My dad was like, "Oh my God." It had come full circle. It's unreal for me personally to go from wanting to be a clown as a kid, never really saying I wanted to be an actor, but that I wanted to be a clown. That line in the episode, "I knew I wanted to be a clown from when I figured out that clowns were just people with makeup," is a direct quote from my life. I said that to my mom at the circus.

As flattered as he felt, Stonestreet had no intention of handing over his creation without some level of collaboration.

STONESTREET (*Cam Tucker*): I was very, very, very direct with Steve in the beginning. I said, "If we're going to do this, I have control over what I look like, what my costume is, what my makeup is. It can't be what your version of Fizbo is. It's my version."

LEVITAN (*cocreator*): He's very passionate about clowning. He doesn't understand the scary clown thing at all. He thinks it's a cliché that people have embraced even though they don't mean it. It actually cracks me up. He gets very angry. He goes on these rants, and I just smile.

STONESTREET (*Cam Tucker*): It's been a pet peeve of mine forever, the reputation of being scary and the makeup mistakes that people make on TV.

CASE (*director/editor*): I'm afraid of clowns. Eric found that out and chased me around in a golf cart. I let him know that isn't helping.

Stonestreet remembers walking on set for the very first time in full Fizbo attire. From being a Kansas farm boy and having his grand-

mother make his cherished costumes to rocking it on a soundstage in Hollywood, stage 5. Art imitating life imitating art.

STONESTREET (*Cam Tucker*): I was so proud. I was wearing my clown shoes that I had gotten made in college. My socks were my socks. Some of the material for Fizbo's costume is made from material I got from my dad's store when I was a kid that I had put aside, for if I ever got to make a clown costume. It's on Fizbo's vest. The red suitcase I carry is mine. That was my parents' luggage from when they were younger. I don't want to take all the credit, because I want to leave some for the wardrobe designer. But it was the execution of my vision, and that was the first time I'd gotten to do it like that. It was like my Robert Plant moment. It was incredible.

SCENE FROM SCRIPT

INT. MITCHELL AND CAMERON'S DUPLEX—BATHROOM—DAY

We are CLOSE UP on Cameron's face, reflected
in the mirror. He stares intently. His hand
comes into frame and smears white grease
paint on his cheek. As Cameron continues
to apply grease paint, we reveal a counter
full of makeup, a red nose, a wig, etc.

CAMERON
(to reflection)
Hello, old friend.

WINER (*director / executive producer*): I was going for the seriousness of the methodology in that moment. To us in the writers' room, Eric's dead-serious approach to clowning made us all giggle. It was a serious shot and expression to doing something that people think is silly.

STONESTREET (*Cam Tucker*): It's not like I was out there as an eleven-year-old putting on the clown makeup every day and working as a professional clown. Life happens. You go to high school and feel, "Maybe I shouldn't do my clowning as much as I used to." Then you go to college. I got into the theater department. I thought, "My only performance background is really clowning. I should start doing some clowning again." And so my clowning came back. So "Hello, old friend" means something to me personally, it's like I enjoy doing this. And I hadn't done it in a long time. And now I'm doing it on a successful TV show.

SCENE FROM SCRIPT

EXT. GAS STATION—DAY 17

The nozzle is in the car. Mitchell stands behind it. A car pulls up, and as it inches forward it slightly bumps Mitchell's leg. He turns around.

                    MITCHELL
          Hey!

                    DRIVER
          Hey, yourself. Move!

The DRIVER, a tough guy in his thirties, gets out of his car and goes to the pump. Mitchell stares at the driver, waiting for an apology.

                    MITCHELL
          You know you just kind of hit me with
          your car.

                    DRIVER
          I don't think so.

                    MITCHELL
No. I'm pretty sure you did because
there's grease on my pants and, oh
yeah, I felt it.

                    DRIVER
Call an ambulance.

                    MITCHELL
I just thought you might want to
know in case you want to be a decent
human being and apologize.

The driver ignores him.

                    MITCHELL
                 (to himself)
Okay. I get it. Ass.

                    DRIVER
What'd you say?

The driver starts to walk menacingly
toward Mitchell.

While you would expect all of Fizbo's story to come from clowning memories in Stonestreet's past, the gas station scene actually came from a thorny experience in O'Neill's life.

O'NEILL (*Jay Pritchett*): I had this black 1997 twin turbo Porsche, a beautiful car. I used to go to this gas station in my neighborhood where I knew the guys. I pull in one day to the far pump. I probably could've gone farther in, but there was no one there but me. I didn't think about it. I got out to put the pump in. I walked around behind the car and was looking at the back of it because it's such a beautiful shape, with the whale tail. This car pulls in behind me. I glanced back. It was a vintage Jaguar Sedan, beautiful car. I noticed there's a guy driving and an old man sitting shotgun next to him. The guy's pulling in slow, slow, and slow, but he kept edging up. I'm standing by my back bumper. The guy kept coming closer and closer and closer. I turn around. Now I'm looking at the guy. He's got sunglasses on, so he's hard to read. But I thought that he's angry. He kept coming, and I just stood there. And he kept coming. Finally he bumped into my leg with his bumper. He didn't hurt me, but he made contact. So I was instantly fucking outraged. I balled my right fist up and pounded it on the hood of his vintage Jaguar. Boom. He jumps out of the car, and I'm thinking it's on.

    Cameron's car door opens, and a large
    clown shoe steps onto the pavement.

                        CAMERON
        Is there a problem here?

                        DRIVER
        What the hell are you?

                        CAMERON
        I'm an ass-kicking machine who will
        rip your heart out of your chest
        and shove it down your throat if
        you don't apologize to my boyfriend.
        Right. Now.

                        DRIVER
        Apologi—? Boyfriend?

                        CAMERON
        Apologize!

                        DRIVER
        Okay! I'm sorry, I'm sorry.

Mitchell looks at Cameron with great
admiration as the driver goes back to his
car.

MITCHELL

Wow.

O'NEILL (*Jay Pritchett*): I came around and went, "You motherfucking cocksucker." He opened the door and stood behind it. I would have had to go around the other side to get at him. And then, I don't know if he either recognized me or changed his mind about confronting me, but he turned around and went to go put gas in his car. The old man was sitting in the front seat, in shock. I said a few other things to them. I was so angry. Then I thought, "Well, he's not going to do anything further, so I'm either going to attack the man or shut the fuck up." So I decided to leave. I put the pump back and said something to him in parting like, "You're a lucky motherfucker." The whole reason I told the story to them was because I thought it was Michael Mann [the producer/director]. I had done the first *Miami Vice*, which was his show. And to this day, I don't know if it was, but I do know he had a vintage Jag and he lived in that area. He was known to have a short fuse, and apparently he thought I hadn't pulled up far enough to suit him and was going to teach me a lesson. He came close to getting his ass kicked. I was happy to have that go to Eric, because it was a much better story with the clown.

LEVITAN (*cocreator*): It was a very compelling story. I think the "Fizbo" plot originally went to a different place, but then we said, "What if that happens to Mitch while Cam is there in his Fizbo costume and Fizbo is the one who protects him and he gets to see Fizbo in a different light?" Thank God we heard that story about Ed, because it gave us a great ending.

Stonestreet found a personal moment in the scene as well.

STONESTREET (*Cam Tucker*): My mom was in town the day we were shooting at the gas station. And my best friend played the guy at the station. That was crazy.

Cameron pulls an old-fashioned alarm clock
from his vest and checks the time.

CAMERON
(nonchalantly)
We should go. We're gonna be late.

WRUBEL (*writer / executive producer*): That was the biggest laugh, maybe in the show, where Fizbo pulls out his clown clock to check the time. That was pitched by Sameer.

GARDEZI (*staff writer*): I pitched that as almost an aside to myself. It got a very big laugh. I was so shocked that that landed because of all the things that didn't land.

Stonestreet went on to win the Emmy that year for "Fizbo."

STONESTREET (*Cam Tucker*): It's hard to surpass that episode as far as overall meaning and excitement. I have other episodes that I have loved doing as much or more, but that's a very hard one to not say, blanketly, is my moment. For that to be the episode I won an Emmy for. That's some crazy stuff there.

The show would also win its first Emmy for Best TV Comedy that year, one of five in a row, making it the darling of prime time and the most successful sitcom coming out of the gate in television history.

O'SHANNON (*writer / executive producer*): Chris tried to give me his car. It was around Emmy time, and he said, "If we win the Emmy, I'll give you my car." I thought he was kidding. He had a really nice car. Anyway, we won the Emmy that night, and afterward he showed up at the party and dropped the car keys into the pocket of my tux. It was a beautiful gesture, but the Midwest in me said, "I love you for doing this, but I can't accept this; it's too big." I realize now I should have kept the car and made him Uber home.

Hawaii

Hawaii became the series' first travel episode, remarkable for a first-year series. Friends, as a comparison, didn't go to London until season 4. A Levitan connection helped cast and crew situate themselves at the high-end Four Seasons.

VERGARA (*Gloria Delgado-Pritchett*): *That was our first trip, and we realized, "Oh, we travel perfectly together." We all had a great time. In the nighttime, we would come together for dinners and drinks.*

LLOYD (*cocreator*): *I think the audience loved seeing them out on vacation, but that was where the Brady Bunch goes to Hawaii came up a lot. Like, is this just going to be a travelogue? What are the stakes? But once we kind of came around to a good version of Phil's and Claire's marriage story, that's surprising.*

Everyone tagged along over the ocean—except, surprisingly, Lloyd. He no longer flew, discovering a self-diagnosed "aversion to chairs in the sky." The last plane that touched ground with Lloyd inside landed in LA the day before ABC screened *Modern Family* at upfronts. After the incredible first year they'd all had, Lloyd's absence felt weird to everyone.

BOWEN (*Claire Dunphy*): *Ty and I were laughing thinking he was going to emerge from the water like James Bond in a wet suit and pull it off and have a tux underneath. It was a little bittersweet realizing* *one of our dads wasn't going to come on the family vacation. That was a little sad.*

Most people, however, remember Hawaii for what many on the show consider one of its funniest moments.

EXT. HOTEL GROUNDS—NIGHT

Phil finds Jay in a hammock in a secluded area.

> PHIL
> Jay? What are you doing?

> JAY
> I'm stuck in the hammock. I laid down and my back went out.

> PHIL
> Don't worry, we're gonna get you out of this thing.
> Grab on.

Phil grabs Jay's arms.

> JAY
> Phil, I'm not sure.

> PHIL
> I'm just gonna rock you. Like a hurricane. I'm kidding.
> You're too old to get that.

Phil starts swinging the hammock.

                            JAY
          Just get someone from the hotel.

                            PHIL
          No, this'll work.

The hammock hits Phil, and he falls over
on top of Jay.

                            JAY
          You're lucky I can't move.

                            PHIL
          By the way, I just want to thank
          you for this trip. It's really the
          vacation of a lifetime.

A YOUNG COUPLE approaches holding hands.

                    PHIL (CONT'D)
                  (to couple)
          Nothing weird.

The couple walks off.

BURRELL (*Phil Dunphy*): *I am forever going to laugh at that scene. We kept tweaking it so that it was more and more intimate in terms of getting closer and closer to Jay's face. I'm supporting my weight above him, and then at a certain point I can't hold it anymore, and then as much as he doesn't like me or disapproves of me, we're forced into a hug and embrace where I'm lying on top of him.*

LLOYD (*cocreator*): *If you're next to someone who you feel's always standing in judgment of you, you don't want to basically be kissing him without permission, which is what that scene kind of became.*

BOWEN (*Claire Dunphy*): *The hammock creaking back and forth, there wasn't a crew member that wasn't sobbing with laughter.*

O'NEILL (*Jay Pritchett*): *That was one of the funniest things I ever did with him.*

BURRELL (*Phil Dunphy*): *I don't know how we ended up getting that scene because I couldn't get that close up to Ed's face and not laugh. I don't know if we got one where I wasn't laughing. The dynamic of Jay and Phil being that close to each other to just about be making out.*

LEVITAN (*cocreator*): *After ten years on set, that's as hard as I've seen people laugh at something, and it was so simple and silly.*

O'NEILL (*Jay Pritchett*): *The soundman in the cabana was above us laughing so hard that he literally fell out the top of the hut.*

Hysterical laughter, perhaps the perfect summation of the juggernaut sitcom's first season.

Lifetime Supply

Every one of Modern Family's *250 episodes has at least three plotlines in play. That adds up to 750+ A storylines in eleven years, more than even* The Simpsons, *which has produced more than 650 A stories over the course of thirty-plus seasons. So where do all these episode ideas come from?*

O'SHANNON (*writer / executive producer*): One source of stories is real life—this thing happened to me or someone I know. Another is simply "What if . . . ?" And then some are based on structural challenges. Let's do a whole episode at an airport gate. Let's do a Valentine's Day story that has three complete stories, that kind of thing.

The series' most memorable stories came from the first option— real life. Levitan and Lloyd gave flexible hours in support of family time but also in hopes of something happening in writers' lives that could be mined for future episodes.

LLOYD (*cocreator*): You try to tap into real feelings that you go through, some of which surprise you in the course of family life.

LEVITAN (*cocreator*): I would often refer to things that happened at my house and get opinions from my whole family about how does this seem to you? Does it seem real?

HIGGINBOTHAM (*writer / executive producer*): I've been in tears in that room, not gushing tears, but I've gotten a tear in my eye talking about something. We share everything.

At the beginning of season 2, in "The Old Wagon," Lloyd turned his story of selling the family car into a personal reflection on the passage of time.

LLOYD (*cocreator*): We had an old Land Cruiser in our driveway that was an eyesore. It had so many different smells from kids, spilled drinks, milk formula left under the seat, a bag of asparagus from a farmers' market that got forgotten and blended with the floormat. It had eighty thousand miles on it and was belching smoke. Finally, God knows how, we got someone to agree to buy it for parts. So they come by to take it away. I'm thinking, "Please don't let it fall apart on its way down the street." Then, as it turned the corner out of my driveway and headed away, all I could see was bringing both of my kids home from the hospital in that car and any number of birthday parties that I had taken the kids to and family vacations or outings we'd gone to. It was suddenly a very moving experience.

Later on that season, in "Good Cop Bad Dog," which introduced Stella the dog,* Gloria brings in Guillermo (Lin-Manuel Miranda), who tries to sell his dog treat invention to Jay. The idea came from Lloyd coming home sometimes and finding some random person waiting in their kitchen that his wife had brought home to talk about some idea.

Levitan's son went through a period of taking awkward photos with weird fake smiles. That became a Lily story in season 6's "Do Not Push." Levitan's obsession with getting a stop sign in his neighborhood became a multi-episode Claire story in season 3, culminating in her running for and losing a city council position to Duane Bailey (David

---

* On-screen, Jay and Stella are tight. Off-screen, not so much. As O'Neill points out, "I love dogs, and this one is particularly sweet, but often with dogs on sets, they come with a trainer. These dogs are working. They're not your usual cuddle type."

Cross). In another Levitan-based story, Claire grows frustrated with Phil's new high-tech remote control (season 1's "Fifteen Percent").

LEVITAN (*cocreator*): My wife at the time really didn't do well with remote controls and methods I had for turning on the TV, to the point that one time I came home and this expensive remote I had bought was in ten thousand pieces by my front door. She had had it.

"Moon Landing," the series' fourteenth episode, retold Wrubel's accidental naked butt touch while changing in an NYU locker room.

WRUBEL (*writer / executive producer*): What was interesting was I thought it would be a Phil story with some stranger. Chris, which is an example of what makes him great, said, "No, no, no. Let's do it between Cam and Jay."

LLOYD (*cocreator*): That was certainly going to be funnier with Cam and a slightly homophobic Jay. Touching wet butts is obviously a splashdown, however, and not a moon landing.

Season 2's "Slow Down Your Neighbors" came from a Wrubel story about his wife trying to publicly shame a neighbor for constantly speeding down their residential street. One of Wrubel's favorite stories, "Chirp" (season 2), focuses on a smoke detector in dire need of a new battery.

WRUBEL (*writer / executive producer*): It was not only annoying but also emasculating, trying to solve this simple household problem that's interrupting my wife's and daughter's sleep. It became my great white whale, tracking down which one was the one that was fucking chirping, and then the added problem of getting up to the height where I could change the battery successfully. It was me at my most inept. Dan went off and wrote a great script.

O'SHANNON (*writer / executive producer*): The whole thing was about Phil lacking confidence in his ability to be a good provider and husband

and the idea that every time he heard the chirp from the smoke alarm—which he couldn't fix—the chirp was basically saying, "You're not a man." It was about showing a side to Phil we hadn't seen. Yes, he's the funny, big-hearted man-child, but he's also struggling with these real adult concerns that he takes on bravely and sometimes alone. It's one of those episodes that really fleshes out the character for me.

"Undeck the Halls" (season 1) came from O'Shannon's childhood, in which his parents bluffed canceling Christmas until someone confessed to gouging a living room wall. O'Shannon also introduced sweet, small moments like collecting heads-up pennies with his daughter to create the world's luckiest dollar. Manny and Gloria did that together in season 3's "Aunt Mommy." A freelancer friend, Jerry Collins, came in with a story that led to Phil and Claire's recurring romantic role-playing as Clive Bixby and Juliana (season 1's "My Funky Valentine").

JERRY COLLINS (*writer*): My wife and I tried to have a sexy night away at a hotel for our anniversary. We had young kids and wanted to recapture that fire from our dating days that had been paved over by parenting. It was one night, so the pressure was on. We decided to go to a sex shop beforehand—we bought oils and toys, et cetera . . . At the hotel, we got a sexy couple massage, ate oysters. We tried so hard to make it sexy that it became hilariously unsexy. We sat there with all this "equipment" and realized that we were still just Jerry and Lori from Sherman Oaks.

In a quiet moment within the writers' room, Walsh let drop that he and his sister had once formed an ice-dancing team, which served as the climax for season 1's "En Garde."

STONESTREET *(Cam Tucker)*: Mitch and Claire are doing their ice-skating scene in the parking lot, where he's lifting her up. We had seen them rehearsing it, but when I saw that with my own eyes, that was beyond fucking funny. One of my favorite moments for Jesse and me is when at the end I tell him, "Now do me." I wanted to throw that in there because, dealing with my feelings about myself and my childhood, I always thought that if I ever wrote a book, it would be titled *Nobody Ever Offered Me a Piggyback Ride*. That's because I was always the one giving people piggyback rides or carrying them. I thought that was a really funny moment to ask Mitchell to lift me.

> *Walsh also recalled from his high school days in Rhode Island, located next to Brown University, ranting about Brown people. He realized how that sounded a little late. They incorporated that into "Starry Night" (season 1). In "Truth Be Told" (season 1), Corrigan and Walsh captured their story about working long hours on a previous sitcom.*

WALSH (*writer / executive producer*): We were leaving after a long rewrite. It's like 2:00 a.m. We've got the windows down, and we're stopped at a red light. I'm venting about the showrunner and his inability to make a decision and keeping us there so late. I turn to my right, and in the car next to me, with his window open, is the showrunner. He's looking right at me. He drives off, and we start to freak out. We're going to get fired. So then Paul and I start trying to figure out, can you even hear a person in another car in traffic? By the time we get home, we've concocted this plan where Paul drops me off, I get into my car, and we drive around the neighborhood speaking at the volume we were speaking before, to see if we can hear each other. It's ridiculous, embarrassing, and an indication of how desperate you are to come up with anything that works. We pitched the story to Chris, which was rather difficult because he was the showrunner from the story.

CORRIGAN (*writer / executive producer*): Honestly, I don't think we've ever gotten an answer about whether he knew it was him.

> *Corrigan went to a Christmas charity event misunderstanding the charitable cause (season 5's "The Old Man & The Tree").*

CORRIGAN (*writer / executive producer*): We assumed it was to raise money for something. A clown came up to one of my kids, played with them for a few minutes, then looked at me and put his hand on my shoulder and said, "Don't worry, I'm sure it's all going to work out." I looked around and realized we were the cause. One of my kids was in line with Santa and about to be handed a free toy. I was like, "Oh my God, we have to get out of here and hide the fact that we're getting into a Cadillac." I did write a sizable check to the charity to make up for all of the free hot dogs we ate.

When Zuker and his wife went to open house night at their twin daughters' elementary school, they decided to divide and conquer by having each one accompany one child to a classroom.

ZUKER (*writer / executive producer*): I was talking to my daughter Charlotte, and I said, "Charlie, so tonight, your mom and I are going to have to split up." She thought about it for a while and then said, "Well, I love you, Dad, but I think Mom will take better care of me." We gave a version of that to Luke and Claire in "Manny, Get Your Gun."

Zuker also turned a potentially life-threatening crisis into a Lloyd-written classic, "Up All Night" (season 1).

ZUKER (*writer / executive producer*): I live in Manhattan Beach, and the firemen and EMT workers are famously handsome. Like, I never had a gay thought in my life until they showed up at my doorstep. So it was two in the morning, and I wake up with some of the worst pain I've ever felt. I feel like I'm going to die. I tell my wife to call 911. I'm writhing in my underwear on the floor. I can't even get into pants, I'm in that much pain. I hear a really loud knock on the door downstairs, and I'm like, "Honey, they're here. Where are you? Where are you?" And my wife comes out of the closet in a sexy dress with some slapped-on makeup. I said, "You got dressed up for the firemen?" It's a story I'd tell at parties and she'd deny until we put it on TV and she liked it.

In college, Richman amassed a stack of sixty unpaid parking tickets on a car registered to his father, resulting in his dad's arrest and his mother having to bail his father out in the middle of the night. That story became Haley and Phil's in season 5's "And One to Grow On." Another time, Richman recalled a snit between him and his partner over awards that turned into a Mitchell-and-Cam story for season 3's "Lifetime Supply."

RICHMAN (*writer / executive producer*): My husband, who's an actor, and I had just bought an apartment in New York, and we decided there would be no show business stuff in it—posters, awards, et cetera. At the time, I had a bunch of Emmys, and he didn't have anything. Then he won a Tony Award, and it went from the awards show to a prominent spot in the apartment. So the next time I went to New York, I brought with me an Emmy and put it next to the Tony Award, which dwarfed it. And that became a story about Mitch and Cam having competing awards. Mitch got some Man of the Year award and Cam didn't like that Mitch put it on the shelf. So he took a childhood fishing award and demanded it be up there.

Ko mined her life into Alex's psyche when she went into therapy (season 5's "Under Pressure").

KO (*writer / executive producer*): The idea was actually Steve's, who one day came into the room and said to me, "You're going to write an episode where Alex has a meltdown and has to go to therapy." Steve knew he wanted me to write it, even before we'd spent a second talking about it. I'm guessing it's because he saw similarities between myself and Alex, especially when it comes to dealing with pressure. Those Alex therapy scenes include some of the most personal stuff I've ever written for the show. Some of the stories she shares, including one about a spelling bee she was in when she was young, came straight from my life. Writing those scenes was weirdly cathartic—it's the closest I've gotten to being in actual therapy.

Jack Burditt has had a series of unfortunate events that inspired episodes in later years, such as a contractor and construction crew he and his wife hired always calling his wife "boss" and treating him like a dope. That became a Cam-Mitchell story in season 9's "Catch of the Day." Another real-life event inspired an Alex story in season 10's "Did the Chicken Cross the Road?"

JACK BURDITT (*writer / executive producer*): My daughter joined the army, and because of her specialty, two guys from military intelligence came to our house to interview the family. I said to one of the guys, "Now that we're all a part of the intelligence community, you can tell me . . . We have aliens and their spacecraft in our possession, right?" My daughter was not happy.

The storyline for Chris Martin, from Coldplay, in season 9's "Brushes with Celebrity" came courtesy of Burditt's once-in-a-lifetime encounter with a Beatle.

BURDITT (*writer / executive producer*): I have a friend, Brent Carpenter, who works with Ringo Starr. They were in New York, and Brent asked me if I wanted to spend the day hanging with him and Ringo. Spend a day with a Beatle? It was going to be one of the best days of my life. About an hour before I met up with them, I started getting a pain in my groin area. Concerning, sure. But it would have to wait, because Beatles. Then the pain got worse. "Fight through it," I said to myself. It was a snowy day in New York City, and now I was sweating buckets. I met Ringo, who couldn't have been nicer even though I looked like a sopping-wet insane person who then slid down a wall and passed out. They called an ambulance, which took me to a hospital, and my fantasy of becoming best friends with Ringo Starr ended in humiliation. I had an infection in my balls—that might not be the exact medical term—but at least we were able to turn it into a story where Phil passes out from the same thing in front of Chris Martin.

Ryan Walls's mother and in-laws like to refer to themselves as "the outlaws." As part of the gimmick, they'd pretend to have secret meetings, which led to the secret spouse meetings of non-Pritchetts in season 8's "The Alliance." Another escapade involved his mother taking airplane pills to calm her during flying (season 8's "Five Minutes").

RYAN WALLS (*writer / supervising producer*): One time, we were traveling as a family and we were on a layover, which is not great when someone is on an airplane pill. She wandered off. My dad came back from getting us food and said, "Where's your mom?" We had to track her down. We found her buying handfuls of hats because she thought we all definitely needed some hats.

Writers' assistant Matt Plonsker learned that kinky people don't just populate dating sites. They also surf eBay, which played into season 9's "No Small Feet."

MATT PLONSKER (*writers' assistant*): One of my girlfriends in college bought a nice pair of Nikes, wore them once, and didn't like them. She knew I'd been selling textbooks on eBay and asked if I would mind selling the Nikes for her. I put them online. I started getting questions from people like, "How sweaty were they?" "Does the sweat show?" More questions came in like, "What do you look like?" I realized this isn't a girl who wants running shoes. It's a creepy dude. So I wrote, "I'm a five-foot-three Asian girl." And these fifty-dollar shoes got bid on for two hundred. My girlfriend and I went to the Salvation Army and bought all the cheap running shoes we could find and ended up making like $3,000–$4,000 selling them one semester.

CHAN (*writers' assistant*): The reason that Jay has his relationship with Stella the dog is because of my husband and how he is with his dog. I'm the one who pitched that original story. Danny was the one who suggested they give me the "story by" credit for it.

Higginbotham, today the father of three with his life partner, went through a period of self-doubt the first time they considered surrogacy. (Season 3's "Aunt Mommy")

HIGGINBOTHAM (*writer / executive producer*): At the last minute, Thanksgiving weekend, I panicked. My sister was going to donate the egg. She was going to go on drugs the day after Thanksgiving. My partner and I went for a run that day, and halfway through, I said, "I don't think I can do this." Someone had made me aware that they don't know what those hormones do long term. They think there could be cancer risks. I thought, "My sister already has three kids. She can't get cancer." I freaked out, I was like, "I'm not doing this. I don't want to have a kid yet."

Lloyd got upset with his son for having an overnight guest of the opposite sex at an age he deemed inappropriate. That became season 7's "Double Click."

LLOYD (*cocreator*): What is Phil really mad at? He's mad at the fact it showed his son's getting older and he liked him young. It also showed Phil was getting older and his son was reaching a point where all of these vistas were opening in front of him where Phil and middle age was feeling like his life is shrinking a little bit. He worked it out with Claire what was behind the anger, at least how justified he was in getting angry at Luke. My son watched the episode, scratched his chin, and said to me, "Well, that clears a few things up."

"The Last Walt" (season 3) came courtesy of Levitan's son be-friending an old man in the neighborhood who subsequently dies. That turned into a two-episode arc with Luke and guest star Philip Baker Hall. It also introduced Claire's habit of smiling when talking about death. Levitan FaceTiming with his daughter sparked an idea that turned into season 6's "Connection Lost," an episode filmed en-tirely on iPhones.

LEVITAN (*cocreator*): I had some text messages and documents open. I realized that's really an interesting snapshot of my life on that screen. I always thought that would be interesting to do something on the computer like that. I told my daughter, and then she texted me a couple of months later this short Canadian film [*Noah*]. I went, "Wow, if they could do something this long and keep your interest, maybe we could do that." We contacted the filmmakers and told them they did a really great job and maybe they could help us work on this. It turned out it wasn't going to work with the schedule we have. Our idea was that Claire was out of town. She's dropped her phone in the toilet and needed to be on her computer and couldn't find Haley. Once we had that, then the thing started rolling. What if there's this massive search for Haley that involved everybody and at the end you find out that Haley has been in the basement the whole time? We basically told the story in real time. Meghan Ganz and I wrote the script together. Meghan got extremely involved in all the details of the production. A lot of people assumed it was an Apple commercial that we got paid to do. But we didn't. We thought that's the way it happens in our lives. For me, what was exciting was after it aired, I got invited up to the Apple campus to screen it for hundreds of employees.

Season 1's "Starry Night" takes a page from Lloyd's own fears of the awkwardness of his children's artistic endeavors as they entered their teen years and turns it into a treatise on celebrating individuality.

LLOYD (*cocreator*): My wife was a dancer earlier in her career and got our kids into tap dancing when they were small. They were really good at it. I was living in fear of that moment when it was suddenly not going to be cool in school for them to be tap dancers. I thought, if we can just get them through this ugly period between age twelve, when kids become monstrous and judgy, to say sixteen or seventeen, when suddenly having different interesting skills makes kids cool, then we would be okay. That sentiment wound up in "Starry Night." Manny wasn't getting on very well in school. He hadn't been invited to a party and was feeling the odd man out because he has peculiar interests. Jay schedules this trip with Mitchell where they're going to bring telescopes and look at the night sky like they used to do as kids. Suddenly Manny's along, and Mitchell's disappointed. He thought Jay was trying to reconnect with him by doing something they used to do together. Then you find out Jay is trying to be a good dad to Manny. He can't help him with his feelings of alienation, but he knows Mitchell went through that, which is quite touching.

In the scene, Mitchell is wearing one of Gloria's dresses after getting sprayed by a skunk in the woods.

LLOYD (*cocreator*): I think there was some debate about getting Mitchell into a dress, which was not my idea, but ultimately great for the episode. It was funny.

EXT. MOUNTAIN FIELD—LATE NIGHT

Mitchell sits with Manny.

                    MITCHELL
          You won't believe this looking at me
          now, but I used to get picked on at
          school, too.

                    MANNY
So Jay told you?

                    MITCHELL
Yeah. They'd call me weird. I was
weird. Fun weird. But this is the
funny thing about growing up.
For years and years, everybody is
desperately afraid to be different in
any way.
And then suddenly, almost overnight,
everybody wants to be different. And
that is where we win.

                    MANNY
I'm sort of counting on that.

LLOYD (*cocreator*): That's more or less a speech that I'd given my kids for years and years. Don't be afraid of being different, because at some point overnight, being different makes you stand out, and it's the coolest thing imaginable. It was nice to finally have a place to put it in an episode. It wound up getting quoted back to my kids from one of their teachers who had seen it on TV. He said, "There was something wise that was on TV that you should all really listen to," and he quoted that speech. It had come full circle.

Chirp

People have many different reactions toward Sofía's accent.

O'NEILL (*Jay Pritchett*): *I have no clue what it would be like acting in another language. I think for me it would be a disaster.*

BURRELL (*Phil Dunphy*): *Her accent is thick enough that it disguises how brilliant she is as a comedian. Sometimes it can seem as if she isn't fully understanding the way the language is laid out for a joke. She uses that to her advantage.*

VERGARA (*Gloria Delgado-Pritchett*): *I realized early on one of my jokes has to always be the mispronunciation thing. Of course, my English is horrible, but I overdo words to make it sound crazier. I realized this is a good thing for my character. When I'm changing the words, I start discovering the character.*

Some people accuse her of faking her accent.

CORRIGAN (*writer / executive producer*): *Sofía said once that her son always told her that the longer she's been in America, the worse her accent has gotten. When she first moved here, apparently she spoke English pretty well.*

VERGARA (*Gloria Delgado-Pritchett*): *It's true. I see recordings of when I was in my twenties and my accent was actually not that crazy.*

Of course it became funny to mispronounce words. I think I got lazy. Now I don't even make the effort.

BURRELL (*Phil Dunphy*): *She laughs about it all the time, about how she should have less of an accent. It's who she is and how her ear works, in my opinion.*

LEVITAN (*cocreator*): *If gibberish comes out of her mouth, she's the first one to laugh. It's very endearing.*

BETH MCCARTHY-MILLER (*director*): *That is her, the way she talks. I can't even tell you how many times I've walked onto the set, given her a note, walked away, and then I hear her turn to one of the other cast members and go, "What did she say?"*

Lloyd often gives her notes using her accent.

VERGARA (*Gloria Delgado-Pritchett*): *In Spanish, phrases are different and have a different rhythm. Once he tells me in my accent and rhythm how he wants me to do it, I totally understand it. He's speaking my language, so I get it.*

Everyone on set seems to do a Vergara impersonation.

ZUKER (*writer / executive producer*): *A lot of people start out doing Sofía, and then at the end of it, for whatever reason, it becomes Count Dracula. I don't know why.*

Writers in general follow certain rules with her accent.
Rule #1: You can only predict the unpredictability of her accent.

VERGARA (*Gloria Delgado-Pritchett*): *I think for the writers, it's been a lot of fun to learn what I can easily fuck up. The things that they think I'm going to be able to say right, I don't, and vice versa.*

BOWEN (*Claire Dunphy*): *She can't pronounce anything, and then she can. She's a conundrum.*

HELENA LAMB (*first assistant director / director*): *If she doesn't know her lines that day and we're trying to feed them to her, that can be its own five-minute bit. That can be really funny if we're not totally exhausted.*

MILLER (*assistant prop master*): *Most of the time, her comedy comes from getting two-thirds of the way through her line and then hitting a word she can't remember, so she picks a word out of the air and throws it in. She couldn't remember* highway *and said, "I was driving on the graveyard." I was driving on the graveyard? Where do you get that?*

Rule #2: She struggles most with English jargon.

BOWEN (*Claire Dunphy*): *They would give her these sorts of idiomatic expressions or American terms there isn't a translation for. They like to watch her massacre them.*

LLOYD (*cocreator*): *And she's great. She always finds her way to the pronunciation eventually, but some of her fits and starts are spectacular at how far off she can be.*

BOWEN (*Claire Dunphy*): *There was an episode where a family has a fire and we were collecting things to give to them. Gloria comes in with this tray of knickknacks, which she's collected to give. Knickknacks has no meaning for Sofía. This word was just nonsense syllables to her. So, every time she'd walk in, she'd say something different like "I bring the snickers-snackers" or "I bring the knocker-noodles." Every time it was different, and every time she made me laugh so hard.*

Rule #3: She flat-out doesn't remember English names.

WINER (*director / executive producer*): *Sofía is so lovely and great to me, but I was pretty sure she didn't know my name the whole first season.*

SAPIENZA (*script supervisor / director*): *I've been on the show from the beginning. A handful of seasons ago, she was in a scene and couldn't get her line out. Normally the actor calls out, "Line" or says, "Iwona,"* but she goes, "Meese [miss]?" Everyone started laughing because they realized she didn't know my name. Jesse and Eric still call me that.

VERGARA (*Gloria Delgado-Pritchett*): *You give me a Latin name like* Enrique Javier, *even if it's super complicated, that I can remember. If it's an American name, to me, it doesn't mean anything. It's like I'm memorizing "rr-rr-rr." Immediately after I say it, it disappears from my head. Ed is the same. I'm always next to him, and he'll ask, "What's her name?" and I'm like, "Why are you asking me?"*

Rule #4: She finds it funny when the writers give her weird or difficult names on purpose.

In season 4's "Mistery Date," Richman had Cam secretly hire a muralist, Abelard, to paint a mural in Gloria's nursery for the baby, similar to what Cam had done in Lily's room.

RICHMAN (*writer / executive producer*): *As Gloria is figuring out that Cam has secretly commissioned his friend Abelard to paint a mural on her nursery wall for her baby, she says, "So this is why you kept me outside all day? So that your friend Abirard could come and paint my present?" There wasn't really a reason to have the character repeat that name. She could have just said "your friend," but because I thought Gloria would struggle to pronounce Abelard, I wrote Abirard in the script just because I wanted to hear Sofía say it that way. And she did it perfectly. It was one of my favorite things written for the show, a throwaway little thing like that. I loved it.*

JEREMY MCGUIRE (*Fulgencio "Joe" Pritchett*): *Shorty wanted to see* Wicked, *and instead of* Elphaba, *she said* elephant. *That was funny. I laughed like crazy.*

Rule #5: She does mind a mispronunciation written into a script, unless it serves a specific purpose.

GARDEZI (*staff writer*): *We had an early table read, and all of the* Jays *written in the script were replaced with* Yays. *I remember seeing that* *and my eyes widened. We're going out of our way to accentuate her ste-reotypical accent. I mean, it's one thing if that's a part of your character and another if it's like, "Give us that cha-cha-cha show." When Sofía got to a Yay, she over-enunciated the J. That was never done again.*

LEVITAN (*cocreator*): *She said she wouldn't say that and then she turned around and said another j word with a y right after that, so there's no rhyme or reason. We weren't going to tell her what she had to say. It worked one way or another.*

An exception to the rule, and a favorite malapropism of many, occurs in season 2's "Halloween" episode. At home, Gloria, feeling insecure about her English, asks Jay if she has a problem with her pronunciation. Jay tries to soothe her as he opens a FedEx-size box she's handed him.

```
                  JAY
     Just little mispronunciations. Like
     last night you said we live in a
     doggy-dog world.

                GLORIA
     So?

                  JAY
     It's a dog-eat-dog world.

                GLORIA
     But that makes no sense. Who wants to
     live in a world where dogs eat each
     other? A doggy-dog world is a happy
     full-of-puppies world. What else do I
     get wrong?

                  JAY
     It's not blessing in the skies, it's
     blessing in disguise.
```

Carpal tunnel syndrome is not
carpool tunnel syndrome.
And bob wire-

                    GLORIA
          Okay, I didn't realize you keep a
          list of all the glorious mistakes.

                    JAY
          I don't find them glorious, I mean
          they're kinda cute-

                    GLORIA
          Gloria's! Mine! You know, I may have
          an accent, but people understand me
          just fine.

Jay opens the box and looks inside.

                    JAY
          What the hell is this?

                    GLORIA
          What? I told your secretary to get me
          a box of baby cheeses.

Jay lifts up a small ceramic figurine of
the Baby Jesus.

                    GLORIA (CONT'D)
          Oh, and I suppose that is my fault?

This scene sets up another of the show's funniest scenes in its history: the House of Horrors.

Halloween

With the success of season 1 behind them, cast and crew couldn't wait to come back from summer hiatus for season 2.

BURRELL (*Phil Dunphy*): Almost greater than any other achievement of the show for me, including the Emmys, was shooting the first episode of season 2. I had shot several pilots before. Two made it to air. Both didn't make it a full season. Showing up for work at the beginning of season 2, I was giddy. I couldn't believe it. We were all part of a TV show that was an actual TV show on the air, and I was still employed, which was hard to believe.

To further ease any uncertainty, Levitan and Lloyd had replaced the standard craft services tent or temporary structure with some- thing more enduring.

SALLY YOUNG (*production manager / producer*): We found the money in our budget and built this really nice kitchen on the stage with built-in countertops, cabinetry, and a nice refrigerator. We put a stationary island in the middle. The first week of shooting, Ty walks in and pushes on the island. Then he pushes on the counter. Then he goes, "Oh my God. They're permanent. We might be here for a while."

Halloween, Christmas, and Thanksgiving, always popular sub- ject matter for sitcoms, all became recurring storylines on the show.

Halloween first reared its pumpkin head in the sixth episode of season 2, subsequently returning multiple times thereafter.

GOULD (*Luke Dunphy*): Logistically, everyone hates the Halloween episodes because the soundstages get warm with all the lights on and we're in stage makeup dressed up as ridiculous things like Frankenstein and zombies. But our fans think those episodes are some of our signature ones.

HYLAND (*Haley Dunphy*): I've had some really great Halloween costumes, like my fireman outfit, and sexy mental patient, which got a lot of flak when I posted a picture of it on Instagram.

Higginbotham and Richman joined the writing staff in season 2, positions they would remain in until series' end. By this point, the showrunner ruckus had morphed into a détente. Each person ran point on alternating episodes, with the other person having significant say. That solution would come crashing down with Richman's first script, the season's sixth episode, "Halloween."

RICHMAN (*writer / executive producer*): I was already a little nervous, and then Steve gave me notes and Chris gave me opposite notes.

MCCRAY (*script coordinator*): Jeff wrote an outline that was hilarious, after breaking the story with Chris. Then Steve gave his notes and didn't understand any of it. He told Jeff to change everything that Chris wanted. And then it went back to Chris and he was like, "What's this? This isn't what we talked about."

RICHMAN (*writer / executive producer*): The notes would invariably be contradictory. They were given separately with no conversation between Chris and Steve about what they wanted. It became too difficult to address, to keep doing passes for them individually when they would have different story ideas.

CORRIGAN (*writer / executive producer*): Once they started arguing, it was out of our hands. It was between Chris and Steve. It was just between Chris and Steve.

WRUBEL (*writer / executive producer*): The process was a nightmare for Jeff. I remember he came into my office and said, "This is insane," and I said, "This is the process."

RICHMAN (*writer / executive producer*): Those writers who had been there before knew what I was going through and were so incredibly supportive. It was a Chris episode. I remember him being incredibly sympathetic to my plight. Ultimately, he said, "I think I'm the one whose notes you need to address."

MCCRAY (*script coordinator*): It was probably the breaking point. The writers finally had to sit down and say, "We can't keep going back and forth being pulled every which way with this. We need to find a new system."

And they did, but first they had to get through "Halloween."

As much as Winer considers "The Bicycle Thief" to be Phil's quintessential episode, "Halloween" in many ways defines Claire.

INTERVIEW

PHIL
We love Halloween. Especially Claire.

CLAIRE
It's my favorite holiday. I've just
always loved scary things. When I
was a kid and a new horror movie came
out, I was always first in line. "One,
please." Then I met Phil.

LLOYD (*cocreator*): The idea is that this button-down housewife, who essentially has four children to rein in all the time, has a real affection for Halloween. Having that as her outlet seemed like a really funny character trait. She's a slightly mad housewife who starts thinking about Halloween around August 10, and that carries her through the next twelve weeks thinking how she's going to do it different this year.

MICHAEL SPILLER (*director*): The passion and attention to detail she throws herself into around the holiday. Other people don't care as much. They have their own crap going on.

```
              PHIL INTERVIEW


                   PHIL
         Someone your age dies, what's the
         first thing you wanna know? Died of
         what? You wanna hear it's something
         that could never happen to you.
         Same with divorce. Tell me it was
         booze, cheating, physical abuse. No
         problem. I'm a monogamous social
         drinker, and Claire only sleep hits
         me. Just don't tell me it came out
         of the blue.
```

RICHMAN (*writer / executive producer*): Phil's feeling insecure that Claire's going to get sick of him the way the next-door neighbor's wife got sick of her husband. All of this leads to the big blowup in act 3 where nobody's talking to each other and Gloria punches Mitchell's scarecrow in the face.

SPILLER (*director*): Phil's insecurity leads to his overcorrecting and trying too hard, acting oblivious to Claire's needs, being super affectionate. There's that moment where she's like, "I've had it; I'm out," and walks out into the front of the house, where Phil joins her.

RICHMAN (*writer / executive producer*): There's a lot of heart when they go outside. There's a lot of "You're stuck with me and I'm not going anywhere."

SPILLER (*director*): I don't think I gave them a single note there. What's doubly impressive about that is when Claire walks out of that house and we cut to the exterior, that was on a different day, different location. One's on a stage; the other's a couple of blocks from the studio. Yet it feels perfectly continuous. Julie was able to get herself right back into that headspace. It's so brilliantly executed on their end.

INT. MITCHELL'S CAR—DAY

Mitchell, in his Spider-Man suit, pulls into his office parking lot and sees his coworkers entering the building, none of them in costume. He ends up calling Cam while hiding in a bathroom stall.

                MITCHELL
           (into phone to Cam)
    There are exactly three people in
    costume here: a tool, a douche, and
    me. And I don't have time to come
    home and . . .

                CAM
    Calm down. Did you bring in the dry
    cleaning last night?

                MITCHELL
    Are you really getting on me about
    the dry cleaning when . . .
           (then, realizing)
    Ohhh! I have suits in the trunk.

                         CAM
        Look at that. Yesterday's lazy cures
        today's crazy.

Mitchell hangs up, looks around and sneaks
out of the car. When he returns, he's in
a suit and tie, which is very tight and
confining given the Spider-Man muscles.

The idea for Spider-Man came from a crossed-signals date Wrubel had on Halloween.

WRUBEL (*writer / executive producer*): She had mentioned her friends were having a party and maybe we'd swing by. My brain started to put two and two together. It's Halloween, and it's a party, so it could be a costume party. On the other hand, I was solidly in my thirties, and maybe we were too adult for costumes. I didn't want to be the idiot in a costume in a houseful of corduroy-clad Los Feliz hipsters. But then, I also didn't want to be the buzz-killing jerk in a plaid shirt talking to a fun-loving C-3PO. So my solution was to find a costume I could hide under my clothes. I found a Spider-Man suit in a costume shop. It fit quite snugly under my clothes. As it turned out, the party was a mix, but I was comfortable wearing what I had on without turning into Spider-Man.

Throughout the episode, Haley keeps modeling risqué costumes that her mother frowns on, such as this one in the Dunphy kitchen.

Haley enters in short black shorts, a
black tank top, knee-high boots, and cat
ears.

                         HALEY
        Check it—I'm a scary black cat.

                    CLAIRE
I'm the only person that costume
scares. Go change.

                    HALEY
To what?

                    CLAIRE
One of your old costumes.
        (dialing phone)
Trust me, I'm sparing you a whole day
of guys asking if you have a rough
tongue.

HYLAND (*Haley Dunphy*): I think Julie's favorite line of the whole show is, "Check it—I'm a scary black cat."

BOWEN (*Claire Dunphy*): Yes, it's my favorite line.

HYLAND (*Haley Dunphy*): I could not imagine wearing those costumes now. It would not be fun for anyone. It wasn't even that much fun for me then. Everything was so short and so tight. I guess my ass cheeks were hanging out of those black shorts because I remember when I turned around Julie seemed like she was going to pass out from being so mortified. She said, "I see your vagina."

    Haley ends up dressing like a scantily clad Mother Teresa, which makes sense to her somehow.

                    CLAIRE
Are you kidding me?

                    HALEY
What? I'm her back when she was hot.

One small running bit through the episode involved a motion-sensitive skeleton that would pop up time and time again to scare Phil anew as his mind raced elsewhere.

MILLER (*assistant prop master*): I was working that skeleton. You pushed a button and the hydraulics would pop the skeleton up. It came up really fast. Julie hadn't been on set yet and was walking up to it. I could have scared the ever-loving shit out of her. Toby [Tucker] looked at me, going, "Pop it. Pop it." Earlier, I'd popped it once and the head flew off. I could see Julie getting close to it, me popping it and the head flying off and breaking her nose. That's the only reason I didn't do it. I think I saved the show.

The episode's climax takes place in a decked-out haunted house for trick-or-treaters in the Dunphy living room. All the characters have congregated together there in costume, opening the door for all the episode's petty arguments and annoyances to surface at once.

CLAIRE BENNETT (*production designer / art director*): You want to believe they could do this in their house. You want it to look good, but we always have to stay grounded.

BERG (*production designer*): Everyone brought their own little things to the set, and we created something that was way bigger than the sum of its parts. Eric's head on the plate. That was actually something we did in the Nine Inch Nails / Mark Romanek "Closer" video, which was a photograph by Joel-Peter Witkin.* It's the most beautiful portrait of a decapitated head on gothic fruit.

Probably not a lot of competition in that category.

---

* Witkin is a contemporary American photographer whose work focuses on darker subject matter, such as death and pieces of corpses—not the type of images to show your child before bed. The image referenced for the Nine Inch Nails video and for Cam is *Still Life,* Marseilles, 1992. According to the Fraenkel Gallery, it is a reinterpretation of Dutch vanitas painting in which Witkin employs a severed head as a flower vase. "Joel-Peter Witkin," Fraenkel Gallery, accessed December 3, 2019, https://fraenkelgallery.com/exhibitions/joel-peter-witkin-2.

VERGARA (*Gloria Delgado-Pritchett*): It was so much fun to see everyone in their outfits.

RODRIGUEZ (*Manny Delgado*): I was super excited. I got to have my face and arms painted because I was Frankenstein. I had this big old prosthetic piece with hair and everything. I was in ten-inch platform shoes. So I was standing tall and thinking, "I hope I don't fall, because that would be totally embarrassing."

Alex, staying true to form, doesn't dress up but participates by sitting in a cage and reading a book.

WINTER (*Alex Dunphy*): I wanted a Halloween costume, and then I get stuck in that cage the whole day. They left me in a cage! I did absolutely nothing. I pretended I was reading and doing homework.

HYLAND (*Haley Dunphy*): I felt bad for her. But also she loves to sit. I had to stand the entire time.

Standing for long periods of time took extra energy from Hyland, who found herself in need of a kidney transplant at the time.

In addition to the Dunphy storyline, Mitchell has to deal with Cam's Halloween PTSD that he never wants to talk about yet always melodramatically does. Gloria feels both embarrassed and pissed by Jay's attitude toward her accent.

WRUBEL (*writer / executive producer*): All the orchestration of the House of Horrors was Chris. The pacing of it, the way it happened, is what he does best, which is choreograph an extended comic scene where everyone has a strong comic attitude that's built up during the episode.

LLOYD (*cocreator*): It was a tricky story to figure out. We got to that idea of all of them coming to Claire's rescue and doing the House of Horrors once and how that plays into all of their individual stories. To have it all come together in that funny little performance within the family was fun. Seeing Ed dressed as a gargoyle or, as Sofía called him, a "gargle." There was a ton to laugh at.

SPILLER (*director*): I think it's so sharp the way that Claire switches into director mode and gives everyone notes. They're so not into it. And Cam's little comment about Claire, his head poking through the table, "That's a lot of complaining from someone who asked for thirds of our tandoori turkey last year." These scripts are so dense with jokes that aren't set up and pay off. So beautifully woven that it takes multiple viewings to truly appreciate everything that's there.

STONESTREET (*Cam Tucker*): It's brilliantly set up by the writers. To play the scene very serious, all of us, in our costumes. That's what's so funny about adult Halloween parties. It's you dressed as Teen Wolf and your friends, dressed in costumes. You're still having the same mundane real-life conversations and arguments that you would have if you weren't in costume.

And then Gloria gets her revenge.

```
The first children enter the House of
Horrors. Gloria pops up from behind the
couch.


                    GLORIA
          (formal accent, not remotely scary)
     Welcome to your nightmare. Ha ha ha
     ha ha.


                    CLAIRE
          (stunned)
     What the hell is that?
```

RICHMAN (*writer / executive producer*): There was this idea to have Sofía try to put on an American accent.

VERGARA (*Gloria Delgado-Pritchett*): They realized it was funny for Gloria to try to speak perfect English.

LLOYD (*cocreator*): She's trying to shove it in Jay's face by speaking very properly. It was goofy and hilarious.

WINTER (*Alex Dunphy*): That wasn't the first take. It was the third or fourth. Sometimes that will happen to Sofía. She'll do it fine in the first couple of takes while she's still figuring it out. On the third or fourth take, I don't know what happens. I think her brain doesn't connect with her mouth.

MILLER (*assistant prop master*): Sofía stands up and says her line, and all of us, to a person, fell down laughing. Who is she doing? What is this read? Pure genius.

WINTER (*Alex Dunphy*): We probably laughed about it for a solid twenty minutes before we could go back and film another take because it was so fantastic.

Next, add in Jay, a sad, ridiculous-looking "gargle."

VERGARA (*Gloria Delgado-Pritchett*): Every time that Ed would approach me with that ridiculous outfit, I couldn't remember my lines.

STONESTREET (*Cam Tucker*): The way he sulks out of the room as the dejected gargoyle was physically the funniest frickin' thing ever.

BURRELL (*Phil Dunphy*): We couldn't get through Ed walking. Something about Ed in that costume tore everyone up.

HYLAND (*Haley Dunphy*): I like to pride myself for not breaking, especially back then, but I could not stop laughing. Thank God I wasn't the only one.

RODRIGUEZ (*Manny Delgado*): You could hear Eric laughing from underneath the serving platter. We couldn't help it.

Stonestreet as an aggrieved head on a platter only added to the madness.

LLOYD (*cocreator*): The idea of Eric, who uses his whole body and certainly his hands in his gestures in his comedy, reduced to a head on a table seemed quite funny.

YOUNG (*production manager / producer*): His head was basically a serving of ham.

BOWEN (*Claire Dunphy*): Between takes someone would take the serving dish off because he was under the table and couldn't leave.

At this moment, Cam finally recounts his childhood Halloween trauma in which a friend empties a bowl of candy from a neighbor's porch into his bag and then, when caught, blames it on Cam. The story culminates with young Cam pissing all over himself. That idea came courtesy of Higginbotham's past.

HIGGINBOTHAM (*writer / executive producer*): I offhandedly said I played baseball for two years, largely from the pressures of being a gay kid and a dancer, that sissy pressure. I was ten or eleven. There was this kid, Marvin Kelly, who you couldn't hit. I always struck out, but they had to shove me in for two innings. So I got up to bat against Marvin and swung. Nothing. Then I swung on the next pitch and people started screaming. I heard the crack, but it didn't register that I had hit the ball. I'm thinking, "Oh my God," and I start to run and in the excitement of it, I completely pissed in my pants in front of a bleacher full of people. It was so humiliating. I came back and wondered, "Do people know?" I had white pants on. They had to know. I had to stink. When I got into the car of my friend's mother who was driving me home, she put a towel on the seat. Yeah, everyone knew.

The show won director Spiller an Emmy and helped propel the series to win its second Outstanding Comedy Series award. It remains a cast favorite.

WINTER (*Alex Dunphy*): It's been ten years since we did that episode. We still talk about it.

BOWEN (*Claire Dunphy*): I remember Eric saying under a silver platter, "I don't want to jinx it, but I really feel like we're making a classic episode of television right now." Who could listen to a guy whose head is under a serving dish?

STONESTREET (*Cam Tucker*): It's one of those moments where you say, "I am going to remember this for a long time." I think we all had that moment in that scene. This is going to be one of our memories of the show that will stand out.

> *As would the next, when Levitan and Lloyd disbanded as a partnership, remaining one in name only.*

Connection Lost

Kobe Bryant and Shaquille O'Neal feuded their way through three NBA championships. Dean Martin and Jerry Lewis spent a turbulent and combative decade (1946–1956) as Hollywood kings and then the next two decades not speaking to each other. Simon and Garfunkel harmonized across five successful studio albums and countless tours but held a cold sound of silence most of the time in between and thereafter. Such things happen in great partnerships with equally powerful personalities.

JAY SURES (*Levitan's agent / copresident UTA*): Writing partnerships are similar to marriages. In many instances, you spend more time with your writing partner than you do with your spouse.

Levitan and Lloyd had an arranged marriage, born out of circumstances, not organic growth. Perhaps if they'd risen through the ranks together as hungry writers or if one had a submissive personality, things would have been different. But by the time they came together, both had their own brand of comedy and way of running a show. Neither had to compromise that vision before, and they didn't want to start now.

RICHMAN (*writer / executive producer*): One could see on *Back to You* that they were very different types of storytellers and leaders. Chris also had a long history with Kelsey and Jimmy Burrows, and they both naturally looked to him for leadership—and that probably bugged Steve. Also, the show was struggling, so there were difficulties in putting out episodes. That exacerbated tensions. You could see the beginning of the erosion of their friendship.

HIGGINBOTHAM (*writer / executive producer*): They're different writers with very different styles. When they listen to each other, they make the best scripts because they complement each other. But I think success makes you think your way is best.

SURES (*Levitan's agent / copresident UTA*): The creative process is a subjective one. It's passionate and can be emotional. I think when you put all those things together, you sometimes find relationships that can't stand the test of those factors. I wasn't a part of that room all the time, but I'm guessing that was part of the case. I've represented probably fifteen writing teams as an agent over thirty years. Only one is still together.

    Daddy and Daddy went their separate personal ways but stayed together for the good of their family, remaining with the show through its entire run, focusing on their half of episodes while staying arm's length away from the other's.

WALSH (*writer / executive producer*): They aren't writing partners. They're co-equal showrunners, both strong willed and confident with their own ideas about what to do. I think it was inevitable that they split up, because they want to be in charge and should be in charge.

LEVITAN (*cocreator*): In the beginning, it was a very practical thing. We're two people. Had we been three people like Casey, Angell, Lee, it would be majority rules. We didn't have that luxury. And at one point, I worked for Chris. So that added a layer of complexity to the relationship.

    People want to find a smoking gun: Colonel Mustard in the library with the candlestick. But life doesn't always work out so smoothly. Sometimes friends can't work together, or live together, or marry each other. It stinks, but it happens.

LEVITAN (*cocreator*): I've thought about this a lot. It seems to me some of the best partnerships in this business are when you have two people with very different skill sets, where you have an alpha and a beta and they're both happy in those roles. One is clearly the more take-charge lead and the other person's very happy to be in a position of power but not necessarily in charge. That's not who we are.

LLOYD (*cocreator*): Some would say it's not surprising that two people who were used to running shows on their own and had a measure of success might not fall into an easy partnership with give-and-take right out of the gate. They would be right.

LEVITAN (*cocreator*): We're alpha males and type As who see the world very differently. We have very different upbringings and very different personalities. I'm a typical neurotic Jew, and Chris is a sort of classic WASP, for lack of a better term. I hope it's not offensive.

In the end, the fissure mostly comes down to differences in story-telling—what they write, how they write it, and what kind of story they like to tell.

CHAN (*writers' assistant*): There were long debates over their differing opinions on how a story should be handled.

LLOYD (*cocreator*): I like it to creep up on you or come in a surprising place as opposed to maybe announcing from the beginning, "This is the episode where, in the first scene, I announce I'm breaking up with my boyfriend."

LEVITAN (*cocreator*): I think Chris enjoys more plot. He likes to have more stuff happening than sometimes I do. I don't need as many beats for it to feel like a good episode or as many twists and turns as he does sometimes. It's not a criticism. It's a stylistic approach.

LLOYD (*cocreator*): I have maybe a little bit more rigid view of what a story is, which is that every scene advance what happened in the scene before. So if you're telling a story whose arc is twenty-two minutes, you have stakes and things the audience cares about. Steve might pitch something and get excited about a particular scene or moment. Then the next day, because he's very good at thinking outside of the box, he'll shake it all up. He'll get a whole idea for a new scene and get very excited about that that day. My thing is we've got to be very buttoned down and disciplined here and follow a story through to a satisfying ending.

LEVITAN (*cocreator*): I completely cop to the fact that I am a bit more of an impulsive person than Chris is, and I'm sure the writing staff would agree. We start stories from different places. I might say, "Here's the thing that's intriguing me this week. What if your kid does something you feel is not so great? How much do you support him, and how much do you let him know he can do better? Where's the line there?" That to me is a very valid place to start a story. That doesn't mean I'm saying, "We're doing a story about that, no matter what." It means I want to pursue this area because I think as a parent, people are interested in this.

LLOYD (*cocreator*): The danger with writing before you know where you're going is you could be doing work that ultimately is going to get torn out. Better to have gotten it all figured out before so that you're not doing unnecessary work. You're not getting that pitfall of falling in love with something and then twisting everything in order to keep it. That's not going to yield good results. But again, that's my way of doing stuff. That doesn't mean it's right, but it's my way of doing it.

LEVITAN (*cocreator*): I don't believe there's one way to break a story. Many brilliant authors say they need to go where it takes them a little bit. I'll start with a notion, but we're not starting writing. We're doing beats to the story. Okay, what's next, what if, what if? Those are starting points. Can it go to a satisfying ending? It's a different way of approaching storytelling.

LLOYD (*cocreator*): It's the same problem with building a house before you have a set of blueprints. Pretty soon, you have a house with a staircase that doesn't go anywhere and a window on the roof. But it can be effective in getting things moving in the right direction. He did push us that way in the pilot.

LEVITAN (*cocreator*): We spent a lot of time during the pilot battling these things out. It wasn't ugly, but I like to work faster, and Chris likes to work very slowly. He walks slowly. We used to go to lunch together on the lot. He walks half as fast as I do. I'm like, "Can we walk faster?" I move fast. I talk fast. I sometimes react too fast. I like forward momentum. Chris is very deliberate and methodical and likes to think things through for a long time. At times, that's fantastic and at times frustrating. So we're different on so many levels that some of this is inevitable.

LAMB (*first assistant director / director*): I heard Chris say, "I'm too old and too rich for this shit." Every time there was a renegotiation, I was always surprised that Chris would come back, but then later on, at the end of season 6 or 7, we were having lunch and he said, "I honestly don't know what else I would do. I don't have hobbies." I understood why he stuck around.

BOWEN (*Claire Dunphy*): The competition between them keeps them both engaged and fully invested in the show. I don't think either wanted to leave it in the hands of the other. And in that, we all benefit.

In addition to their differences in style, Lloyd has a strong aversion to public speaking. Levitan does not, and so he appeared in public to accept awards on their behalf. For both of them, the "damned if you do and damned if you don't" circumstances became a further source of friction.

LLOYD (*cocreator*): I know what I can do and what I can't. That is firmly in the *can't* category. A stage is a place for actors. If I were good at getting up and talking in front of people, that might have been something that I could have enjoyed. I was always massively uncomfortable doing that, and so I avoided the whole thing.

LEVITAN (*cocreator*): There's two showrunners, and one of them doesn't want to be there. Because I'm not bothered so much about public speaking, it fell on me, and I didn't make a big deal about it. I tried to always be gracious and mention Chris and never tried to look like it was my accomplishment. I literally went multiple times to him and said, "Please, just get up there with me and stand there. You don't have to say a word. Otherwise, people are going to wonder, 'Where's the other guy, and why is there just one person?' It doesn't reflect well on me. I don't like the feeling of it, like in some weird way I'm taking credit." Yet what choice do we have? He couldn't and wouldn't.

LLOYD (*cocreator*): There are people that will say to me, "You're a moron. Why wouldn't you get out there and grab that award and have everybody watch you?" They're assuming that would be a pleasure for everyone. I don't feel I was missing anything other than a night of excruciating anxiety, so I think I made the right choice.

LEVITAN (*cocreator*): I didn't think that was fair, and I didn't like it. It put a little bit of a weird spin on winning. Those should have been nothing but happy moments, but there was always a bit of weirdness like I have to feel strange about this, people saying nice things about me after a speech or being up there. The first Emmy, I have a big picture of me and the cast. It's one of the favorite pictures I took in my life, and it hurt because Chris isn't there. Why isn't he there? It looks like me and the cast. I didn't choose that, but it almost looks like I did.

LLOYD (*cocreator*): I hope that no one ever interprets it as my being disdainful for awards or that Hollywood thing where some people say we're all creatives and there's no room for competition and all that. I love the competition and that we won all those awards.

Lloyd would rather pursue activities he enjoys, like playing basketball, which became his annual Emmy ritual. He'd turn his trusted flip phone off during the game and then back on afterward to see whether his show won or not.

Amazingly, out of all this friction, came a diamond in the rough, an effective way of producing a television show—a so-called happy ending. They took joint custody of the estate, splitting the show in two. In doing so, they kept the set fresh and prevented burnout in the writers' room.

RICHMAN (*writer / executive producer*): You're very grateful to have that variety. If you work ten years on a show with one leader in one style of storytelling for twenty-two episodes a year, it can be very difficult to keep your interest. This way, we go from one style of storytelling to another. The writers move pretty effortlessly through that.

> *The writers maintain the ebb and flow so that both halves make one cohesive whole. The audience doesn't notice. Cast and crew haven't had a problem because neither showrunner carries their feelings onto set. Perhaps the greatest oddity concerns both turning a blind eye in many ways to each other's work.*

LEVITAN (*cocreator*): It feels like a weirdly competitive environment, everyone wanting their shows to be the best and all that. It's utterly complicated.

LLOYD (*cocreator*): There's a hundred episodes of a series that I cocreated that I've never seen. And that's not a typical situation. But I know that if I watch certain episodes, the same things that bothered me about them at the table read, and that weren't changed, would make me nuts. That's probably just me, by the way. I don't want to be bothered, so I don't invite that irritation into my life.

LEVITAN (*cocreator*): There are many of his episodes I haven't watched partly for the same reason. I find certain episodes frustrating. We see the world differently, and so I get it. That's definitely an issue.

LLOYD (*cocreator*): I do feel a little bit proprietary about the characters. When I see things being done in a way that I wouldn't allow them to be done, they jar me. But that doesn't mean that would be my reaction every week. It might be only occasionally. But it's a thing that I've learned to avoid, and that's okay. There are *Modern Family* fans that would win trivia contests about our series way faster than I would because there's lots of things that have happened on the show that I'm not even completely aware of.

LEVITAN (*cocreator*): If I sat down and watched one of his episodes, I don't think it would fill me with enjoyment necessarily. But then occasionally I'll stumble on something. Certainly there are many episodes that I admire that he's done. And all of his episodes have moments I certainly admire. Chris is a very smart guy.

LLOYD (*cocreator*): People who are not in this situation would never understand it. If someone comes up and is very complimentary about an episode that I didn't have too much to do with, I say that's good for the show. It's lovely that they liked the series, and that's always a good thing.

LEVITAN (*cocreator*): I don't ever hear the audience say, "That show's really different than the week before." People like the show.

LLOYD (*cocreator*): I'll go one step further—there are people who will come up to me and say, "I watched the show this week. It was such a great episode. And I knew it was one of yours right away because of this, that, and the other." And it wasn't one of mine. So there is a homogeneity to the episodes at a certain point because we have a staff that works on both of them.

LEVITAN (*cocreator*): I wish it weren't this way. It's not the way I like to live my life. I would like us to be friends again, but there are times you realize this relationship has gotten a little negative and toxic and I can't seem to fix it, and short of saying, "Let's go into counseling together and talk out some of these issues," I don't know what else to do.

LLOYD (*cocreator*): The fact that we arrived at a survivable way of doing things as early as we did, where we split the episodes, is a good thing because I can't fight the same fight every week. That's going to not only make me crazy, that's going to make the staff crazy.

WINER (*director / executive producer*): I saw the division as tremendous self-awareness on their part and an excellent use of their experience. That way no one is chasing their tails like on "Fizbo."

BURDITT (*writer / executive producer*): If I ever created another network sitcom where you have to do twenty-two or twenty-four episodes a year, I'd probably do it that way, too.

BOWEN (*Claire Dunphy*): It makes a lot of sense to divide and conquer the workload and not burn out.

Visitation rights resulted in an odd-even streamflow in which one gained custody of the writers' room one week while the other supervised their episode onstage. The following week they swapped, back and forth, for an entire season. The next year, they exchange odd episodes for even and even for odd. That way, each gets the opportunity to do season premieres and season finales every other year. Only during summer preproduction, in which the staff comes together to lay the groundwork for next year's stories and arcs, do the showrunners cohabitate for any length of time within the same space, which can be uncomfortable and tense for writers.

LLOYD (*cocreator*): You could tell when Steve and I would argue. It still happens, not frequently, but you can see the staff members who were from divorced families because they're the ones that hide under the table more because it calls up ugly memories.

LEVITAN (*cocreator*): It doesn't make sense to sit there and argue things out forever. Because ultimately somebody's got to win. So we said, "Why don't we take turns on who gets to win? It's a time-saver."

LLOYD (*cocreator*): We fell into a workable procedure, which is when it's my episode, he's free to give his thoughts and notes. I digest them and take what ones I think are valuable and discard the ones that I don't. And exactly the same process happens on his episodes. I'm sure he feels like his notes should be listened to on mine more than they are. The same goes the other way. There was no better process than that, that we could think of. It's kept things relatively harmonious for a long number of years.

So, in a house divided, Daddy and Daddy alternate rushing home from work to go to the other's house to critique the dinner they've prepared for their kids. Somehow it works.

WRUBEL (*writer / executive producer*): I just assumed I was in a production of *You Can't Take It with You* or some classic comedy where the eccentricities of the family are never commented on.

HIGGINBOTHAM (*writer / executive producer*): They'd both rather have their own shows, and at this point they do. I don't need them in the same room again. Mommy and Daddy are happier when they're separate. Let them be separate.

LEVITAN (*cocreator*): It's a difficult thing, but kids of divorce, they adapt. Our writers have handled it well. They often get more responsibility thrown on them, and the best of them welcome that and fill the gap. If we were a very united front, it would be me and Chris and then, a tier down, these other people.

LLOYD (*cocreator*): It puts a different pressure on the staff members than you would have on most shows, but it could be said that they're coming out of this experience with an extra level of training, because they lived in two different systems.

KO (*writer / executive producer*): Their tastes are pretty far apart, which was part of why the show worked. But it really was like working on two different shows.

HIGGINBOTHAM (*writer / executive producer*): This is a fucking cakewalk. There's dysfunction so much greater than we've experienced here. Neither one of them is an asshole or credit hog. We're home at dinner most of the time. We get to have lives and be successful. There so much gratitude around what we had and the fun that came with that.

BOWEN (*Claire Dunphy*): It's Daddy and Daddy, and they're mythical to all of us. And then they got divorced and, as with any parent, they become people. They're just two humans who couldn't get along. It was exactly that.

Perfect Pairs

So exactly how do two writing rooms work?

Every week, one showrunner has the run of the place, while the other handles the stage. After the table read, typically on Wednesdays, the on-set showrunner comes to the writers' room, gives feedback, which often includes the question, "What are we caring about?" and then quickly hightails it out of Dodge and back to stage 5. The other showrunner rewrites their script with writers for the remainder of the week.

HIGGINBOTHAM (*writer / executive producer*): If you're in the room breaking the story and have been since the first idea came up, and thought through it, and asked a million questions about it, you think there's something there to care about. But when you're not in the room that broke it, it's harder to latch on.

Over the course of a season, the writers go back and forth between showrunners.

LLOYD (*cocreator*): It's not like we have a blue team and a red team and they're always criticizing each other's work. You can be on the blue team one day and the red team the next. The teams are constantly shifting.

WALSH (*writer / executive producer*): Whichever room you're in is the correct room that's making stories the right way, and you can't believe what they're doing across the hall. Then two weeks later, you've switched and you're like, "Oh, those people over there. They're completely off. We've got it figured out."

ZUKER (*writer / executive producer*): Both rooms can be fun, and both rooms can be hell. I definitely know if someone's working in one room for a couple of episodes; often they're eager to go into the other room.

Choosing teams comes with its own challenges, however.

MCCRAY (*script coordinator*): It's like gym class in high school. It can get weird because hard feelings can happen.

WALSH (*writer / executive producer*): I'm sure we've all taken turns feeling like we were on the outside of the staff.

CHAN (*writers' assistant*): I think there are definitely two factions because the same group of people are always in Chris's room and in Steve's room starting out the season. They try to mix it up, but then those writers come back into their original rooms.

The writers' room subdivides into one team breaking a new story and a second room revising that week's table read. When they finish revisions, they lock the shooting script so filming can begin the following Monday.

Certain plotlines remain with one showrunner.

WALSH (*writer / executive producer*): Gloria's sauce business. You'll never see a Steve episode with that or a Chris episode with the Nerp offices. I don't think Chris has ever set foot, story-wise, in a Nerp office.

CORRIGAN (*writer / executive producer*): I don't think Chris has ever said the word *Nerp*.

If a writer believes in an idea, they have been known to work the system.

PLONSKER (*writers' assistant*): If you don't get any traction in one room, then the next week you're a brand-new writer with a brand-new idea. You can change notes or mix characters around.

BURDITT (*writer / executive producer*): It's like going to Dad after Mom said, "No."

Each environment has its own flavor.

RICHMAN (*writer / executive producer*): You can't say one is better or easier than the other. They're both really valid, and they've assembled a staff that can meet the challenge of different kinds of storytelling. Your job is to serve the leader, so you try to get into the head of whoever is steering the ship and build that with him.

Lloyd's room mirrors a popular college course that always fills up as soon as class registration opens. The professor, with his scholarly acumen and biting wit, can be rigid at times, but mostly challenges his students and mentors their efforts.

LLOYD (*cocreator*): Somebody comes in with an idea, and then four to eight hours later or even three days later, it's ping-ponged its way through different people's brains into something great. No one can take full credit for it. None of us are smart enough, creative enough, or good enough on our own to have come up with what we now have. It runs through everybody.

WRUBEL (*writer / executive producer*): Chris went to Yale. Everything he approaches is slightly more academic. He grew up in the shadow of his father. I think that he's probably always navigating his dad's voice in his head.

GARDEZI (*staff writer*): Chris writes all his scripts by hand on a legal pad, which is really amazing to see. We were talking once about the fear of what would happen if your episode got lost. He, in a very matter-of-fact way, said, "I would rewrite it." We asked, "What do you mean?" He replied, "Every script that I write, I memorize." He thought that it was something that everyone could do.

He adheres to a stricter regimen for conflict and resolution. Every story beat has a purpose.

WALSH (*writer / executive producer*): In season 1's "Travels with Scout," Paul and I were in the editing bay watching the episode. About two-thirds of the way through, Chris says, "Please hit Pause." The editor paused the scene. Chris asked, "What do I hope happens in this TV show?" No one had an answer, which was his way of pointing out the characters really didn't have a drive at that point and that was why it wasn't moving forward. It was very uncomfortable. I never made that mistake the same way again, because I didn't want to live through that twice.

In season 3's "Virgin Territory," Lily's doll gets broken. Phil drives Lily, Haley, and Alex to the mall for doll triage. In the car, Alex makes a biting barb that clues Phil in that Haley's lost her virginity. Phil feels traumatized and Haley, guilty and chagrined. In talking about the doll during its treatment, father and daughter indirectly navigate through their issues.

LLOYD (*cocreator*): When Phil talks to Haley through a broken doll and lets her know that he's struggling with her having lost her virginity, but he will always be her dad, that to me is both complex and highly emotional. It's one of my favorite scenes that we've done. That's always the thing that I'm aiming toward.

Everyone contributes ideas and elements to the story cauldron.

WRUBEL (*writer / executive producer*): Chris is happy to take his time and little by little, chip away, chip away, chip away until they've got something. He would always say, "We need seven good ideas to make an episode." He wanted a stew of good ideas he could build as a master puzzle maker into a well-constructed story that drove to a great ending.

CORRIGAN (*writer / executive producer*): When you had a story come out of Chris's room, you knew what you were writing. You knew what the scenes were and what the structure of those scenes were for the most part.

KO (*writer / executive producer*): Even when you thought you were done and the episode was ready to be shipped, he'd ask if there was one more twist to be had. And there usually was. It forced you to step up your game in a great way.

Taking that next step in a story can take time.

MCCRAY (*script coordinator*): We'd go forty-five minutes of silence with people sitting there and wondering what's going on. Like, "Why aren't we talking?" It's Chris ruminating things over.

Much as every class has a clown, Lloyd's room had O'Shannon the first five years, a longtime colleague from Frasier who liked to play comedian to Lloyd's straight man.

O'SHANNON (*writer / executive producer*): I was a bit intimidated when I met him. I heard he was very quiet, very austere. But it turned out that Chris is as playful as I am. He has a very silly side to him, and he can break down giggling. When I learned that, it became my daily goal to make him laugh.

LLOYD (*cocreator*): He'd play this character who was an overeager staff member that wanted to be by my side and do funny bits, but be super deferential. I would always placate him, but always find excuses to move away from him. He called himself "my show buddy." During *Frasier,* he ended up writing an entire song called "Showbuddies," renting out a studio and doing a giant production number.

O'SHANNON (*writer / executive producer*): One time, I got up to leave the room for something, and I announced that Chris would be in charge while I was not here. And Chris quietly said, "I'm always in charge." And I said, "So you're in charge when I'm here, but also when I'm not here, right?" And he said, "Yes," and I turned to the room and said, "Well, you heard it—while I'm gone, Chris is in charge." I started to leave, but he stopped me to correct me, and it went around like that for a while. That's the kind of thing we could do for half an hour. I'm surprised he never fired me really.

Levitan's room felt less like a classroom and more like a campus co-op gathering, everyone gathered around, talking freely.

LEVITAN (*cocreator*): I like stories that come from real life or at least feel like they do. I want people to watch and think, "That could actually happen," or even better, "That's happened to me."

WRUBEL (*writer / executive producer*): Steve is less patient with chipping away. He wants to take a giant stab at the piece of marble immediately, so he knows what he's looking at.

HIGGINBOTHAM (*writer / executive producer*): What I like about Steve's storytelling is you're dealing with the consequences of a big inciting incident. And while you don't build to a bigger comedic scene at the end, you are building to an emotional resolve about something significant that has happened. Chris's and Steve's styles are so different in that way.

MCCRAY (*script coordinator*): Steve's a very visual person. We use this program, Scapple, that puts digital index cards up on a giant screen so you can see scenes and story beats and move them around like in *Minority Report*. He needs to be able to see the story in front of him.

PLONSKER (*writers' assistant*): Steve's more a fly on the wall. Everyone's talking and joking around. Once something starts to gain momentum, Steve will perk up, hear the idea, either stoke the flame or pick out the elements he really likes and continue moving forward. It's growth from the writers, and he corrals the energy.

WALSH (*writer / executive producer*): Steve is less adamant about endings making stories. We've done some episodes that had their high point early and we made our peace with it. "Career Day" [season 4] has a funny scene at the top where Phil's presenting the world of real estate to Luke's classroom. He speaks to himself on video and winds up making a fool of himself.* We spent a day or two trying to put Phil's presentation scene at the end of the episode, but eventually decided that it wanted to be at the beginning. To Steve's credit, he's gutsy that way.

WRUBEL (*writer / executive producer*): In my episode "Door to Door" [season 3], he had this vision of intercutting everybody going door-to-door for different purposes in the middle of the show. I was against it and he was insistent on it, and after the show was done, it was a pretty fun section. I was wrong, and he was right.

WALLS (*writer / supervising producer*): This is so annoying, but I heard this phrase "burstiness" on some podcast. Basically, burstiness is in a room where people are pitching ideas and you're creatively building off one another. I think when it comes to rapid-fire pitching or putting ideas out there, Steve's room is probably looser and closer to burstiness.

CORRIGAN (*writer / executive producer*): In rewrites with Steve, a lot of stuff could be thrown out and rewritten because it wasn't figured out to begin with. So you leave, you come up with a lot, you fill in a lot of blanks, and the chances of hitting the target on those is a lot smaller than it is with Chris because you haven't talked about it.

LEVITAN (*cocreator*): I like to leave room for writers to discover little side trips that are interesting or insightful. I don't want a story to feel like it's been painted by numbers. Sometimes I like or maybe need to see how an episode flows before every beat is locked in.

RICHMAN (*writer / executive producer*): Steve could have a scene in the middle of the episode that doesn't advance the story, but emotionally he

---

* Walsh realized later he was inspired by the 1973 Albert Brooks comedy album, *Comedy Minus One,* in which Brooks gives one side of a comedy routine and the listener is supposed to read the other part of the act. It's an interactive exercise in futility because the timing purposefully never works out between the listener and Brooks.

thinks it's important to have those characters do whatever they're doing emotionally. It's up to you to figure it out, because you can't pitch on that. You can have an idea on what they want to say, but you have to dig around and figure out how to write the scene.

WALSH (*writer / executive producer*): "The Incident" [season 1] was an episode that Steve really believed in. He broke it loosely. The staff was afraid we were going to have to rewrite it because it didn't make sense to anyone and very few people had faith in it. Steve went off to his office, wrote it, brought it back, and we were like, "Crap, this is good." We were completely wrong to doubt it. It was pretty amazing.

Levitan and Lloyd have the final say about their own pluses and minuses within their spaces.

LEVITAN (*cocreator*): I think I have a good sense of the big picture of things. I feel like I have a fairly good gut instinct about what an audience wants to see and a pretty strong bullshit filter. I don't like fake moments. I try to stomp them out wherever possible. I think I'm a fair person and that I treat people with respect. I'm not one of those showrunners who rules by fear. I hope to be well liked among the people I work with, and that goes from the intern to the stars of the show.

LLOYD (*cocreator*): My strength is in storytelling. You're listening to a bunch of ideas, synthesizing them, and saying, "Okay, we're going to take it in this direction." But you're trying to still encourage people by saying, "I liked this idea because . . . ," or "I thought it was a better idea because . . . ," sort of marshal that along to get the best from everyone without alienating anyone. That's not a thing you're called upon to do in life that much. But it's a thing I've done for twenty-five years.

LEVITAN (*cocreator*): I think I could improve on my focus, especially lately, as my life has taken some twists and turns. That's been an issue for me. One of the things that people make fun of me for is having this weird, they call it the "bad smell face," where if I don't like something, you can see it on my face. I'm often rolling something through my head and thinking how it feels to me and don't realize I'm doing it. People don't always feel supported when they pitch something and I make that face. I'll also have a certain tone, which was the tone of my household growing up, which was direct. It sometimes conveys much more negativity than I ever intended. I'm working on that.

LLOYD (*cocreator*): I have been accused of being stingy with praise. I think my only justification is my focus is elsewhere, but it is part of the job, too, to encourage people who are really giving their all to the show. It's a team effort, and as a person at the top, you have to be cognizant of how hard people work and absolutely reward and thank them for that. They're making your show better and putting money in your pocket, and you should thank them. If I failed at that, then it's a valid criticism.

This Old Wagon

In the pilot, Manny gets distracted in the middle of a soccer game by the sight of Brenda Feldman, a sixteen-year-old girl who works at a novelty photo kiosk. After the game, Jay drives his family to the mall so that Manny, the aspiring lothario, can attempt (and fail) to woo his Juliet. That simple car ride became the litmus test for hundreds of car scenes to follow over the course of the series.

LEVITAN (*cocreator*): Cars are where many important conversations take place. It's where so much of modern life is lived, especially in Los Angeles.

WRUBEL (*writer / executive producer*): We didn't want to be in houses all the time. In a world in which people go from house to house or house to job, you have to drive.

LLOYD (*cocreator*): I don't agree. You're always looking for stories to have some urgency to them. Out of 120 episodes I've overseen, 118 take place in one day or half a day, because the shorter time span lends urgency. A car scene does the same thing. You feel the urgency about getting on with your goal. It's a luxury of a single-camera show.

Many television shows use cars for action: a fast getaway, backseat fornicating, throwing a body in a trunk, freewheeling. On Modern Family, *car scenes mostly serve as a vehicle for conversation.*

WRUBEL (*writer / executive producer*): They're like these weird little one-act plays that take place within a confined space.

BURRELL (*Phil Dunphy*): You get to focus on the nuance of dialogue. Sometimes, I feel like they're the best part of an episode because it's so contained and focused. There's no expectation of movement or anything kinetic. It feels like there's room for a little bit of awkward silence or, nerdy actor term, *having a beat.*

HYLAND (*Haley Dunphy*): I tend to like them because we'll always somehow start singing and dancing in the car, kind of a like a road trip.

RODRIGUEZ (*Manny Delgado*): You have to pretend you're driving. You have to check the mirrors and do the proper things you do when you're driving. Obviously, the steering and wheels are all locked. You can't really steer. If you do try to move it, it will lock and you're like, "Damn, I hope they didn't see that." I remember someone telling me over the walkie-talkie, "Rico, you didn't put the car in drive." I didn't even know that was a thing. I was twelve or something.

Any TV viewer can spot a green screen background used in a car scene: the flat-looking cars, the poorly lit backgrounds, cars in the background disappearing and reappearing, the appearance of cowboys or alien ships like they did to parody car scenes in the movie Airplane. *It distracts from actors and conversations.*

WINER (*director / executive producer*): There was some debate before we started shooting the series about how to execute the car scenes. For me, no matter how good the technology, I can always tell when a driving scene is being faked on a soundstage. After doing several camera tests, we decided there was no replacement for the extra effort it takes to actually tow cars around the streets with the actors inside. The feeling of reality we were going for with the show required it.

Oftentimes, production employs a car mounted onto a tow rig, driving down a street.

LISA STATMAN (*director / assistant director*): When we shot the pilot, in order to capture the documentary style and get all the coverage at once, the DP, David Hennings, came up with lipstick cams that we placed inside Jay's car.

TOBY TUCKER (*camera operator*): We rigged little cameras on the dashboard in different quadrants of the car. There were no camera operators.

STATMAN (*director / assistant director*): Because it was an SUV, we could put the sound mixer in the back, turn on the cameras, and have Ed "free-drive" [not tied to a rig].

FERGUSON (*Mitchell Pritchett*): No one can really communicate with us. I felt like we were in charge of the show in a way that we had never been before. It's very intimate.

STATMAN (*director / assistant director*): Baggs [James Bagdonas] revised Hennings's design by spreading three cameras on a hood mount.

SPILLER (*director*): There's a tunnel shot straight through the window and then two side angles—one through the driver's side and one through the passenger window that get all the coverage without ever moving the camera, mounts, or lights. We'd then drive the rig off the lot and around the studio neighborhood until we have the scene.

STATMAN (*director / assistant director*): A four-page scene with five actors in the car would traditionally take a minimum of five to six hours. On *Modern Family,* Baggs made it so we could finish that same scene in roughly an hour, two tops if there were technical problems. And it looked as good.

SPILLER (*director*): These driving shots look great, but they're a pain in the ass to shoot. Everyone sitting on the camera car is under a tent of heavy black film fabric. You're breathing fumes from the generator.

HIGGINBOTHAM (*writer / executive producer*): There's exhaust coming out of the truck. It stinks like crazy. If you do long shoots on hot days, you get off feeling you need a little water and lung cleansing.

ZUKER (*writer / executive producer*): It's really fucking uncomfortable. It sounds like Hollywood people complaining, but you're sitting on these corrugated metal benches, traveling backward.

WRUBEL (*writer / executive producer*): That truck was a gateway to vomiting, although I never did.

In the car, due to sound constraints, actors have to make do with the elements.

BOWEN (*Claire Dunphy*): It's not fun when Sound says you have to turn off the AC or heat. It turns into a coffin in there of either heat or cold. Are you kidding me? We just drove past a fire engine, helicopter, and garbage truck, but we have to turn off the AC or heat to keep the sound pure?

Directors find them boring, too.

MANCUSO (*director*): Cars are as much a character of the show as the interviews are, but when I see it in a script, I go, "Ugh." They're preset cameras. Instant interaction is hard. I don't like talking into a microphone to an actor. I like talking face-to-face. It's my least favorite thing in the show, to be honest.

HIGGINBOTHAM (*writer / executive producer*): You're only honing performance and making sure you're getting the right energy and build for the scene.

Sometimes the actors catch a quick twenty winks.

WINTER (*Alex Dunphy*): People used to laugh at me because I have narcolepsy. It used to be much worse when I was younger. We'd be in the car and sometimes I would fall asleep in between takes or if we were driving back to stage on the rig. That was entertaining for my costars.

HIGGINBOTHAM (*writer / executive producer*): For an episode I'd written in season 5 called "The Late Show," we were shooting for an entire day. The entire third act took place in a restaurant. It was thirteen pages. Shooting ended with Ty and Julie in a car. I think we put them in a car at 2:15 in the morning, fourteen hours after we started. As we were driving and setting up the shot, they both fell asleep. And it was adorable watching the two of them. They were talking to each other, trying to stay awake, and then they both gave up and closed their eyes until we could find a place to shoot the scene.

BURRELL (*Phil Dunphy*): It was neither the first or last time that Julie and I have fallen asleep near each other in between shots. Especially shots when we're in bed. We're big fans of having a nap. We've both dozed off multiple times in between shots.

BOWEN (*Claire Dunphy*): We talk about naps the way some people talk about sex. We'll whisper, "Did you get it?" He's like, "Yeah. I don't want to make you jealous, but I caught like ten in the corner." "You didn't." "I did."

In between takes, the actors have time to kill to talk with one another.

BOWEN (*Claire Dunphy*): There's a very lovely sense of intimacy you get from being in a car with one other actor because you don't often get that feeling that there's no crew around even though there's cameras everywhere.

WINTER (*Alex Dunphy*): It's a good time to have conversations and make jokes without the hustle and bustle of what's going on onstage.

FERGUSON (*Mitchell Pritchett*): I totally agree. Some of my favorite moments have been in the car with some of my cast members. It feels like we've secluded ourselves into our own little bubble and we get to enjoy each other. It feels very free.

BOWEN (*Claire Dunphy*): We'll forget that we're mic'd, though. Then all of a sudden, someone will come in on the little voice-of-God microphone and laugh or add something.

HYLAND (*Haley Dunphy*): Yeah. Someone talks on the God mic, and you're like, "Oh, fuck, I hope I wasn't talking shit about anybody that can hear me right now."

HIGGINBOTHAM (*writer / executive producer*): I remember I shot with Ed and Sofía in a car in Burbank. They were chatting away wondering why they had to come to Burbank. Why do they have to drive all the way across town for this one little scene? And I'm thinking, "Do you know we're listening to you right now? We all had to drive over here, too."

ZUKER (*writer / executive producer*): In an early episode, there was a car scene between Ed and Rico. On the way back, Ed starts coaching Rico. He says, "Rico, point in the script where you think you get the idea to ask me this question?" And Rico points out the line. Ed says, "Nope, I said something two lines ago that got Manny thinking. That's where that question started to germinate in your head. The next two lines you're thinking about the question and then you ask it." He communicated to this eleven-year-old boy this fundamental thing in acting where you're not just acting on your line. It's a buildup of emotion.

VERGARA (*Gloria Delgado-Pritchett*): He always takes time that nobody else takes to really guide them. I think Rico's acting is a part of Ed's teaching.

LEVITAN (*cocreator*): I think that I picked up things as a director from listening to him.

Ed O'Neill's Book of Acting

Sandy Meisner. Lee Strasberg. Stella Adler—elite acting teachers all. None of their theories, however, come with the calm and consciousness of Ed O'Neill.

Mention Ed O'Neill's Book of Acting to anyone on set, and they give that knowing look followed by a laugh. Over the course of eleven years, the cast has learned and practiced what Burrell refers to as "a Zen tone on how to do the least amount possible in your work." Over time, Burrell has compiled the master rule list of inertia, which, for the first and last time, he and O'Neill share in their entirety here.

RULE #1: IS THERE ANY REASON THIS SCENE CAN'T BE IN A CAR?

O'NEILL (*Jay Pritchett*): If you sit in a car, number one, you sit. Always sit. If you can sit, sit.

BURRELL (*Phil Dunphy*): *When we're acting in a car, we're always shot from the waist up, so Ed's in shorts and flip-flops, even if he's in a tuxedo on a way to a wedding. He can have his coffee below the frame, too. And there's no blocking, meaning there's no rehearsal. You get in the car and start filming.*

Rule #2: Why stand when you can sit? Why sit when you can lie down? Why lie down when you can be off-screen?

O'NEILL (*Jay Pritchett*): It's an old military thing I adapted. I often give a director a reason like, "I think it's more casual if I'm seated." The director will say, "You should probably stand halfway through the scene and walk over there, for variety." I may try it and then say, "That doesn't work for me. It's awkward. I think the whole scene plays better if I'm seated." They usually go along after you try it their way once.

Rule #3: When your dialogue's over, find an exit.

BURRELL (*Phil Dunphy*): Ed'll finish a line of dialogue, slap a table as if he's putting punctuation on the end, like, "All right then, I've made my point," and then exit.

O'NEILL (*Jay Pritchett*): *If you get out of a shot, you're done. If you stay in the shot, you stay in the next setup. If they have to cover it from another angle, and they will, and you're still standing there, you're in the shot. Whereas if you finish, you're gone.*

Rule #4: Always go back to your trailer.

BURRELL (*Phil Dunphy*): When a scene's over and we're going to the next setup, they'll ask if you want to stay or go back to your trailer. Ed's philosophy is always go back. You'll be more comfortable in your trailer.

O'NEILL (*Jay Pritchett*): *If they see you on set, they're relaxed. They can take their time with whatever it is they have to do. But if you leave, you're gone. Now they get a little nervous. He or she's not here.*

Plus, you need to get away from it. You can't stay there all day long. It's tiring.

RULE #5: ALWAYS PLAY A SICK PERSON.

O'NEILL (*Jay Pritchett*): Because then you can lie down.

RULE #6: ABS (ALWAYS BE SHOOTING).

BURRELL (*Phil Dunphy*): When you're getting ready to do a scene, the director will ask, "Do you guys want to do a read through?" Ed will say no. Then they'll say, "Do you want to rehearse it?" Ed will say, "Let's just shoot the rehearsal." And then when you shoot the rehearsal, Ed will say, "Okay, I think we got it."

O'NEILL (*Jay Pritchett*): *When you come to set, you know the scene. We don't get paid to rehearse. If they're going to ask, "Do you want to rehearse one?" I always say, "Why don't you shoot it?"*

RULE #7: IF YOU HAVE NO LINES, NEVER REHEARSE.

O'NEILL (*Jay Pritchett*): I never rehearse if I don't have dialogue. I say, do it with the second team.

BURRELL (*Phil Dunphy*): *Unless you're dancing. He holds out a caveat for dancing.*

O'NEILL (*Jay Pritchett*): *Especially if you're not a dancer. That's obvious. And if you have no dialogue, don't get wired. They always want to wire you in case you utter some sound. It takes a couple of minutes to wire. I always tell them, "I'm not going to utter a sound. I'm not speaking."*

RULE #8: WHEN YOU'VE SHOT A SCENE FOR A WHILE AND THE DIRECTOR SAYS, "LET'S GO AGAIN," ALWAYS ASK, "WHERE FROM?"

O'NEILL (*Jay Pritchett*): A director loves to see a scene all the way through without stopping. I know we have the beginning of the scene, and they know it. But we may not have the end. So every time there's a reset, I'll say, "From where?" You keep saying it, and it gets the director thinking, "We probably have the beginning." If it's too many takes, sometimes I'll say, "Okay, one more," and I'll go either too low in volume or too big on the take. In video village, they'll go, "He's done. Check it. Move on."

RULE #9: IF THERE'S FOOD IN THE SCENE, ALWAYS BE FINISHING YOUR LAST BITE.

O'NEILL (*Jay Pritchett*): It's dangerous to eat and talk. I take an empty fork or spoon and put it in my mouth. On action, I'll take it out and start chewing, like I just put it in with food, but there's no food. I'm not eating anything. Get the napkin. Wipe. But I'm not eating anything.

BURRELL (*Phil Dunphy*): *If you go back and look through eleven years of filming Ed's plate, Ed has it set up where he's essentially at the end of the meal. He's developed a masterful fake chew. It's the Daniel Day-Lewis of fake chews.*

RULE #10: HOLD THE BABY.

O'NEILL (*Jay Pritchett*): If you're holding the baby, you go home with the baby. That's not always true, but you try.

Rule #11: Always ask about a neighborhood's restrictions.

O'NEILL (*Jay Pritchett*): It's nice to know you have to be out by a certain time. Hopefully there's a curfew. That's true in most neighborhoods. It's mentally relaxing to know we have to finish by seven, that we can't go further. Also, it's nice to know location stuff like flight patterns of airports. These are things I think about.

Rule #12: Always palm your props.

O'NEILL (*Jay Pritchett*): Oftentimes, when you're putting something in or trying to take it out of your pocket, like coins or keys, it doesn't go smoothly, and son of a bitch, that's another couple of takes. So I palm it. I have my hand in my pocket. I act like I'm fishing for it, but I've already got it. So it's smooth and it saves time. Ty loves that because he's into magic.

Rule #13: Too many takes makes it worse.

O'NEILL (*Jay Pritchett*): Usually you should have it at four or five. After that, you start to get stale. I have done takes where I didn't have it and then around take eight or nine, I've got it.

Rule #14: Light every inch.

O'NEILL (*Jay Pritchett*): It helps not to be confined to a specific narrow box of space. Because then you're thinking too much again. If you're in a general well-lit area, then they can pretty much see you.

BURRELL (*Phil Dunphy*): Ed believes in lighting every aspect of the room so wherever you walk in a scene, it's still usable on-camera. You don't have to stop and relight it.

Rule #15: Paralysis by analysis.

O'NEILL (*Jay Pritchett*): I was a handball player. They used to say when you were trying to figure out a guy's game too much, you were overthinking things. You can overthink anything in a scene. The perfection aspect can ruin it. It wears people out, and it's silly. Keep it simple and relax a little bit.

Do You Believe in Magic

Inside a nondescript room in building 104 on the Fox lot, *Modern Family's* cast, writers, producers, and invited guests have assembled for a lunchtime table read of Corrigan's and Walsh's "Paris" script, the series' last family vacation episode. While settling in, the cast partakes from another amazing lunch buffet whipped up by Stephen Brenes and his assistant, Jesse Cervantes. Last week, they served dim sum as an 11:00 a.m. snack. Come on! How everyone on cast and crew doesn't weigh four hundred pounds, I will never know.

The cast sits behind a row of adjoining laminated school tables with that unmistakable fusion maple color. Folded paper name tags mark everyone's place.

The audience, seated in two sections of metal folding chairs, about five rows deep, consists of perhaps seventy-five total. Beckham sits nearby with his kids. Rodriguez's sister and mother, regulars on set, take their seats. The writers sit together off to the far right. Every seat has a script to follow along.

This being a Levitan episode, he sits up front. Lloyd hangs back by the door. Vergara opens her script, knowing that Rodriguez will have highlighted her lines for her, like he has done since season 1. Rodriguez thinks Vergara would laugh at the ritual's origins. "She's sometimes late to table reads. So one particular day, she was running late. I know how she highlights her scripts because I sit next to her. So I highlighted and dog-eared it and she was ready to go. She comes in and goes, 'Oh my God, I have to highlight my script.' She looked and saw it was already highlighted. She looked at me because she knew I did it and thanked me. The next week at the table read, she looks at her script and it's not highlighted. I didn't think to because she was early this time. She said, 'Rico, hurry and do my script.' Since then, I highlight it every week. I love Sofía so much. I would do anything for her." Vergara likens it less to a ritual and more to a tradition. "I used to make my son, Manolo, do little things like that to make him feel like he was working. Eleven years later, Rico knows it's his job now."

The cast reads the script in real time. Today's favorite mispronounced Vergara word? *Squirm,* which she turns into "squeem."

Upon the reading's conclusion, O'Neill, ever the cheerleader, gives his usual stamp of approval. "It's simple. It's funny. It's smart." Someone brings in a surprise birthday cake for Ferguson. He gives a short emotional speech, reflecting, "This is the best job I ever had, which I know sets an unfair precedent to the spin-off." Everyone cracks up and then disperses soon thereafter.

Thirty minutes later, the writers have converged around the outer conference table in the writers' room to hear Lloyd share his notes. Levitan sits at the opposite end.

In the script, Claire's storyline revolves around a torrid affair she had thirty years ago with a Frenchman, Guy, in which they promised to meet again on this day, a date she's long forgotten. Lloyd questions Claire only saying to Guy, "Nice to see you again," and then turning away from this man and his broken heart. "I also don't believe Claire says, 'Oh my God, this poor guy has been in love with me for thirty years,'" says Lloyd. "She doesn't know that. He could have been married for twenty-five years. He's embarrassed because she isn't leaning into the moment."

The biggest issue Lloyd has concerns Mitchell and Cam's story. "What are the stakes?" He likes Mitchell being instantly recognized as an American by his clothes. But then what? And Cam discovers another Fizbo clown, resembling his own creation. Did he steal Cam's act? Did Cam steal his act? Is there any way to care more about that story, to give it more stakes?

"One of the tricky things here is the metaphor being a comedian stealing jokes," says Levitan. "It's the ultimate taboo. Cam gets to go on and essentially kill and then someone steals his jokes as opposed to you're about to go on, you're nervous and getting ready, and then he looks over and there's somebody there who's already him [playing Fizbo]. It would ruin that experience that he built up in his head. He wants people in 'Paris' to experience this."

And with that, Lloyd disappears like Batman into the night, except the clock reads 2:00 p.m. Levitan splits the room into two. In "the big room" goes Levitan, Walsh, Zuker, Lloyd's brother Stephen, and Morgan Murphy to revise "Paris." This room, incidentally, with its two glass walls, one emblazoned with the Pritchett's Closets & Blinds logo, doubles as Jay's business place.

In the B room, a smaller space, like the kids' table at Thanksgiving, Richman, Walls, Higginbotham, and Vali Chandrasekaran work on an upcoming story. Burditt works alone in his somewhat bare office on a script that Lloyd asked him to cowrite with him for next week's table read.

Lloyd hasn't taken a script credit in several years, making this a big deal. One would assume he will have one more for the finale. Levitan will write a script this year as well, a similar situation and big deal. Although not writing together, they leave as they came in, creating story, emotion, and hopefully laughs.

Lloyd's script, "Legacy," holds a Kid Gavilan bolo punch—the death of Phil's dad, Frank. The show has dealt with death before, outside and within the family (the Dunphys' elderly neighbor Walt and DeDe Pritchett). Lloyd wants to handle this one differently as well as the message behind it. "We were looking for some weightier events to deal with in our final season," recalls Lloyd. "It was an opportunity to examine how Phil got to be Phil, but also to bring a new perspective to Phil's penchant for silliness—that it's actually more philosophically based. The world, and people, need a cheerleader, and Phil knows he's good at that, and is happy to provide that, even if it means suppressing some of his own emotions to that end."

Lloyd denies it has anything to do with his dad, in the conscious mind anyway. Burditt concurs. "Chris used what he felt best fit with Frank and Phil as characters," says Burditt. "But we didn't discuss our own personal feelings. Maybe that's the Catholic in us." Lloyd handled two of the episode's stories, that of Phil and Frank and one involving Mitchell and Claire. "Just like I always prefer playing basketball with players that are better than me, I love writing with someone who can write circles around me," shares Burditt.

The ending, a treatise on life and wonder, comes from a feature film idea Lloyd has kept in his back pocket for years. "It's based upon a news article I read years ago," confides Lloyd. "It occurred to me it might make for a nice way to honor a father who has passed." Burditt sums it up more directly. "Reading Chris's Phil-Frank scenes slayed me. It made me miss my dad."

The script goes under several revisions on its way to the finish line. In a few instances, he moves scenes around. The biggest change, however, comes with the story. "In Claire-Mitchell, it was to get a bit more comedy and urgency into their drive—a real desire to catch their dad and step into the conceit of them being detectives trying to put clues together to catch a criminal," Lloyd shares. "In Gloria-Cam, it was to see Cam's nemesis earlier, creating drive, and to streamline the argument between Gloria and Cam over approach." And therein ends the master class for the day.

Back in the big room, Levitan and company slowly work their way through revisions. Levitan comes to a conclusion about which way he'd like to go with the Fizbo setup. He tells the room, "I think it's, 'I'm about to go on. Someone's doing my act.' I think that moment will land more. He's looking at a clown who looks exactly like him. The metaphor is the comedian who comes on before, stealing or doing all your jokes."

Elsewhere, small changes in the room pertain to dialogue.

```
                    OLD SCENE


                     MITCHELL
         We're all so proud of you, Dad. I'm
         glad that we get to be here for this.


Jay crosses off to deal with the luggage.


                      CLAIRE
                (Calling after Jay)
         Wouldn't miss it for the world.
                (Then to Mitchell)
         We can bail on the reception, though,
         right?
```

NEW SCENE

                    MITCHELL
          We're all so proud of you, Dad.

                    CLAIRE
          We love that we get to be here for
          this.

Jay crosses off to deal with the luggage.

In the new version, both of Jay's kids show pride in their father. Claire's feigned and slightly cold disinterest disappears.

A big debate in the room involves a single joke. Levitan begins by framing the skeleton of Jay taking in the occasion of his winning a prestigious closet award. "I wish my old man could be here to see this. Funny, he stormed the beaches of Normandy and I'm getting the closet award. Who's the bigger hero now?"

The room comes alive as everyone throws in suggestions about a new punchline. Some get ignored, some talked over, others considered and then dropped. Everyone wants to be the one to land the joke. It feels like an episode of *Match Game* with Gene Rayburn:

I wish my old man could be here to see this. Funny, he stormed the beaches of Normandy, and I'm getting the closet award, blank . . .

People shout out punchlines:

Two American heroes in one family.
We both left our mark in Europe.
This country brings out the best in both of us.
A couple of heroes.

The room grows quiet as everyone regroups. Suddenly, out of the blue, Walsh speaks up. "We keep topping each other. Who knows what Joe will do?" The room cracks up. Drop mic. Winner. Moving on, they try to come up with funny names of other closet businesses. The script already has *Heinrich Müler of Berlin's Closet-stadt, Susan Sasaki of Tokyo's Closets and Canned Whale Meat.* The room cleverly adds as possibilities *Warsaw Wardrobes, Finnish Unfinished Closets, Norway's Affordable Closets, and Das Closets.*

In the second room, most of the conversation revolves around Alex's plight, working for a non–environmentally friendly conglomerate and perhaps walking off into the sunset with her fireman ex-boyfriend. In a surprise, Arvin Fennerman, one of Haley's old lovers, will be returning for episode 15. Alex always had a thing for him. Perhaps Fennerman's scientific theory came to the wrong Dunphy conclusion? That remains to be seen. I have been told she will be quitting her corporate job to work on a scientific project with him. The rest remains a mystery. Levitan teases his appearance for me. "In creating a world of characters, it's nice to revisit some after a while because, as in life, people have a way of coming back, leading us to reflect on where we are in our lives since last seeing them."

The writers also talk about Mitchell and Cam's ultimate fate. Looks like through a series of circumstances, another baby lurks on their horizon. That requires a bigger house. And then wouldn't you know, Cam gets offered a job back in Kansas to coach football. The writers wonder aloud if for a cherry on top of all of their life changes, would it be funny if they see someone giving away a dog while driving to handle all of these problems and then adopt that, too?

They debate over timing. Should they find out about the baby at the end of episode 14 or the beginning of 15? In episode 15, their storyline involves looking for a new house while Phil stages theirs. No one knows about episode 16, but it could be a Haley episode, perhaps with Claire.

Just another day writing a hit TV show.

Caught in the Act

HALEY, ALEX, AND LUKE INTERVIEW

ALEX
It's our parents' anniversary so we're
surprising them with breakfast in
bed.

HALEY
They're impossible to buy for. We
think. We've never really tried.

LUKE
I was going to make them another
piece of macaroni art, but I just
wasn't feeling it this year.

INT. DUNPHY HOUSE—UPSTAIRS HALLWAY—MOMENTS
LATER

Carefully balancing the tray with fancy
china and a flower in a vase, the kids
quietly approach their parents' bedroom
door.

```
                    ALEX
                 (whispering)
            Okay, ready?


                    HALEY
            One, two, three . . .


     They throw open the door—


                    KIDS
            Surpriiiiaaaaaaaaah!!!


     Their enthusiasm immediately turns to
     horror.
```

WRUBEL (*writer / executive producer*): I think what was inspired is that it starts with sex. We didn't play into any of the tropes of debating sex. There was something surprising about that.

SPILLER (*director*): The whole episode hinges on the kids walking up to a door, opening it, and seeing something that will scar them forever.

RICHMAN (*writer / executive producer*): Oh my God, when they open that door. I don't know that people remember much else from the episode.

SPILLER (*director*): I feel like we were pushing the boundaries of prime-time TV standards and practices. Yet it's not a sexy moment. It's a funny and horrific moment for any parent that's had something similar happen. For the kids, of course, they'll never be the same again. I'm so thrilled with the way that worked.

The impetus for the scene came from an unfortunate experience Levitan and his wife had on a houseboat with a daughter.

LEVITAN (*cocreator*): I was on vacation with my whole family. My wife and I were engaged in adult activities in our bedroom, and all of a sudden we heard our door open, heard our daughter gasp, and then the door quickly closed.

MORTON (*executive producer*): I didn't have that happen in my life, but all kids wonder what the hell their parents are doing.

HYLAND (*Haley Dunphy*): I was fortunate enough to have it happen at a very, very, very young age. So it wasn't seared into my brain.

LEVITAN (*cocreator*): It was something that so many people have experienced. I experienced it as a kid and still remember it. I'm sure my daughter will never forget it.

SPILLER (*director*): The fact that it's one shot, the children innocently walking up to that door. That's what makes it real.

```
                    CLAIRE (O.S.)
               (horrified)
        No!

The kids scream and drop the tray. By
the time the camera swings over to Phil
and Claire in bed, they are frantically
covering themselves with the blanket. We
see nothing inappropriate: no side boob,
no outline of Phil's package, etc.


                    PHIL (O.S.)
        Nothing's happening!

The kids bump into each other, slam the
door, and run off back downstairs.
```

SPILLER (*director*): In my notes I wrote, "Make sure they have a tray that doesn't break because I want to be sure they can drop it." I also feared we wouldn't cut around to the kids seeing it.

GOULD (*Luke Dunphy*): There's this photo of us looking in for the first time during rehearsal to see our TV parents fake being naked in bed. All of us are turning around crying, laughing, and being horrified.

LEVITAN (*cocreator*): "Doing sex" is the way my son phrased it. Which I thought was off enough that it felt right.

> *It went in the script. The writers pushed the awkward situation with the sexual position, one of the first times if not the first time, seen on a family sitcom.*

SPILLER (*director*): They had to be doing it doggy-style.

HYLAND (*Haley Dunphy*): Michael? I did not know that about him. But wow.

SPILLER (*director*): It's more horrifying. And they could both turn and see the door instantly.

HYLAND (*Haley Dunphy*): It makes sense. With Claire's past, I feel like Claire would be the real leader in the bedroom. Sorry, Ty.

BOWEN (*Claire Dunphy*): You need to believe that these people are sexually into one another and they have chemistry. They're grown-ups. It also helps answer some questions about how these people get along. It excuses a lot of other quirky things they say or do.

WINTER (*Alex Dunphy*): We all got our own great jokes. I thought it was funny, my washing out my eyes.

LEVITAN (*cocreator*): One of the best jokes in the whole script—which, as I recall, is a Dan O'Shannon line—was when Luke says, "What were they doing?

and Alex says, "Nothing!" and then Luke says, "Whatever it was, it looks like Dad was winning." It's a killer joke. It never fails when I show that clip.

It did fail with one person, however—Gould. He had no idea what any of it meant.

GOULD (*Luke Dunphy*): I really didn't understand when I first walked in what the joke was. I thought they were supposed to be pretending to have sex. That's not sex.

BOWEN (*Claire Dunphy*): He's literally looking at us doing something that he doesn't know what it is. And he couldn't ask.

BURRELL (*Phil Dunphy*): We're doing fifteen takes with ten-year-olds and putting their parents and guardians in that position of having to talk them through what was happening.

RICHMAN (*writer / executive producer*): I remember giving Ty a line in the interview. Claire's saying she feels terrible, and Ty says, "They weren't there when we started." And then I gave him the line, "In fact, you weren't even there when we started."

Intimacy on a TV or film set, in front of a bunch of union workers and cameras, doesn't radiate sexy.

BOWEN (*Claire Dunphy*): Whenever they do naked stuff, there's nothing that could be less sexy. There's nipple covers to keep you from seeing nipples. There's a boob cover if you're supposedly naked or in bed and they don't want to see anything. I can't stop myself from drawing smiley faces on them or a happy and a sad face like a drama and comedy mask because they're so dumb.

BURRELL (*Phil Dunphy*): That scene is less awkward than having an actual sex scene, which I've had the misfortune of having to do a few times in my career, as has Julie. When you're doing a still version of it, it's less awkward, but you're still hanging out in flesh junk bags.

BOWEN (*Claire Dunphy*): Some flesh-colored sock over his business. You get to this point where you're lying there wearing your happy-and-sad-face boob covers going, "This is so dumb. It's so fun, but boy, is it dumb." We can get the giggles pretty good.

RICHMAN (*writer / executive producer*): I found them to be extremely protective of each other, like a couple.

BURRELL (*Phil Dunphy*): In one of those takes, I accidentally ended up taking the whole sheet with me, and Julie was left wearing nothing but her flesh bikini. I had to reevaluate my quality as a teammate. I apologized profusely and re-strategized.

BOWEN (*Claire Dunphy*): We would take breaks in shooting, somewhat in that position, but not consciously, like I would fall to the side and he'd be sitting there with his flesh-colored sock on. At some point, I said, "I'm so glad that this is you. There are about one million people that doing this with would be horrible." With him, it's another day at the office. Never once have I felt degraded by any of those scenes because there's always so much humor, and Ty's the greatest person alive.

The buildup and payoff of one famous scene, that takes up almost this entire chapter, lasts less than thirty seconds. It occurred three minutes into the story, meaning the writers had nineteen more to fill.

WRUBEL (*writer / executive producer*): It was challenging structurally to tell that story with this giant event at the top. What happens after that? It got a little talky without a lot happening. We spent some time trying to figure it out. I still think the best scene is the first scene, but all the writers contributed, and Steve was open as to what the episode would be after the big opening.

RICHMAN (*writer / executive producer*): You break a big story with four or five characters. Somebody isn't handled yet, so you have to come up with a story for them. The sex story included Gloria and Jay. So that left Mitch and Cam.

WRUBEL (*writer / executive producer*): I think it's an example of the staff pulling together in a friendly way that was fun to make that episode better, including Chris, who had a strong point of view of what happens in the second act of this episode.

> *Wanting to go home, Richman took a page from his own life that he knew would slide in perfectly.*

RICHMAN (*writer / executive producer*): I was staying at a friend's house with some other friends. I spilled a glass of wine onto an expensive new rug and knew this friend was going to go crazy. We realized that if we turned the rug around, the stain would be hidden under the couch and she'd never find out about it. It's the perfect crime. They never get caught. Everyone in the writers' room was like, "That's so unlikable. They have to get caught." I thought, "Oh my God, they're talking to me and having a big judgment about the fact I never admitted to my friend that that happened." So they do get caught in the episode, and then because it won a fucking Emmy, my friend watched it and I was caught fifteen years later.

> *Although the opening scene stands out, to cast and crew, another subtler scene comes to mind as important.*

LEVITAN (*cocreator*): What I think made that episode very special is that scene where the kids are outside the gas station talking about what they saw and then realizing that with all of their friends' parents getting divorced, how great it is that their parents still have sex and love each other. That's what gave that episode some real depth and heart we're always looking for. It kind of all came together.

BOWEN (*Claire Dunphy*): That was the first time there was a scene with just the three Dunphy kids. You realize that usually a lot of TV kids don't work without the adult foil or they are the foil for the adult. But these guys were not only working on their own but foiling for each other. It was so complex what they were doing as total second nature.

WINTER (*Alex Dunphy*): We practiced our lines a lot, which is something we still do. Before rehearsal, during, after, in the van over.

BOWEN (*Claire Dunphy*): Sarah playing Haley being dumb trying to protect her brother in a very earnest way. And Alex knowing the truth of the matter, but also trying to protect him and not be a know-it-all, and Luke still not really sure what the fuck is going on.

WINTER (*Alex Dunphy*): It was a nice feeling to be able to show them that we didn't need to be in a scene every time with an adult in order for it to be funny. As a kid actor on a show, you do think about that. They're testing you, and it felt good.

HYLAND (*Haley Dunphy*): I felt proud that the writers entrusted us to carry a scene on our own. That was really great.

BOWEN (*Claire Dunphy*): It was an amazingly complex and lovely little scene. They're both trying to explain without saying and still trying to protect the innocence of this kid. It made me realize these kids are fantastic. They don't need an adult there to hold a scene together. They were 100 percent doing it on their own, more than they could have known.

We Need to Talk About Lily

Lily—baby girl, adopted from Vietnam.

Deadpan is definitely my thing.

— AUBREY ANDERSON-EMMONS

What happens when baby twins you've cast in your pilot have a growth spurt during summer hiatus? You find new babies. And when those new babies throw temper tantrums and break into a waterfall of tears every time they cross the threshold of your soundstage? You stop using babies.

JIM HENSZ (*director / assistant director*): There's an old Hollywood saying, "Don't act with children or animals." Either they pull focus because they're great or they can't pick up cues.

WEBER (*assistant producer*): Anytime I work on a show where there's a baby involved, it's a challenge on all aspects of production.

The tangled casting saga of Mitchell and Cameron's adopted Vietnamese daughter, Lily Elizabeth Tucker-Pritchett, started simply enough, with baby twins in the show's pilot playing the same part. By California law, they can only be on set for limited amounts of time.

SHARON SACKS (*studio teacher*): Newborns [fifteen days old] up to six months can only be under lights and on set working for twenty minutes and at the work site for two hours between 9:30 a.m. and 11:30 a.m. and 2:30 p.m. and 4:30 p.m. For babies six months to two years, they can be on set for four hours but can only work two. And then once they reach two years old until five years old, they can be at the workplace six hours and work three.

In the four-month interim between filming the pilot and the series' first episode, the twins had sprouted, necessitating Lily's recasting. Because casting directors don't pre-read babies, this task fell outside casting director Greenberg's realm and within that of the Extras Department. The casting associates ended up selecting a new set of one-year-old twins, Jaden and Ella Hiller, to take over the role.

LLOYD (*cocreator*): They weren't called upon to do very much except be there and react a little bit.

WINER (*director / executive producer*): If you look at those early episodes, you'll see they have this hilarious deadpan that weirdly functioned as a punchline to Cam's and Mitch's occasional hysteria. It really seemed like baby Lily was judging them harshly, which was hysterical. But as time went by, we realized their deadpan nature on set was evidence of their dislike of being there.

STATMAN (*director / assistant director*): They were screaming at the top of their lungs, which became the bane of everyone's existence, especially Eric's and Jesse's.

FERGUSON (*Mitchell Pritchett*): It was the reality of the situation Eric and I were in. We were the characters who had a baby, so we had to deal with it.

STONESTREET (*Cam Tucker*): They were happy-go-lucky, seemingly normal, regular functioning kids off set. The moment they stepped onto stage 5 and saw us, however, it was like, "No, thank you. We're done."

O'SHANNON (*writer / executive producer*): I think they developed the power of speech to say, "This job is ruining our souls. Get us off this set."

When not crying, the twins still managed to readily express their moods.

MCCARTHY-MILLER (*director*): In the episode "Two Monkeys and a Panda" [season 2], the baby was supposed to clap, but she didn't want to do anything. So we said, "We'll put someone underneath her to put her elbows together, so it'll look like a clap." If you play the scene back, you'll notice that the baby's fists are clenched. She was so mad we made her do that.

CASE (*director/editor*): They had the baby in a Diana Ross wig for shooting a calendar. If you study her face, you can see she'd been crying. Her little nose is red.

Sometimes the editors managed to make something out of the tears.

MILLER (*assistant prop master*): At the end of "The Bicycle Thief," during the montage, you see Cam and Mitch, and Lily is crying and crawling away from them. It's perfect.

O'SHANNON (*writer / executive producer*): The best shots we got were them sitting there like blobs. And if a kid is doing that for two years in a row, the audience starts to worry, "What's wrong with this child?"

All the actors' performances took a back seat to the babies' temperament.

FERGUSON (*Mitchell Pritchett*): They rule the day with whatever they're in the mood to do. I remember trying to get through scenes without them crying, hoping our performances were up to par.

STONESTREET (*Cam Tucker*): What's very frustrating is how you'd read about people saying, "Oh my God, how did they get Lily to do those things in those scenes?" And I'm like, "Are you kidding me?" What you're seeing on-screen is the only thing that we could get them to do. Our performances were secondary to takes with kids not crying. There's no other way to say it.

HENSZ (*director / assistant director*): Sometimes Eric would walk off. Sometimes he'd stay and engage. There were different ways of handling it.

STONESTREET (*Cam Tucker*): It was hard. I'd get frustrated. It's like, "Why do I have to come to work every day and feel like I'm abusing a child? How is this fair? Why is this okay?"

LAMB (*first assistant director / director*): It just wasn't where they wanted to be. They weren't with their mom. They didn't know any of the people. The lights were on them. They're eighteen months.

Sometimes they replaced the baby with a doll.

MILLER (*assistant prop master*): I had one I used quite a bit. It was silicone and stupid heavy. If I had to guess, I'd say thirty pounds. The boys had to deal with that a couple of years.

STONESTREET (*Cam Tucker*): That baby was *so* heavy. It was at its heaviest in the car carrier. I remember thinking when it was in the car seat that it felt like a bag of pig feed. Those are fifty pounds.

Cast and crew did as best as they could in hopes of finding a baby whisperer who could calm the hysterics.

FERGUSON (*Mitchell Pritchett*): I babysat for lots of families in between jobs when I was doing theater in New York. So I'm very comfortable with babies. I'd sing to Ella and Jaden to try and get them to calm down. My go-to song was "A Bushel and a Peck" from *Guys and Dolls*. The poor crew was so sick of that song, but it was one of the few things that quieted them down. I was constantly bouncing around, singing "A Bushel and a Peck" right up until action, and then we'd try and get a few lines in and then the baby would start to get fussy and we'd have to start over and try and figure out something else.

HENSZ (*director / assistant director*): The teacher would give them Cheerios or find iPad devices with things to push.

SACKS (*studio teacher*): I'd lie on the floor, use finger puppets.

HENSZ (*director / assistant director*): Anything you could do to try and make the kids comfortable with a bunch of grown men and women standing around with big intimidating-looking lens and lights everywhere and a boom that keeps flying over their heads.

LEVITAN (*cocreator*): All of a sudden, you're trying to do scenes more quietly or a little gentler, and you're not doing it the way you want to because you're feeling tight now. We were all pretty unhappy with that situation.

LLOYD (*cocreator*): At a certain point, you go, "This isn't good for these kids or the show. If they hate being here so much, why are we putting them through that?"

HIGGINBOTHAM (*writer / executive producer*): There was a very quick and big discussion like, "We're making these kids miserable. Family is more important than the business. Everyone knows that. Let them go and have lives."

LEVITAN (*cocreator*): The last thing we want to do is make anyone miserable, especially children. It wasn't even a close call. We had to make a change.

They didn't ask the Hiller twins back for season 3.

O'SHANNON (*writer / executive producer*): Fans of the show would say, "How could you fire those little girls?" It was hurting them to be there. We probably saved their lives. To this day, those kids probably switch through channels and start crying when they see *Modern Family.*

The writers decided to boost Lily's age for the next season, evolving her from a motionless sack of potatoes with eyes to a real person, with limited communication skills.

LLOYD (*cocreator*): We decided Lily's getting to an age where she can be a talking character and have opinions. So let's open our casting a little bit.

GREENBERG (*casting director*): I was assigned to find a four-year-old Lily. I read ninety-four three- to five-year-old Asian actresses. I didn't care about their real age, I needed them to play the age Chris and Steve wanted. We even tested the Hiller twins [the parents had hoped their children had outgrown their aversion to being on set—they hadn't]. We thought it was the right thing to do.

The Hiller family happened to live in the same area of the San Fernando Valley as four-year-old Aubrey Anderson-Emmons and her mother, Amy. The families occasionally bumped into each other at a local playground, where the girls would romp around together. Amy had been working in Hollywood for more than twenty years by then. She understood the ins and out of the business and didn't feel a great affinity for either.

AMY ANDERSON-EMMONS (*Aubrey's mother*): I know what it's like to be a working actor and struggle. You audition, audition, and audition, book stuff here and there, have lean times in between. It wasn't what I really wanted for Aubrey.

Aubrey hadn't expressed any interest in acting anyway. She preferred singing, dancing, and watching kids' TV shows like The Fresh Beat Band. *A fateful snapshot would change all of that, however. On a lazy spring afternoon in April of 2011, during another chance encounter with the Hiller twins at the playground, Aubrey's mom took a photograph on her smartphone of all three kids looking mesmerized by a ladybug.*

AMY ANDERSON-EMMONS (*Aubrey's mother*): They were sitting there, bing, bing, bing, three in a row, taking turns holding this ladybug. The daughter-in-law of my agent at the time is an actress and good friend. I'd shown her that picture because I knew she was a *Modern Family* fan. She said they looked like triplets. Cut to July, when they're recasting the role. My friend told my agent about the picture.

AUBREY ANDERSON-EMMONS (*Lily Tucker-Pritchett*): Her agent agreed that I looked a lot like the girls that played Lily before me, so she told my mom I should audition for the show.

Her friend Romi Dames sent the picture of the girls along with the following email to casting associate Hooper.

Subject: Adorable Asian 4 yr. old

Hi Allen!

This is kind of random, but I heard that Modern Family was looking for a 3-4yr old girl that looks like Lily, and I happen to know one. She's my friend's daughter, she just turned four a few weeks ago, and she is totally adorable and a little ham. Her name is Aubrey, and she actually hung out with the girls who play Lily in the park one day, and this is a picture of them hanging out together. They look SO similar, I had to ask her mother which one her daughter was. (Aubrey's the one facing the camera in the red shirt.) My agent is going to get her up on the breakdowns asap to submit her, but I thought I'd email you in case it's a time crunch.

Just thought it might be helpful! :)

One friendly paragraph and primitive emoji got the ball rolling.

AMY ANDERSON-EMMONS (*Aubrey's mother*): She really felt strongly that Aubrey would have a good chance of booking it. I was thinking, "She's never auditioned for anything in her life. She's not even going to know what to do."

Amy had a difficult decision to make. Knowing Hollywood, should she shun the spotlight for her daughter or play it out with her and see where it goes? She turned to Aubrey for help.

AMY ANDERSON-EMMONS (*Aubrey's mother*): I tried to explain to Aubrey what it meant to be on TV. "When you turn on the TV and see *SpongeBob,* it looks like they're having fun all the time, but it's a job, a serious job, and you have to work like an adult. You can't goof around. So I want you to think about this seriously." I think in her head, she was thinking about *SpongeBob.* She said, "Yeah, I want to be on TV because it would be all about me."

Aubrey met with Greenberg and got an instant callback to meet the producers, along with two other child actresses, for a chemistry read with Ferguson. Levitan and Lloyd whipped up a test scene for them to perform.

AUBREY ANDERSON-EMMONS (*Lily Tucker-Pritchett*): We were in the Tucker-Pritchett house sitting on the couch, and there was a camera and quite a few people in the room. Jesse was super nice.

FERGUSON (*Mitchell Pritchett*): It was weird doing a test with children. Basically, I sat on the set and had a conversation with them for a little while, and then we read the scene. They were all very different in their own ways, but all of them knew their lines.

LEVITAN (*cocreator*): What we liked about Aubrey is she played everything deadpan. It felt the opposite of a typical TV kid.

AMY ANDERSON-EMMONS (*Aubrey's mother*): I think Jesse really liked her. There was one line that was a non sequitur, because that's how four-year-olds talk. She's having this dialogue with him, but then all of a sudden, she's supposed to say, "Why is your hair orange?" It didn't make sense in the context of the dialogue, so she kept forgetting that line. And Jesse kept trying to help her by raising his eyebrows to his hair, giving her a visual cue. Steve said, "Okay, let's do it again. Jesse, don't help her." He really wanted to make sure she could do it. She paused a little, and then remembered it. Later, when we were on our way out, Steve leaned out the door and said to us, "Thank you for not crying."

Anderson-Emmons won the part. The writing staff then went to work on Lily, framing the character to be sassy and succinct, with a poker-faced stare and still mannerisms that emphasized her train of thought.

RICHMAN (*writer / executive producer*): She was a miniature Thelma Ritter, throwing off one-liners to her parents. I think she was really fun.

LLOYD (*cocreator*): Aubrey was a big boon to the show because she was funny in the way she could pop the balloons of her sometimes pretentious dads. Suddenly, there was a new element in that household that really helped us.

HIGGINBOTHAM (*writer / executive producer*): There was an organic nature to how flippant, funny, dry, and cutting she could be, because she was in a house with two gay guys who have very specific voices, very specific ways of expressing themselves. They're acerbic. They're sarcastic. They're dramatic. We thought, "We can get away with having this deadpan little girl with so little emotion." She heard her fathers say these things, so now she's parroting it, like my children do constantly.

On her first day of shooting, for the third season episode "Phil on Wire," Anderson-Emmons met the cast.

GOULD (*Luke Dunphy*): I felt an instant connection with her because I had started acting at a very young age. She was hiding behind her mom's leg. The new craze at the time was the iPad 1, and I had one with me. It had a bunch of games on it. So I pulled it out and started playing with it. She gasped, and I let her play. It opened her up.

Her first scene called for her to approach a miserable Cam, in the midst of suffering through a juice diet, and say, "We hided, but you didn't seek." The director called, "Action," and waited and waited.

FERGUSON (*Mitchell Pritchett*): I think she had a moment where she thought, "I was in this place before when I met this redheaded guy, but now he's acting like the guy on TV, but we're doing it in a place without a ceiling. It's all very weird." So she goes, "Are you real people because you live in a fake house?" I thought that was such a bold and kind of Zen statement. That's a great question. We aren't real people, and we do live in a fake house. It was a lot for her to take in. But she did a great job.

She also had her first encounter with Vergara.

STONESTREET (*Cam Tucker*): Mitch and Cam were on a juice cleanse, and Mitch has lost his mind. We come back to Jay and Gloria's to pick up Lily, and we're wolfing down these muffins, eating muffin after muffin after muffin, not knowing they were dog muffins for Stella. Gloria was supposed to carry Lily in and find us eating these muffins. It was the first time Aubrey had really ever been around Sofía, and she wouldn't stop playing with Sofía's boobs.

AMY ANDERSON-EMMONS (*Aubrey's mother*): She looked at Sofía's chest and honked it with one hand. We were all watching on the monitors. I was freaking out.

AUBREY ANDERSON-EMMONS (*Lily Tucker-Pritchett*): What child can say that? I honked Sofía's boob.

STONESTREET (*Cam Tucker*): Aubrey was squeezing and pushing on them. Like, "Oh my God, what are these things?" I remember thinking, "Aubrey, you're expressing exactly my thoughts when I first met Sofía." We were laughing so hard. Sofía was laughing, too, telling her, "You have to stop doing that now. You have to stop pushing on my boobs."

VERGARA (*Gloria Delgado Pritchett*): That always happens to me with little kids when I carry them. It gets very awkward because they start touching them in front of people. It's a weird thing. I'm having a conversation and the whole time she's playing with them in front of everyone.

During a lapse in Anderson-Emmons's breast obsession, the cameras rolled. Gloria brought Lily into the kitchen to react to her dads devouring muffins.

AMY ANDERSON-EMMONS (*Aubrey's mother*): I'd shown her some episodes so she'd know who everyone was and what they looked like. She still didn't have a concept that she was on the show at that point.

LEVITAN (*cocreator*): When the scene was done, she looked at Eric and Jesse and said, "You look like those guys on *Modern Family*." It was such a bizarre moment, but got a big laugh.

Anderson-Emmons stayed in touch with the Hillers. They got their kids together a few times afterward.

AMY ANDERSON-EMMONS (*Aubrey's mother*): I sent the mom a message, out of goodwill. I didn't want there to be any hurt feelings. She was very sweet. She said, "We're so excited that it happened for you guys. It couldn't happen to nicer people." There used to be a Johnny Rockets at the Calabasas Commons. We came and ate there with them once and then walked around. Every once in a while, somebody would walk past us and their heads would explode because all three Lilys were in one place together.

AUBREY ANDERSON-EMMONS (*Lily Tucker-Pritchett*): They would say, "Oh, are you triplets?"

AMY ANDERSON-EMMONS (*Aubrey's mother*): It was very weird.

Unlike the Hiller twins, however, Anderson-Emmons never formed an aversion to lights, camera, and action. What scared them enthralled her.

HOOPER (*casting associate*): We were in Jackson Hole, Wyoming. One day, after she'd gone to wherever they were filming, she was in the shuttle van coming back and seemed a little upset, and somebody said, "Aubrey, are you okay?" And she went, "No, I want to keep acting!"

She would.

Dude Ranch

A lot of prep work and stress goes into planning a family vacation. The same thing happens with a TV family. During preproduction for season 3, the word on where to vacation came down from above: dude ranch.

WALSH (*writer / executive producer*): We thought instead of writing the travel episode at the end of the season, let's write it at the beginning. We'll have more time to dedicate to it and we can really get it right. What happened instead was we spent six weeks over the summer debating whether it should be a half hour or an hour.

MORTON (*executive producer*): Steve wanted to do an hour episode, and Chris only wanted a half hour.

LLOYD (*cocreator*): I was open to an hour, but we needed to follow the same rules we always do, which is every scene needs to build on what happened in the one before.

LEVITAN (*cocreator*): Think about great westerns. You can afford to take some time with long streaking shots that take you into a scene and let it breathe. It was so unbelievably beautiful there that everywhere you shot looked good. And that was great.

LLOYD (*cocreator*): To watch them ride over a mountaintop into a sunset because it would be cool to see isn't good storytelling. That's letting the location dictate what we're doing. And that's not what should be happening.

The location should be secondary. We're in the "Bradys go to Hawaii" territory then.

WALSH (*writer / executive producer*): It became tense because the clock was ticking. It was time we should have spent breaking other episodes.

O'SHANNON (*writer / executive producer*): The show was a half an hour and then an hour and then a half hour and then an hour. Do that twenty times. It was a war, and Brad, Paul, and I were in the middle of it.

WINER (*director / executive producer*): Chris's point was that he had never, ever seen a half-hour comedy successfully expand to an hour. Two back-to-back half hours, sure, if they aired them that way. I think Steve was coming at it from the point of, "Let's break new ground."

HIGGINBOTHAM (*writer / executive producer*): We would take a vote. We'd think it was done and then it would come back up again. "Well, here's why I think maybe we should revisit this," and you'd be like, "I thought we were done."

Flat 301 couldn't go anywhere until the issue got resolved.

MORTON (*executive producer*): Finally I go, "This is crazy. We need a decision because we can't plan it all out." I went up to the writers' room and said, "Guys, we're going to solve this." Two hours later, there was still no decision, just intransigence. I started to understand how frustrated the writers were getting.

O'SHANNON (*writer / executive producer*): It would have made a perfect forty-five-minute episode, because there was some good stuff that got cut and then some of it was a little rushed. But then on the other hand, it might have dragged if it had been an hour so . . .

RICHMAN (*writer / executive producer*): Brad, Paul, and Dan had to write a forty-five-minute draft that was in the middle to see if there was enough story for an hour.

LLOYD (*cocreator*): After giving it a fair try, we couldn't come up with a way to make it an hour. And it's a shame because it would have made the cost of doing that episode easier to bear. But the decision was we tell the best stories we can tell on the show even if they are costly. So that's what we did.

LEVITAN (*cocreator*): We would have had to add another story or beats to it to fill out the time, but I maintain it would have been a better one-hour episode. Instead we cut the heck out of it to fit everything in. I don't think it was the right call. But we'll debate that until the end of time.

LLOYD (*cocreator*): It was not the first nor the last protracted disagreement between Steve and me and not the first or last that it came down to ideas about storytelling.

While the writers worked on the script and the parents quarreled, Morton, the wizard behind the curtain for travel episodes, put feelers out for a usable dude ranch with easy access for a production crew. They looked in Northern California and Colorado, but logistics negated them all. Then they got a new lead—Lost Creek Ranch in Jackson Hole, Wyoming.

YOUNG (*production manager / producer*): My sister had run the chamber of commerce for some time in Jackson Hole. She did a lot of research for us and found a high-end dude ranch that was interested because they were fans of the show.

Once production kicked into gear, the cast flew in. They got a hero's welcome.

YOUNG (*production manager / producer*): No one had seen the new Lily yet, so when she got off the plane, they put her on top of a horse of the mounted police right there on the tarmac. They had a marching band, and a little affiliate TV station in Idaho came in to cover it.

Morton had set everybody up in condos at the Snow King Resort. Just outside the hotel, you could ride the Alpine Slide, in which you could zip a cart down the side of a mountain, 2,500 feet's worth of track.

GOULD (*Luke Dunphy*): It was a land luge, a cart you sit in with handles you push forward and go on this big track. Whenever we weren't working, we were racing each other.

To get to the ranch required a caravan of vans and a forty-five-minute ride every morning and end of day.

MORTON (*executive producer*): It was a bumpy ride to the ranch. One day, Reid wasn't supposed to be working until about two in the afternoon. At seven in the morning, we're in a van starting to go down the street, and we look back and Reid's running alongside the van. So we stop and go, "Hey, Reid, what's up?" And he says, "I wanted to see if I could get a ride." We said, "But you're not shooting until two o'clock," and he says, "I mean, who wants to miss those pancakes? Am I right?"

REID EWING (*Dylan Marshall*): I'm always running somewhere for some weird reason, chasing after something. I wanted breakfast and to be on set and enjoy the atmosphere. Getting to travel for work is one of the best parts of being an actor.

Tim Blake Nelson guest-starred as a cowboy named Hank, their guide at the ranch.

GREENBERG (*casting director*): We made offers to John C. Reilly, Kurt Russell, Timothy Olyphant, Josh Holloway, Kevin Bacon, and Thomas Haden Church. They read the script, then passed. We wanted to make an offer to people including Sam Rockwell, Owen Wilson, George Clooney, and Mark Wahlberg, but were told they wouldn't be interested.

WINER (*director / executive producer*): Tim was the perfect choice for that character.

```
              MITCHELL INTERVIEW

                     MITCHELL
       I realized if we were going to raise
       a boy, I needed to butch up my life.
       I want to be able to teach my son all
       the things my dad taught Claire.
```

ZUKER (*writer / executive producer*): I'm not sure if this inspired what we were doing, but when I found out we were going to have a son, I had a friend, who's a jock, teach me how to throw a football. I'm not an athletic guy. My dad never threw a ball with me. So I had a friend take me to the beach to practice for my son. I think that was an element of Mitch trying to butch it up.

To that end, in a later scene, Mitchell and Luke blow up a bird-house with a firecracker.

```
EXT. DUDE RANCH—DAY

Mitchell runs up to Cameron and Lily.

                     MITCHELL
       I did a boy thing! I blew up the
       birdhouse!
```

ZUKER (*writer / executive producer*): I've said for years that it doesn't matter what kind of man you are—Gandhi, Tommy Tune, or the Rock—men like blowing shit up.

By this point, Haley had gotten together and broken up with Dylan multiple times. Jackson Hole became something bigger. Dylan got left behind permanently.

EWING (*Dylan Marshall*): I was really sad when Haley broke up with me in season 1. I was really sad when we broke up at the end of season 2.

After that, I was like, "If you guys want to use me, great, and if you don't, don't." It's their thing and not mine. I have no right to tell them how to do their job.

CORRIGAN (*writer / executive producer*): At the time, we thought dumping Dylan was smart. We'd had him on the show for two years and didn't know quite what else to do or new wrinkles he would bring. We thought it was a funny way to say goodbye.

O'SHANNON (*writer / executive producer*): I put one joke in where Dylan says to Claire, "You want me to leave?" and she says, "No, it's actually the opposite," and Dylan says, "I want you to leave?" We couldn't help it. We were piling on these dumb jokes because they cracked us up.

HIGGINBOTHAM (*writer / executive producer*): They were in the forest and Dylan says, "I've never been this far from home before." Then he would take a step and go, "Now I've never been *this* far." And he would take another step . . . I was like, "That's funny, but he's concussed. Something is wrong with him."

CORRIGAN (*writer / executive producer*): The other joke was when they find Dylan in the woods and Haley yells, "Where are you?" and he replies, "Wyoming." I had the pleasure of pitching both of those and then for years hearing how horrible they were.

Alex got her first kiss in the episode.

WINTER (*Alex Dunphy*): People tease you in a good way because you're having that kiss. It was really funny and nice that I was part of the cast in that way that I got the teasing.

WALSH (*writer / executive producer*): People internally didn't love the Alex boyfriend character. And I understand some of the criticism. It's one of the hazards of travel shows, because you have to make compromises. Internally, it was never a favorite.

WINTER (*Alex Dunphy*): It was not my first kiss. In some interviews, I was told to say it was my first kiss, but in honesty, it wasn't.

> *During off-hours, cast and crew mingled together, taking in the local nightlife.*

VERGARA (*Gloria Delgado-Pritchett*): We always try to do things because when we're in LA, we don't see each other as much. When you're on a trip, we make the effort to try to do everything together as much as we can.

CORRIGAN (*writer / executive producer*): I remember walking around Jackson Hole with the cast, shocking people out in the world seeing the *Modern Family* family together as if they were a real family. It was fun to experience that through their eyes. Of course, sometimes you see a celebrity, but seeing the actor act like their character in the real world is surreal.

HENSZ (*director / assistant director*): There was a real big night in downtown Jackson Hole where the cast and crew all went out country western dancing at the local bar.

LEVITAN (*cocreator*): It was beautiful. People really liked the area and going out at night to this country western town and country bars. A bunch of people bought western clothes and cowboy hats.

CORRIGAN (*writer / executive producer*): One night, we were at a restaurant and they handed us the dessert menu. Ty saw something on the menu called *sweet corn crème brûlée*. It sounded like a fantastic exclamation for Phil. I think he wound up using it in an episode once.

BURRELL (*Phil Dunphy*): The amount of ridiculous things said in screams on our show boggles the mind.

BOWEN (*Claire Dunphy*): I remember giving Ty a bear-fur jockstrap because they sold them there and I thought that was pretty funny.

BURRELL (*Phil Dunphy*): That was for future sex scenes. I'm sure I've got it somewhere.

When on a dude ranch, you have to do the outdoors.

HENSZ (*director / assistant director*): There was the whole horseback riding sequence. Anytime you put a bunch of non–horseback-rider actors on horses, there's a little bit of tension there and it's less controllable.

VERGARA (*Gloria Delgado-Pritchett*): Eric didn't like the horseback riding. I don't think he had ever done it. But he did a pretty good job once he got on the horse. It's hard. It's a scary thing. I grew up riding horses, so I was super comfortable and having the best time.

STONESTREET (*Cam Tucker*): I remember seeing all the horses being brought out for everyone and then seeing mine. Mine was like a draft horse. Others were smaller and I thought, "Good. I don't want to hurt any horses in the making of this TV show."

AUBREY ANDERSON-EMMONS (*Lily Tucker-Pritchett*): Everybody got to ride horses. I've been riding horses since I was little, but they wouldn't let me because I wasn't old enough. So I started crying.

The production crew had their own adventures in the great outdoors.

JOSH ELLIOTT (*on-set dresser*): Our trucks were far away, and I had to run back to it. It took forever. On the way back once, I decided to take a shortcut over the fence and into a non-maintained field to the other side and hop the fence. Well, Little Red Riding Hood left the path. I got halfway there, and I hear, "Halt!" I stopped and turned around. And there's a ranger there. He says, "Don't move." I asked what's going on, and he says, "Sssssshhhhh." He pointed down. I saw dirt coming out of the earth. He told me to back up very slowly. I got about five feet away from a badger. When he backed out of the hole, he was about two feet wide and a foot thick and looked like three feet long. He was not attractive, and he was pissed. So I screamed and ran away like a little girl and went the long way.

WALSH (*director / executive producer*): Those travel episodes in general are more crowd-pleasers than writers-pleasers. They're light by nature. I hear about them a lot from civilians, but internally, it's never what the writers are talking about.

In terms of vacations, Jackson Hole ranks as one of the best for cast and crew. The next one, also in season 3, proved more magical, however—a Magic Kingdom, in fact.

Disneyland

Disney owns ABC. ABC airs Modern Family. *Not unexpectedly, Disney executives saw a marketing opportunity. They had ABC reach out to* Modern Family *and ask them to film an episode at Disneyland.*

WRUBEL (*writer / executive producer*): I don't know if that's the best reason to do something.

HIGGINBOTHAM (*writer / executive producer*): The question we were asking was, "What about going to Disneyland makes this worth doing? Otherwise, let's not do it."

LEVITAN (*cocreator*): When I was a kid, that stupid Hall of Presidents that nobody really thinks about made an impression on me. We came up with this idea of having the ending voice-over be President Lincoln and have that relate to the story. So we went back and listened to what he's actually saying and reverse engineered it. We came up with this very heartfelt, touching story about the last time Jay had been at Disneyland with Mitch and Claire was when they were kids. His plan that day was to go home and tell his wife that he wanted a divorce.

JAY INTERVIEW

                    JAY
When Claire and Mitchell were young,
their mom and I were going to take
them to Disneyland, but that morning,
DeDe and I got into this huge fight
over something or other, surprise,
surprise, and I ended up taking them
on my own. Claire's biggest fear was
running into the evil queen.
My biggest fear was that I married
her.

Harsh words, perhaps, but by establishing such animosity up front, it elevates the potential for a more emotional payoff in the end. This became the core of the episode.

Before moving ahead, however, with their plans, the producers wanted certain assurances from Disney.

LEVITAN (*cocreator*): We didn't want to look like corporate shills, like we're doing a Disneyland commercial. So we said, "We have to be able to do it in a way that we think's appropriate. We want to be able to talk about the long lines and the weird things people do there. That's the only way we'll do it—if you're not censoring the content." And they agreed to it, which was cool.

YOUNG (*production manager / producer*): When the Dunphys are getting ready to go, Claire tells everybody to eat up, because "the happiest place on earth is also home to the most expensive churro on earth." They let it in. Or when Phil and Luke wait in line for an hour at Indiana Jones and then there's a height restriction. They get excited when Luke passes only to come to a sign that says there's a forty-five-minute wait from here. Disney was gracious for letting us have some of those jokes.

CINDY CHUPACK (*writer / co-executive producer*): I think the only thing Disney didn't let us do was have a costumed character in the park take its head off to reveal the person inside—which, in this case, would have been Dylan. It was explained to me by our park contact that for children who believe, that would be like seeing your favorite Disney character get decapitated. In the end, I think it was actually funnier that Haley was forced to play the whole scene with Dylan as Little John. And when we filmed, seeing my (at the time) two-year-old daughter's excitement over meeting "the real" Mickey and Minnie Mouse, I could see the wisdom in the decision.

At what point shall we expect the approach of danger? By what means shall we fortify against it?
   —ABRAHAM LINCOLN, GREAT MOMENTS WITH MR. LINCOLN

A million things can go wrong with a location shoot. That comes from a loss of control, like a production crew has on their own stage. Now, add in going to the trademarked "Happiest Place on Earth" during open hours, with fifty thousand people alongside you. That doesn't sound like a place "Where Dreams Come True" but rather a living nightmare.

HENSZ (*director / assistant director*): That it was an operating park was certainly a challenge. It was some of the busiest days there.

BOWEN (*Claire Dunphy*): We were there on leap day to make it crazier. Every four years on leap day, Disneyland and Disney World stay open for twenty-four hours, so people can go to both. It's the most crowded time you could possibly be there, because it's got this insane bunch of red-eye Disney junkies coming in.

JAMES "BAGGS" BAGDONAS (*director of photography / director*): We had to move from one side of Disneyland to the other. Every move was basically like going through a stadium to get through all these people and capture the scene. The logistics were one of the hardest things we've done.

Disneyland, however, had their crackerjack troops at the ready.

YOUNG (*production manager / producer*): Disney's people understand logistics like no one else. On the day of shooting, we'd tell them what ride we were at and all of a sudden, there'd be an army of twenty of them walking with us. Within fifteen seconds, they'd create a web around us with stanchions and tape. They were masters at it.

GOULD (*Luke Dunphy*): When you wanted something, it would magically appear. One time, I said, "A Dole Whip sounds really good right now." I wasn't even asking for it. And one appeared in a size they don't even carry.

They had to improvise to handle all the lookie-loos.

LEVITAN (*cocreator*): People would stand at the perimeter of the circle staring at the actors while we were shooting. It looked very odd. But there was no way to get them to not do that. As soon as you say, "Don't look over here," that's exactly what people are going to do.

BAGGS (*director of photography / director*): We used a long lens and filmed as far away as possible so the background remained a little out of focus. For the dialogue scenes, we used backgrounds that wouldn't be so much about people as it would about a ride or something iconic in Disneyland.

LEVITAN (*cocreator*): Somebody came up with the brilliant idea that we'll put Disney characters near our actors and they'll do a dance or whatever and it'll look like everyone is looking at those characters like people do. It worked beautifully.

The cast stayed at the Disneyland Hotel during filming. Perks included access to an empty closed park during off-hours.

BOWEN (*Claire Dunphy*): It was cool to be walking through the park at four in the morning. There's always a version of Walt Disney's opening day address coming over the speakers. You can't hear it during the day, because it's too loud. But if you're there at four in the morning, you can.

GOULD (*Luke Dunphy*): There were no security guards. So I figured it would be the best opportunity to do parkour for the first and last time in my life inside Disneyland. I ran around Frontierland jumping off park benches and running up the side of Thunder Mountain.

Let reverence for the [law] be breathed by every American mother to the lisping babe that prattles on her lap; let it be taught in schools, in seminaries, and in colleges; let it be written in primers, [in] spelling-books, and almanacs.
   —ABRAHAM LINCOLN, *GREAT MOMENTS WITH MR. LINCOLN*

When it comes to the magical world of Disney, no one on Modern Family *loves all things Disney more than Hyland.*

BOWEN (*Claire Dunphy*): She was weeping at points with joy over things we were doing, places we were eating, experiences we were having.

HYLAND (*Haley Dunphy*): The first scene I shot was on the Rivers of America. Afterward, they said, "Okay, let's take you back to the greenroom." I'm like, "Cool." So we start walking toward the Pirates of the Caribbean ride. I know that the Dream Suite is above that ride. That was a space that Walt was building because the apartment that he and his wife normally stayed at was above the fire department on Main Street. I'd been trying to stay there for years, but you can't unless you're a sweepstakes winner or an invited guest by Disney. My heart started pounding, like, "There's no way we're going to the Dream Suite. There's no way that the Dream Suite is our fucking greenroom." And then they opened up the doors. I walked through it and started crying.

RODRIGUEZ (*Manny Delgado*): Each room has a theme. Since some of us still had to do school, we got Walt's kids' bedroom. Every inch of that building was so beautiful and amazing.

Disney-obsessed fans know all about Club 33, located at 33 Royal Street, an exclusive and secretive club at the park. Much like Yale's underground, undergraduate Skull and Bones society, members can't talk about it unless they want to be killed . . . with kindness, this being Disneyland.

HYLAND (*Haley Dunphy*): Club 33 is a members-only restaurant. It's the only place that you can get alcoholic drinks in Disneyland other than Star Wars: Galaxy's Edge.

Club membership costs about the price of a Mercedes-Benz SUV. Modern Family *got a freebie.*

LEVITAN (*cocreator*): Everyone was curious about that place.

HYLAND (*Haley Dunphy*): We had dinner in the Trophy Room. They had animatronics of vultures and birds in there, like the Tiki Room. Walt used to take his meetings there with business partners. You can either take the stairs to get there or this gorgeous glass elevator. Walt saw it in Paris and wanted it but was told he couldn't have it. So he sent his imagi-neers [the Disney geniuses who design and build park attractions] over to Paris to study it and then re-create it in Disneyland. At least that's what I was told. So of course I took the glass elevator, because why wouldn't you?

Hyland had no idea about the biggest surprise coming her way.

HYLAND (*Haley Dunphy*): On the last day of filming, Steve called me and said, "Hey, I heard you cried when you walked into the Dream Suite." And I said, "Steve, do not make fun of me. I'm not here for it." And he said, "Well, we have it throughout the rest of the week. My wife and I were going to stay in it tonight, but I think that you should." I started crying even more. So I got to stay in it, and it was a very wonderful and magical experience.

If destruction be our lot, we [ourselves must] be [the] author[s] and finisher[s]. As a nation of free men, we must live through all time[s].

 —ABRAHAM LINCOLN, *GREAT MOMENTS WITH MR. LINCOLN*

In the episode's other storylines, Jay tells Gloria not to wear high-heeled shoes to the park, which of course she does. Manny worries about a stock market project at school instead of having fun. Claire tries to break Haley's propensity for dating bad boys by setting her up with a supposed mensch. Haley ends up instead bumping into and getting back together with Dylan—who, unbeknownst to everyone, now works at the park. Phil feels old for getting queasy on rides with Luke. Fortunately, he learns he only has the flu. And Mitchell and Cam deal with leashing Lily to keep her from escaping.

AUBREY ANDERSON-EMMONS (*Lily Tucker-Pritchett*): They told me to bark.

LEVITAN (*cocreator*): It's funny how leashes disturb people. People have very strong feelings about that.

AMY ANDERSON-EMMONS (*Aubrey's mother*): They meet a mom who has twins who are on leashes, they tried to get Julie's twins to do it. They didn't want to.

LEVITAN (*cocreator*): When two dogs come up to each other and they start doing that twirly thing where they run around in circles, we thought, "Wouldn't that be great if that happens with the kids on a leash?"

In between setups, they'd go behind the curtain or sneak off to play.

LEVITAN (*cocreator*): We ate in the area in back where all the Disneyland cast members eat, so you see the characters walking around. Half are in costume, half aren't. It was very fun to see how things work behind the scenes.

RACHAEL FIELD (*associate producer*): Julie emailed me and said she would pay me any amount of money to not celebrate her birthday. But then at Disneyland she made a passing comment that it's okay. We ended up getting Minnie Mouse and bringing a cake out. It was a whole big embarrassing thing, which I worried she was going to kill me for, but she loved it.

RODRIGUEZ (*Manny Delgado*): Eric kept trying to get me to get on Space Mountain because he knew I was scared to get on it. Finally, he said, "I got you. You're good." So when they said, "Whoever wants to go on Space Mountain, let's go," he looked at me and I looked at him and said, "All right, let's do this." After, he said, "See, I told you you'd be fine." And then I got on again.

GOULD (*Luke Dunphy*): Whenever we were done working and weren't in school, we'd go out with a guide and use front-of-the-line passes to go on rides over and over. For the episode, me and Ty had to ride Big Thunder Mountain Railroad like eight times. To this day, I don't like that ride because of that. Going on anything eight times in a row with a film crew as you're saying lines ruins it for you.

CHUPACK (*writer / co-executive producer*): I felt for Nolan and Ty. I remember brainstorming about the perfect tag for the episode and finally landing on the idea of simply showing Phil trying to act excited but secretly feeling sick on Big Thunder. I still laugh every time I watch that tag. It's a great example of how Ty could take one line of stage direction and spin it into comedy gold.

Neither let us be slandered from our duty by false accusations against us, nor frightened from it by [the] menaces of destruction to the Government nor of dungeons to ourselves.
—ABRAHAM LINCOLN, *GREAT MOMENTS WITH MR. LINCOLN*

The Pritchett family journey for the episode concludes being seated before animatronic President Lincoln reciting some of his greatest speeches in Great Moments with Mr. Lincoln. In Jay's voice-over, he recounts what happened at the end of his last visit here with his children, the day he decided to tell their mother he wanted a divorce.

```
              JAY INTERVIEW

                    JAY
          I don't know what happened. Maybe
          it's what robot Lincoln said about
          a man's duty or keeping the Union
          together, maybe I chickened out.
          But I realized staying with my kids
          was more important than leaving my
          wife. That's not the right decision
          for everyone. But it was the right
          decision for me.

                  LINCOLN
          Let us have faith that right makes
          might and in that faith, let us, to
          the end, dare to do our duty as we
          understand it.

                    JAY
          So I stuck it out until they were
          grown.
```

LEVITAN (*cocreator*): He stuck it out for another ten years. It's a very sad and touching moment.

HIGGINBOTHAM (*writer / executive producer*): And then to show him now, sitting there with his kids as adults. I think that made it worth doing.

LEVITAN (*cocreator*): It breaks with a great joke when Jay's retelling this story in an interview. I've shown that clip dozens of times in speeches or panels, and it never fails to get a very big laugh.

Gloria calls to Jay from off-screen.

                    GLORIA
        Jay, you want to join me in the
        Jacuzzi?

                    JAY
        And the universe rewarded me.

The field trip proved more than worthwhile after all.

Express Yourself

From the very beginning, pilot director Winer wanted to establish a visual language for interviews so that people could focus on what a character says and not get distracted by where they say it.

WINER (*director / executive producer*): You create this understanding and covenant with the audience. If we were changing locations all the time, the simplicity of that language wouldn't be nearly as elegant. There's computational time needed in the audience's mind.

All the homes use one locale, except the Dunphys', which originally started out with two.

CASE (*director/editor*): We did this thing in the pilot where we did interviews on the couch and in the kitchen. They were called *formal* and *informal*.

BURRELL (*Phil Dunphy*): In the kitchen, it was as if the filmmaker was pulling you aside. There must be so many versions of those because there would be the scripted one and then my lesser-improvised version and then a series of alts and different ideas.

During that first season, to help the actors get in the moment, Winer would sit in the room with the actors and ask a question that would warrant the scripted answer.

WINER (*director / executive producer*): I wanted them to feel like they were really answering questions. I encouraged them to improvise their way into and out of the scripted response so that ultimately when we put it in the cut, it would truly feel like an excerpt from an interview. I felt it was giving the actors something.

The writers still loosely follow the motif.

WALLS (*writer / supervising producer*): When we're writing an interview, we might ask, "What do you think the question is here?" because they're obviously answering it after the fact or before they do it, like, "What are you hoping for this Father's Day?"

The show—for the most part—adheres to the script. The actors, however, sometimes find space to run with ideas in alternate takes.

LAMB (*first assistant director / director*): Because we do fewer takes, people stay excited, fresh, and crisp. So when we do interviews, we have more time and breadth to play with it. For Ty and Chris, it's their playground. It's hysterical and funny every time.

LEVITAN (*cocreator*): Ty's the one that will say in an interview, more than anybody, "Let me try one for me." It'll be not a little word change but a whole different interview that he's thought up himself, and it's often hilarious.

BURRELL (*Phil Dunphy*): Because there's no blocking, I deal with them different. I don't have to be as memorized as for a regular scene. I don't have to talk and chew gum, so to speak.

FERGUSON (*Mitchell Pritchett*): I definitely feel like it's the place where we have the most freedom. Eric is such a great improviser. I come from the world of theater. I can definitely improv, but I really love a script. He comes from a different world, and he brings that energy into our interviews. I love going on that ride with him because I feel safe with him, whatever he's doing. He'll have ideas and suggest different takes or suggest an alt line. The writers have always been very generous in letting us play in those moments, like the episode where Eric and I are doing the Venn diagram [season 4's "Schooled" episode], putting our arms together.

SPILLER (*director*): I think Eric and Jesse are so inventive. Their little mannerisms, particularly in the interviews, were so telling. Like Jesse touching his forehead with his thumb in some weird way and Eric's flourishes and theatricality and wearing his heart on a sleeve.

FERGUSON (*Mitchell Pritchett*): Eric and I once talked about switching chairs at some point to see what would happen if I was on the other side of him. It was meant to comment on a scene, when we were Ferberizing the baby and were frazzled and realized we were in the wrong chairs and were going to maybe get up and move. That never became a thing.

STONESTREET (*Cam Tucker*): The one interview that really sticks out in my mind is in the episode about Meryl Streep ["The Bicycle Thief"].

INT. MOMMY AND ME CLASS—DAY

A song ends and everybody claps. Cam is standing
with Helen.

                    CAMERON
          So, seen any good movies lately?

                    HELEN
          Well, my husband and I just rented
          Mamma Mia! last night. I liked it,
          but I'm not sure Meryl Streep was the
          right choice. What did you think?

Cameron looks like he's about to explode.

(above) Jesse Tyler Ferguson and Sarah Hyland during filming of the final season episode "The Last Christmas." *(Courtesy of Larsen & Talbert Photography)*

(below) Ed O'Neill goes over a point with director Jason Miller. *(Courtesy of Larsen & Talbert Photography)*

(left) Julie Bowen checks out her sides for her next scene. *(Courtesy of Larsen & Talbert Photography)*

(below) Ty Burrell and Ariel Winter, looking like real-life father and daughter, watch the production crew in motion. *(Courtesy of Larsen & Talbert Photography)*

A heavenly view from above shining down on Sofía Vergara during rehearsals. *(Courtesy of Larsen & Talbert Photography)*

(top) The *Modern Family* production family. *(Courtesy of Larsen & Talbert Photography)*

(middle) The hall of actors: headshots of every performer who has ever guested on the show line the two hallways outside Casting. *(Courtesy of Larsen & Talbert Photography)*

Wardrobe houses eleven years' worth of outfits for cast members. *(Courtesy of Larsen & Talbert Photography)*

(left) Rico Rodriguez and makeup artist Melissa Sandora, looking impressed with each other in the makeup trailer. *(Courtesy of Larsen & Talbert Photography)*

(below) Ed O'Neill leans on his partner Sofía Vergara during rehearsals. *(Courtesy of Larsen & Talbert Photography)*

Jesse Tyler Ferguson and Eric Stonestreet, with a platter of cheeseballs in front of them, enjoy a moment of bliss during rehearsal. *(Courtesy of Larsen & Talbert Photography)*

(left) Ariel Winter creates her own spotlight during rehearsals. *(Courtesy of Larsen & Talbert Photography)*

(above) Cocreator Steve Levitan *(left)* proudly looks on during preparation for filming an ensemble scene at the holiday dinner table. *(Courtesy of Larsen & Talbert Photography)*

Julie Bowen gives a friendly wink to Eric Stonestreet, her self-described brother. *(Courtesy of Larsen & Talbert Photography)*

(above) The writers' room outer conference table along with gaming distractions to free the creative mind. The glass room in the background doubles as Pritchett's Closets & Blinds. *(Courtesy of Larsen & Talbert Photography)*

(below) Phil Dunphy (yes, that's a mustache) wants to help you find a home (taken in Christopher Lloyd's office). The Pop! action figures are of the cast. The framed picture *(right)* are four members of the show dressing as Clive Bixby. The bottle of booze is for writer's inspiration. *(Courtesy of Larsen & Talbert Photography)*

EXT. GERARD: Everyone gets into their cars. Phil circles back, puts on a hoodie, punches in a code, and enters the bldg.

GERARD – LOBBY: Phil runs into Higgins who asks if he can be of service. Robot rolls by. Higgins explains the robot is the "cop" of the

down." The kids behind h
her. Gloria starts down
and Spidermans herself

(above, left) Color-coded storyboard cards used for season 11's "The Prescott." *(Courtesy of Larsen & Talbert Photography)*

(above, right) Fire Chief Sarah Hyland and pregnant first assistant director Helena Lamb on the set of season 6's "Halloween 3 Awesomeland." *(Courtesy of Helena Lamb)*

(right) Best buddies Nolan Gould and Ariel Winter take a selfie after a table read. *(Courtesy of Andy Gordon)*

Julie Bowen and Jesse Tyler Ferguson share an off-camera laugh inside the Pritchett household. *(Courtesy of Andy Gordon)*

(above) From left: Jay, Claire, Mitchell, and Cam take in a gust of anger blowing from Hurricane Gloria calling out Luke for kissing Manny's ex-girlfriend in "The Last Christmas." (Courtesy of Larsen & Talbert Photography)

(left) Nothing says twenty-one-year-old like a selfie, such as this one taken during a break in filming by the always amiable Rico Rodriguez. (Courtesy of Larsen & Talbert Photography)

Front left: Ty Burrell, Jesse Tyler Ferguson, and Sarah Hyland joke between takes. No, Ferguson isn't a two-handed drinker—they're props. (Courtesy of Larsen & Talbert Photography)

(*left*) Sofía Vergara, her dog, and the Prescott robot have a conversation during filming of "The Prescott." (*Courtesy of Marc Freeman*)

Haley and Dylan, the glowing parents with their new baby twins in the season 10 finale, "A Year of Birthdays." (*Courtesy of Steven Miller*)

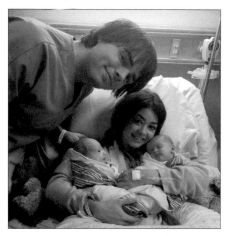

Borderline creepy baby dolls that double for Haley's twins, Poppy and George. (*Courtesy of Marc Freeman*)

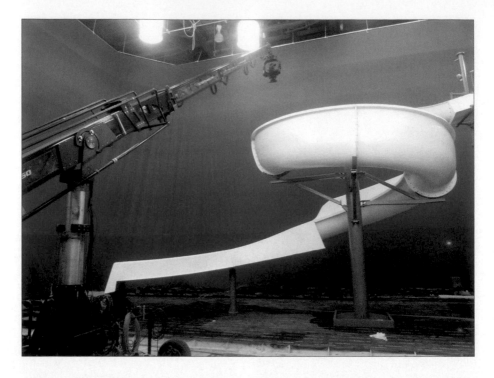

(*above*) On the Fox lot, the trucked-in and assembled seventeen-foot water slide with a blue screen behind it. The screen will be filled in later with a background to match that of the next photo (*below*), the one shot at a downtown location, the Level. (*Courtesy of Marc Freeman*)

(*below*) The bottom of the water slide that through the magic of post-production, will be made to look seamless with the slide from the previous photo (*above*). (*Courtesy of Marc Freeman*)

(left) Sofía Vergara practices her pronunciation. *(Courtesy of Larsen & Talbert Photography)*

(below) Ed O'Neill holds court with his on-screen and off-screen family. *(Courtesy of Larsen & Talbert Photography)*

(above) Julie Bowen enjoying an Ed O'Neill story on set in Mitchell and Cam's living room. *(Courtesy of Larsen & Talbert Photography)*

(right) After director Jason Miller yells cut, Nolan Gould, Eric Stonestreet, and Rico Rodriguez can't help breaking into a smile. *(Courtesy of Larsen & Talbert Photography)*

(above) Jesse Tyler Ferguson gets up close and personal with his friend (and one of the writers of "The Last Christmas") Abraham Higginbotham. *(Courtesy of Larsen & Talbert Photography)*

(below) Michael Bagdonas, son of director of photography Baggs, does his assistant cameraman magic on a scene with Jesse Tyler Ferguson and Sarah Hyland. *(Courtesy of Larsen & Talbert Photography)*

Father and son Pritchett, Ed O'Neill and Jeremy Maguire, on Lake Tahoe for season 9's premiere episode, "Lake Life." *(Courtesy of CeCe Maguire)*

(left) Pepper Saltzman (Nathan Lane), wedding planner from Lubbock, Texas, with his husband and planning partner Ronaldo (Christian Barillas). *(Courtesy of Steven Miller)*

From left: Writer/executive producer Brad Walsh, cocreator Steve Levitan, and writer/executive producer Paul Corrigan listen in on guest star Peyton Manning's story. *(Courtesy of Brad Walsh)*

(above) Qantas welcomes *Modern Family* to Australia, the most trying and divisive trip in the history of the show. *(Courtesy of Steve Levitan)*

(below) The shell of the train that Claire Bennett designed for the season 7 episode "Crazy Train." Visible green screen was replaced with actual footage of the train ride from Los Angeles to Portland. *(Courtesy of Claire Bennett)*

(above) Haley distracts Cam with a selfie to gain access to information on his phone in "The Last Christmas." *(Courtesy of Larsen & Talbert Photography)*

(below) Stuntwoman Julie Bowen flips backward out the window of Mitchell and Cam's living room and somersaults below camera line and out of view. *(Courtesy of Larsen & Talbert Photography)*

(above) The cast rehearses a holiday dinner at Mitchell and Cam's dining room table, where secrets and future plans get revealed. *(Courtesy of Larsen & Talbert Photography)*

(below) From left: The Dunphy household set and Mitchell and Cam's condo underneath a sea of rafters. Up front, a crew of caterers from a local vendor make submarine sandwiches for the cast and crew. *(Courtesy of Larsen & Talbert Photography)*

CAMERON'S ORIGINAL INTERVIEW

CAMERON

Excuse me, Meryl Streep could play
Batman and be the right choice. She's
perfection. Whether she's divorcing
Kramer or wearing Prada, and don't
get me started on Sophie. Oh my God,
I'm tearing up just thinking about it.
                    (losing it)
She couldn't forgive herself.

Stonestreet took it one step further.

STONESTREET (*Cam Tucker*): The tag is me. That's all improvised. What it was is me doing the interview and then, once we had it, me continuing on and on. Chris was like, "Oh my God, that was so funny." And then, unbeknownst to me, he put that in as the tag that week. I had no idea until I watched it.

STONESTREET'S ADDED IMPROVISATION

CAMERON
          (crying)
She couldn't forgive herself, and . . .
she had to choose! And I think
because now I have—we have—we have
L— . . . we have Lily, it's so hard to
imagine being put in that position.
If I had to choose Lily or Mitchell,
I mean, I would choose L— . . . I
don't know!
                    (gets up; walks off)
I just, I don't know! I don't know! I
don't know!

Bowen, at one with the camera, hates doing interviews alone.

BOWEN (*Claire Dunphy*): To me, it's actors' hell. You have the same two guys, Toby the operator and Noah the focus puller, sitting there in front of you. You're chatting, and then from the other room, voices are telling you to do something as you stare into camera, and then there's silence . . . whisper, whisper, and then someone gives you notes. It feels awful. There's nothing to do but stare into the camera. You don't learn how to talk into the camera in acting school. That's a tough one to do in character and convey any humor.

CORRIGAN (*writer / executive producer*): I know she hates those interviews. But she's really good at it. She did one where Phil is going to do some comedy at a real estate banquet. She had to do this thing where she laughs, but not with her eyes, and she managed to do that. It was remarkable.

ZUKER (*writer / executive producer*): One of my favorite Claire moments of all time is "The Butler's Escape" [season 4]. She's sitting there smiling and being patient. You know exactly how she feels about magic and this story. She's communicating it absolutely perfectly doing nothing.

BOWEN (*Claire Dunphy*): Ty has the longest freaking dialogue about the dumbest, craziest thing in magic, this whole made-up "Butler's Escape."

```
             PHIL INTERVIEW

                  PHIL
     It goes without saying that the
     Butler's Escape . . . is one of the
     most challenging feats of escapology
     an illusionist can perform. It's
     based, of course, on the well-known
     story of the Earl of Flanning's
     manservant, Percy, who was imprisoned
     in the Tower of London . . . and, as
     we all know, refused to take off his
     uniform when he was shackled.
```

```
Famously, as the, uh, tower guard,
Gert, slept, Percy freed himself and
leapt over the sleeping guard, giving
rise to the popular expression Percy
jumped the Gert.
```

WRUBEL (*writer / executive producer*): I wrote that as a Phil interview, and then Chris had the idea to put Claire in it and not say anything.

WALSH (*writer / executive producer*): Phil has most of the real estate in terms of lines, and yet there's a whole scene to be watched on Julie's side of the screen.

SPILLER (*director*): Their whole relationship is reflected in every beat of that.

BOWEN (*Claire Dunphy*): All I had to do was listen to him, and it was magnificent. It showed how much I love and adore this man, but how ridiculous he is all at once.

Perhaps the funniest interview moment, a classic on the show's blooper reels, involved Phil's mispronunciation of the word mnemonic.

```
          PHIL INTERVIEW


               PHIL
Well, you can't be in sales and not
remember people's names. That's why
I like to use what they call "mina-
monic" devices. They're little tricks
to help you remember. Um, like the
other day, I met this guy named Carl.
Now, I might forget that name, But he
was wearing a Grateful Dead T-shirt.
What's a band like the Grateful Dead?
Phish. Where do fish live? The ocean.
```

```
          What else lives in the ocean? Coral.
          Hello, "Coral."


                    CLAIRE
          I think it's mnemonic.


                    PHIL
          I-I think I'd remember.
```

BURRELL (*Phil Dunphy*): Julie didn't see that one coming. We added that on the day, the fact that Phil didn't understand how that was pronounced. It got Chris and me laughing before we sat down to do the interview.

BOWEN (*Claire Dunphy*): "Mina-monic devices." That was it. There must be an hour of me laughing.

LLOYD (*cocreator*): He said *mina-monic* about eighteen times and she laughed about eighteen times. It was killing them to not get through it, but they could not get through it.

BOWEN (*Claire*): For the most part, we really try not to break because if someone's doing something that funny, you don't want to trash the take. I try really, really hard to put my fingernail into my hand or bite the inside of my face, but with *mina-monic,* I didn't see it coming and it was right there. That's the genius of Ty.

LLOYD (*cocreator*): He said it with such a straight face as though he absolutely believes that was how that word was pronounced. They could not stop laughing. It's absolutely infectious.

BOWEN (*Claire Dunphy*): It gets to the point where it was definitely disrespectful, but we don't make a common practice of that. So I hope we're forgiven.

LLOYD (*cocreator*): They don't realize that I could have seen them do it another twenty-five minutes and broken up that many more times, because it was delightful every time.

Grab It

Modern Family *has a legendary reputation in the industry for production speed, taking the single-camera format and speeding it up exponentially. While other sets endure a lot of Fraturdays (where Friday night turns into Saturday morning),* Modern Family *production days typically whiz by.*

MORTON (*executive producer*): *In one hour of production, you typically spend forty-five minutes doing production and fifteen minutes doing the scene. Comedy's about freshness and spontaneity. No one's funny at two in the morning. My goal was to flip the equation.*

LEVITAN (*cocreator*): *We wanted to get to the funny part sooner and then be allowed to spend some time, when things aren't quite working, without feeling like you're under such a gun to get moving.*

Some of it comes from camera placement.

SAPIENZA (*script supervisor / director*): *On a regular show, you set up two cameras. You shoot a master, then set up your cameras in one direction to get one actor's dialogue. Then you turn around and focus on shooting the same thing from the other side.*

CASE (*director/editor*): Modern Family *does something called cross coverage. If I'm shooting a shot of Gloria talking to Jay, Camera A is shooting Gloria and Camera B is shooting Jay. The cameras are off angle enough that you can shoot them at the same time, and the lighting is universal so you can shoot both directions at the same time.*

TUCKER (*camera operator*): *We don't do a separate wide master establishing the scene. We don't do a medium and tight shot. We do all three in one setup. Start wide, stay below the light, avoid the other camera, and push in to the close-up.*

BAGGS (*director of photography / director*): *It lends itself to more voyeuristic moments that capture the spontaneity. The cast knows what camera will probably be on them. They can play to that camera and still make it look as if it's natural, like you captured it for the first time.*

TUCKER (*camera operator*): *Baggs has the task of lighting the scene, which is an incredible challenge. You can't put lights where you normally would because the other camera is going to see it.*

BAGGS (*director of photography / director*): *I knew I was going to have to be fast and compromise, so during setup, I think, "What's the most important thing here in terms of light and composition?"*

It can take time for guest stars to pick up.

BAGGS (*director of photography / director*): *They're kind of waiting for their close-up. We tell them, "You're on-camera all the time. Everyone's on the same time throughout the scene."*

ADAM DEVINE (*Andy Bailey*): *That's not how regular TV shows work. Usually they march in to get their close-up, and you're prepared for it. It's freeing and fun here. It makes you be fully prepared for every scene.*

CHRIS GEERE (*Arvin Fennerman*): *I love the pace. It's like doing a play in a little way. Walking into rooms on different cues and then exiting the rooms and waiting for others to go in and out.*

BAGGS (*director of photography / director*): *Our operators are basically storytellers.*

TUCKER (*camera operator*): *Just capture what happens. It's a matter of, if you see something, go grab it. If you have to completely whip across the room to go get an actor who just all of a sudden comes in the door, that's our game, you can do that.*

BAGGS (*director of photography / director*): *Operators listen to the scenes and know where they want to be. One take could be different from another. People are pretty amazed when they see it from behind the scenes. It looks simple, but it's extremely hard to do.*

TUCKER (*camera operator*): *Chris has been big about not wanting the moment where something happens and the lens zooms in to go "ba dum dum." You don't want to sell the joke. You want to pick and choose when to do those zooms and camera takes.*

BAGGS (*director of photography / director*): *It's very difficult at times to know where not to be. We made a lot of mistakes in the beginning. I think what organically grew was the actors got to know our operators and the operators got to know the actors.*

Sometimes characters break the fourth wall, letting the audience in on a moment or having a character embarrassed by it.

BOWEN (*Claire Dunphy*): *We had an operator early on who was operating Camera A. When somebody pulls the focus on the camera suddenly, you can see the movement in the lens. I remember feeling like I am having a relationship with the operator and camera because I would look up inside the camera, and as I was doing it, see the focus pull. I'm not going to lie, that was deeply satisfying. It meant that he, as an audience member, knew that this was the moment and we were exactly together.*

BURRELL (*Phil Dunphy*): *Being able to look to somebody outside of that world either for help or for confirmation and/or checking on them to see if they caught you doing something embarrassing—that's something I'm going to miss. It gives you an extra element to work with that I consider a luxury.*

Baby on Board

On multiple occasions, like Mitchell and Cam's wedding or Haley's pregnancy, the writers developed a season-long story arc. They tried this for the first time in season 3, with Mitchell and Cam deciding to adopt a second child. In hindsight, some of the writers feel they erred by introducing the storyline without knowing its conclusion, because they had to make sure it paid off somehow.

ZUKER (*writer / executive producer*): We fought over it for the better part of the year. We actually did an arc where they decide to adopt a boy. Steve, and he had supporters in this, was thinking they'd adopt a young African American kid. To half of us, me included, we felt that was a little anachronistic. Like what you don't want to do today is have the white couple rescuing the black child.

LEVITAN (*cocreator*): I thought it would be interesting to add to the multicultural nature of this family.

ZUKER (*writer / executive producer*): I have many friends who have adopted African American kids, but on television, you ask, "Who are this kid's parents? What was going on?" And we didn't want to have a wisecracking city kid in there because it's too hard to avoid all the trappings that go with that.

LEVITAN (*cocreator*): I think people get overly politically correct at times, worrying about the way things will look. It didn't mean they were rescuing a race by any means. I thought it would have been an interesting way to add a few more issues to that family.

The writers ultimately gave up on the baby idea entirely.

LEVITAN (*cocreator*): We'd just been through Mitch and Cam raising Lily. To start that all over again ultimately didn't feel like we were going to get that many fresh stories.

But because they'd teased a baby all year, they had to deliver one. They did, but from an unexpected source.

O'NEILL (*Jay Pritchett*): Steve told me, "We're thinking of having Gloria pregnant." I thought it was a very funny idea. Jay would think, "What the hell, how could this possibly be?" It gave us room to do a few funny things. I said, "Fine with me. I'm not pregnant. I don't have to put the thing on."

WRUBEL (*writer / executive producer*): We thought that house would get the most jolt of energy from a baby. It seemed like it would help give all those characters more things to play.

They revealed her pregnancy on season 3's last episode, "Baby on Board." The episode focused on the heartbreak of Mitchell and Cam's final failed attempt at adoption, cleverly played out within a humorous real-life telenovela to soften the drama.

LEVITAN (*cocreator*): The soap opera conceit was a way to handle what otherwise could have been a pretty maudlin situation at the hospital. Two characters who are working so hard to adopt a baby and ultimately couldn't and the heterosexual couple accidentally having a baby that they weren't even trying for. We hid the ball well with Gloria's car sickness. I think it's all really earned by the time we got to it.

Mitchell and Cam give up on the adoption idea while lying in a field, staring up at the same stars from "Starry Night."

STONESTREET (*Cam Tucker*): They always try to end the season with all of us together. This was us laying in the dirt.

FERGUSON (*Mitchell Pritchett*): Eric and I looking up at the stars. It was at night and freezing. We were far from the studio, far away from everyone.

Levitan took certain liberties with directing the sequence, breaking the mockumentary shooting style to better capture the emotion of the moment.

LEVITAN (*cocreator*): I thought it would make that scene better. I got a directing Emmy for it.

FERGUSON (*Mitchell Pritchett*): It was very emotional. There are those rare moments on our show where we get to dive deep, and that was one of them.

STONESTREET (*Cam Tucker*): I'm always melancholy and sad at the end of a season anyway.

FERGUSON (*Mitchell Pritchett*): Eric and I were walking back to our cars knowing we wouldn't see each other for a few months.

STONESTREET (*Cam Tucker*): Having an hour to drive home after that. "See you." "See you."

FERGUSON (*Mitchell Pritchett*): We thought, "Okay, that was weird."

Gloria's pregnancy led to the birth of Fulgencio Joseph "Joe" Pritchett. Lloyd wanted a name that seemed very Colombian and that could create conflict between Gloria and Jay, who just wanted a baseball player's name: Joe. Fulgencio comes from Fulgencio Batista, Cuba's president before Castro's Cuban revolution. Much like Lily, multiple babies and toddlers played Joe (Rebecca and Sierra Mark played baby Joe; Pierce Wallace played toddler Joe). Then the producers decided to bump up Joe's age in season 7 so the show could ditch another sack of potatoes.

LLOYD (*cocreator*): We were finding it a little difficult telling Jay-and-Gloria stories. So having a kid would free up some new story directions.

HIGGINBOTHAM (*writer / executive producer*): I think the goal was to bring a boy into that house, who was the son Jay always wanted, a rough-and-tumble, sports-centric, athletic kid. We thought that would create a funny conflict with Mitchell, a forty-two-year-old man, jealous of his four-year-old brother [technically, half brother] for having the relationship he always wanted with his dad, and Claire, who thought she was Dad's little boy.

Greenberg pre-read 221 three- and four-year-olds. One of them, three-year-old Jeremy Maguire, had never aspired to be an actor. He got discovered, however, singing his ABCs in the middle of a Home Depot by someone at a talent agency. Maguire signed with the agency soon thereafter. Over the next several months, he auditioned for five television commercials, amazingly booking them all. Next came a Sarah Silverman pilot. By the end of the year, he had a longer résumé than many actors ten times his age. Then came Modern Family.

CECE MAGUIRE (*Jeremy's mom*): On his first audition, he met with Jeff and Allen. When he finished, Allen mentioned that Jeremy said he was going to meet up with Peter Pan and conduct the parade at Disneyland. We'd planned to do Disney that day. I hoped he didn't just talk about Disney. Apparently, he didn't. He had a callback two days later. Rachael Field walked him back and forth. When Jeremy came for his final audition, he remembered her name. She was blown away by that, this little three-year-old.

FIELD (*associate producer*): He was so sweet and composed. He's very good at picking up on people and wise beyond his years.

Greenberg brought fifteen kids to producers. Four, including Jeremy, did a screen test with O'Neill and a production crew.

GREENBERG (*casting director*): It's very intimidating to have a sound boom over your head where people are lighting you and putting makeup on you and there's a couple of dozen people in the immediate vicinity rushing around. You want to see how a child behaves in that atmosphere.

Maguire, fortunately, had his trusty cape on to calm him.

JEREMY MAGUIRE (*Joe Pritchett*): Every event I go to, I always wear a cape. The cape is the thing that makes me look dapper and chic.

Yes, he said "dapper and chic," which sounds even better when spoken by an eight-year-old.

CECE MAGUIRE (*Jeremy's mom*): I think it helps him feel comfortable doing what he does. When he showed up for his final audition, Jeff was walking with him and said, "Jeremy, I think you should keep your cape on."

GREENBERG (*casting director*): I loved the idea because it's such a real kid thing. I thought that was a great touch.

CECE MAGUIRE (*Jeremy's mom*): They had him do his lines, and he didn't miss a beat. Ed did it about three times with him. Then they asked him to do other things like knock some blocks on the floor and run off. He said, "Oh yeah, and then I could jump off the chair like this." They all started laughing because he was adding to what he could do.

Maguire won the role. Everyone else seemed to understand that except for him.

JEREMY MAGUIRE (*Joe Pritchett*): When I was working on my first episode, I really got weirded out. I thought it was a commercial. I didn't know what a TV show was. I learned it that year.

It took O'Neill time to warm up to Jeremy.

O'NEILL (*Jay Pritchett*): I'll be honest with you, I may have been a little late to the party with him because I felt early on that he was a little too cute. I worked with him. I would give him specific instructions like, "Don't go there. Stand here. When I tell you to, go move there."

ANDREW BROOKS (*associate producer*): It's so funny to watch. An eight-year-old kid is getting a master class from Ed in acting.

O'NEILL (*Jay Pritchett*): I felt like I needed to teach him something that I didn't think he was getting. Not from the lack of trying but from a lack of experience.

JEREMY MAGUIRE (*Joe Pritchett*): He's really smart with how he goes over the lines with me and gets me all my cues.

O'NEILL (*Jay Pritchett*): I don't praise him every goddamn time he opens his mouth, which is what was happening with guest directors desperate to get their shot. It doesn't mean anything after a while. I'd tell him, "I don't understand what you're saying. Speak up." And then when he got it, I'd say, "Now that's a good job." He's a sweet kid.

JEREMY MAGUIRE (*Joe Pritchett*): He's basically my acting teacher, because I've never had one. He's super funny, a little inappropriate, but really funny.

> *For the entire series, the writers, self-admittedly, have struggled at times with his dialogue. Much as TV fans squirm at "jumping the shark" moments, so, too, do they squirm at the mention of Oliver, the cloyingly cute cousin of the Bradys introduced in the last handful of* Brady Bunch *episodes as a desperate attempt to recapture the lost prepubescence of the teenage Brady children.*

ZUKER (*writer / executive producer*): Some other writers may have stronger feelings about the character. I like him and think he's been reliable.

HIGGINBOTHAM (*writer / executive producer*): You want the kid to be funny, which often leads you to going over the top with it. The challenge is how do you make a kid funny while letting them still have a kid's voice?

MORTON (*executive producer*): On a personal level, I'm tired of babies, but I don't have to write twenty-two episodes a year. This was an area ripe for telling stories.

HIGGINBOTHAM (*writer / executive producer*): I don't think we've succeeded with him all the time. I think that you have to watch how precocious and articulate you make him. I think sometimes we write Joe speeches that make me cringe. Like, really? Where is he getting these words except from a comedy-writing team?

LLOYD (*cocreator*): Jeremy is precocious, so he was talking a lot better than most kids his age. It made it seem like a bigger cheat than it was.

LEVITAN (*cocreator*): If we're giving him moments that are too cutesy, that's our fault, frankly, because we're giving him those moments.

ZUKER (*writer / executive producer*): We're successful with Joe when the story's more about how our adult characters are reacting to Joe rather than Joe leading the deep emotions. Joe's best when he has one or two lines that are super quick. I came up with a line where Jay was being really goofy with Thomas Lennon [season 10's "Can't Elope"] and Manny says, "I never thought I'd say this, but I miss Jay's toxic masculinity." It just sat there. So, I had Joe say, "At least he's not your real father." I think that's a good way to use him. Don't make it the "Joe show."

Off-screen, everyone enjoys the Jeremy show.

VERGARA (*Gloria Delgado-Pritchett*): He's a little genius since he was really young. So many intelligent and funny things come out of his mouth.

ZUKER (*writer / executive producer*): It's very weird to see a kid as sharp as he was when we hired him. His ability to memorize was preternatural. It was incredible.

MCCARTHY-MILLER (*director*): We were doing a scene where it had to look like he was biting Manny's friend, grabbing her by the leg. We get his teeth on the jeans but they came off in the middle of the scene. He reset himself and continued the scene. It was unbelievable. He's five years old.

JEREMY MAGUIRE (*Joe Pritchett*): I don't feel now like I work on commercials anymore. I work on the same TV show over and over again. On hiatus weeks, I really miss everybody. I just miss people.

Phil's Sexy, Sexy House

Fans of the show know the three home interiors very well. They come courtesy of production designer Berg, he of CSI *(2000–2015) before and* Gotham *(2014–2019) afterward. A natural, logical progression of set design to and from* Modern Family, *said no one.*

For Mitchell and Cam's abode, he chose a Spanish-themed duplex with stucco walls and a red-shingled roof.

BERG (*production designer*): *The exterior's a few blocks away from the studio. Stylistically, it reminded me very much of what I call "the flats" in LA. Inside, that house smelled so bad from a pet bird that I couldn't spend a minute in there. I never really got a sense of how it laid out, so I was free to design it so it was a more workable space for stage.*

Because the designs don't match, the camera never follows anyone into the home. The backyard proved problematic as well.

BENNETT (*production designer / art director*): *We tried to shoot there once, but spatially it was very restricting. We ended up building one here on the lot. It's a patch of lawn called the Writers' Lawn. It's surrounded by Fox buildings. It's an undertaking whenever we need that set because we have to completely transform it.*

BAGGS (*director of photography / director*): We make three sides with fencing and greens. We have a false wall, which is the back of the house. That's great art directing.

BERG (*production designer*): It was such an ill-conceived plan. As we got to needing it more and more, Fox progressively became more and more restrictive with how and when we were able to use and prep it. It became like the most sacred ground on the lot. Not fun.

The interior motif comes from Berg's own life.

BERG (*production designer*): It was modeled after the apartment I first lived in when I moved to LA. It was an old Spanish-style apartment on Cochran Avenue that had depressed arches like what transitions from the living room into the dining room of Mitch's and Cam's set.

BENNETT (*production designer / art director*): The archways define the space and create wonderful depth for the interviews with the long hallway.

BERG (*production designer*): The colors were a muted pastel, which was a little depressing, but I wanted less of a splashy feel. The saturation of color on Friends was the exact wrong way to go. My attack on it, from reading the script, is "Let's make this thing real, authentic-looking."

The Pritchett household has a modern art deco exterior that would seem to cater toward Jay's tastes. The interior, however, with its rich textured colors and wild animal-striped furniture, is all Gloria.

BERG (*production designer*): The whole criteria for the exterior of that house was it needed to be near Steve Levitan's house. I guess Steve wanted to walk there. That's how it came to me. The houses were all inappropriate except for this one house, which was very workable, interesting to look at architecturally, and believable that Jay, with his wealth, would conceivably have done well enough to live in.

WINER (*director / executive producer*): *In the pilot, you didn't see any of the house. All you got was a bit of a vibe of an upscale designer-furnished place. It's very different than what ended up being in the show, but no one noticed that switcheroo.*

BENNETT (*production designer / art director*): *The backstory was the place had been Jay's bachelor pad. There's definitely signs of that from the leather couches, the bar, and the dark wood furniture. And then Gloria moves in and brings her feminine and fiery touches to things. So we were able to bring in this red color, which brought the space alive. We've taken hints of that throughout the show.*

BERG (*production designer*): *The barstools are zebra prints. That's definitely in reference to Gloria.*

BENNETT (*production designer / art director*): *There was a contentious issue about the foot painting in the foyer. It's a red painting that has different ladies' legs and feet. I'm not a huge fan of it, but some people loved it. It's no longer on the set because Sofía didn't like it.*

BERG (*production designer*): *A lot of the photography in the house were images I had taken out on the desert in Palm Springs. There's one very large painting on the second run of stairs. It looks like a '70s graphic. It was an homage to Roy Lichtenstein's brushed-stroke paintings. I painted it on a piece of paper and then had it scanned and did a vector drawing of it. For the black-and-white photograph above the mantelpiece, I wanted an Albert Watson type of look, which is a blowout shot of the family over a white background.*

RODRIGUEZ (*Manny Delgado*): *We had to take family photos depicting Jay and Gloria's wedding. Sofía had a wedding dress on, and Ed had his tux on. They're both happy, and I was smiling. They said, "Rico, frown in this one like you're upset, like you hate Ed." So that's the photo that they used.*

BENNETT (*production designer / art director*): *When Joe was born, we made sure he was added with baby photos and moments in a family's life you document. That's important to me, keeping these sets alive. We need to believe a family is living in these houses.*

The Dunphy house exterior, located in Cheviot Hills near Fox Studios, offers a classic two-story, traditional home with an interior that Berg feels suggests the dueling styles of Pottery Barn and Restoration Hardware.

WINER (*director / executive producer*): *The actual interior of the Dunphy house came from a house we found in the Pacific Palisades. In some ways, we copied it.*

Most television shows only build a series of ground-floor sets for interior shooting. Winer wanted something different. To save money, the set used recycled pieces from the recently canceled *Samantha Who* (2007–2009) set.

WINER (*director / executive producer*): *We built a functional double-decker set, which is unusual in broadcast TV. Because of the doc style, I felt like there'd be great utility if you could follow characters from one room to another. You really needed to see them move through the set.*

The Dunphys tend to congregate in the kitchen and den, which offers a wide space for actors and crew.

BENNETT (*production designer / art director*): *There are little tricks. The kitchen island can roll to allow camera position or blocking. We finished the island countertop this year because we had a prop last season where Alex was smashing a puzzle that she couldn't solve on the counter. It took massive chunks out of the wood. The backsplash tile's also very fake. We actually used vinyl, which proved problematic because the glue would melt and the tiles would fall off. That was embarrassing.*

BERG (*production designer*): *When we did the breakfast room off the kitchen, we were a day or two away from shooting when Jason came on set. He turned his head sideways a little bit, regrouped himself, and then asked, "Is there any way we can make the set four feet wider?" It was literally a finished dress set at that point. I said, "Of course there is, Jason; we have to rebuild it." We did, and it was a much better set for it.*

BENNETT (*production designer / art director*): *We have a door-jamb in the Dunphy kitchen. When the kids were on set, they would mark their heights as they grew season to season. It's a nice touch that will never make it to camera.*

On the staircase wall hang family pictures that came from the actors' personal collections.

BENNETT (*production designer / art director*): *It's trying to make the space tell the story of this family. Over the years, whenever there's an opportunity, like when Manny and Luke graduated, we made sure to get some good snapshots that we could add to the wall. When we did the trips to Australia and Wyoming, those were great opportunities to get candid photos, too.*

At the bottom of the staircase rests an existential dining room, one that exists only as a doorway that leads to nowhere. Apparently, the Dunphys don't believe in fine dining.

BERG (*production designer*): *It was a complete afterthought. For one of the episodes, we needed another route out somehow into a different room, so we opened that space up. Because of the way the stage was positioned, we only had four to six feet of depth to work with to create the illusion of a dining room.*

BENNETT (*production designer / art director*): *It's a random space. There's a running joke about why the family never goes there.*

Yet they have no issue traveling to Las Vegas and Australia as they did in season 5's two travel episodes.

Las Vegas

The "Las Vegas" episode, like many of the show's greatest achievements, evolved from one simple idea.

WALSH (*writer / executive producer*): Bill, Paul, and I got it into our heads that it would be cool to write a farce. We asked Chris if we could explore the idea, and he gave us the go-ahead. Then we realized that we didn't really know how to write a farce.

LLOYD (*cocreator*): Farce is a challenge in storytelling. It's all split-second timing, lots of people with lots of stakes that are running counter to one another. Everybody with a very clear drive, but all in conflict in as close a quarters as possible. It's a massive puzzle.

WRUBEL (*writer / executive producer*): Chris had done one of the great TV farces of all time, "The Ski Lodge" episode on *Frasier*. So we had a feeling he'd be into it. In typical Chris fashion, however, he never wants to repeat himself, so the challenge became, "How do we do this?"

CORRIGAN (*writer / executive producer*): The *Frasier* farces often used sex as the key drive for characters. Since we have three happy couples, we had to find a way to add motivations that didn't raise questions about their relationships. The example that I held in my mind was an episode of *Cheers,* "An Old-Fashioned Wedding." It's probably my favorite episode of TV, and it was written by David Lloyd.

WRUBEL (*writer / executive producer*): We tried to give everybody something to play. It was a little sad because the kids weren't in it. But once we landed on the fact that it was just the adults, I thought that became an interesting challenge, too.

WALSH (*writer / executive producer*): It was so confusing. We had to draw a map of the Vegas hotel suites on a dry-erase board. We made a magnet for each character and started moving them around as we broke the story because, otherwise, we couldn't track their movements.

LLOYD (*cocreator*): There was tremendous contribution from everybody to get that right, because there were so many questions that had to be answered to get everybody's drives figured out in a semi-believable way.

PATTON OSWALT (*Ducky*): That's a very specific genre, feel, and taste, and I thought they really nailed it.

They brought in Gail Mancuso to direct the symphony of complexity.

MANCUSO (*director*): It's the single hardest episode I've ever done in terms of blocking and tracking; not only the physicality of it but the emotions and where the jokes are. In a farce, everyone's going from room to room. I had to color code my script. Phil and Claire's room was yellow, the hotel hallway blue, Mitchell and Cam's orange. I had to make sure we're in the right set when we're back on set.

Production designer Bennett, in a ridiculously short amount of time, created a seamless re-creation on stage 5, down to the doorknobs, of the interior of the Mandalay Bay hotel in Vegas, where they shot parts of the episode.

CORRIGAN (*writer / executive producer*): Everything in the hotel's hallway is in Vegas. Everything in a hotel room we shot on our sets, except what was in the bathroom. Claire made it blend seamlessly, and you can't discount Gail's direction to make it look seamless.

MANCUSO (*director*): The actors literally turned it over to me. They said, "It's in your hands," because it was so busy. The ins and outs, the scenes and how they all connected, there was no way an individual actor could really understand it all. We had to build up to the breakneck speed of the third act that held a lot of comedy.

LLOYD (*cocreator*): I had some reservations about whether it would work in our single-camera form and how our actors would take to a different pace and style than we're used to. And they loved it. They took to it instantly. By the end of it, everyone was like, "We've gotta do more of those."

MANCUSO (*director*): Day one in Vegas, I remember watching a scene I had just blocked and thinking, "Wow, this is going to be something special." That rarely happens.

Because the casino remained open during the shoot, the crew had to take precautions to protect cast members.

VERGARA (*Gloria Delgado-Pritchett*): Vegas is always hard because you're in those hotels where there's so much people.

LESLIE MERLIN (*assistant director / key PA*): We were filming a shot with Sofía. She really had to go to the bathroom, but people know we're filming. She made me go check that no one was in the stalls so that while she was in there, no one was going to take photos of her.

INT. CASINO—NEAR ELEVATORS

Jay rounds a corner and approaches an elevator.
A SECURITY GUARD stops him.

                    SECURITY GUARD
          Sorry, sir. This is a private
          elevator.

                           JAY
          No need to apologize. I'm glad you're
          on top of this stuff.

Jay produces his silver card.

                     SECURITY GUARD
          That's only for the Excelsior level.
          This elevator goes to the top floor.

                           JAY
          I thought the Excelsior was the top.
          Sixty-two.

                     SECURITY GUARD
          Mandalay Bay has sixty-three floors.
          The top floor is Excelsior Plus.

The security guard waves a couple of people
through after they flash him black key cards.

                           JAY
          Wait, they're allowed up there?
          They're wearing dungarees. This can't
          be right.

WRUBEL (*writer / executive producer*): Whenever I would go to Vegas, my friend would book a suite on whatever the fancy floor was. But there'd be an elevator that goes above my floor. I wondered, "How do they get up there?" I thought I had VIP tickets to Coachella one year, and then I saw there was another entrance and I was wondering, "How do they get those seats?" I'm always feeling even if I get a good deal, someone has gotten a better one.

For Gloria and Jay's story arc, the writers harkened back to Barkley, the life-sized dog butler (from the season 1 episode "Not in My House") that Jay had won in Vegas. Its presence constantly scared Gloria, leading her to refer to it as "diablo" and "an unholy mix between man and beast."

In "Las Vegas," Gloria spies in a store's window display Rebarka, a female version of Barkley. The script describes her as "half-dog, half-French maid." Gloria fears she will become Jay's next purchase.

LLOYD (*cocreator*): Gloria buys it herself so that Jay can't and hides it in a hotel room. Ultimately, she gets locked out of her room. She's naked and has to change into Rebarka's outfit. Somehow, her appearance in that outfit winds up being the culmination to a magic trick that Phil does to try and impress Ducky, the magic elder. That's a fair amount of work to get all of those pieces to interlock. I think it took us more than three weeks to figure out every element of that.

INT. HOTEL—PHIL AND CLAIRE'S ROOM

Phil throws down a smoke pellet. Smoke billows. Gloria emerges through the smoke wearing Rebarka's French maid outfit.

                    GLORIA
        Hola.

                    DUCKY
        Amazing! You lull me in with the
        hackey quick change, and all the
        while, you're turning a fake dog into
        a hot maid.
        That's brilliant. That's magic.

                    PHIL
        No. That's . . .
                (striking pose) . . .
        Metamorphosis!

A beat, then Gloria curtsies.

PATTON OSWALT (*Ducky*): Ducky was very, very serious about what he does. It's very much like a 1930s screwball movie, so I didn't have to get that deep into the character. It was more like, "Can I serve certain traits that make the characters in the scenes funny?"

While in the casino, Mitchell bumps into Langham [Fred Armisen], an old flame that he hasn't seen in years, and his partner, Tim. That meeting triggers Mitchell and Cam's storyline concerning a misunderstanding of intentions with a past lover.

GREENBERG (*casting director*): Fred Armisen happened to be on the list of names to play the bath butler. They saw his name and said, "Why don't we use Fred for this other part?"

MANCUSO (*director*): When we first met Langham and his fiancé in the lobby, I asked Fred, when he walks away, to throw one lingering look back at Mitch and think about what could have been. It's a small nuance, but it set up his attitude in the episode. He took the ball and ran with it.

Langham sidles up next to Mitchell, who's on a roll at a blackjack table. A misinterpreted conversation ensues, culminating with Mitchell accidentally leaving the table without his room key. Langham takes that as an invitation. Mitchell, meanwhile, takes his winnings and plans a surprise romantic-themed "techno-bath" bath for him and Cam, courtesy of the bath butler.

ZUKER (*writer / executive producer*): When I think of Vegas, I have more than once been dragged to one of the nightclubs where I have the rare honor of being the oldest and creepiest person in them. It's all that crazy techno stuff. I thought maybe someone wants to carry that experience into the bathtub.

Meanwhile, Cam returns from a bachelor party he attended behind Mitchell's back. Mitchell discovers the betrayal.

Cam enters to discover a bathroom transformed into a dance club: lasers, fog, thumping music. Langham is in the tub. Cam sees the back of his head and immediately shuts the door, unseen by Langham.

> LANGHAM
>
> Oh, don't act so shocked. You told me at the bachelor party you two lead separate lives.

> MITCHELL
> (to Cam)
> You went to the bachelor party?

> CAMERON
>
> Yes, and I felt bad sneaking around, but I shouldn't have now that I see what you're up to.

> MITCHELL
>
> I'm not up to anything! I left my room key by accident.

> LANGHAM
>
> We're all obviously tense. Let's take a deep breath, get in the tub.

> MITCHELL
>
> It's not happening!

STONESTREET (Cam Tucker): The way Fred delivers *"We're all obviously tense. Let's take a deep breath, get in the tub"* like he hasn't abandoned the idea we're going to get in the bathtub with him. Talk about a choice of how to deliver a line. This is why he's Fred Armisen.

And then came the bath butler.

WALSH (*writer / executive producer*): Paul and I wrote a pilot years ago with a bath butler in it. "Shockingly," it wasn't produced, so we thought, "Guess we'll never get to do an episode of television with a bath butler." Somehow *Modern Family* afforded us that opportunity.

CORRIGAN (*writer / executive producer*): We were in Vegas. We knew we wanted to be slightly extravagant. We thought the idea of a bath butler was hilarious.

LLOYD (*cocreator*): This ridiculous character, the bath butler, sees all of this madness going on around him and acts like nothing's wrong with it. He takes his bath accoutrement very, very seriously.

INT. HOTEL—PHIL AND CLAIRE'S ROOM

Phil removes an antique-looking case from his suitcase and unlocks it. There is a KNOCK at the door. Phil tosses a blanket over the case and opens the door to reveal HIGGINS, an officious English butler.

                HIGGINS
  Mr. Dunphy, I presume.

                PHIL
  Yes. Hi.

                HIGGINS
  I'm your butler, Leslie Higgins. It's
  a boy name where I come from. May I
  come in?

LLOYD (*cocreator*): *Butler* sounds English, and it was hard to think of anybody who could be funnier doing that than Stephen Merchant. He has that really unique English ability to be very sophisticated, deft with language, and perfectly ridiculous. So we really fell in love with the idea of his doing it.

MERCHANT (*Leslie Higgins*): The fun of it is this person, who's masterful at his job and who has seen the most diabolical things in his time, is a soul of discretion. Nothing fazes him. He's the guy trying too hard to impress his patrons. I think it's a little bit John Cleese and a little bit Stephen Fry who used to have a comedy sketch with Hugh Laurie.

Everything went swimmingly with Merchant's casting, until it didn't.

GREENBERG (*casting director*): We asked his agent, because we always ask for foreign actors, "Are his work papers in order?" And he said yes . . . but he didn't get them to us. And when he finally did, they weren't in order.

YOUNG (*production manager / producer*): Usually work visas are only good for one project. And somehow that got misunderstood.

MORTON (*executive producer*): The morning of the table read, we found out Stephen's work visa was only good for a project at HBO [Merchant's *Hello Ladies*]. He'd have to apply for this special visa, which can take a week or two.

GREENBERG (*casting director*): It's hard to make it happen quickly these days, post 9/11.

Merchant knew nothing of this as he arrived for the table read.

MORTON (*executive producer*): I'd never met Stephen before, and I had to tell him he can't work because he's not legal. He said, "Well, that's disappointing," and I said, "Yeah. We tried to get ahold of you to stop you." He said that as long as he was there, he'd like to do the table read, and I said, "I can't ask you to read it, but if you happen to read it, fair enough." He sat in, did the table read, and was brilliant.

MERCHANT (*Leslie Higgins*): One of my occasional talents is cold readings. I don't mean cold readings in a psychic, magician sense, but reading things without much prep.

MORTON (*executive producer*): We had Fox attorneys and the best immigration attorney connected to Fox see if we could expedite all of this. Unfortunately, we were also battling a three-day weekend. It didn't work out. We got word Saturday afternoon that he didn't get his visa.

GREENBERG (*casting director*): We ended up offering the part to James Corden, who was in London. We didn't make the offer until late on Friday, however, and we needed him to fly to Vegas on Sunday. He told me had we asked a day earlier, he may have been able to pull it together, but he couldn't. So, we offered it to someone we had used on *Frasier* and was wonderful. He flew up on Sunday for costume fittings and then started rehearsing on Monday.

MORTON (*executive producer*): What I didn't tell anyone was that at eleven in the morning on Monday, our attorney texted me that Stephen's paperwork had been processed. Around 12:45, we did a scene with the other actor. It was really flat compared to what Stephen did. So we finished and went to lunch. I went over to Paul, Brad, and Bill and said, "What do you think?" They said it wasn't great, and I said, "No, it was terrible."

MANCUSO (*director*): It wasn't that this particular actor wasn't bringing it. He was doing a great job, but we had all heard Stephen's take on it already.

MORTON (*executive producer*): I said I had a crazy idea. I'd found out a couple of hours earlier that Merchant's visa had cleared. I didn't know where in the world he was right then, but if for some reason I could get him here this afternoon, we could flip the schedule around and shoot some other scenes. They went, "Yeah."

MERCHANT (*Leslie Higgins*): I'm sitting in my little writing office on the Disney lot, working on an episode of *Hello Ladies,* when I get a call from Jeff saying they sorted out the visa problem and could I get on a plane immediately to Vegas? They didn't even have time for me to go back to my house to get any clothing or a toothbrush. They said, "We'll buy you that stuff if you jump on a plane." So I subsequently found myself in a car with only my wallet and phone on the way to the airport.

MORTON (*executive producer*): We had ninety minutes to get him to LAX. With traffic from Burbank, that's no easy thing.

MERCHANT (*Leslie Higgins*): It was quite a frantic chase against time.

LLOYD (*cocreator*): Fitting that it was farcical.

MORTON (*executive producer*): The gods were smiling on us, and he made the flight.

MERCHANT (*Leslie Higgins*): Only I didn't have my passport at the time, and I didn't have a U.S. driver's license yet. I only had my UK license, which didn't seem to convince anyone that I was worthy of flying. The United Kingdom is obviously a deeply mistrustful country in the eyes of airport people, and so there was much back-and-forth with them about whether I'd be allowed on the plane. Eventually, someone said Britain was a trusted ally of the U.S., and they let me on.

Back in Vegas, they had the awkward task of letting the other actor go.

MANCUSO (*director*): It's always horrible, not that it happens a lot. No one wants to do it.

MORTON (*executive producer*): We explained the situation. To his credit, he said he thought we should do what was best for the show. He was a gentleman and couldn't have handled it more professionally.

MERLIN (*assistant director / key PA*): I then had to do what I call the "Hollywood Switch," having one person come in and making sure the other person doesn't see them. You're just trying to be respectful through the process. They know that you know. You know that they know. You're trying to make sure that person is comfortable and that they're not left standing on the sidewalk.

While waiting for Merchant, they filled in the rest of the cast about what had transpired. They feared telling O'Neill most, because it would require the watch tapper to stay an extra day.

O'NEILL (*Jay Pritchett*): I had one scene left to shoot, a short scene with the bath butler. So I go to the location, which is the next hotel over. I'm in hair and makeup. I'm ready to go. I walk to the set, and there's people milling around. Somebody says that there's this little snafu. I said, "What's going on?" They said that they'd gotten Stephen. I'm standing there, my flight's in a few hours. I said, "Where is he?" They said, "Well, this is the problem. He's at LAX." I said, "Now, as we speak?" They said they're going to try to get him on the next flight here. I asked, "Where's Ty? In the next room? Excuse me a minute." I walked into the next room, and there's Ty. I trust Ty's judgment. I said, "Ty, I only have one question for you. Is this worth it?"

BURRELL (*Phil Dunphy*): I said, "Yes, he's incredible. He's that funny," and he really was.

O'NEILL (*Jay Pritchett*): I said, "Done." Not another word spoken. I walked back out, said "All right, we wait." It was worth it.

Merchant learned his lines on the airplane.

MERCHANT (*Leslie Higgins*): I landed in Las Vegas, took a car straight to the hotel, went straight into costume, and the next thing I know, I found myself in a corridor doing a scene with Ed O'Neill. I used to write an occasional column for a British magazine in which I would write about my comedy heroes, one of whom was Ed as Al Bundy. I thought it was such a funny, fantastic performance. So I was a little intimidated working with him because that was my first scene up, lines barely learned, no time to meet, greet, and prepare.

O'NEILL (*Jay Pritchett*): The fucking guy shows up. We share a couple of pleasantries. "Hi." "Hi." And we shot the scene. He was spot-on. I think we did it in two takes.

> JAY
> I need a couple primo cigars ASAP. I'm
> not a real stickler about how they
> got in the country.

> HIGGINS
> Consider me the answer to your Cuban
> Missile Crisis.

MERCHANT (*Leslie Higgins*): We got through it great and were off to the races really.

INT. HOTEL—PHIL AND CLAIRE'S ROOM

> PHIL
> Hang on, do you know where I can get
> a cape pressed quickly?

> HIGGINS
> Opera or superhero?

> PHIL
> I'd rather not say.

> HIGGINS
> I overstepped by asking.

Higgins hands Phil a brochure.

```
                    HIGGINS (CONT'D)
        Before I go, I should tell you about
        our luxury bath service. We have five
        outrageously decadent baths I can
        prepare at a moment's notice. (re:
        menu) The Pharaoh's Fantasy takes a
        dash longer because our Nubian lives
        off-site.
```

MERCHANT (*Leslie Higgins*): The thing I loved with Ty is that we had that ping-pong, very fast, back-and-forth. It's not something I get to do often, and I love that. It's *A Night at the Opera,* Marx Brothers rhythm.

BURRELL (*Phil Dunphy*): He's good company on set, which can't be underestimated. Talk about the joy of doing bits on set. I had so much fun doing ridiculous bits with him.

MERCHANT (*Leslie Higgins*): Ty and I got into some weird improv conversation about robots. We were very amused by the idea that we'd have robot replicas of ourselves. The Ty-bot 3000 that we could send out to social events. We giggled like schoolchildren about that.

BOWEN (*Claire Dunphy*): Stephen Merchant I couldn't look in the eye. I have a problem where if I find somebody attractive I can't be anywhere near them. I have a fantasy that in another world, had we met at another time and place, we would have had beautiful babies together. He's so deeply funny. I feel like there's nothing I could say or do that wouldn't make me look like a buffoon. He has that incredibly subtle, hilariously weird sense of humor. And it would kill me.

CASE (*director/editor*): Ty doesn't break much, but when he was with Stephen, he had a really hard time not laughing.

MERCHANT (*Leslie Higgins*): I've got a weird man-crush on Ty. I feel like I want to go 'round to his house and just hang out. You know the idea, that you want to make someone your friend but they're busy getting on with their life and can't factor you in.

BURRELL (*Phil Dunphy*): Sometimes when a guest star is as good as Stephen, they end up working harder because everyone wants more of it. Chris had a million ideas just to hear them come out of Stephen's mouth.

LLOYD (*cocreator*): That's accurate. That guy made me laugh very hard.

BURRELL (*Phil Dunphy*): I remember doing tons of takes. Stephen had several of his own ideas that were hilarious and ended up in the final.

The episode ends with Higgins holding the door open as the scantily clad Kilty Pleasures troupe of men kick their way into the room to Scottish-themed dance music. Mitchell, Cam, and Claire follow them in from the hall, and Phil enters from the adjoining door:

```
          HIGGINS
     This reminds me of my late
     grandfather.


               PHIL
     He was Scottish?


          HIGGINS
     He was a stripper.
```

MERCHANT (*Leslie Higgins*): I ad-libbed the line about the stripper.

When Merchant got back to LA, he found a surprise message on his phone.

MERCHANT (*Leslie Higgins*): I had a message from Ed. I didn't even know he had my number, but I had a message from him, lovely and complimentary.

It was a real thrill. That was completely unsolicited praise from Ed. I found him completely a joy.

MANCUSO (*director*): At the Emmys before the telecast, I saw Ed on the red carpet. He pulled me aside and said, "I just want you to know, whatever happens, that was a hell of an episode that you directed." And then I won the Emmy later that night.

O'NEILL (*Jay Pritchett*): I thought that was one of our best shows, period. Just the moving in and out of the doors, the timing of the rapid lines, the misdirection, the misunderstandings. I love that kind of stuff.

WRUBEL (*writer / executive producer*): And then shortly after that, we went to Australia. It was a lot of travel toward the end of the season, and that had a hand in people getting tired and irritable.

Australia

Much as the sun rises every morning, so, too, does the restlessness of sitcom writers on a long-running series. Many aspire to develop their own shows, be the big cheese in charge for once. Some just grow tired voicing the same characters over and over again. Story engines become harder to come by. Repetition settles in.

WRUBEL (*writer / executive producer*): I was on *Will and Grace* from seasons 4 through 9. I saw how, at a certain point, successful shows, no matter how great, start to repeat themselves a little bit. There's a limited number of stories you can tell. That's the life of any series. You can't stay on top forever.

WALSH (*writer / executive producer*): Dan said we started off telling stories from our lives. They were the anecdotes we always told at parties, things that happened to us along the way that seemed funny or unique. By season 5, he said we were scraping the bottom of the barrel of our lives.

O'SHANNON (*writer / executive producer*): I felt I was repeating myself, and I wasn't as productive as I'd been in earlier seasons.

ZUKER (*writer / executive producer*): I definitely had these moments around season 5 or 6, where I was out with my family, or friends, and I was like, "God, I wish my kids would do something interesting right now so I could write about it."

For a show in its fifth season, with four consecutive Emmy Awards for Outstanding Comedy Series already under its belt, the writers' room (outside of women writers; more about this in the chapter "Truth Be Told") had very little turnover. Some important creative people, like Winer, had already moved on. But the core family had remained intact until outside influences tested them.

ZUKER (*writer / executive producer*): Our contracts were up. It's pretty common for higher-level writers to check your market value out in the world. So a lot of us went out and met with other studios to see if it's time to jump ship or is Fox going to pony up and pay for us.

WRUBEL (*writer / executive producer*): Everybody who had been there from the beginning was getting wooed for new opportunities, and that was seductive. It opened my eyes to what else I might be able to do in my career.

Contract negotiations with the studio didn't go well, leading to grievances and grouchiness that created family strife.

HIGGINBOTHAM (*writer / executive producer*): Usually the people who were there the first year, whenever they renegotiated, they negotiated together. The fifth year saw the people from the first season negotiate separately. Some came back feeling valued, some felt they weren't, and some said after five years, they wanted to try something else.

LLOYD (*cocreator*): In success, that's one of the fallouts. People become a little competitive. They want credit and money, and those things are their due, but they're sometimes difficult because a studio arrives at how much people should get paid based upon their years of experience, which isn't always a fair factor to bring into it as opposed to how much they're contributing on the show.

RICHMAN (*writer / executive producer*): Everybody was an all-star. Everyone knew how to write the show and was a contributor. Every single person felt an investment in this very singular experience.

O'SHANNON (*writer / executive producer*): The studio tossed out kind of a take-it-or-leave-it offer for seasons 6 and 7, which made my decision easier. Of course, if they'd offered more, I would have stayed and happily repeated myself for a few more years, but I think it was the right time for me, creatively.

WRUBEL (*writer / executive producer*): The studio was cheaper than they needed to be, I think. They could have made it very easy for me to stay. At a certain point, with all things being equal, I did what I thought would give me the biggest challenge.

CORRIGAN (*writer / executive producer*): Brad and I didn't know the numbers. I prefer being ignorant. I enjoy that. I don't want to know I'm being undervalued.

WALSH (*writer / executive producer*): We were making numbers we thought we'd never see. So it was hard to figure out what's being valued or undervalued. What does that even mean in this context?

RICHMAN (*writer / executive producer*): That was a very, very tight group for the four years I had been on it. This was the first time it felt not that. It was a very close family, and then suddenly it wasn't.

By November, Wrubel and O'Shannon let the showrunners know that they wouldn't be back for season 6. Another important member, Ben Karlin, in the room since 2011, also decided to move on. Everything came to a head that year with the episode "Australia."

HIGGINBOTHAM (*writer / executive producer*): "Australia" was a nightmare. To me, it's the moment of the show I'd love to forget—the only one.

O'SHANNON (*writer / executive producer*): It was always tense getting toward the end of the season. We had something we used to call "the drive for five"—getting those last episodes written in time, with little to no fuel left in the tank. So we were in the thick of it, heading toward the big Mitch-and-Cam wedding, when "Australia" happened.

*By this point, the show had traveled multiple times. In those epi-
sodes, the writers followed normal story development practices: story
first, story second, story third. With "Australia," the writers found
themselves forced to reverse course, writing for a locale instead of a
relatable situation.*

O'SHANNON (*writer / executive producer*): The trip to Australia was
planned long before the episode was figured out. And so it became, "Let's
figure out an episode to justify this trip we're all going to take." I think
when we saw the first table read for that, some of us were like, "Really?
We're going to Australia for that?"

WALSH (*writer / executive producer*): Travel episodes are difficult to
break because you have to come up with what some would say is an excuse,
but more charitably a reason that it's happening. "Australia" ended up taking up quite a bit of time, again at the end of a season, so that put some
stress on the staff.

LLOYD (*cocreator*): It's not a story to say they're going to Australia. Something actually has to be happening to them. And there's a limit to the number of things that can go wrong when a family's on vacation. When we
can find a story that's interesting and emotional, with that backdrop, we're
great. But that's tricky, which is why we tend to do a limited number of
them.

*Some of the cast, ready for a summer break, didn't feel very excited
about the whole idea.*

STONESTREET (*Cam Tucker*): We've always been so proud of our show
being story driven. I think people were on the fence about "Australia." How
relatable is it that we're going to Australia?

O'NEILL (*Jay Pritchett*): It's like fifteen hours on a fucking jet out of LA.
I'd rather skip location shooting altogether. I want to work in the studio.
Our best shows have always been done there.

Morton helped change hearts and minds by finding sponsorship with companies like Qantas Airlines and amazing hotels for their stay. Simply put, he arranged a high-class, low-budget trip.

SAPIENZA (*script supervisor / director*): We had a Qantas plane that said *Modern Family* on the side of it. It was so surreal.

O'NEILL (*Jay Pritchett*): We flew to Australia first class, which is pretty special.

AUBREY ANDERSON-EMMONS (*Lily Tucker-Pritchett*): They called us up and asked, "Are there any snacks you want for the trip?" And Mom told me to list some stuff. I was listing a whole bunch of stuff to give them some options. And they literally bought all of it. It was insane. It was amazing.

FIELD (*associate producer*): I got to fly with Jeff [Morton] and Eric. If I didn't have to leave that pod for the rest of my life, I would have been happy. We had butlers. I ended up sitting next to Rose Leslie from *Game of Thrones*, who is a huge *Modern Family* fan. We became buddies.

ELLIOTT (*on-set dresser*): They gave us pajamas. We had our names embroidered on them. Little pillows on our seats saying, "Qantas loves *Modern Family*." There were fairies flying around with mints. It was incredible.

Zuker and Ko wrote the episode and thus traveled to Australia, too. Being a Levitan episode and one he'd opted to direct meant he'd not only be going, too, but leaving a week early to help scout locations.

LEVITAN (*cocreator*): You couldn't really go and do much scouting before we wrote it, so we did our best to figure out what we thought it would be like. When I arrived with the advance crew, there was media waiting for us. Some city official gave me an official bush hat.

And so began three weeks of paradise.

Meanwhile, back at the ranch in LA . . .

LLOYD (*cocreator*): There was resentment because it took a bunch of people out of commission and left the rest of us behind to do key episodes at a time when there wasn't a lot left in the tank.

RICHMAN (*writer / executive producer*): The people that stayed back felt shorthanded. The show was at the top of its game, so the urgency of staying really good was pretty prevalent.

O'SHANNON (*writer / executive producer*): We'd go on social media and see pictures of the others having a great time in Australia while we were knocking ourselves out to write the last episodes. By then, we were all frazzled and tired of each other.

HIGGINBOTHAM (*writer / executive producer*): Everybody was so mad. It was crazy. Two writers got to go. They were working, and we all knew they were working. But people acted like at the last minute a couple of writers and Steve jumped on a plane and took a vacation. And that's not what happened. I never minded that Danny and Elaine went to Australia. They wrote it. I didn't want to write it.

KO (*writer / executive producer*): I was assigned to cowrite the "Australia" episode with Danny, which I was happy to do. As I remember it, none of the other writers expressed any interest in writing it. If it had been up to me, we would have shot it last so everyone on staff would have been able to go. I don't think anyone at the time had any idea it would end up breeding resentment from some of the other writers. It's unfortunate, because it was otherwise an amazing experience.

ZUKER (*writer / executive producer*): That episode without a doubt could have been shot at the end of the season and more people could have gone. It wasn't our decision to do it before a two-part finale. I think there were some missteps made along the way. What we felt bad about was that we were in the crucible of a situation we neither encouraged nor would have done that way ourselves.

BURRELL (*Phil Dunphy*): Elaine and Danny felt terrible about it. They felt so stressed out and shitty that I don't think they had the vacation the other writers thought they had. They didn't have a good time in Australia, feeling the waves of resentment coming from across the ocean.

At the same time, on the other side of the world in the land Down Under, the cast encountered Beatlemania—or, in this instance, Mod-ern Family-mania.

FERGUSON (*Mitchell Pritchett*): People would be waiting outside of our hotel. Every time we'd leave for set, there'd be people wanting autographs.

BOWEN (*Claire Dunphy*): Jesse is a magnet because he's redheaded and has a red beard. I don't look anything like Claire. I look like a sweaty four-teen-year-old boy, and I like that. If I walked with other members of the cast, it'd get challenging.

FIELD (*associate producer*): We were shooting on Bondi Beach. Julie, Jesse, and I ended up taking a walkabout. They didn't think they'd be rec-ognized, so we were walking and this massive school of girls came by. We had nowhere to go. So I had Jesse and Julie face the ocean, and I stood be-hind them pretending I was on my phone so no one would see their faces. The girls walked by, and we were fine.

FERGUSON (*Mitchell Pritchett*): There was one day when I was out ex-ploring the city on my own and I ran into Sofía. She had a big hat on and sunglasses. No one was bothering her because she can slip under the radar when she's incognito. We're talking, and the minute people heard Sofía's voice, they realized it's her. People started coming up. She told me that I had to leave her alone so people would stop knowing it was her. "Walk away from me. I'll meet you at a café." We ran our separate ways.

VERGARA (*Gloria Delgado-Pritchett*): Sometimes I can get away with blend-ing in. But if they see us together, they immediately put two and two together.

O'NEILL (*Jay Pritchett*): Sofía and I went to dinner one night at this restaurant near the opera. The people went nuts when we came in. You have to understand. We were the only show in town.

On the other side of the world, the entire writing staff focused on Mitchell and Cam's marriage—except for Brad, Paul, and Bill, who, having just returned from Vegas, had to write the "Sleeper" episode by themselves. Phil's storyline in that episode didn't land well with some.

HIGGINBOTHAM (*writer / executive producer*): A lot of us were like, "Are we seriously doing Phil with stress-induced narcolepsy?" It feels like the moment when we went broader than we had ever gone in terms of the reality of these people. It felt huge to me, like we're changing the tone of the show a little bit. And poor Brad, Paul, and Bill were tasked with writing this thing.

WALSH (*writer / executive producer*): There were a couple of rooms breaking groundbreaking TV, and some of those people were upset with the group of people in Australia having fun shooting. But the one thing everyone could agree on was that Bill, Paul, and I were writing an awful episode of television. It felt a little thankless, but it had to be written.

In the land Down Under, cast and crew, however, felt very thankful for staying at their own private resort on Hayman Island. The resort itself, closed for modifications and upgrades, had made an exception for Modern Family.

FIELD (*associate producer*): There was a masseuse on staff, and we were taking helicopter rides. I felt like I was in an episode of *The Bachelorette*.

ELLIOTT (*on-set dresser*): There was lobster, crab, sushi, and fillet and chefs and bars. Everything was free. It was like you just walked into *Defending Your Life*, that Albert Brooks film.

GOULD (*Luke Dunphy*): Me, Ariel, and Ty went scuba diving in the Great Barrier Reef. I was having a blast [Gould has become a certified scuba diver since]. Ty was super nervous at like ten feet of water. He looks down and sees me thirty feet below doing stunts. He was super jealous and super blown away.

WINTER (*Alex Dunphy*): There were pools in a couple of rooms. You walk in the doors and there was this living room and you walk out the living room doors and there was this big open area with a pool and hot tub in your room, in the middle of your living room and then your bedroom. It was crazy.

TUCKER (*camera operator*): My room had a big, huge balcony overlooking the ocean. I sent my wife a picture. She was at home pregnant with our second child and wasn't happy with me.

HYLAND (*Haley Dunphy*): We did that barrier reef helicopter. That was really, really dope.

RODRIGUEZ (*Manny Delgado*): Everything you saw us do in the show we got to do. Climb the Sydney Harbor Bridge, the helicopter ride over the Great Barrier Reef. Everyone, the crew and cast, were able to do that if they wanted to.

> *Not everyone in the cast wanted to climb the bridge, though, but they had to.*

LEVITAN (*cocreator*): There were some members of the cast not entirely comfortable with heights. So that was a bit of a tense moment, and we had to coordinate with a helicopter shot.

WINTER (*Alex Dunphy*): It's beautiful and amazing to do, but for somebody so terrified of heights, it was horrible. I was so silent, which isn't like me, looking at the back of the person in front of me, staring at the top and being silent walking down doing the same thing.

BOWEN (*Claire Dunphy*): I'm glad I did it, but it was really scary. I remember the helicopter that was supposed to come right at us and then up, a sweeping movement. They were practicing it, getting their bearings, while we were up on top. We were like, "We don't need to be practicing it." It was a little scary.

HYLAND (*Haley Dunphy*): I think Nolan and I were the only ones that were supercool on the bridge. I was doing ballet on that bridge. I was thinking, "This is amazing. I love this."

For readers who want to travel to Australia, remember to wear sunscreen at all times.

GOULD (*Luke Dunphy*): Someone forgot to run sunscreen into my eyebrows, which is not a thing most people have to do, but because I'm so pale I have to do it. The sun burned my eyebrows red, so I'd have to come in ten minutes early so they could figure out ways to color them in.

HYLAND (*Haley Dunphy*): It was the morning, and I was having my coffee. I saw some of the cast and crew down the beach. I'm out there talking to them for twenty, maybe thirty minutes tops, and I get back to my room and my back kind of itches. I look in the mirror and I am a lobster.

And beware of all creatures great and small.

LEVITAN (*cocreator*): Australia has a lot of things that can kill you, so we had to make sure that whenever we were shooting in the woods, people were constantly making big noises to scare away anything that could bite you. Then when we were all in the water, we wore these crazy full-body suits so if anything touched you, you wouldn't get stung.

ELLIOTT (*on-set dresser*): We got to one of the locations, and there were a couple of park rangers in this tall grass with these tall sticks. I asked what they're doing. They said looking for snakes, and they mentioned what kind of snake. I looked it up. It was a snake that when it bites you, you have ten seconds, and there are no antidotes. You're on to the next life. I looked at one of my buddies on the show and said, "You want me to handle it for you?" He said, "Yes." So in the episode, I was the kangaroo rapidly punching Phil.

Hyland had perhaps the worst moment.

HYLAND (*Haley Dunphy*): We were doing this event, and there were a bunch of fans out front. I saw this group of schoolgirls, and I told them, "I'll be back to take pictures." They got pushed to the back by the adults and stuff. And I think it was the third or fourth picture that I was groped by a middle-aged man-fan who apparently had already been arrested for groping other women. He grabbed my ass real hard. I was wearing a dress. I had two security guards around me and my ex-boyfriend and the guy did that. I pushed him off of me, wagging my finger, yelling and cursing, "Don't you fucking touch me!" Once they realized something was happening, he was tackled to the ground, and they rushed me inside. I really just wanted to go out to take a picture with those schoolgirls. I felt bad that they didn't even get that.

In the midst of their outback adventures, they did a videotape read of the "Sleeper" episode. The lack of an audience sucked the life out of the reading.

MORTON (*executive producer*): The table read didn't go great.

MCCRAY (*script coordinator*): You want it to be live to have that better sense of the jokes. We had to watch it on video, and then subsequently everyone there started badmouthing the script.

WALSH (*writer / executive producer*): I think their notes weren't received well given they were coming from a bunch of people Instagramming how much fun they were having in Australia.

CORRIGAN (*writer / executive producer*): Even among the people in Australia, there was diverging opinions about the wisdom of sending those notes.

MORTON (*executive producer*): I think Steve may have given some of his thoughts. I don't think Chris appreciated that.

CHAN (*writers' assistant*): I remember Chris being pissed off. He wrote them an icy email.

KO (*writer / executive producer*): For whatever reason, the icy reply was addressed to Danny and me alone—not to Steve, who had sent the original email. That felt to me like misdirected anger. But it's not like there was time to sit around and have a group discussion about our feelings when we got back. Whatever ill will there was had to be pushed aside while we all rewrote the last two episodes together.

LLOYD (*cocreator*): It was a lot of miscalculations on the part of a few people, but we got through it.

WRUBEL (*writer / executive producer*): Familiarity breeds contempt. I truly believe we all loved each other in our own dysfunctional way, but by that point, people were looking for a reason to be annoyed. The episode and that table read gave them a reason. It was stupid.

LLOYD (*cocreator*): Here's the thing about table reads, and it goes across the board. The writers laugh like hyenas at everything because they've all contributed stuff, so they're inclined to like their own material. And if it gets laughs, you're going to be spending less time at the office rewriting lines. That's every sitcom I've ever been on. So that table read was being judged by people who were eight thousand miles away and had none of the jackals in the room with them.

ZUKER (*writer / executive producer*): Everything Chris said is true. It's a very hard thing to do, and I think the misstep was, given that there was so much resentment toward the fact that we were in Australia, that Steve should weigh in with notes. There's no way that looks good from our standpoint if they're perceiving us on vacation and saying, "Here's what you guys should do." It's not a good situation. Steve did not take that advice on that particular one.

LEVITAN (*cocreator*): Everyone was in a great mood heading into the table read. We had just shot a really funny scene with Ty and a kangaroo. We then went into a rec center where the crew and guests watched the table read. It didn't go well. I just wanted to make sure the writers at home knew that and didn't just blame it on the audio of the feed. As I recall, we sent word back (in a very nice way) that it didn't get a ton of laughs, and we offered whatever suggestions we had, just as we would have done at home. I believe the angry response to those notes was more about people being mad that some of us were in Australia while others were working hard at home.

KO (*writer / executive producer*): Danny and I made it clear we didn't think it was a good idea to send notes on the table read, but the email was sent anyway. I wasn't even aware Steve had actually sent it until after the fact. Eventually, the resentment faded, and we all moved on.

Everyone in the writers' room had to and did. After all, they had a wedding to plan.

The Wedding

Much like popular, long-running shows such as Friends *and* Seinfeld, Modern Family *focuses on humor and relatability, rarely delving into politics and causes. But in the few occasions where the show did, it went big. The season 5 finale, "The Wedding," concluded a yearlong arc about Mitchell and Cam's marriage. Television rarely had gone down that path. In 1991, the Fox sitcom* Roc *(1991–1994) aired the first gay marriage on network television. In 2008, ABC's* Brothers & Sisters *(2006–2011) aired the first gay marriage between series regulars. Mitch and Cam's nuptials felt different, perhaps because the times felt different.*

RICHMAN (*writer / executive producer*): You can't watch our show, especially in the early seasons, and think that couple has any less of a right to be a family legally than any of the other two families. If you love those characters, how can you then go, "But still they're less than?"

FERGUSON (*Mitchell Pritchett*): There was such momentum to have this moment with Mitch and Cam. My husband, Justin, was working on Proposition 8, which was going into deliberations that summer. The writers wanted to break stories for Mitch and Cam getting married, so a few of them called Justin and said, "How's it looking? Do you think we'll be able to do this story?" Justin was working a little bit like an insider voice, relaying what he knew.

They got the green light. As a result, season 5 started with a proposal.

RICHMAN (*writer / executive producer*): I knew more than any episode in the life of the show, I wanted that one. And then I got to write it. I can still get emotional about it.

FERGUSON (*Mitchell Pritchett*): What they ended up doing was so beautiful, having them want to make a big moment out of their proposal and then settling on this very quiet one that wasn't romantic.

RICHMAN (*writer / executive producer*): It's the middle of the night, and they're by the side of the road with a flat tire.

STONESTREET (*Cam Tucker*): It was chilly. We were overlooking the San Fernando Valley, and I remember thinking, "Wow. I can't believe I'm here, in such a big part of a big TV show, in such a huge moment for the character I get to play."

FERGUSON (*Mitchell Pritchett*): They're both on their knees changing the tire, and they look up at one another and say, "Yes," at the same time.

RICHMAN (*writer / executive producer*): They knew what the other was thinking. I remember sitting at my computer writing the ending, and suddenly I had tears in my eyes. It didn't affect me that way breaking that story. I never expected the emotion of that one word, "Yes." It was so satisfying.

From that moment on, the writers knew where the season would end: with a wedding.

LLOYD (*cocreator*): It was a big, splashy season-ender. Normally, I would only have episode 2 to figure out, but I had to figure out both halves and get them written. That was a workload that wasn't easy to accomplish at that time of that season.

HIGGINBOTHAM (*writer / executive producer*): It was such a group effort. The first part had my, Jeff's, and Ben's name on it. The second one had

Chris's, Dan's, and Meghan Ganz's. We broke them as fast as we could, two episodes in four days' time, writing them in three days.

FERGUSON (*Mitchell Pritchett*): A lot of the writers, and specifically the gay writers, were so emotional about this movement toward marriage equality. They were funneling it into their art, and I was funneling it into Mitch and Cam. It was exciting. It was very easy to ride those emotions from your real life into your artistic life.

LLOYD (*cocreator*): There was giant acrimony between Mitchell and Jay and various subplots, like getting Cam's family in and losing wedding venues that had a big impact on the characters. You need stuff of that scale, in my opinion, to do a double-length story.

HIGGINBOTHAM (*writer / executive producer*): I remember Steve coming back and saying, "I'm going to help you make this work to the best of my ability, and I'm not going to change anything, because I wasn't here for it. I didn't break it. I don't want to piss anyone off. I'm getting on board. Let's make it the best version of what you decided."

```
          MITCHELL AND CAMERON INTERVIEW

                    MITCHELL
          My mom can't come to the wedding. She
          was on a yoga retreat, fell out of a
          warrior pose, and broke her hip.


                    CAMERON
          Should we consider the possibility
          that someone pushed her?


                    MITCHELL
          Cam, please. They were a bunch of
          peace-loving yogis who spent two
          weeks in a rain forest with my
          mother. Of course someone pushed her.
```

MCCRAY (*script coordinator*): We were trying to get Shelley for the wedding. It became difficult.

RICHMAN (*writer / executive producer*): Shelley wouldn't come. She was a significant part of the original breaking of the story and didn't drop out until an inconveniently short time before. That took adjusting.

LLOYD (*cocreator*): It was DeDe's son getting married. It was a natural one for her to appear in. She said she was not going to be available for a reason that seemed a bit mysterious, but we covered it in the episode, and it wound up not being a big problem.

> *In one minor subplot, the dry cleaners, closed for the day, prevent Cam from getting his tuxedo. He and Mitchell improvise a plan, sending Lily through the cleaner's open-drop slot to retrieve it.*

EXT./INT. DRY CLEANER

Lily is inside standing on a counter. Mitchell and Cam stand outside calling instructions into the open drop slot.

                    MITCHELL
      Okay, now press the green button and
      look for number five-one-eight-zero-
      seven, and when you see it come by,
      press the red button to stop it.

Lily presses the button and the rack starts moving.

                    CAMERON
      I'm so glad you're here. I get us into
      these situations, I freak out, and
      you always fix the problem.

                    MITCHELL
Well, we each have our gifts. It's
just easier for me to stay calm in
the face of—
                (freaking out)
Oh my God!

ANGLE ON: Lily has somehow gotten caught on the
rack, and it carries her away with the moving
clothes.

                    LILY
Wheeeeee!

AMY ANDERSON-EMMONS (*Aubrey's mother*): She actually got to ride the conveyor for real, which I think every kid has dreamed of.

AUBREY ANDERSON-EMMONS (*Lily Tucker-Pritchett*): I loved that so much. I literally wanted to go the whole entire way through the rack.

AMY ANDERSON-EMMONS (*Aubrey's mother*): She's like, "Keep going! Keep going!" And I'm telling her, "We can't send you up into the rafters."

Ronaldo and Pepper handled the wedding arrangements.

CHRISTIAN BARILLAS (*Ronaldo*): It was written in that Pepper and I were getting married and honeymooning in Europe, but then they edited that out in order to keep us around for the wedding.

NATHAN LANE (*Pepper Saltzman*): They decided to use Pepper as their wedding planner, and then everything went wrong. They kept losing venues and going to another place.

INT. PEPPER'S CAR

Pepper and Ronaldo are up front. Mitchell and
Cam are in the back with a crate between them,

its top slightly ajar. Monarch butterflies fly
about.

                    CAM
    They're eating me!

                  PEPPER
    Well, who told you to jostle the
    crate?

                 MITCHELL
    One got in my mouth!

LANE (*Pepper Saltzman*): We had to be in a car with all the monarch butterflies. Only there weren't butterflies, they had to be added later, so we had to fake it, screaming like big girls.

The largest conflict came from Jay and Mitchell.

FERGUSON (*Mitchell Pritchett*): There was a very emotional scene where Jay says, "I don't even understand why you need to get married," and Mitch basically uninvites his dad to the wedding. My father was at my wedding and had a great time and danced and is 100 percent supportive of my marriage and of Justin, but there was something very easy about tapping into that feeling of disappointing your parents and them disappointing you. Looking at these people who you thought could do no wrong and realizing they're flawed human beings.

O'NEILL (*Jay Pritchett*): I love the relationship. It's a comedy law. You go one step forward and one step back, but the steps forward are always so sweet and the steps back are always so funny. Jay just can't wrap his head around the fact that the kid is gay. He tries. He loves the boy, but he can't quite make that jump.

MERLIN (*assistant director / key PA*): I remember having that conversation myself. You can love someone, but why does it have to cross the boundary? The fact that the show was willing to have that conversation . . .

BARILLAS (*Ronaldo*): It felt bittersweet and ironic for me to be part of that show. I grew up in Guatemala and stayed until I was almost eighteen. My parents still live there, and so culturally, they're always behind. I remember feeling such pride in what I was achieving in my career, having come from so far away, and at the same time, feeling sad about certain aspects of my personal life. I don't know that the show helped me have conversations with my parents. We've never talked about it. I got married several years after the episode. My dad and I are in a really good place finally, but he wasn't at my wedding. It took that to jolt something in him that if he's going to be a significant part of my life, he's going to have to change. We've had our own Mitch-and-Jay journey.

The wedding took place ironically at a scenic spot overlooking a Donald Trump golf course.

BOWEN (*Claire Dunphy*): A gay wedding overlooking a Trump golf course, how great was that?

ZUKER (*writer / executive producer*): I was in a Twitter war with Trump. So I have some pictures of me flipping off the sign.

LLOYD (*cocreator*): A special element was that it was the final episode for Dan and Bill. I said, "As a going-away gift, I want to take you guys out and buy you Armani suits, but your part of the bargain is you have to be a gay couple in attendance at Mitch and Cam's wedding." And they were more than happy to comply.

O'SHANNON (*writer / executive producer*): It was bittersweet. It wasn't just an emotional episode about the characters. It was the end of a five-year stretch of my life.

WRUBEL (*writer / executive producer*): At the time, it felt like the end of an era. In some respects, perhaps it was. Dan was such a key voice for the show.

EXT. COUNTRY CLUB—SUNSET

In the back, Mitchell and Cam wait to follow
Lily up the aisle. Pepper pushes Lily down the
aisle. Jay joins Mitchell.

>   MITCHELL
>   We're starting, Dad. You should take
>   your seat.

>   JAY
>   Actually, I was thinking you and I
>   would take a walk.

Jay offers Mitchell his arm. Mitchell smiles and
takes it. They start slowly up the aisle.

RICHMAN (*writer / executive producer*): We had been playing that for a few episodes, that they were going through a rough patch. It was really, really moving to be there and watch it get resolved.

FERGUSON (*Mitchell Pritchett*): It was very easy to get caught up in the emotion of it.

O'NEILL (*Jay Pritchett*): I was choked up a little myself, just the look on his face.

LAMB (*first assistant director / director*): The notion of Jay saying, "Let me show you how much I love you. I'm going to go against all my instincts and prejudices and show up for you right now." That to me was a message of such hope that I cried like a baby.

LLOYD (*cocreator*): If you go back to the pilot when Jay's pretty dismissive of Cam and Mitchell's relationship and now he's walking his son down the aisle, I think it was moving for the audience for the same reason it was for us. It seemed like a genuine evolution on the part of this character. That was nice to see.

BOWEN (*Claire Dunphy*): Jesse was not married in real life yet, and neither was Eric, so it was like seeing them get married. It really was special. I cried at that one, absolutely.

STONESTREET (*Cam Tucker*): I was emotional in the role and personally at that time. It felt important, and I was proud to have a front-row seat with Jesse.

FERGUSON (*Mitchell Pritchett*): It felt like a moment. I was so proud to be part of a show that was going to show these two men getting married. I loved that we got to be part of that celebration.

BURRELL (*Phil Dunphy*): I felt really lucky to be alive at a time doing an episode like that, having lots of friends planning to get married or actively choosing not to get married. But it felt like a real special moment and an amazing thing that we were able to do.

LLOYD (*cocreator*): We had gay people on our staff and in our cast, up and down the organization. I think it was monumental for them to see this couple become married. And that was moving for me to see how moved they were.

BARILLAS (*Ronaldo*): I felt like I was a tiny part of something much bigger than me with the show in general and that episode in particular. You felt that living rooms across the country had brought these two characters into their lives and helped evolve the culture into a level of acceptance.

MERLIN (*assistant director / key PA*): I'm so glad the whole world got to experience that. People need to see good things.

With the sun going down quickly, they almost lost the light, which would have required a reshoot and probably a lack of the same level of emotion as the first time. Baggs, with his lighting bag of tricks, how-ever, somehow preempted that.

LANE (*Pepper Saltzman*): They filmed the entire ceremony.

Stonestreet's parents attended.

STONESTREET (*Cam Tucker*): The football player Golden Tate was there playing golf and watched us shoot the reception stuff.

YOUNG (*production manager / producer*): He was a big fan. I knew Ed was a big football fan. I went over to tell him, and he said, "Oh my God. Golden Tate's here? I have to meet him."

The wedding's conclusion strayed away from the script. Statman, directing the episode, wanted a sweet Modern Family–style montage of the season. Lloyd preferred more of a misdirect.

STATMAN (*director / assistant director*): The entire montage sequence I shot tied all the storylines together and gave them an ending. What I had to do to keep the sequence was take out two of the gags of Ty and Julie doing magic tricks together. Chris was going back and forth. Ryan [Case] would text me, "montage back in," and then six hours later, "montage back out." It didn't make the final cut. That's the only time I thought Chris made a bad decision, because when all the reviews came out for that episode, they said there were too many storylines and we weren't focused on the immediate family.

ORIGINAL ENDING

```
              CLAIRE (V.O.)
Sure he was warm and funny and
loving, but was he everything
I wanted for my brother? I wondered,
"Is he really the best person?"
```

INT. RECEPTION AREA—LATER

The crowd has moved indoors for dinner, dancing, etc. We see that Claire is giving her toast.

                    CLAIRE
        No, I'm the best person.

People laugh. We dissolve to scenes of the celebration:

        —Mitchell and Cam cutting their cake.
        —Barb and Merle (Cam's parents)
         dancing. Jay and Gloria dancing.
         Lily and baby Joe dancing.
        —A videographer's POV of several
         wedding guests wishing Mitchell and
         Cam well.

A crowd has gathered expectantly as a garter flies in and is caught by Phil. A second later, another garter flies in.

Over this, we hear:

                    CLAIRE (V.O.)
        But it's not who either of them is,
        it's who they are together. Great
        dads, great partners, and now, I'm
        pleased to introduce to you for the
        first time ever—on our fourth try—two
        great husbands, Mitch and Cam.

We cut around for reactions from the crowd, including Haley, who looks a little wistful. Back to the dance floor as Cam and Mitchell bow.

Pepper steps out applauding, then extends his arms to present the newly married couple to the crowd. As he does, several butterflies fly out of his jacket sleeves. The crowd oohs at the magic. Phil reacts jealously as Claire squeezes his hand.

It really comes down to a preference of a long or short version.

REVISED ENDING

                    CLAIRE (V.O.)
          I wondered, "Was he really everything
          I wanted for my brother? Was he
          really the best person?"

INT. RECEPTION AREA—LATER

The crowd has moved indoors for dinner, dancing, etc. We see that Claire is giving her toast.

                    CLAIRE
          No, I'm the best person.

People laugh. We see guests react.

                    CLAIRE (V.O.)
          And now, I am very pleased to raise
          a glass and introduce for the first
          time ever—on our fourth try—great
          husbands, Mitch and Cam.

Mitchell and Cam dance.

FERGUSON (*Mitchell Pritchett*): When Justin first met me at the gym in West Hollywood, his opening conversation to me was he'd just watched the pilot of *Modern Family* and was working on Proposition

8. He felt the show was really going to do great things for marriage equality. I think it did. I think all of these things when you step back and look at the full picture we are all part of that tapestry of making it happen.

RICHMAN (*writer / executive producer*): My generation of gay men did not grow up with the idea that marriage was even a possibility. Marriage was not something that I expected or even really wanted. I think the proposal episode, more than the wedding, spurred a real sea change in my thinking in terms of my own wanting to get married. All of a sudden, it meant a lot to me to be part of a family. Legally, in every aspect, I wanted a thing that I never thought that I would want. I don't think my partner was like me. He was like, "What? Really? We want to do that?" I thought, "I can't be writing these people moving forward in their lives and have myself be standing still." You can draw a direct line from writing those episodes to my desire to move forward, to take another step in my relationship like those characters were doing.

The federal law for same-sex marriage passed in 2015. Richman married his longtime partner in 2018.

Game Changer

I just wanted Mitch and Cam to show that they can make as many mistakes raising a child as a straight couple. Like that's the goal. We're all the same.

—ERIC STONESTREET

Can a TV sitcom really influence our culture, or does it merely reflect it? Probably both. What Modern Family *achieved with Mitchell and Cam's parenting and marriage sent a clear message without preaching; provided an avenue for discussion without directing; opened a door for acceptance without forcing. In so doing, it helped change the conversation and educate some in need of it.*

LEVITAN (*cocreator*): It wasn't like we set out to do a show that makes a statement about gay families. It was, "Let's present these characters realistically." And then because we did, all these good things happened.

LLOYD (*cocreator*): There was no political agenda. No thought that this was going to normalize this behavior for some people who found it challenging or threatening. That was a very happy consequence.

FERGUSON (*Mitchell Pritchett*): I think that for many people, Mitch and Cam are their gay friends. A lot of people don't know any gay people, but they know Mitch and Cam, which is really cool.

STONESTREET (*Cam Tucker*): I said from the beginning, I want my character to be relatable, fun, and cool to everyone; that he not represent gay people but represent people—parents, boyfriends, girlfriends, aunts, and uncles, whatever.

FERGUSON (*Mitchell Pritchett*): Mitchell's not only a great gay character, but he's also a father, son, and brother. I feel like being gay is so far down the list of things that are interesting about him.

My mom definitely referenced Cam and Mitch when I proposed to my wife. She said, "Well, they did it."

—LESLIE MERLIN

Much as everyone wants somebody to love, so, too, does everyone want cultural figures that align with their own experiences. As TV series such as Will and Grace *or superheroes such as* Wonder Woman *and* Black Panther *have shown us, dollars and diversity don't represent polar opposite ideas. That false bill of goods comes courtesy of your friendly neighborhood narrow-minded executive. At the same time, seeing representation can sometimes evoke unpredictable emotions.*

HIGGINBOTHAM (*writer / executive producer*): My partner often talks about the first time he saw *Will and Grace*. He thought, "Oh no, are people going to be okay with this?" There are people on TV acting the way that you always felt like you had to hide. There's so much pressure from our world to live in secret. We're raised with that fear inside of us: "Don't let anyone see you."

RICHMAN (*writer / executive producer*): Without *Will and Grace*, there is no *Modern Family*. But while Sean [Hayes] and Eric [McCormack] are geniuses, they were only relatable as far as they were fabulous. They looked fabulous. They didn't have kids. They lived larger than life. A kid watching *Will and Grace* could say, "I could grow up, be gay, funny, and wear great clothes." Our characters showed them something different. For me as a gay person, I go, "Oh my God, some twelve-year-old gay boy or girl is watching this and is going to grow up thinking, 'I'm going to get married and have a family.'" That thought didn't exist for me when I was growing up.

It makes people realize that sexuality is not as much of a chasm as they expect it to be.

—JESSE TYLER FERGUSON

The writers took it slow the first season, wanting to draw people into the normalcy of Mitchell and Cam's world. Some people in the LGBTQ community objected to the lack of physical affection.

LEVITAN (*cocreator*): If you want to change hearts and minds, then you don't do a lot of things in the beginning that will make people go away. You want them to invest in the show. Then you can slowly let these characters evolve. Then whatever they do, the audience will accept.

FERGUSON (*Mitchell Pritchett*): I think Mitch and Cam were under a bit of a microscope in a way that the other couples weren't. It goes back to the gay community being very excited that we were on TV, but at the same time, we were meant to represent an entire community, and that's not doable.

O'SHANNON (*writer / executive producer*): In the "Airport 2010" episode [season 1]; there's a scene where Claire and Phil get together after fighting and they kiss. Mitch and Cam reunite in the same scene and hug. I think it's because those two moments are right next to each other that it's hard not to compare and go, "Oh, how come the straight couple can kiss and the gay couple has to hug?"

STONESTREET (*Cam Tucker*): It bothered me that people thought we were intentionally trying to make Mitch and Cam not affectionate. I told Jesse, "This is where I yield to you and you tell me."

FERGUSON (*Mitchell Pritchett*): I do feel it's important to see a gay couple showing affection that speaks to visibility. These characters do need to be aspirational and feel real, so I took the criticism with a grain of salt. But at the same time, I thought maybe we should show a little bit more affection. I always look for opportunities with Eric to kiss him or be closer to him or infuse the characters with behaviors that a couple would have. He's very open to that. I love that we addressed that issue of Cam and Mitch not kissing in an episode.

That episode became season 2's "The Kiss."

FERGUSON (*Mitchell Pritchett*): Mitchell always had a hard time showing affection, and his dad never kissed him. Their family forces them to kiss. That was the pinnacle of the scene, the emotional release. Then Claire and Jay kiss, and in the background, Mitchell and Cam kiss, in a way that's without fireworks, fanfare, or close-ups. It's not "a thing." It's real life. I thought the writers handled that so beautifully.

Rather than darkness and hate, it allowed the light in.
—HELENA LAMB

STONESTREET (*Cam Tucker*): I was on a Sirius radio show in New York. This woman with a strong Southern accent called in. She said, "I wanted to let you know that I'm a big fan of the show. My husband's an over-the-road truck driver, and because of your show and Mitch and Cam, you guys have shown him that gay guys aren't after his behind but are actually people, too, and fun." I was like, "I'm sorry, what?" That's exactly it. That's the reach I wanted to have. I told the lady on the phone, "Ma'am, please pass this message along to your husband. I have never met him. I don't know what he looks like. But I can assure him that no one is after his behind. No one, man or woman."

VERGARA (*Gloria Delgado Pritchett*): One of the things that I hear a lot of people say is "You made me understand my son," or "You made my life so much easier with my family. You guys have been portraying a gay couple, not men in a G-string in a parade."

FERGUSON (*Mitchell Pritchett*): The thing that I've gotten several times that is really cool is there are a lot of straight couples who come up to me and say, "My husband is such a Cam." They talk about when they Ferberized their baby. I love their relating to these universal themes that happen to be happening to a gay couple.

HIGGINBOTHAM (*writer / executive producer*): I was at a dinner, and this woman said she had a funny story to tell me. "All my life, I knew my dad was homophobic and racist. He had a hard time watching *Modern Family* because of Cam." So I'm thinking, "He's a boilerplate homophobe. What's the end of this story? It feels like a hate crime." She said, "I asked him about it, and he said it's because Cam reminds him so much of my mother and it drives him insane." That's a funny way to tell me this character is relatable. A little dark, but such great progress.

STONESTREET (*Cam Tucker*): I was at the Out100 party in New York, and this guy came up to me and said that he'd recently come out to his mom. He told her his friend Bill, who she always thought was his best friend, was not his friend but his boyfriend. And he said she paused for a minute, stopped and looked at him, and her first question was "Well, who's Mitch? Who's Cam?" And I thought that's pretty awesome.

I think a lot of people saw in them themselves.
—ABRAHAM HIGGINBOTHAM

FERGUSON (*Mitchell Pritchett*): Eric and I have both met kids who have said they were able to come out of the closet because of Mitch and Cam. It started conversations with their parents, or there have been mothers and fathers who said they were able to accept their child because they had a conversation about Mitch and Cam.

STONESTREET (*Cam Tucker*): I was in Australia doing a talk show when the stage manager passed me a very sweet note that read, "I want to let you know I'm an audience member and a lesbian. My partner and I have a daughter, and she came home from school very upset because she was being made fun of for having two moms." They eventually got together with the person making fun of them. They all watched *Modern Family* together and said, "Our life isn't much different than this. These happen to be two men. We're two moms. Can we all move past this type of thing?"

RICHMAN (*writer / executive producer*): My husband was recently shooting a movie in Israel. *Modern Family* is apparently really popular there. I couldn't believe the reaction. But the best one was his twenty-three-year-old costar, a gay man, who literally cried when he met me. That sounds insane, but the show was so important to him as a gay kid in Israel in a country that's not as tolerant to gay people as in America. It was very gratifying.

To see how a TV show can change people's minds means it never should have been that well founded in the first place for them.

—Helena Lamb

Mitchell and Cam also had a profound impact on crew members working within it.

MERLIN (*assistant director / key PA*): I grew up in New York and didn't come out until I was twenty-six years old, because I wasn't sure about what my family would think. I'm not saying these shows are making it easier, but kids are coming out younger. They're able to talk to their families easier. It makes it more acceptable. It's no different than having *Black-ish* or *Transparent*. It makes it okay where it wasn't okay.

FERGUSON (*Mitchell Pritchett*): Growing up gay in Albuquerque, New Mexico, there were shows like *Will and Grace* that I could look to like, "Okay, that's something that represents me or the person I want to become," but I didn't feel there was really a show that encapsulated what it's like to be a normal gay man or woman raising a family. What I love to think about is that the show's going to be on forever in reruns, and there'll be kids in Albuquerque, New Mexico, or wherever they are and they'll look at our show and it will be aspirational for them.

LAMB (*first assistant director / director*): I'm a gay woman. I have a wife and two kids. I was raised in a Southern Baptist household. My parents weren't accepting of me. They didn't come to my wedding. My mom never said *wife* to me. She couldn't use that language or talk about it. My father died not knowing I was five and a half months pregnant. My mom didn't want to upset him because my gay children would be such an abomination. He rode that out to the end. My mom came out the first or second season, and I put her in the background of a scene with Jesse and Eric. They were incredibly lovely to her and made her feel like a big star. My mom walked away saying, "I love Jesse and Eric. They're the nicest men." Years later, when Jesse married Justin, my mother said, "Will you do me a favor? Tell Jesse that Mrs. Lamb said he and his husband were so handsome at their wedding." That's literally the first time my mother had ever addressed a gay wedding. My mom's now very involved with my family, loving and accepting. I'm a walking testament to the fact that this TV show changes people's lives in the sense of saying, "I don't have to agree, or really accept, but it's my job to be loving because you're my family."

FERGUSON (*Mitchell Pritchett*): I know how much work went into Proposition 8. I would never, ever take any responsibility for that. I certainly would include our show as part of the pop culture talking point during that time, and I do think that minds were changed. I do think that we were a reference point for a lot of people. I do think that being in the zeitgeist in that time was important.

The Great Debate

Creativity doesn't come from conformity. The Modern Family *writers' room occasionally had heated debates about plotlines and character actions.*

Dirty Clowning

Regardless of where you fall on the clown spook spectrum, you probably don't want to talk about clown sex. Yet in the Modern Family *writers' room, that very topic came up with Fizbo.*

WALSH (*writer / executive producer*): We got to the point of, "Why doesn't Mitch like this clown?"

MCCRAY (*script coordinator*): There was a storyline that Mitch hated Fizbo because they had some drunken sexual escapade. It was more a farcical thing, and Steve was grossed out by it basically. He's always been leery of sexualizing Mitch and Cam.

CORRIGAN (*writer / executive producer*): The crux of the disagreement was between Chris and Steve. Chris found that to be really funny. And Steve, I think, was really nervous about the new show doing something that graphic or salacious. They both felt very strongly about it.

LEVITAN (*cocreator*): I thought it was a little weird. I thought it was far funnier that every time he's in this costume, Mitch keeps rolling his eyes. That to me is a gift that keeps giving. Whereas if every time Mitch gets turned on, I personally find that odd and distasteful. But again, we're individual people with individual opinions, and they are all valid.

LLOYD (*cocreator*): It was never a big part of that story. There was something tawdry but funny about the idea that Mitchell gets turned on by the clown. The counterargument is that it's a bit much or isn't it enough that we're getting American to embrace this gay couple? Let's not push our luck by making one a weird sexual fetish. It was debated, and we went away from it.

The Condom Conundrum

The great condom debate of 2012 over Claire sending Haley off to college with condoms, pitted Zuker, who thought it way out of character, versus Levitan, who considered it a reflection of the world today.

ZUKER (*writer / executive producer*): Yes, Claire knows Haley is sexually active, but it didn't seem real to me for that character to send her daughter off to school with condoms. Others said that seemed like something a mom would want to do, to make sure she's safe. That to me seemed like a line she wouldn't cross.

LEVITAN (*cocreator*): For me personally, it was a no-brainer. As I recall, when my daughter was leaving for school, my ex-wife did the same thing, which I agree with totally. People are going to do whatever they're going to do, and better to be safe than sorry. This is supposed to be *Modern Family,* and it seemed an appropriate move for responsible parents trying to raise responsible kids. Danny being the big voice on the other side was pretty unexpected for me. He's typically a pretty forward-thinking parent.

CHAN (*writers' assistant*): Typically, if I happened to be the only woman in the room at the moment, Steve would often look to me like,

"Do you think that's okay?" I didn't think there was anything wrong with that at all.

HIGGINBOTHAM (*writer / executive producer*): It became an intense argument for the entire time we worked on the episode. Then it became a recurring joke on the show after the episode aired.

ZUKER (*writer / executive producer*): I suppose it's a good story point, because there was debate in the room about it, but that never felt real to my experience.

WRUBEL (*writer / executive producer*): Danny really dug in on that issue. Typically, I would agree with things Danny was saying. In that instance, I was inclined to go with Steve. Steve had a very firm opinion about what he wanted, and I knew Danny was going to lose.

ZUKER (*writer / executive producer*): I can't deny that it was entertaining. Dealing with a kid's sexuality is weird. What's great about our show is when our characters talk about it. It's always been fun to address those things head-on. Conflict and awkwardness are always good for comedy.

Baby Talk

Pregnancy came up often as a hot topic for almost every character. The biggest debate concerned the timing of Haley's pregnancy, which started as early as season 5 and finally came to fruition in season 10.

RICHMAN (*writer / executive producer*): We knew we needed to evolve Haley and keep her at home.

MCCRAY (*script coordinator*): The whole debate was really a clear divide between Chris's and Steve's room. Most of the people in Steve's room were on board with it, and most of the people in Chris's room were not.

CHAN (*writers' assistant*): Chris suggested if we want to make someone pregnant, maybe have it be Claire. At her age, that would be surprising.

LLOYD (*cocreator*): I thought of keeping Phil and Claire young and vital. Having a kid of their own is more energetic than having them be grandparents.

BOWEN (*Claire Dunphy*): I would have loved to be pregnant. But it's too late in the season. We would never see her baby.

ZUKER (*writer / executive producer*): There was always a possibility of getting Claire pregnant even before we got Gloria pregnant. I wrote the episode "Snip" [season 4] about Phil's vasectomy, and one of the things we liked was leaving the option open for them.

LEVITAN (*cocreator*): Because we had done Gloria and Jay having a baby, I don't think that there was much enthusiasm in the room for Claire, frankly. Their being grandparents felt like a different thing.

HIGGINBOTHAM (*writer / executive producer*): I was one of the proponents of it happening earlier with Haley and Andy. I wanted to play with the conflict between Claire and Haley. Sins of the mother, so to speak.

HYLAND (*Haley Dunphy*): In season 5, I was saying, "I want Haley to get pregnant. I want her to be a young mom. I think that would be hysterical. I want her to have her own picture frame." That was my goal.

RICHMAN (*writer / executive producer*): The room was divided. Many people thought Haley's pregnancy was sad. A young girl like that having a baby. And then a lot of people thought the Claire thing was sad, too. I was really against the Haley pregnancy when it was first introduced. In that way, I sided with Chris in that she was twenty years old. How are you getting away with not even considering terminating this pregnancy?

CHAN (*writers' assistant*): We were discussing if it was going to be Arvin. The episode where Haley passes out and ends up in the hospital. We had talked about it being that episode. One of the arguments was it was too soon in their relationship for that to happen. Steve's argument to that was, "In real life, those things happen."

LLOYD (*cocreator*): She's getting pregnant with a guy she's barely met. There's no way they're not at least discussing having an abortion. It would be a giant break in the character's continuity if she said she definitely wants this baby. She's a party girl, the textbook example of someone who would choose the abortion route. We would have to deal with that, which was another reason not to do it at that age.

LEVITAN (*cocreator*): It would have been more controversial, and frankly, I find that interesting. And Claire was about that age when she got pregnant, so it made sense for a lot of reasons, but I understand that we don't all think alike.

LLOYD (*cocreator*): I think some people probably thought we'd be getting into real stuff. We can sit here and talk about how much comedy there is to mine from that, but I don't know that we're going to find a real fun spin on that. I think we made the right decision in waiting.

RICHMAN (*writer / executive producer*): Ultimately, we all were on board the way it happened. We waited, and I think that was the compromise.

LEVITAN (*cocreator*): When Haley got pregnant, it was still something, but it wasn't as much as if she had been a bit younger.

Lost Horizons

Not all ideas make it to the finish line. Some make it further than others, before their timely or untimely demise.

LLOYD (*cocreator*): You can fall in love with a scene, but that's not a good enough reason to say we have to have it in a show. It's not a story yet.

ZUKER (*writer / executive producer*): You start in Mitch's and Cam's house. Phil and Claire come down for breakfast, and the Dunphy kids are all there. Why are they in this house? You have to go back and figure out why people aren't where they're supposed to be. We never did figure that one out, but I thought it was a strong opening to a show.

WALSH (*writer / executive producer*): For a while, we were going to have Phil build a building.

CORRIGAN (*writer / executive producer*): Phil was going to take his real estate agent career to the next level. We sat there for a day thinking, "This is going to be great." A week later, we were like, "There aren't that many stories."

LLOYD (*cocreator*): We had Sofía running for school board at one point. I think we toyed with the idea of Mitchell working with his father, but Claire seemed to make more sense.

MCCRAY (*script coordinator*): The clown funeral episode [season 3's "Send Out the Clowns"] with Lewis [Bobby Cannavale] originally had a very dark turn to it that was fought all the way through the table read. Lewis falls off a parking garage and dies. It may be funny that a clown dies, but it was so not our show.

RICHMAN (*writer / executive producer*): It was a clown suicide or accident. It happened in front of Mitch, Cam, and *Lily*! It was insane.

CHAN (*writers' assistant*): There was an idea where all three families share a vacation house, but each stays at different times. It was basically that something the first family leaves behind creates a story for the second family and then something the second family leaves behind creates a story for the third family, and then it was all supposed to come together in the end.

ZUKER (*writer / executive producer*): What I've always liked about my relationship with my wife is that one of us will get a really stupid idea and then the other one will say it's stupid. Then we avoid a lot of heartache. But occasionally, we will both get the same stupid idea. And that happened when we adopted a potbellied pig. For the longest time, we were working on an episode where Phil and Claire did that. And then somehow the pig got stuck in one of the walls. To this day when we go down a road that is not fruitful for a very long time, it's the pig in the wall.

O'SHANNON (*writer / executive producer*): We went pretty far along with the pig. For a while, Chris was determined to make that an episode.

KO (*writer / executive producer*): I even wrote an outline for it—before we decided to toss it. There were a lot of funny elements, but in the end, it never quite came together. It was also one of the first (if not the first) times we paired Phil and Cam together for an entire story. We were surprised at how challenging it was to make that particular dynamic funny. We realized it was probably because Phil and Cam are both such positive characters by nature. There wasn't anyone there to balance them out or check their spontaneous impulses. It was hard to drum up conflict between them.

WINTER (*Alex Dunphy*): I know they were thinking of doing an escape room episode. I'm an escape room queen. I love them. Steve and Chris both asked me about them.

KO (*writer / executive producer*): There was a Haley-Luke story that wasn't exactly rejected, but never made it to air. It was about Haley graduating from community college on the same day Luke was scheduled to take his driver's test. Neither of them told the rest of the family what was going on, and they realized it's because they've both lived in Alex's shadow for so long. It doesn't matter what they accomplish in life, because it will always pale in comparison to what Alex has achieved. And they really bond over that. In the end, Luke surprises Haley by showing up at her graduation and cheering for her. It was actually a really sweet story for the two of them, but we had to cut it for time. For a couple of years, we talked about inserting it into another episode, but sadly, we never did.

O'Shannon, five years removed, almost came back in season 10 to do an episode he'd thought up.

O'SHANNON (*writer / executive producer*): I was watching a later episode and remembered how little the kids were when we started. I began to wonder if there were enough outtakes and unused footage that—with some clever editing, maybe some digital work with wardrobe or character placement, some off-screen and over-the-shoulder voice doubling—we might be able to craft the beats of a story. Unfortunately, there wasn't enough footage to make anything of it.

Perhaps the one that stuck around longest involved Cam and Claire.

WRUBEL (*writer / executive producer*): They realize that they're married to people who wouldn't enjoy a warehouse sale, so they decide they'll team up and go to one together.

RICHMAN (*writer / executive producer*): They're known for spending wildly at sales for stuff they didn't need just because it was 50 percent off.

LLOYD (*cocreator*): They go on a budget. Neither was going to spend more than $200. Within thirty seconds, Cam had spent his full $200.

RICHMAN (*writer / executive producer*): Cam sees a scarf for $200 marked down from $600 and buys it immediately. It's in the smallest bag imaginable. And now he has to sit there while Claire carefully combs through racks and racks of clothes and takes hours to decide on her $200. And he's freaking out because he wants to be shopping. That's all the way the story got.

LLOYD (*cocreator*): We would move away from it for six months, and then we'd say, "Oh, wait, we had that wonderful story where they go to the mall." I'm sure we said that five times over the space of five years, the great mall story, which every time we looked at it was like, "No." It was actually a terrible story that was about six pages long.

Truth Be Told

As pointed out to me in numerous conversations, Modern Family *gained an industry reputation over time for letting women writers go or not asking them back. Every year, anywhere from one to three women worked on the show (often out of fifteen total writers). Typically, they didn't get asked back. Some of the male writers I spoke with said they sensed a disconnect but didn't understand why. No one pointed fingers at anyone as much as raised questions about the issue. While many staff writers, men and women, past and present, remain friends to this day, they look at the situation through a different lens. Some of the show's female writers sat down to reflect on their time on the show and the issue as a whole.*

CHUPACK (*writer, season 3*): I loved writing episodes, loved the actors, made some lasting friendships with other writers, won an Emmy for my season there, and will always have *Modern Family* on my résumé, which is invaluable. But at *Modern Family,* more so than on any other show I've ever written, it felt like you had to prove yourself every day. This was true for all of the writers, but it was especially challenging for the new girl, since that was a place where almost every year there was a new girl trying to prove herself in a roomful of men who had been there from the beginning.

CHRISTY STRATTON (*writer, season 8*): It was absolutely a challenge—every day, with every pitch, I couldn't help but think of the women who came before me and wonder if I was doing enough to avoid their fate. It was hard not to be in my head the whole time. That said, I enjoyed my season there. Getting to be on set with those gifted actors, seeing my name in the credits, going to the Emmys—being on that show made me feel like I had finally arrived. And the times I was able to make Chris Lloyd laugh are among my career highlights.

JESSICA POTER (*writer, seasons 9 and 10*): Yeah, I was warned the show didn't have a great history when it came to retaining women, so of course I was nervous about my reproductive system interfering in my ability to do my job. But there were other obfuscating factors. I came in season 9, when the other fourteen writers had a shared history working together on this show (or shows prior). I was the only lower-level writer. It was my first staffing job. I was much younger than most of them. I knew nothing of the Lakers *or* the Clippers. A tough time was going to be inevitable.

DAISY GARDNER (*writer, season 6*): You're talking about a show where no female writer lasted for the run of the entire series and where only one female writer was consistently retained and promoted. The best advice I got came from a former *Modern Family* female writer before I started. She told me to learn all I could from the room, then scan the doors for the exits. You don't go to Bluebeard's castle as the new wife and say, "I can change him!"

CHUPACK (*writer, season 3*): I had heard from my agent and other writers that *Modern Family* was a tough place for women. But I loved the show, and I had a lot of experience behind me, so I felt certain I could break that pattern and be the one female writer—other than Elaine—who they realized they couldn't live without. But I couldn't figure out how to contribute like I normally do. Once you start to lose confidence, or second-guess, there's a chilling effect that happens that isn't good for the show or for you as a writer.

GARDNER (*writer, season 6*): For the first few months, the other writers recounted in detail the reasons that the previous women didn't work out: one had a high-pitched laugh, one had the gall to decorate her office, one took time off to be with her kids on Jewish holidays, one talked too much, one didn't talk enough, one needed a few mental health days after a pet died . . .

CHUPACK (*writer, season 3*): I think I was the one who had the high-pitched laugh, and I was definitely the one who decorated my office. I do that at every job—hang a few pictures, bring in a throw blanket . . . I thought about not doing it at *Modern Family* since I knew women don't last long there, but it felt defeatist.

GARDNER (*writer, season 6*): By the way, Cindy's script was nominated for an award that year! The weird thing was the room didn't usually have a problem with the women's writing. The vibe was more, "Here's what was wrong on a very personal human level with the women that came before you." Then it would be time to pitch. I'd open my mouth and be like, "Mee-ble marble murp!" It was not cool.

CHUPACK (*writer, season 3*): They did that to me, too—joked about why previous female writers hadn't worked out. It had the quality of making you think you were on the inside, like you were passing the test. And of course the next year I was one of the women they were complaining about to the new girl.

STRATTON (*writer, season 8*): We were doing an episode about our characters going to the Women's March. The showrunner wanted it to say something bigger about feminism and women's issues. Elaine had gone for the day. So it was me in a room with a dozen men. We were all pitching ideas. Several times, I struggled to get my pitch in over the men's pitches. I looked around to see if anyone would make eye contact with me—I thought, "This is exactly the type of thing the story should be about! It's happening to me right now!" After my pitches were rejected (as well as theirs), the showrunner announced, "Go home and ask your wives what issues they have with being a woman." I jumped outside of my body for a minute and begged myself not to yell, *"Hi! Hello! I'm a woman, and I'm right here!"*

POTER (*writer, seasons 9 and 10*): Yes, it felt terrible to be on the other side of arguments to do with what it feels like as a woman, or would a woman do *x*. If there had been more women to have differing opinions, it wouldn't have been as frustrating; I'm easily cowed into thinking I'm the weirdo anyway. I will say I don't think there was anything malicious going on. The staff would go out of their way not to interrupt me and to give me credit. I think I did succeed creatively on the show and made many lasting friendships. I wish being worried about my status there hadn't factored into it.

CHUPACK (*writer, season 3*): At the end of the season, I was wondering if I should pack up my office in case they let me go, or leave it decorated for next season. It felt like either decision would be bad luck. I left it decorated and ended up going in late one night the week before season 4 was to start and emptying it out very unceremoniously after hearing I wasn't being asked back.

Lessons learned from the experience, good and bad, they took with them.

GARDNER (*writer, season 6*): The skills, talent, and collective institutional comedy writing knowledge of the *Modern Family* room are beyond impressive. I'm grateful to have observed writers working at the top of their game, and I'm glad I got to contribute to it. I enjoyed and appreciated everyone on an individual level.

STRATTON (*writer, season 8*): I learned the value of a talented, devoted, supportive production crew.

POTER (*writer, seasons 9 and 10*): I learned how to break stories and refine jokes, and I am grateful that they gave me my first writing job and asked me back. It was so cool to work alongside such a deep bench of hilarious writers. In terms of what I'd do differently if I ever get to run a room, I would definitely want the staff to be more balanced, gender-wise.

CHUPACK (*writer, season 3*): I would say that for any new writer, especially if you're in the minority because of your gender or ethnicity or sexual orientation or age, it's important to feel that once you're hired, you're on the team. You're not there on a trial basis, and you're not being judged daily. Everyone should want you to succeed.

Many women writers have encountered similar experiences in other writers' rooms.

STRATTON (*writer, season 8*): A big challenge is when you're the only woman on staff, getting people to relate to your personal stories and episode ideas. There's no one able to support you with a "That happened to me, too!"

POTER (*writer, seasons 9 and 10*): Totally. It's important to have more than one person who can speak to a specific life experience and back others up with the stamp of, "Oh yeah, that is a thing!"

CHUPACK (*writer, season 3*): I love how Christy and Jessica just illustrated their point by validating each other's experience of not getting your experience validated.

STRATTON (*writer, season 8*): When your room is mostly men, the most interesting stories often go to the male characters. I pitched this idea once: What if Gloria, who grew up poor, had a room we have not seen that she has hoarded wall-to-wall? The room pitched on it for hours. But by the end of the day, the story had morphed into Jay being the hoarder.

GARDNER (*writer, season 6*): Great rooms are starting to look more like America in terms of diversity and gender balance.

CHUPACK (*writer, season 3*): There needs to be an atmosphere of mutual respect, trust, and fun so that you can throw out and build on ideas without being afraid of sounding stupid or exposing too much about yourself. If you want writers to share their most embarrassing, unflattering moments—which are often the most comic—they need to feel safe, like they are among friends.

Some have seen change, hopefully a sign of better things to come.

GARDNER (*writer, season 6*): There isn't a huge "women aren't funny" bias with millennials. They grew up watching Tina, Amy, Julia Louis-Dreyfus, and the *Broad City* gals. Millennials expect that both partners in a marriage will be equal. When funny young dudes come to work, they feel comfortable working with women.

For aspiring women writers, these veterans offer some advice.

CHUPACK (*writer, season 3*): What matters is your writing. Great writing will open doors for you. If doors aren't opening, go back to the writing. Go to storytelling shows and try telling stories. Try stand-up. Try improv. Write essays. Write a blog. Write a play.

POTER (*writer, seasons 9 and 10*): Believe in yourself. If you can make yourself laugh, someone else will laugh at your work, too.

GARDNER (*writer, season 6*): Believe in your own bag of bullshit. It's yours. Never stop writing it.

STRATTON (*writer, season 8*): I would tell young women that being fired from a job is not a career-ender.

CHUPACK (*writer, season 3*): Pay attention to what show or magazine or production company is doing the kind of writing you love. Look for female role models and see how they've done it. Read profiles and listen to podcasts about women in the business. Women will help you, so pay it forward as you rise up the ranks and help the women who come after you.

Brushes with Celebrity

Lots of celebrities have appeared as guest stars on the show, some unknown at the time like Stranger Things' *Millie Bobby Brown (on-screen for all of ten seconds),* The Walking Dead's *Lauren Cohan (another blink-and-gone appearance), or* Last Man Standing's *Kaitlyn Dever (a youthful Manny crush). Other times, casting made them celebrities, such as when Greenberg worked diligently to cast one of the first transgender child actors, eight-year-old Jackson Millarker, for a role as a transgender friend of Lily's.*

The show also got its share of movie stars, perhaps no bigger than the first two to appear, Ed Norton, a theater friend of Burrell's, and Elizabeth Banks, a friend of Ferguson's.

FERGUSON (*Mitchell Pritchett*): Liz is one of my oldest friends. We were at a birthday party for Busy Phillips. Our show was so fresh then, and we were basically asking anyone to be on it, not that Liz is anyone. She's a movie star. So we started pitching her ideas and decided at that party that Liz was going to be on our show.

ELIZABETH BANKS (*Sal*): I remember being a bit tipsy at Busy's party and talking with Jesse and Jason [Winer] about the show and what kind of role I could play. As I was throwing an arm over Jesse's shoulder, it felt like I was already playing a version of Sal.

A much milder version, considering what audiences would learn in subsequent episodes about her.

BANKS (*Sal*): Sal's a commitment-phobic narcissist who's emotionally lost and needs constant validation. She's that friend we all had in our early twenties, who always knew where the party was, hustled nonstop, was sexually promiscuous, and challenged your boundaries. She would sleep in your bed or in your car. Some of the best nights of your life were spent with her, but then you outgrew it and she never did.

Sal didn't handle Lily's adoption well, to say the least, mumbling to herself in front of Mitchell and Cam, "You should kill that baby," followed later by the equally soothing "I will throw her in the ocean."

BANKS (*Sal*): Mitch and Cam's marriage and kid feel like a betrayal not only because it means they've moved on but because it feels a little like they're judging her for not doing the same. Lily is the new lady in their life, and Sal doesn't like being replaced. My favorite exchange between Sal and Lily is Lily missing my wedding and saying, "I'll come to the next one." She totally has Sal's number.

As did Banks the show's.

LEVITAN (*cocreator*): Elizabeth had one of the funniest ad libs I've ever heard on set, when Mitch jumps on Cam's back and she says, "Well, that's one mystery solved."

BANKS (*Sal*): My favorite line was "Sometimes when babies come this early, they're black." Although I was disappointed when I came back with a white son—I'd really hoped they'd go for it. I was delighted that I was raising him to emulate my two favorite people.

Much as DeDe played a significant part in the Pritchett family's life series, so, too, did Manny's dad, Javier (Benjamin Bratt).

BENJAMIN BRATT (*Javier Delgado*): Javier is your archetypal ne'er-do-well, a charismatic rogue and vagabond whose main goal in life is to seek out pleasure and adventure. He's got charm and mystery to burn, and enough danger to make him an intriguing friend, but he's a terrible father and a worse husband. Still, I tried to play him as someone who has genuine love and affection for his son and simmering heat for his ex, though he would never admit it. He likes Jay and respects that he can give Manny and Gloria the stability he never could. He's the eternal bad boy, which doesn't make him a bad guy, you just wouldn't want to be married to him.

Bratt's Modern Family *career got off to a rocky start.*

LEVITAN (*cocreator***):** At the table read, we could barely hear him and were like, "Uh-oh. This isn't going to be funny."

GREENBERG (*casting director***):** He's the most fun, charismatic guy to be around, but when we started reading him, like many film actors, he did it really under, really quiet, and really low.

BRATT (*Javier Delgado***):** It was a total disaster. They were looking for a full-blown performance, and I obviously didn't get the memo. Typically, table reads are for the actors and writers; it's about process, and for me in this case, about discovery, an attempt to find a way into the character before making any definitive choices about how to portray him. So I played it all under, noncommittal, very low key, which is my way, and it bombed spectacularly. To make matters worse, this was not a table read in the traditional sense but more like a house party. There were no less than fifty people in that room, and it was apparent they were there for the show. The main cast was dialed in, and we were all laughing out loud. The room was rolling, giddy with laughter, a runaway train of comedic brilliance, and I got left behind at the station. The louder they got, the quieter I got. Just . . . awful. But I was never worried. I'm a red-light ball player, always have been. When the cameras roll, I'm going to give you what you need, which is when it really matters anyway.

GREENBERG (*casting director***):** It was Ed who said, "Give him a chance. He can do this." And he was so much better when the cameras were rolling.

BRATT (*Javier Delgado***):** Ed knows I love him. We met back in the late '80s on a cop drama, when I was a kid starting out, and he was already a big star on *Married with Children*. He's the same guy he was back then, an old-school cat, very warm and affable, quick to share a story and bring you in.

Phil's dad, Frank [Fred Willard], appeared fourteen times on the show, sometimes via Skyping from Florida while other times appearing at Phil's doorstep.

WILLARD *(Frank Dunphy)*: I was the nutty, good-humored father, passed down to Phil, to explain why Phil was always joking and doing silly things. I would have some jokes I would start and Phil would finish with the punchline, because he grew up hearing these things. My take is that rather than being bored with it, Phil loved it and, as he grew older, played right into it. In other words, like father like son.

BURRELL *(Phil Dunphy)*: Fred's by far had the most influence as a comedian on me. He's been working with a lack of self-awareness as a comic device forever, and it feels like I just co-opted the whole thing. I completely ripped him off, and that's what sons do from fathers.

WILLARD *(Frank Dunphy)*: Frank was very evasive in their relationship, so there was a little bit of uneasiness. He didn't want to get anything too teary. He wanted to keep everything light and aboveboard. Never getting too close, too personal, a little standoffish—he would do that with his jokes. And that's what he passed on to Phil.

The last episode of the first season, "Family Portrait," included a storyline in which Phil and Gloria end up on the kiss cam at a Los Angeles Lakers game at Staples Center (look closely and you'll see Levitan seated next to Gloria).

LEVITAN *(cocreator)*: We needed someone from the Lakers to do this little bit. We of course said Kobe [Bryant], and they said, "Kobe never likes to do these things." We said, "Ask him anyway," and he said yes because apparently he really liked the show. He came on set. I told him it would mean the world if he'd come with me up to the writers' room and surprise everybody. So Kobe and I are driving in a golf cart back to the writers' room. I want the entire lot to see me driving around with Kobe. We didn't pass a single person. It was suddenly a ghost town. But we did bring him up to the room, everybody freaked out, and he was very gracious.

MORTON (*executive producer*): The Lakers were very cooperative. They did the kiss cam moment at a prescribed time. We had our cameras rolling then. We may have also shot it beforehand in case something went wrong.

Chazz Palminteri appeared several times as Shorty, an old friend of Jay's, a bad gambler who sets off Jesse's gaydar.

GREENBERG (*casting director*): The character's name is Shorty, so we originally offered it to Joe Pesci, who's a short guy, and he passed. Chazz is a very tall man. They loved the idea from the get-go.

O'NEILL (*Jay Pritchett*): Chazz goes to meet Steve and Chris, and they say, "Of course we're going to change the name." And Chazz says, "You know what? Keep the name. I like it." A lot of times in the neighborhood, a guy gets a nickname for the opposite. A tall guy, you called *Shorty,* a fat guy, you call him *Skinny.* You know?

CHAZZ PALMINTERI (*Shorty*): Shorty is a working-class guy like Jay. They grew up together, were best friends, and love each other. I think they secretly looked up to each other.

GREENBERG (*casting director*): Ed and he are really good buddies. It was always a treat when he was there. He had the best time.

PALMINTERI (*Shorty*): Ed's a very giving actor. When we talked about Shorty in the first episode, you weren't sure if Shorty was gay or metrosexual. I told Ed it would be great if we kept it that way. He said, "Yeah, let's go for it, whatever's funny or good." He was never worried about his own ego. He's one of those giving actors who lets the actors around him shine, which is great.

Comedian and actor Rob Riggle appeared multiple times as Phil's real estate agent nemesis, Gil Thorpe.

GREENBERG (*casting director*): They wanted someone there to really get under Phil's skin and be a real dick, and that's in his wheelhouse.

ROB RIGGLE *(Gil Thorpe)*: Playing Gil Thorpe was pure joy! He's such a jerk. Phil Dunphy is the nicest guy on TV, and Gil is his nemesis. Whenever something goes wrong for Phil, Gil always seems to be around to witness it!

Thorpe, a fun character to write for, tickled Levitan, enough so that he considered spinning him off to his own series.

LEVITAN (*cocreator*): It seemed like that character was larger than life. I thought it was worth exploring at least. Brad and Paul initially seemed intrigued by the idea. As soon as it got in the press and became a big deal, however, it put Brad and Paul under the pressure of that, so we just bailed on it.

LLOYD (*cocreator*): Steve had a fair amount of belief in it, but because it was going to be a character from our show, he needed me to sign off on it. I said, "To be honest, I don't see the potential you see." It seemed like he was a good supporting character. I didn't see too much of a future for this.

In season 3's "Punkin Chunkin," and in one of the last season's final episodes, Josh Gad played Kenneth Ploufe, a former geeky neighbor who idolized Phil and annoyed Claire to no end. That he ended up an internet billionaire only adds salt to her wound.

GAD (*Kenneth Ploufe*): What I loved about Kenneth was he was essentially what Phil could have been. He had gone off and become a billionaire.

BOWEN (*Claire Dunphy*): They had a special handshake that went on for hours. You sit down and watch at a certain point.

LLOYD (*cocreator*): I have a soft spot for adults acting stupid, and those complicated handshakes are a common enough thing in our culture. There couldn't be too many steps to it as far as I was concerned, because it showed what made these guys like each other. They were both men-children.

GAD (*Kenneth Ploufe*): Ty and I more than anything love doing physical comedy and making ourselves look like idiots. There was this very simple blurb in the script that described this handshake that the two of us had. Of course Ty and I chose to take that little blurb and expand upon it and make it something so much more insane, ridiculous, and stupid than I think anyone had anticipated.

BURRELL (*Phil Dunphy*): They were stupid things to make us laugh. Chris contributed a lot to those.

GAD (*Kenneth Ploufe*): One hundred percent. Conceptually, he gave us a jumping-off point of what he was thinking. And then Ty and I took and made it much more unnecessarily complicated than it needed to be. Our MO was to make Chris laugh as much as possible, not really thinking that we were going to lose half a day working on this handshake for the joy of making Christopher Lloyd laugh his ass off.

BURRELL (*Phil Dunphy*): At a certain point, somebody had to pull us back because we made the shake too long. We can't make this thing any longer than it is. It was cracking us up.

GAD (*Kenneth Ploufe*): At the time, Ty and I figured that would be the entirety of the episode. We didn't think there was much need for story in that particular episode, just a ten-minute handshake.

LLOYD (*cocreator*): People still stop Josh on the street and want to talk about or do the handshake.

In season 3, Levitan cast Kevin Hart in two episodes as Andre, Phil's next-door-neighbor, over-the-fence buddy. They had done a comedy pilot years before called Dante *(2005). Hart even got to do an interview with Phil on the Dunphy couch, a rare occurrence for a non-family member.*

In season 4's "Mistery Date," Phil invited a new friend, Dave (Matthew Broderick) from the gym, over to watch a football game involving their alma mater. While both have best intentions, they wildly misinterpret the other's.

RICHMAN (*writer / executive producer*): We had tried to break Phil's gay date for three years. Then we finally got traction on an interesting take on it. As we were breaking it, I went to Chris and said, "Matthew would be so perfect for this. Because the whole story was going to be just Ty and this other character, which is something we rarely do—send one of our characters off with a guest star for the whole episode—it would need a comic actor who could go toe to toe with Ty, and that's a tall order." And Chris, who doesn't really like "stunt" casting, feeling that famous actors take you out of the story, was, to my delight, immediately on board. So I called Matthew and said, "I'm writing this part."

MATTHEW BRODERICK (*Dave*): Jeffrey described what was going to happen. It sounded very funny, and I really liked Ty's work, and Nathan [Lane] had already done a few episodes, so I had been quietly annoyed that I hadn't.

RICHMAN (*writer / executive producer*): I said, "You're going to have to take it on faith, because it won't be completed in time for you to read and say no."

BRODERICK (*Dave*): I was doing a play at the time. I flew out on my day off. I learned the part on the flight out, all my lines except one scene I didn't notice. I got there, and they said, "Now we're going to shoot the scene at the gym where you're on the phone." And I said, "What phone. What gym?" I had totally skipped that scene. I had to learn it while they were lighting it.

At the gym, Phil learns he and Dave went to the same college. He invites him over to watch a football game. Dave, a friend of Cam's (perhaps the only one with a traditional name), mistakes it for a date.

BRODERICK (*Dave*): Dave's being urged to get back into the dating waters. I felt like he was somebody who often misunderstood people around him. And he of course very much misunderstands Phil. He sees every sign incorrectly. I thought that was a funny situation.

When Phil accidentally spills margaritas on both of them, they remove their shirts so Phil can throw them in the dryer. Within the farce setup, Dave thinks they're removing their shirts for something else. This culminates with a bare-chested hug when their team scores.

BURRELL (*Phil Dunphy*): We both had a hard time getting through it. That has to have been one of the toughest scenes I had in terms of breaking.

BRODERICK (*Dave*): I laughed a great deal. It's uncomfortable to take your shirt off, particularly on TV. That was part of it. I felt that added a lot to the humor of it.

Sadly, Dave hasn't been seen or heard from since.

RICHMAN (*writer / executive producer*): Matthew complains that Nathan has done it a million times and we've never had his character back.

BRODERICK (*Dave*): That's a running joke, but it's not really a joke. I'm constantly angry at him for not having me back. But he says it's a one-off or some TV term like that. I felt Dave could be fleshed out.

In season 5's episode "The Help," Peri Gilpin played a prostitute who winds up spending a night in the Dunphy basement with Phil's father.

WILLARD (*Frank Dunphy*): Frasier always accused Peri's character [Roz] on that show of being oversexed. I remember I came face-to-face with her on set and said, "This is Frasier's worst fear of how you'd end up."

PERI GILPIN (*Jeannie*): To get to be in a room with Fred was amazing. We were backstage, and he started improvising with me. "I had no idea." "Are you sure you need this much money?" "Why didn't you tell me before?" We're not even onstage.

WILLARD (*Frank Dunphy*): It's a little game to pretend the scene has started. It helps me get into character, and it lightens the mood. You come in already warmed up.

Gilpin took a little time figuring out her character.

GILPIN (*Jeannie*): I was trying to figure out who she was, because I'm not aware of middle-aged hookers. I don't know where they hang out, how you get one.

LEVITAN (*cocreator*): I think Peri had this idea of us as this wholesome show. We needed to let her know it was okay to really go for it—the more outrageous, the better.

GILPIN (*Jeannie*): He said, "You're being Nice Peri." I said, "What do you want?" He said, "I want Slut Peri." And I was like, "Okay, I'll give you Slut Peri." My kids were in elementary school then. The head of the school is Jane Leeves's [close friend Daphne from *Frasier*] father-in-law. He walks out of his office and says, "I caught you on *Modern Family* last night, and now I have to explain to my nine-year-old what a hooker is." The wife of the art director from *Bob's Burgers* teaches there. I'm like, "He's even worse than I am."

In season 7's "Playdates," Mitchell cashes in on a sloppy, hand-drawn, last-minute birthday gift certificate, courtesy of the Dunphy children, promising him a Fun Day—a present they think he'll never actually use. Then he does. Driving him blindfolded around the neighborhood, they end up buying a map to the stars' homes with the intent of taking him to the abode of his favorite performer, Barbra Streisand.

RICHMAN (*writer / executive producer*): The minute someone said that idea, I thought, "I'm so fucked."

MORTON (*executive producer*): Jeff wrote material for her concerts. He knows her.

RICHMAN (*writer / executive producer*): I really, really like her and have worked with her a long time. We have a great relationship. But in no way did I ever want to use our relationship to get her to be on the show.

> *In the storyline, the kids take Mitchell to the wrong house. Streisand no longer lives there. Ray Liotta does. The bit became Liotta, who none of the kids recognize despite his fruitless attempts, claims to be friends with Streisand and offers to take them to her house.*

RICHMAN (*writer / executive producer*): I knew she was never, ever going to make an appearance, and I wasn't going to put myself in the position of asking her. Then it was a question of "Can you get her? Does she like you that much? Are you going to be able to do this?" So it became, "Do you think she'd record a voice-over and Mitchell could have a conversation with her through her gate?" The production side said, "We can do it any way she wants to do it. We could send somebody there. She could literally do it on her iPhone and send it in." Again, I am dreading asking, but now I have to because it's also a really funny bit. So I call her manager and lay out her part, and he talks to her and calls me back and says to call her. So I do. She picks up the phone and says, "What?" in a really funny way, so I knew that she would be a little on board. I described it to her and sent her the lines, and she thought it was really funny. She even pitched a joke that made it in, which was [when] Ray asks her if she'd sing "Happy Birthday" to Mitchell, and she says, "I'm not singing into my gate, Ray."

> *ABC, of course, marketed the hell out of it, drumming up interest by teasing the audience with ads about a mystery guest star while playing "People" or "Don't Rain on My Parade" underneath it.*

RICHMAN (*writer / executive producer*): It was insane. She was in it literally thirty seconds. It could have been Cher or Bette Midler if Barbra wouldn't have done it, but nobody had connections to any of those people.

Many of the name guest stars that we've gotten we got because someone knew them.

> Season 8's "Do It Yourself" introduced Peyton Manning as Coach Gary, whom Gloria hires to teach Joe how to throw a baseball. Jay, of course, gets jealous, only to find out Coach Gary took the gig for Jay's mentorship in opening his dream business: Gary's Gazebos and Sheds.

LEVITAN (*cocreator*): I always said to Peyton, "I'm going to write something for you." Brad had one of his kid's coaches who he was a little jealous of, and that seemed like a good story area for Jay.

WALSH (*writer / executive producer*): He was my youngest son's coach, who my oldest son to this day refers to as "Coach," even though he's never been on a team with this man. I felt slightly threatened by it. So the idea of having Jay slightly threatened by that amused us.

PEYTON MANNING (*Coach Gary*): The idea was I was a coach helping out their son with sports and Jay was offended because that was his job, but the real reason I was there was to get business advice from a guy I looked up to. After Jay realizes that, I become his protégé. He gives me advice, and it ends with the infomercial for Gary's Gazebos and Sheds.

LEVITAN (*cocreator*): It was funny. You could see how hard he works and why he's such a success. He was really going over this thing ahead of time. "Tell me about Gary. Tell me who he is."

CORRIGAN (*writer / executive producer*): At some point, we said the deal with this guy is he's a goofball. I think that that was all he needed to figure it out.

MANNING (*Coach Gary*): I think growing up with two brothers, Cooper and Eli, we said, "You'd better have thick skin and be able to laugh at yourself and take it as well as you dish it."

JEREMY MAGUIRE (*Joe Pritchett*): Peyton Manning was cool. He taught me how to throw a football.

MANNING (*Coach Gary*): I chose to do it for one reason and one reason only: a fun experience. I think some people said after that, "Oh, I guess you're going to go into acting now?" I said, "No, I'm a fan of the show."

The episode's tag became an ad for Gary's business. Walsh and Corrigan have the words posted on their wall.

IS THIS YOU, SITTING IN AN EMPTY YARD, WISHING
YOU HAD—A GAZEBO? OR A SHED? THEN CALL GARY'S
GAZEBOS AND SHEDS, BECAUSE WE ONLY DO ONE THING:
SELL, INSTALL, AND SERVICE GAZEBOS AND SHEDS.

Queer Eyes, Full Heart

And by the way, we need to stop having friends with names like Andre.

—MITCHELL PRITCHETT

Before becoming parents, Mitchell and Cam kept up a busy social calendar with their oddly named friends.

LEVITAN (*cocreator*): It was a dream of ours for Mitch and Cam to have this crazy collection of strange friends.

CORRIGAN (*writer / executive producer*): The idea for names started with Chris. He was watching an awards show where someone was thanking their friend Longinus.*

LLOYD (*cocreator*): It was the director Danny Boyle. He had just won an award for *Slumdog Millionaire* and said, "I must correct an injustice. I thanked everyone in sight except our wonderful choreographer, who deserves so much thanks." Then he proceeded to thank someone named Longinus. I thought, "Wow, that's a name."

---

* Longinus's first appearance is in "Dance Dance Revelation" in a department store giving sample splashes of a male perfume. Phil, after a rough day with Jay, gets mad at Longinus for spraying him before asking. Phil then takes out his frustration on Longinus by chasing him around the store and spraying him.

RICHMAN (*writer / executive producer*): Chris is responsible for every one of those crazy names of Mitchell's and Cam's friends: Longinus, Crispin, L'Michael, J'Marcus . . .

LLOYD (*cocreator*): I've always been interested in names. One of my favorite Bob and Ray radio routines is when they were working at an insurance company. They decided to list the names of people who had been good-paying customers for forty years. In a very stentorian, serious way, they ran off a list of about sixty names. The way that those names varied, one to the next, utterly comprised small-town America. It made me laugh so hard. I guess this is my attempt to imitate that.

> *No friend looms larger than Sherman "Pepper" Saltzman, Mitchell and Cam's wealthy, pretentious, condescending, and flamboyant friend.*

I haven't been Sherman since I got on that bus in Lubbock thirty-five years ago.

—Pepper Saltzman

LLOYD (*cocreator*): Pepper began as an off-screen character. It seemed like someone who was a little bit peppery in their life; a little bit of attitude; a little bit of someone who could agitate Mitch and Cam. But they also felt they needed a sprinkle of him in their lives. So the name Pepper seemed right. Saltzman was a funny discovery, a funny capper to that.

RICHMAN (*writer / executive producer*): Pepper was this bigger-than-life person, referred to in multiple episodes in the first season, that we'd never seen. In the second season, we wanted to cast him before he became Maris on *Frasier.* She became uncastable because the more you made jokes about her, the more physically impossible it became for an actor to inhabit that. She was too weak to push down a theater seat. She didn't have enough blood warmth to activate an elevator button. They didn't want that to happen with Pepper.

GREENBERG (*casting director*): Nathan Lane was the prototype for the role. But some people felt he was too on the nose to use, so we had auditions. I put actors on tape in New York and we found some people that could do it, but nobody's Nathan Lane.

BRODERICK (*Dave*): Nobody else but Nathan could remotely do that. He's a genius.

RICHMAN (*writer / executive producer*): I couldn't believe there was any conversation about Nathan being right for the part. I was thinking, "You'd be fucking lucky to get him."

LANE (*Pepper Saltzman*): Jeffrey's an old friend. He contacted me and said, "We'd love you to do this." Based on having seen the show, it being such a phenomenon, and how extremely funny it was, I thought I should make an effort to do it.

FERGUSON (*Mitchell Pritchett*): Knowing that Nathan Lane is interested is one of the first moments when I realized we had a show that meant something to other people; people I really admired and respected loved the show and wanted to be a part of it. That was really meaningful to me.

CORRIGAN (*writer / executive producer*): When we introduced Nathan as Pepper, Jeff wrote some of the lines, dictating them, channeling the character. It came up almost fully formed. What you see on TV is what he pitched.

STONESTREET (*Cam Tucker*): In the first episode, Pepper's talking about being ridiculed and a laughingstock. I say to him, "You're not a joke, you're Pepper Saltzman." That line has stuck with me forever.

I hope you like blueberry scones and Dusty Springfield.
—Pepper Saltzman

RICHMAN (*writer / executive producer*): Because Nathan worked so much on Broadway, all of his scenes had to be done on a Monday, his day off. He'd do a show on Sunday, fly out on Sunday night, work with us on Monday, fly back either Monday night or Tuesday morning, and be onstage Tuesday night.

LEVITAN (*cocreator*): He'd always laugh his way through the first run-through of a scene, just thoroughly enjoying hearing it and seeing everybody's reaction to it, laughing and rolling his eyes at the same time, like he can't believe we're doing this.

LANE (*Pepper Saltzman*): It always made me laugh that Pepper was shocked by the size of Mitch and Cam's apartment. In "The Wedding" episode, he references that he always assumed there was a much nicer part of it that they weren't showing him.

I grew up golfing with my father, the great Hyam Saltzman. Or, as he was known around the clubhouse, Chad Treadwell.
                                                              —PEPPER SALTZMAN

LANE (*Pepper Saltzman*): Every now and then, you would learn some little tidbit from his personal life. The most outrageous may have been he had a son who was a Navy SEAL, but he couldn't talk about it.

WALLS (*writer / supervising producer*): Pepper is so delightful because you can send him off to Laos to get a monkey chin implant without showing him and it's funny, but when you have Nathan, it's the best.

LANE (*Pepper Saltzman*): Initially, you find out Cam, in a moment of shame, dated Pepper very briefly. It wasn't until much later that you find out he was a wedding planner. The writers eventually gave him Ronaldo, his assistant. They quickly got married, adopted a child. There was a moment where he was having trouble with his business. He had to take on budget weddings.

Sorry, I'm in a mad rush to the mashed potato bar to restock something called fixin's. *If you ever felt anything for me, you'll push me out a window.*

—PEPPER SALTZMAN

LANE (*Pepper Saltzman*): I was always tickled if I could get Jesse and Eric to break up because they've been doing this for so long. That made me very happy.

FERGUSON (*Mitchell Pritchett*): He does take great pleasure in that. I've noticed this even with his work onstage. I think that's what makes him such a charismatic performer, because he doesn't take it too seriously. He has this very grounded sense of himself.

LANE (*Pepper Saltzman*): There was one time where they force me to eat Cheetos. We did a few takes where I did quite a thing trying to eat a Cheeto and then spit it out. They both lost it. They didn't think I would go that far, but I did, because when you're Pepper Saltzman, you just have to.

FERGUSON (*Mitchell Pritchett*): There was a stunt and Nathan had to make noises for what the stunt player was doing. Nathan was sitting in a chair under an umbrella, basically screaming, grunting, and yelping. Even then, he was trying to make us laugh in a scene where he was clearly off-camera. It's part of what makes working with him such a joy. It feels like play.

CASE (*director/editor*): Nathan was always improvising. He'd suggest, "Is it okay if I do this?" And then it would be the funniest thing you've ever heard. Like when Pepper's horrified when someone asked where the ketchup was. He's acting like he's being killed. "Just bring the pump." Chris said someone should be walking by carrying bananas, like what is the worst catering at a wedding? We kept putting these funny bits in.

HIGGINBOTHAM (*writer / executive producer*): Nathan will bring what he has to bring to sell it. And the character is so specific. It allows us to play a little bigger with him. He's a little larger than life, so we get to push those boundaries and let him be as dramatic, gay, condescending, and oblivious as a person can be, which makes us laugh. He's a little bit our Karen Walker.

LANE (*Pepper Saltzman*): I think my all-time favorite line is when Pepper gets very upset and storms out of Mitch's and Cam's apartment. I flip my hand backward, look down, and say shamefully, "Sorry. I thought I was wearing a cape today."

I hate sports and nature and sherbet. God, do I hate sherbet. There's ice cream and sorbet and nothing in between.
— PEPPER SALTZMAN

LANE (*Pepper Saltzman*): I hadn't been on the show in a while. I had just done *The Iceman Cometh* in Chicago. *Iceman* was a life-changing experience. I showed up to *Modern Family* and thought, "Let's do something different with Pepper. It doesn't have to be over the top and so flamboyant." After about three minutes, they said, "Oh no. You have to bring up the energy, go crazy, do that thing you do." So, that all went out the window.

The show introduced the love of Pepper's life, Ronaldo. In season 5, he quickly emerged as a favorite recurring character who blended well with Pepper's capricious nature.

BARILLAS (*Ronaldo*): I was doing *The Motherfucker with the Hat* at the Southcoast Rep in Costa Mesa. I felt really good about my work, so I invited Abraham, who's a friend, to come down there and check it out. I knew he would respond to the writing. We had a similar aesthetic in terms of comedic sensibility and making things über real and grounded.

HIGGINBOTHAM (*writer / executive producer*): You live in a big city and terrible things happen all the time. But the worst thing is when one of your friends says, "Can you come see my play?" Fortunately, I went and holy shit, he was so funny and good. He literally got a standing ovation on his exit. He stole the show.

BARILLAS (*Ronaldo*): Months later, Abraham said he pitched this character modeled after what I did in the play. I, of course, thought it was super exciting. If it all works out, I'll go and have a couple of lines in the show. When I got the sides, I looked at it and thought, "There's so much for me to do." And then to see that my material was opposite Nathan was even juicier and hard to wrap my brain around.

LANE (*Pepper Saltzman*): Pepper is not particularly nice to Ronaldo in the beginning. He's just his assistant. Then he realizes that he cares for him. That was very touching. We had a lot of fun doing that.

LEVITAN (*cocreator*): We saw how funny Christian was and decided, "Let's get them together."

BARILLAS (*Ronaldo*): Ronaldo is trying his best to create a world in which Pepper can show up as his best self so that he doesn't get in his own way.

LANE (*Pepper Saltzman*): Christian's the sweetest guy and so terrific in that part. And because of his accent, he became a funny parallel to Sofía.

BARILLAS (*Ronaldo*): My accent's modeled after the accents that I heard growing up in Guatemala, but I also play with certain sounds because I know that they're funny.

If anything terrible should happen, don't feel an obligation to attend my memorial: New York or LA.

—PEPPER SALTZMAN

LANE (*Pepper Saltzman*): At a certain point, I thought maybe the world has had enough of Pepper. I had just won the Tony for playing Roy Cohn in *Angels in America*. My career was going in a different direction, and I thought, "Do I keep doing this?" So I said to Jeffrey, "Just kill him off. Have a funeral and clip show."

WALLS (*writer / supervising producer*): The pitch was he didn't trust his friends to eulogize him properly, so he would perform his own eulogy.

MCCRAY (*script coordinator*): He preplanned his own over-the-top extravagant funeral complete with a hologram of himself.

LANE (*Pepper Saltzman*): Jeffrey thought it was a funny notion. There's a little bit of Tom Sawyer watching his own funeral. There was a lot of joking about that. But he said the writers were very upset by the notion of killing Pepper. They thought it was too sad. "We can't kill Pepper. Everyone loves Pepper."

Lane garnered three Emmy nominations for playing Pepper. At one point, the show loosely chattered about giving Pepper his own series, aptly titled A Dash of Pepper.

LANE (*Pepper Saltzman*): They bandied it about at one point, but not terribly seriously. It was a reaction to spinning off Rob Riggle's character as a competitive realtor. I was like, "How many episodes has he done? Why don't you spin off Pepper, for God's sake? You've given him a partner, a child, a business. What more do you want?" I joked about *A Dash of Pepper,* but it never came to any serious discussions. It's more fun than anything else, although Mel Brooks thought it was a really good idea. Mel likes *Modern Family.* He'd watch it and say, "Why don't they make a show for you with that Pepper fellow?" He's much better as a spice than a main ingredient.

Mother!

DeDe Pritchett played an important role in the development of her children, Mitchell and Claire, and the misery of her ex, Jay. That made her an important element of the show, one never fully realized, however.

WRUBEL (*writer / executive producer*): Early on, Steve and Chris wanted to address the issue of DeDe. Who was this person? Somebody pitched, what if they hadn't seen her since "the incident"? So we then went back and figured out, what was "the incident"?

The answer became season 1's fourth episode, aptly titled "The Incident." It recalled DeDe's inappropriate behavior at Jay and Gloria's wedding. To decide who would play DeDe, Greenberg put together one of his signature lists.

GREENBERG (*casting director*): We offered it to Dianne Wiest, who passed. This was before *Modern Family* had aired. Once it did, Dianne's agent called back and said, "We see the show now and she regrets she didn't do it, and if anything ever comes up, please keep her in mind." Meanwhile, I prepped ideas for who else could play the part. When I said Shelley Long's name to Steve, that was it.

LEVITAN (*cocreator*): *Cheers* is one of the reasons I'm in this business, so I'm obviously a big fan of Shelley's.

LLOYD (*cocreator*): My dad worked on *Cheers*, and I was a massive fan.

Some of the cast couldn't contain their excitement.

FERGUSON (*Mitchell Pritchett*): I have something for people who have been in this business for a long time. I want to sit down with them, ask questions, and hear as many stories as I possibly can. I once sat next to Angela Lansbury at the opening of a show. At intermission, I had to go to the bathroom so bad, but I wouldn't let myself get out of the seat because I had fifteen minutes with Angela Lansbury and I wasn't going to give them up for anything. That's basically how I feel about Shelley Long.

GREENBERG (*casting director*): I'll never forget that first time we see her on air when she's in the same frame as Julie. They had the exact same colored blond hair. You really bought her as Claire and Mitchell's mom. She seemed right for Ed's first wife and the antitheses of Gloria. It made so much sense.

Her character, however, made less sense.

LEVITAN (*cocreator*): That character had to be somewhat unlikable because you needed to root for Jay and the kids. You don't want to think she's the victim. Jay has this young wife. You want to be on Jay's side and say she was a pain in the ass. Shelley portrayed that really well.

HIGGINBOTHAM (*writer / executive producer*): From the very first moment I saw her in an episode, I thought, "Oh my God, they did that thing where they made the woman crazy and everyone loves Dad." It became my goal to humanize her as the series went on.

LLOYD (*cocreator*): I think we wrote her a little too daffy, a little too mean. I think the way that we wrote her and the way that she took the character veered us off to a place that maybe we didn't want to revisit as much as would have been ideal.

On Cheers, *Long had a well-known reputation for being a perfectionist.*

DAVID ISAACS (Cheers *writer*): She liked to talk about the part. She needed to line it up in her mind, which caused her to ask more questions. That was her process. You could be annoyed, but if you get it on the stage, so what?

PETER CASEY (Cheers *writer*): She could overanalyze, but she never did it to be difficult. She had questions and some things needed to be fully explained. If you had a good argument, she was fine with it.

Whatever her process, in the end, she always delivered.

O'SHANNON (*writer / executive producer*): I went to a *Cheers* reunion, and they showed a compilation of highlights from the series. There, on this large screen, was Shelley Long in her prime. She could spar verbally, do physical bits with the best of them, make you cry if necessary. I understand she could be a headache to deal with back then, but you couldn't argue with the results. She was magic.

Modern Family proved less than magical. Long, well into her sixties by then, understood the multi-cam world, not the single cam one, which requires some adjustment. Furthermore, the show's rapid pace added another new wrinkle, as it did with other guest stars occasionally.

FIELD (*associate producer*): I honestly think at this point in her career she was used to a slower pace.

LLOYD (*cocreator*): She felt, as a lot of our guest actors do, that they're stepping into an environment where everybody knows each other's rhythms and you don't. She didn't know if she was going to be able to go as fast and didn't want to be the one that holds up the show.

RICHMAN (*writer / executive producer*): She isn't a bad person. We have had those. You could see there was real struggle happening so you could be much more sympathetic than someone being mean.

SAPIENZA (*script supervisor / director*): She did one episode where she was wearing a scarf [season 4's "Arrested"]. I don't know if it was helping her as a distraction or her being anxious, but she kept pulling it out of her purse or shoving it back in or putting it on. It got to the point that this scarf was the center of attention of everything she did.

HIGGINBOTHAM (*writer / executive producer*): She was the Lucille Ball of her time, and that's a lot to live up to at sixty-nine when you're having trouble remembering lines. She was so apologetic when she'd mess something up. I said to her, "You're not messing up your lines more than anyone at this table, people who work here every week. Don't worry about it."

O'NEILL (*Jay Pritchett*): You could tell that she wasn't confident. She was nervous. We all tried to make her feel at home and comfortable. I think we finally achieved that with her, where she really enjoyed us and doing the show. I really liked her. I felt she was really trying and she wanted to do good. I'm always sympathetic to that. That's a horrible thing to struggle with. It's a form of stage fright, and it can really screw with your head. I think every actor has gone through some part of that. I know I have.

RICHMAN (*writer / executive producer*): Ed was very sweet with her. Ed was always a calming presence.

BOWEN (*Claire Dunphy*): Ed will always surprise you. He's the one who will pick up a little bird when you think he'll step on it. He really took care of Shelley.

RICHMAN (*writer / executive producer*): In the episodes when you watch her, she's good. Was it worth what the actors and crew had to go through to get a performance that could be edited into one? People would disagree about that.

Vergara, for one, had her issues.

VERGARA (*Gloria Delgado-Pritchett*): One of the first things I did with her was she had to choke Gloria [in season 1's "The Incident"]. Shelley had long nails. She scratched my whole neck, scratching and choking, but I wanted to finish the scene. I didn't want to complain, because I knew it was going to be a whole drama and it was going to be longer. I told Ed, but I didn't stop the scene. I said, "Let's do it until we get it and that's it." And that was it. We got it.

> *In her last few seasons, they figured out an amicable way to handle the situation.*

FIELD (associate producer): She's a wonderfully sweet lady. She likes a good handhold, and luckily that is our specialty at *Modern Family*.

GREENBERG (casting director): I said, "Why don't we get one of our PAs to run lines with her, pick her up, and be with her on set so someone can give her attention the whole time?" and that's what we did. It was very helpful, and she felt more prepared.

MORTON (executive producer): She really liked him. We called him the "Shelley Whisperer." He gave her confidence and made her feel listened to, and that made all the difference in her last episodes.

LLOYD (cocreator): From my standpoint, she could be a handful, without a doubt, but what we wound up with on-screen was really good. I take some of the blame. I think we could have conceived that character in such a way that it would have been easier to bring her back. I think Shelley felt some of that frustration, too. She wasn't quite sure what she was playing or who she was. I think we maybe rushed the development of that character a little bit.

GREENBERG (casting director): It was frustrating for them because it was such a rich character and they wanted to use her.

BOWEN (Claire Dunphy): Think of all the stories we could have told with the mom. I never wanted Shelley to die. I thought there were so many great stories we could still tell, and it would expand our horizons so much. The writers had a different point of view, and that's that.

LLOYD (cocreator): I think it was a missed opportunity on our part, because she was a very significant character in the lives of three of our cast members.

BOWEN (*Claire Dunphy*): It was a pleasure to watch Shelley warm up to us over the seasons. When I got divorced, she reached out to me in such a kind and motherly way because she had the same experience, and I really got to connect to her as a person. I felt like she was really part of the family right before they killed her off. I was really enjoying working with her, especially in an episode where we all went to a wedding together.

LLOYD (*cocreator*): They go to a family wedding. They're not sure DeDe was even going to be there. She comes and joins their table. They're all cringing because Dad and Mom are going to fight. And Dad and Mom get along great. They dance together. Mitchell and Claire have a sad moment where they say, "Where was that? Why did we have to deal with all of the tumult in our household if they were capable of getting along like this?" I think it's a sentiment that kids from divorced households know. It felt real, and they played it beautifully. Frankly, it was nice to see them getting along. They couldn't have gotten along fifteen to twenty years ago, where they were in their lives. Now they're able to, and everybody's emotion made sense. Claire and Mitchell's regret made sense. Jay and DeDe's affection toward each other makes sense because they had a huge, long history together, and they were remembering the good times. It was a very complicated, fraught moment, and Shelley was great in it.

Crazy Train

All good things must come to an end, including consecutive Emmy wins for Outstanding Comedy Series, as happened to Modern Family *in its sixth season. The surprise that year came less from the loss than for what transpired afterward.*

GREENBERG (*casting director*): *Sarah says, "What do we do now? I don't know where to go." I thought that was sort of cute.*

HYLAND (*Haley Dunphy*): *If you go up onstage and back to do press, they bring your car to you. And it was very strange. Even Ed was like, "What happens now? Where do we get our car?"*

BOWEN (*Claire Dunphy*): *Ty and I were laughing at ourselves. What arrogant assholes are we?*

Awards aside, the show still had lots of innovations to discover. In season 7's "Crazy Train," the entire cast ventured north by train to attend DeDe's wedding.

WALSH (*writer / executive producer*): *That episode was inspired by a train trip Paul and I took. For some reason, we always romanticized train travel. So we thought, "Let's take one hiatus and take the train up the coast to Portland. On the way, we'll think up a great pilot and maybe even write it." What we discovered was that train travel isn't as romantic as we imagined. It's more like a moving hotel run by* the DMV. We didn't come up with a pilot or anything else other than an affection for air travel. But there was one thing . . .

CORRIGAN (*writer / executive producer*): There's this horseshoe turn right around San Luis Obispo. There's only two in the country. When you're on a train for thirty-six hours, anything that can be made a big deal out of by the crew is, so they spent hours and hours talking about this horseshoe turn and how exciting it was. Spoiler alert—it's not that exciting, but it worked out well in the episode.

For one of the plotlines, Phil and Cam help a mystery novelist figure out how a character in his book can shoot someone in the front of the train from the back of the train without being seen. Their answer? The horseshoe turn.

Typically in train episodes, editors use stock footage of a moving train to establish location. They then go inside the train, a soundstage set with green screen outside the windows.

Modern Family production designer Bennett went one step further, designing a car from scratch that the art department and production staff then built and installed on an airbag so that the compartment moved like a train. They did all of this in one week.

BENNETT (*production designer / art director*): It took us a while to figure out how we were going to shoot it. We did a lot of legwork to see if we could use a practical train. Can we actually go on a journey somewhere? How would that work? How could we control the light and all the other factors that go with a moving vehicle? I scouted train compartments to see if we could realistically, with the smallest camera profile, pull it off on a real train.

The first shot, at a train station, comes from the real deal.

HENSZ (*director / assistant director*): It's a frame of a train pulling out of Union Station in Los Angeles. I happened to be down there scouting, trying to get a sense of what we need. And while I was standing there, a train was getting ready to leave the station. I stole that *shot on my iPhone. We managed to do a little CGI and flip it because the train was going in the wrong direction.*

Bennett ultimately decided to use the familiar confines of stage 5.

BENNETT (*production designer / art director*): *Once you decide you're going to do it on a soundstage, there are so many different options open to you. I don't want to ever build the set and wish we really did this or that, so it's figuring out our requirements and how are we going to interact with the green screen and move practically with special effects.*

The train came together remarkably quickly.

BENNETT (*production designer / art director*): *We had some elements of a carriage and some walls. We had to build the base, ceilings, and windows. We then built our own version, a lot longer. The doors were a complete fabrication. I had to hire set designers and more construction workers and then run and gun and go for it. We had a main carriage and then the actual train compartment for Manny and Luke's rendezvous. We had the long, narrow corridor where Phil and Cam get slammed against the train window as they try to figure out the novel's plot. That was a separate set.*

HENSZ (*director / assistant director*): *There was basically one train car shell that she redecorated with different chairs, colors, and arrangements for every car in the sequence. We had to schedule that and design it so, say, the first-class department one day, the bar car one day, the different passenger cars, the forward car, and the one that Gloria gets locked in, in the back.*

BENNETT (*production designer / art director*): *It comes down to details. Trying to make it believable, adding trim, handles, and signage that make it seem real and believable. We established what we could change dressing-wise, which was the curtains and seating. The set decorator had the challenge to find the right seats and the quantity to* change out. Some of those seats were more for modern planes and not trains, but we made modifications to make that work.

All the footage zipping by the windows throughout the episode, playing over a green screen, comes from the actual train trip.

HENSZ (*director / assistant director*): *The payoff for that episode was the turn in the track. The writers had specifically written for that, so with myself and the visual effects guys, we hopped on the train and did that trip. Along the way, they shot plates of what's actually outside the train windows. Then later in post, we realistically placed what would be outside the windows at each point of that train trip. So I think it came together quite nicely.*

CORRIGAN (*writer / executive producer*): *When I told people who watched that that was not an actual train, they were shocked.*

HENSZ (*director / assistant director*): *I got calls for weeks after, asking, "What trains did you guys go on? Where did you go to do that? How did you do that?"*

WALSH (*writer / executive producer*): *Paul and I are talking about a pilot right now, and at different points during the writing, we've thought, "What would Claire do with this set?" I've never thought in those terms before—what would a specific art director do with my writing? But she's so good that it's exciting to think about how she would influence your show.*

STONESTREET (*Cam Tucker*): *I like to compliment Claire on everything I know for a fact she doesn't do. When we were at an outside graduation ceremony, I complimented her on the turf of the football field. "Claire, this turf is beautiful. How did you get this turf done so quickly and wonderfully? And oh my God, these clouds look so real in the sky." On the lot, "I love what you did with the rafters. You made it look like a real soundstage."*

KO (*writer / executive producer*): *If you ask me, Claire Bennett is the MVP of this series. There's nothing she can't do.*[*]

CORRIGAN (*writer / executive producer*): *Every once in a while, we say that she's a miracle worker. I think that's not far from the truth. That train is as good an example as there is. It's entirely made of wood, and she designed it.*

---

[*] Bennett says one of the most outlandish things she did was for season 9's "It's the Great Pumpkin, Phil Dunphy," in which she had to find giant pumpkins for pumpkin boating. "Contacting a stranger in Oregon who grows pumpkins for a living and then bringing him to Hollywood to be our pet pumpkin wrangler is as weird as it sounds."

The Day We Almost Died

Sarah Hyland has been very transparent about her health issues with kidney dysplasia and endometriosis. To date, she has gone through upward of sixteen surgeries. No one would wish that on their own worst enemy, least of all on the endearing and unassuming Hyland. Throughout her illness, she has never held a pity party for the public to attend, never become a wounded diva of the soundstage. She's always shown up to work on time and performed on cue. The show, in turn, has accommodated and supported her medical procedures, including two kidney transplants.

She continues today to triumph over her health challenges. Not "triumphed over" as in over and done but "continues"—an important turn of the phrase here. Invisible illnesses such as hers don't disappear as much as they become, in the best of situations, manageable.

HYLAND (*Haley Dunphy*): I'm always in a state of pain. I don't think people really understand that. If anybody does, it's Julie because she's a mom, plays my mom, and has been around me more than anybody out of this cast when I'm in the hospital.

O'NEILL (*Jay Pritchett*): She's had a tough time. There were lots of days when she'd be in the makeup chair in the morning and you could see she wasn't feeling good. And you felt so bad. You'd think, "Can you do anything, say anything, bring her anything?" But she was there. She showed up, all the time, unless she was in the hospital.

HYLAND (*Haley Dunphy*): The first few seasons, you'll see a lot of Haley leaning on stuff—against a table, with her arm on the wall, at the end of the staircase banister—always, leaning. It helped with the pain a lot because it was very hard to stand up straight on my own.

LEVITAN (*cocreator*): She doesn't go around advertising it, but you'll know when it's not a good day for her, physically speaking, because she's not being chipper.

MILLER (*assistant prop master*): We've never lost time because of her, and that's the highest compliment I can say.

BOWEN (*Claire Dunphy*): She looks like you could break her over your knee, because she weighs about ninety-five pounds soaking wet, and she's so tough.

HYLAND (*Haley Dunphy*): Toward the end of my real kidneys, before I had the first transplant, I could barely be awake for six or eight hours at a time. That was really hard, the fatigue and constant pain. Like on a scale of one to ten, twenty pain.

LLOYD (*cocreator*): I don't think we knew the extent of her health issues, which makes me retroactively that much more impressed with her. When you calculate backward with physical pain, a lot of worry and sitting in a lot of doctor offices and scheduling things that have big consequences. That's a lot for a twenty-year-old to be dealing with.

LEVITAN (*cocreator*): She really does her best to hide it. There are days where it's overwhelming for her. I could think of a couple of times where she was shaking and pulled it together for a take and then was bad again. But she always pulled it together. That's amazing to me.

BOWEN (*Claire Dunphy*): When we were doing "This Old Wagon," we were in Griffith Park. It was day and warm. Haley famously doesn't wear sensible clothing, and Sarah was wearing some little skirt. But then it was turning into night and getting cold and we were going a lot longer than we usually do. She already runs cold, and you add cold to that and she's in a miniskirt and sandals, and I'm worrying she's going to shiver herself to death. We did the final shot where we have fireflies in a jar. We've walked away from a disaster of a day, but we're still a family. They wanted us to do it again, which meant walking back up the hill. We'd done it a bunch of times already, and I see Sarah doubled over and shaking. I scooted over to her and said, "What do you think? Do you have it in you?" She looked at me like I've never gotten a look from her before and said, "Always." And straightened up and marched up the hill and I thought, "Do not mess with her. She's all pro."

HYLAND (*Haley Dunphy*): Any sick person will say, "I'm fine," especially in their workplace, because they don't want it to define them. There are some sick people that feed into that victim card and all they become is their illness. I tried very, very hard not to be that.

Sometimes within episodes, directors had to get clever to mask her condition, such as a poolside moment in season 5's "A Fair to Remember."

MCCARTHY-MILLER (*director*): She was supposed to be lying at the pool in a bathing suit. She wanted to have a cover-up on, but the producers were saying she's supposed to be lying by the pool. She was really uncomfortable about it. She said, "All I have to do is sit up and you'll see a roll and that's going to be on Instagram and I'm going to be body-shamed."

HYLAND (*Haley Dunphy*): Do you know what FUPA is? *Fat upper-pussy area.* When they put a kidney in you, they put it in the front. I call it my KUPA, my *kidney upper-pussy area* because it sticks out, like you're pregnant from the side. Not great for bikinis [she ended up wearing a bikini top and denim short-shorts]. I was still on Prednisone then, and my body was still very much adjusting to my first transplant, and so I gained thirty pounds. I really wanted to be covered up.

MCCARTHY-MILLER (*director*): I found a thing where we put a towel on the chair sideways and then she could lie back in her top. Then when she goes to sit up she can take the towel and put it around her. She said that was perfect.

There was definitely a learning curve for production.

HYLAND (*Haley Dunphy*): I had picked a dialysis center five to ten minutes away from work so I could do the workday. I did dialysis Tuesdays, Thursdays, and Saturdays. Even on one of my days off, I came over the hill to go to dialysis. Early on, I saw we were shooting the next day in the Pacific Palisades. I told them I can't do that. One of the producers said, "Yeah, you can, what are you talking about?" I said, "I won't be able to get back to dialysis by 3:30." And he said, "Can't you just move it to the next day?" I explained it doesn't work like that.

Typically, different families shoot on different days, so no cast member has to be on set all five days of the workweek, which provides scheduling flexibility.

MCCARTHY-MILLER (*director*): There are things that you have to work around when someone is having health issues, and Sarah definitely has had them on and off. When she had a second surgery, we had to shoot a bunch of scenes from another episode so she could go and have surgery and recover and not disappear from the show.

WRUBEL (*writer / executive producer*): Jeff protected her and created time for her to be off the show. We understood that was more important than anything we were hired to do. If it meant having less of her in an episode, we would do that or not be in an episode, we would do that. Sarah's hilarious and brilliant, so it was a bummer, but there was never a question of how it would be treated. Her health was a priority.

Toward the end of season 8, in the episode "Pig Moon Rising," Hyland had to push a car with Ferguson. When off-camera, she hobbled on crutches, a side effect of medication.

HYLAND (*Haley Dunphy*): One of the most painful things I've ever had was when doctors put me on water pills, which caused me to have gout. I had old king's disease at twenty-six years old. And I pushed a car in neutral in heels, when I could only walk with crutches. I did it and it was fine. I kept myself together but was quietly crying to myself in the bathroom.

> *The ninth season began with another travel episode, "Lake Life." This one took place in Lake Tahoe. Hyland had started dialysis a few months earlier in May.*

GOULD (*Luke Dunphy*): She was really ill there. It shows how much of a trooper she was because the nearest dialysis to Tahoe was an hour and a half away. So she would shoot a scene, drive an hour and a half, go get her blood pumped in and out of her body and filtered, and then drive back to set and keep working.

HYLAND (*Haley Dunphy*): I had a chest port I couldn't get wet because it could get infected.

> *Nothing to worry about on Lake Tahoe . . .*

GOULD (*Luke Dunphy*): We were shooting on the lake. Ariel, Rico, Sarah, and I all get into an inflatable swan, drifting off and leaving Alex's boyfriend on the island.

RODRIGUEZ (*Manny Delgado*): I was at the front of the boat and closest to Ariel, and Nolan was closest to Sarah. He said if anything happens, he'll go for Sarah and I go for Ariel.

> *Anything happened.*

GOULD (*Luke Dunphy*): The inflatable bird popped. We were only in about three feet of water, but I was really worried about Sarah's IV, so I jumped in the water and lifted her up and out. But my jumping off caused Ariel's side to fall farther into the water.

WINTER (*Alex Dunphy*): I was on the very back, so it just screwed me. I fell right in.

HYLAND (*Haley Dunphy*): Ariel plunged under. I felt so sorry for her.

WINTER (*Alex Dunphy*): I got sacrificed. I absolutely got sacrificed.

RODRIGUEZ (*Manny Delgado*): I picked her up right away to make sure nothing else happened before the clothes sink you down.

HYLAND (*Haley Dunphy*): She was like, "I'm okay. Is Sarah okay?" It was so sweet.

GOULD (*Luke Dunphy*): We had to spend an hour going back to hair, makeup, and wardrobe. I don't think Ariel's ever forgiven me for that.

WINTER (*Alex Dunphy*): I'm pissed because Nolan is my best friend and WTF.

The whole Tahoe ordeal took its toll on Hyland.

O'NEILL (*Jay Pritchett*): I was trying to catch a flight out of Reno and was being driven in by one of the drivers. She was in the car, because she had to go do a dialysis, and was sleeping. I thought, "It's not late." She was knocked out. I felt bad for her.

Hyland had her second kidney transplant on September 19, 2017.

HYLAND (*Haley Dunphy*): They were kind enough to write me out of a few episodes after the second transplant because that had to take place while we were filming. I went back to work the second or third week of November. You're supposed to be in recovery for three months, and I went back less than two months later.

BOWEN (*Claire Dunphy*): Once she got the second kidney, it was such a huge winner. That first kidney was never a winner. The second kidney, it was night and day.

An extenuating circumstance occurred later in the season with Geere.

GEERE (*Arvin Fennerman*): We were in the van with the makeup department, me and Sarah in front. There was an accident. Sarah went forward in her chair and then actually pulled back. Then I went in front of her to try and save her.

HYLAND (*Haley Dunphy*): It was hysterical. I had already been back in my seat for what felt like two full minutes and then his arm out of nowhere goes "Whoa."

GEERE (*Arvin Fennerman*): We joked afterward that I would be the worst superhero in the world. It was a bit of a nickname from then on.

HYLAND (*Haley Dunphy*): Everyone asked if I was okay. And I said, "Yeah, I feel fine," forgetting that adrenaline masks pain. Physically from the naked eye, I was completely fine. I already had a hernia from when they removed the old transplanted kidney months before the second transplant. It turns out that that car accident actually made my hernia ten times worse.

In the episode, Haley meets Arvin's parents, which included Sarah Burton portraying Arvin's mother.

HYLAND (*Haley Dunphy*): I'm working with Richard Burton's fucking daughter, and I can barely stand up straight. I'm in searing pain. I had this huge monologue, and I was freaking out because I kept fucking up the words. I kept having to stand up and storm off, and I was hurting so much. And then I had a scene later, where I had to be storming down the street, and then faint. I was under the assumption that there was going to be a stunt double there, since it wasn't too long after my transplant and they didn't want anything bad to happen to it. And there was no stunt double.

Hyland did the scene without letting anyone know her circumstances.

HYLAND (*Haley Dunphy*): I got in my trailer, and I, like, took off my clothes to hang up my wardrobe and I realized my stomach on the right side was protruding even farther than the KUPA. And I thought, "That's not good." And so I had to wear a waist trainer every day for the rest of the season until I could have a surgery to fix it.

Looking back and forward, Hyland has no regrets.

HYLAND (*Haley Dunphy*): Being on *Modern Family* for eleven years, not all of it was a walk in the park. I've had a lot of ups and downs, but there was always a handful of people who had my back no matter what. Eleven years of a lot of Tylenol, wearable heating pads, and naps later . . . I wouldn't change it for the world.

Graduates

Imagine that instead of going through your awkward teen years at school, you went through them in everyone's living rooms. Winter, Rodriguez, and Gould did just that from ages ten to twenty-one. On set, their TV parents served as pseudo-parents and role models, giving them structure and guidance.

LEVITAN (*cocreator*): I will consider us a gigantic failure if these kids come out worse for having been on our show. We've tried to create a family atmosphere on set. Julie is very much a mother figure to Sarah and Ariel, and Ty is very much a father figure to Nolan. And the way that Ed and Sofía look after Rico. That helps a lot.

VERGARA (*Gloria Delgado-Pritchett*): Rico comes from a very traditional Latin family. They have taken such good care of him. It's been amazing to see him grow up on set.

O'Neill remembers from early on Rodriguez's contagious excitement and appreciation for the work and life, something he maintains to this day.

O'NEILL (*Jay Pritchett*): Rico and I were on a cart on a golf course. We're waiting to do the shots, and I'm thinking to myself, "This golf course, it's kind of a piece of shit." Rico's looking around saying, "Wow, isn't this great?" I looked at him, and I was going to say, "What are you talking about?" And he said, "It's just beautiful. Aren't we lucky we get to ride around on golf carts and they bring us coffee and doughnuts?" I looked at him, and he looked like a little angel to me. I thought, "Oh my God, how can I not go his way on this?" I was like, "Yeah, you're right. We're really lucky. It's great out here." I told that story to him when he got a little older, and he always laughs, kind of amazed. Like, "You didn't think it was great?"

ZUKER (writer / executive producer): I have three kids, my twins are precisely the same age as Nolan, Rico, and Ariel. I always joke, it's been fun to watch the kids who make me money grow up with the kids who cost me money.

Most children don't have jobs, nor do they fear public recognition when out and about.

AUBREY ANDERSON-EMMONS (Lily Tucker-Pritchett): Some people try to get my autograph and sell it online. It's really annoying. I'll tell them politely, "I have to go home. I need to go to bed," and they'll start yelling at me and being disrespectful.

CECE MAGUIRE (Jeremy's mom): We've always told Jeremy, "People will recognize and maybe want to meet you, and if you're okay with it that day, you can say yes." But there are times when we're trying to eat or something, and people will say, "You look like that kid on *Modern Family*." I told him it's okay to say, "Yeah, I get that a lot." They don't question it.

AUBREY ANDERSON-EMMONS (Lily Tucker-Pritchett): The main question I get from everybody is, "What is it like being famous?" and I answer, "I don't know. What is it like being normal?"

Much like California laws regulate the amount of time kids can be on set and the money parents can take, so, too, does it mandate the amount of time they must be in school. Depending on the kids' ages, they have a minimum requirement of hours that they must spend in the classroom every day on set. If they have a busy day coming up, they can bank hours on slow or off days so they can film more on shooting days.

RODRIGUEZ (*Manny Delgado*): Child actors work a lot on-screen and off. Not a lot of people realize that. We have to learn our lines and blocking and also get at least three hours a day of school, and if you don't keep above a C+ average, you can't get a work permit. When I would go rehearse, I'd then go back to school for a twenty-minute block. During lunch, everyone got an hour. I got thirty minutes and then had to do thirty minutes of school.

For eleven years, the children of Modern Family *have learned from studio teacher Sharon Sacks, affectionately known on set as "Miss Sharon." Part teacher, mother, advocate, regulator, and friend, she's managed to create a supportive and safe haven in her classroom in which kids can be themselves.*

SACKS (*studio teacher*): They were never famous to me. That's my philosophy. They don't get away with stuff because they're on a TV show. I wanted them to get an education. I wanted them to feel like they had some type of school experience.

On set, she plays the role of good and bad cop, making sure everything and everyone adheres to child labor laws.

GOULD (*Luke Dunphy*): Miss Sharon is awesome. Words can't describe how she helped shape me into the person I am. She looked out for us and would tell us if we were being obnoxious children, but then she also realized we were young kids. She'd let us run around and shoot rubber bands and Nerf guns at each other.

Gould and Rodriguez set up a sign-up sheet once for a Capture the Flag Nerf gun war at lunch. The props department modified the Nerf guns to shoot faster Nerf pellets. Bryan Cranston—Walter White himself—was directing that week, signed up, and ended up on Rodriguez's team. You want Heisenberg on your team, not against it.

SACKS (*studio teacher*): I felt that they didn't get enough exercise, so we would sneak around the lot and run around. I made them set up a basketball net so they could play basketball every so often.

RODRIGUEZ (*Manny Delgado*): We'd read books together and have open discussions about them. During the season, we'd pick a good day and she'd take us to a museum. Afterward, we'd go to the farmers' market. She wanted to make sure we were well-rounded and educated people so that when this show was over we'd have something more than acting. We'd have an education.

WINTER (*Alex Dunphy*): Sharon is one of the most important people in my life, the queen of my life. She motivated me to like school and want to keep doing my schoolwork and keep moving forward with certain things that I was struggling in. For me, she went above and beyond emotionally. Yes, she was technically my studio teacher. But in reality she's my family, my life, and like a mom to me.

One fun schoolwork creation became the studio newspaper, Modern News.

WINTER (*Alex Dunphy*): We really loved doing it because we got to interview crew and cast members, and then we'd get to write it up. It's like you're being a little journalist.

RODRIGUEZ (*Manny Delgado*): She'd edit it and put it all together. We'd print copies, and then the day that it came out we'd go all around set and distribute the newspaper like in the old times, "Newspaper here! Get your newspaper!"

Gould, a MENSA member and certified genius in his own right, graduated high school at thirteen so he could work longer hours, a move in support of his career.

O'NEILL (*Jay Pritchett*): I used to kid him and say, "Let's talk about string theory." And he'd look at me and say, "Let's not, Ed." I'd ask him, "Why? Don't you think I can handle it?" And he'd just look at me and smile. Of course the answer was, "No, you can't handle it."

Every year, they'd have a classroom holiday party.

SACKS (*studio teacher*): Just for us. I have a menorah and a fake Christmas tree. I decorate the room, and we all exchange gifts.

WINTER (*Alex Dunphy*): Her Christmas parties were super awesome. We'd have these little presents that we shared with each other.

SACKS (*studio teacher*): The one thing I always ask for is a picture with them. Even though the three of them have graduated now, they still come with gifts for the little kids. That to me is more important than anything that happens on set. It's our tradition. And they look forward to it. They're always texting me, "What does Aubrey want? What is Jeremy into?"

Not surprisingly and despite attempts to filter mouths, there's a fair amount of swearing on set. The kids managed to minimize the collateral damage by making a swear jar or shouting, "Bubble gum!" over their bad words.

GOULD (*Luke Dunphy*): At a certain point, it was a dollar a curse word. One time, Julie was walking into the van and wasn't aware that we were sitting inside. She put a string of curse words together about someone, all in good fun. That constituted twenty-five dollars. At the end of the year, we'd give the money to charity.

BOWEN (*Claire Dunphy*): I have a terrible mouth. I was constantly turning to a kid and saying sorry.

AUBREY ANDERSON-EMMONS (*Lily Pritchett-Tucker*): Everybody on set cusses except for Jeremy.

JEREMY MAGUIRE (*Joe Pritchett*): I say, "Bubble gum," or "Wash your mouth, buddy."

CECE MAGUIRE (*Jeremy's mom*): When Jeremy started on the show, he didn't really know what a curse word was. One time Sofía said the F-word, and Jeremy said it back.

JEREMY MAGUIRE (*Jeremy's dad*): Sofía said, "You're not allowed to say that word!" He said, "Well, you say it all the time."

The show covered a similar storyline in season 3's "Little Bo Bleep" in which Lily uses the F-word—bleeped out, of course. Some parents, referred to as anti-cursing crusaders, raised a ruckus about it, but fans supported the story.

Between all the time spent in school and on set, a lot of child actors achieve traditional rites of passage later than other kids.

GOULD (*Luke Dunphy*): Ty taught me how to throw a football. He might have taught me how to throw a baseball. He taught me how to ski.

MILLER (*assistant prop master*): I taught Ariel how to ride a bike. I was pushing her around on a soundstage because we had an episode where she had to ride one. She also learned how to swim in Hawaii. We were all yelling encouragement from the sidelines.

GOULD (*Luke Dunphy*): Typically, once every summer, Ty and I go on a TV father–TV son vacation. This year, we went rafting the Grand Canyon. One year, we went skiing together.

MERLIN (*assistant director / key PA*): Rico got his permit because he had to drive in a scene. Ariel, too. I taught them mostly on the golf cart. None of them were behind the wheel until they drove the cart.

RODRIGUEZ (*Manny Delgado*): In season 1's "Fears," Manny gets invited to this birthday party at an amusement park. I was scared to ride roller coasters. I didn't want that scene to be the first time I was on one because I probably would have cried. So I asked Helena [Lamb] to ride with me, to make sure I was okay. I gripped her arms so tight. I did it and loved it and was so relieved.

GOULD (*Luke Dunphy*): The coolest is Ty taught me how to shave. My dad was in the military, so he traveled around a lot. Ty went out and bought me my first-ever shaving kit. I have a photo of him teaching me in my trailer.

Gould struggled through puberty in the spotlight.

GOULD (*Luke Dunphy*): I've never talked about it, but I had a human growth hormone deficiency. Basically, my body wasn't starting puberty and wasn't going to without intervention. So my doctors ran some tests, and I ended up having to give myself human growth hormones. That's one of the reasons you'll notice there's this one season where I go from a baby to a weird man-child with a deep voice and facial hair.

O'NEILL (*Jay Pritchett*): All of a sudden, he shot up like a weed. He looked great. I was so happy to see that.

Once puberty kicks in, so do the hormones, to the point that you can literally smell them. In Gould's case, that led to navigating the dating world.

GOULD (*Luke Dunphy*): Eric introduced me to my first dating app. I'd just turned eighteen, and he said, "You have to get on this. It's only for people within the industry. You're way more likely to meet someone that isn't going to take advantage of you or use your star power."

STONESTREET (*Cam Tucker*): I was very encouraging. I reminded him that he has a lot going for him and that any girl would love to have the opportunity to date him. And that you have to be picky and learn how to figure out what people's intentions are.

GOULD (*Luke Dunphy*): I wanted to be on it, but I didn't want the iTunes charge to go through my mom's credit card because then I'd have to have a talk with her about it. So we set it up through Ariel's credit card.

MERLIN (*assistant director / key PA*): He came to me for advice about how to kiss a girl because he knew I kissed girls.

RODRIGUEZ (*Manny Delgado*): I had my first kiss on set in front of my whole family. That was crazy.

GOULD (*Luke Dunphy*): My two sisters on the show and I were shooting a scene about Luke texting two girls at the same time and getting all of this advice from his sisters. It ends up working out poorly for him. And as we yell, "Cut!" we literally went back to writing a text to this girl I liked. It went poorly for me. I got friend-zoned really hard.

WINTER (*Alex Dunphy*): Conversations about sex, sometimes you don't want to hear it from a parent or learn about from the internet. You want to learn them from people you trust.

SACKS (*studio teacher*): We'd be in class, and she'd give him a sex talk. And poor Rico. I'd say, "Rico, shut your ears." I'd have to walk out of the room. She was very sassy about everything when she was fifteen and sixteen.

LLOYD (*cocreator*): Ariel became the go-to for the two boys on set dealing with their love lives or awkward teen stuff, which was kind of cute to see. She was like Alex in that way.

> *Winter has enjoyed some of the rites of passage with her peers that come with age.*

WINTER (*Alex Dunphy*): Eric would talk to us when we were kids, but it was a little harder because we were kids. I remember I was working on my sixteenth birthday or the day before and hadn't seen him yet that day. He looked over at me from across the room and flipped me off.

STONESTREET (*Cam Tucker*): I said, "I just feel like I can finally do that to you, adult to adult," like I was welcoming her into a different sort of club.

WINTER (*Alex Dunphy*): Honestly, it was fantastic. I was so happy about it. Yes, now he sees me as an adult. We're adults. We're friends.

As part of her evolution, Winter eventually tried a real high school and took it upon herself to bring Gould to events so he could have the social experience, too. Gould felt appreciative but had no regrets.

GOULD (*Luke Dunphy*): There are awesome things in high school, but there's also a lot of drama and bullying. Hanging out with Ed on set is way cooler than going to some dude's lame house party.

AMY ANDERSON-EMMONS (*Aubrey's mom*): Ariel was glad she was able to go to prom and do normal teenager stuff. I think Aubrey definitely is starting to think she wants to do those things, too. The entertainment industry isn't going anywhere anytime soon.

AUBREY ANDERSON-EMMONS (*Lily Tucker-Pritchett*): Everybody says that high school's like the time of your life, but it might be really, really bad. I want to go to a regular high school. Even though it might be insane and crazy.

Gould and Winter, in growing up together, have become thick as thieves.

GOULD (*Luke Dunphy*): I could talk for hours about Ariel. She's my big sister. I look up to her a lot. I genuinely don't know what I would have done without her.

WINTER (*Alex Dunphy*): We grew up together. Now that we're adults, we're going through similar things in our lives. We help each other out and are there for each other. It's interesting to find a connection like that. I'm not a super spiritual person, but I don't know another word to put on it. Instant family.

As for money, they've managed to save, and income will continue to flow in through syndication long after first run episodes end. Gould and Winter have their own homes. They all have cars. Gould's only other major purchase has been paying off his mom's mortgage.

GOULD (*Luke Dunphy*): That was a big deal for me. I owe *Modern Family* a big thank-you. It helped lift my family out of a bad situation.

SACKS (*studio teacher*): Only 15 percent of a child's income is put into a trust. I've seen parents who take their kids' money many, many, many times that you don't hear about. You're on a show for three to four years. One year, the parents are driving the Honda and after a few years, they're driving up in their Mercedes with their Gucci purse.

And what advice do the actors have for young aspiring actors?

GOULD (*Luke Dunphy*): Keep good people around you, who are genuinely looking out for your best interests. Make sure your agents and managers care about you as a person. Have a life outside of acting. You have to have something else you're passionate about because acting is so hot and cold. If acting falls through, find something else, because there's so much else in the world besides this.

WINTER (*Alex Dunphy*): The industry is rough, and 75 percent of the time, you'll face rejection. What helps is to have things you enjoy outside of the business to keep yourself occupied and grounded. Find a hobby or something else you love on the side! Lastly, when you're on set, be kind to everyone and professional! There are hundreds, if not thousands, of people who will audition before and after you, and if you aren't prepared and ready to do the job, someone else will be. If you are lucky enough to get the job and be on the set, remember that you need to put 110 percent into it. The hustle is forever!

Message Received

Social media offers so much potential when used with best intentions. It can prove a slippery slope for young actors, however, leading to everything from cyberbullying to trolling.

WINTER (*Alex Dunphy*): When I was twelve, I started going on social media. The show had gained notoriety, and people were commenting on everything. Being a child in that aspect is really difficult because people on the internet, it doesn't matter how old you are, you could be five, eight, thirty-one. Honestly, you could be any age. They'll say the same things about you.

HYLAND (*Haley Dunphy*): I'm a big fan of social media and its worst critic. I think the potential that it has can change the world. And that's why I really love it. I hate it because it gives people, hiding behind their computer, the ability to say whatever they want without consequences. And that can be very, very dangerous.

WINTER (*Alex Dunphy*): I developed much earlier than a lot of other girls. And everything I was wearing, people would say, "Ariel Winter dresses like a slut." It happens to all people in the public eye. But when you're a child, it's worse because you're trying to figure out who you are, trying to navigate the world with everybody else trying to navigate it for you.

SACKS (*studio teacher*): It really bothers me with Ariel because she's not a mean person. She's very empathetic and has a really good heart. I worked on *Hangin' with Mr. Cooper* and *Dr. Doolittle* with Raven-Symoné. She's another one that has had terrible things said about her and is also a wonderful person.

WINTER (*Alex Dunphy*): It's honestly hard to believe sometimes that people can say those things and move on with their day. It's hard when people make rumors about you that aren't true. It's hard when they make rumors that are true, but they don't know it. It's hard in general.

STONESTREET (*Cam Tucker*): I told Ariel sometimes I'll look at her posts on Instagram and go through and report people that are mean to her. It helps me go to sleep. You can't believe the things that people write about those girls. It's pretty crazy. They can't win.

AUBREY ANDERSON-EMMONS (*Lily Tucker-Pritchett*): I say don't look at it. Shut it out. It's not good for you. It's just not good for you.

WINTER (*Alex Dunphy*): I used to get really upset. I used to want to write anything back that I thought, to hurt them as much as they were trying to hurt me. And it never worked. I'd get into more fights online with people who keep writing back to me and writing back and writing back. Then I find myself getting angrier and writing more negative things toward them. And then honestly, I'm looking at my responses and going, "What is the difference here? I didn't start it. And maybe I'm not saying things that are as negative. But I'm defending something that I don't need to. It's unimportant."

STONESTREET (*Cam Tucker*): A lot of people will say, "Don't post anything." Well, that's not fair. Like the only two choices are don't wake up and be a fucking asshole to somebody you don't know on Instagram or not post something? Those are the options?

GOULD (*Luke Dunphy*): They want their fans to know who they are, what their likes are, what their bodies look like when they post bikini photos or nice dresses. Obviously, that opens you up way more for people to say bad things about you.

LEVITAN (*cocreator*): Ariel has chosen to become very outspoken and brave on the issues for which she's been attacked: body shaming and sexuality. I applaud her for that. She's a very smart and tough woman. She's had her missteps, her moments when we say, "Hey, maybe you shouldn't do this or wear that." My daughters, I'm sure there are moments when I was horrified at what they were wearing, but they didn't have to walk around the red carpet or have ten million people comment on it.

WINTER (*Alex Dunphy*): I don't particularly want to put my entire life out there. I don't think that you have to. I don't think that you should. I used to be more interested in doing that. Then as I got older, I said, "People are talking more about things that aren't true about you because you're sharing different aspects of your life." I'm of the mind-set that I don't think every single aspect of my life needs to be online. I want to keep some parts close to me because it's my life. I'm sharing as much as I feel comfortable with at this moment. I'm still trying to gain all the confidence to be able to post this photo of myself and who cares if somebody says this, that, whatever. I'm near there, but I'm not fully there.

GOULD (*Luke Dunphy*): I don't invest a lot of time in social media or reveal my true self on it. I don't really tell people how I feel about things. I relegate it more to posting things about the show, my other projects, cool things I'm doing. The more open you are on social media, the more you open yourself to trolling.

WINTER (*Alex Dunphy*): Women are, in my opinion, attacked harder online than men. I feel like people are waiting and waiting, excited to see a young woman fail. They can't wait to see the crash and burn. Women are watched really closely and intensely to see if there's anything that they do wrong or that they can call them out for.

HYLAND (*Haley Dunphy*): A few years ago, I was on dialysis and was down to like seventy to seventy-five pounds. People were saying I was too skinny, eat a cheeseburger, that kind of stuff. And I was letting it go. But when they started saying that I was promoting anorexia, I'm not going to stand for that. That's when I wrote a really long response. The only thing I regretted was a lot of outlets picked that up. But at the same time, I got a lot of responses from women and men with illnesses all over the world saying, "Thank you. I tried to explain this to my friends or family and they don't understand. To have a familiar face as a voice makes it more acceptable for me to be going through this and for people to understand better." It was things like that, that make me happy that I'm so loud and opinionated, unapologetically so.

WINTER (*Alex Dunphy*): I try and say to myself, "Those people that are writing something negative just want some attention and recognition." I think just writing back, you're just creating . . . a bigger stage for them to write more things and for people to follow them more and for them to hate on other people. And that's not something that I'm going to give them. Only somebody who is wildly unhappy with their own life would do something like that to somebody else.

SAPIENZA (*script supervisor / director*): Ariel just turned twenty-one. Recently someone wrote something about her weight loss. She had changed a prescription, and people were so quick to call her out. When I read that, it made me teary, but then I sent her a text saying she's such an amazing woman and so strong and rises above it all.

FIELD (*associate producer*): I think young girls see you can be who you want to be. The two of them speak out about stuff that they're dealing with. This is who I am, and if you don't like it, I don't need to hear about it.

HYLAND (*Haley Dunphy*): Most of the times when I clap back, it's because a funny retort pops into my head and I can't not say it because it's too funny. I'm trying to not to do that as much anymore, because it really fuels it.

GOULD (*Luke Dunphy*): I think they've handled it really well. I've tried to avoid it, and they've taken it head-on.

BROOKS (*associate producer*): As an eighteen-year-old, I would have crumbled like a piece of graham cracker. I admire them for keeping their cool and taking that in stride.

HYLAND (*Haley Dunphy*): I always said when I was a little girl, I want to be a successful working actress. But the only reason why I want to have notoriety is so that I have a soapbox to stand on and speak about what I believe in and raise awareness for things that don't have it. So that's why I really like social media. It's to be able to talk about things like invisible illness, mental health, or domestic violence situations. It's hard for some women to have a voice.

WINTER (*Alex Dunphy*): I want to be able to talk about whatever's necessary that can possibly help another person on social media. That's always very important to me. But these days, I've scaled back on doing that.

HYLAND (*Haley Dunphy*): People say, "You're so inspiring. You do all of this stuff and don't care." And I'm like, "Oh yeah, that's right. So many people are looking at this." And then other times, I really make a point to be able to be a voice for those who don't have one.

WINTER (*Alex Dunphy*): I had somebody write me a comment and say, "You focus so much on the negative comments, and you don't really comment on the positive ones." That really hit me because it was true. You go through looking automatically for the negative comments, you take the positive ones for granted, and the majority of the comments in your section are positive. So now I try and focus more on the positive instead of negative, which is something that I feel like we all need to do a little bit more.

Knock 'Em Down

A refrigerator door's open-and-close shuffle leaves Claire dropping a bowl of batter and slamming a carton of milk into a closed door. Such physical humor has been a part of Modern Family's *DNA since day one, scene one. Most people associate such comedy with Burrell.*

BURRELL (*Phil Dunphy*): The pilot really set the groundwork for getting to do all kinds of fun, physical things that were a great challenge. As Chris would put it, it was a mutual love of those guys loving to see me suffer, wanting to put me in situations where I was being abused, and me loving being in those situations.

> *Phil balancing on a high wire. Phil launched in a jet pack. Phil swinging on a trapeze. Burrell did all of those stunts and countless stumbles, bumbles, and falls, often leaving him banged up.*

BURRELL (*Phil Dunphy*): It's not combat, so I don't want to overstate it, but you pick up your share of injuries doing bits. There's no doubt about it. But they're always worthwhile.

LLOYD (*cocreator*): We had him on a hover board where he not only had to maneuver around the kitchen, he had to tidy up the kitchen and sweep and mop while having a conversation with Gloria. He spent forty-eight hours figuring it out and did it flawlessly.

BURRELL (*Phil Dunphy*): That one probably debilitated me the most. I woke up after shooting that and couldn't get out of bed. My lower back around my tailbone and all the muscles I had used in those seventy-two hours were completely seized up. I honestly was bedridden, which is a little bit embarrassing. But it's always super fun. I always feel honored when they ask me.

Some of the physicality ends up being a Hollywood smoke-and-mirrors cheat, such as Phil getting hit by a car with Haley behind the wheel, practicing for her driver's test (season 1's "Run for Your Wife").

That scene incorporates a "Texas Switch," in which the camera, actor, and stuntperson do a complex dance that makes it look like an actor has performed some death-defying feat when in truth they didn't.

BURRELL (*Phil Dunphy*): When I come into the driveway, the camera goes over to Julie. I dive out of frame, and the stunt guy swings back and gets hit by the car before you can recognize who it is. That was a very brave stuntman. He was a young, rubberized, third-generation stuntperson, which you find a lot of on TV sets. He broke the windshield from the impact.

WINER (*director / executive producer*): The stuntman then falls out of frame as Ty pops up into frame.

BURRELL (*Phil Dunphy*): That's all one shot. The stuntman rolled over the car and then I jumped up from the back of the car, which is crazy to think about.

Sometimes they leaned too heavily on Burrell's talents, taking away from the relatable comedy.

O'SHANNON (*writer / executive producer*): For a while there, he couldn't walk across a room without tripping over something or banging his head because he was so funny. There were times we had to police ourselves and say, "This guy can't be Inspector Clouseau."

CORRIGAN (*writer / executive producer*): We had to take a break from having Phil fall because it's funny in the moment, but we're really damaging the character if we rely on that too much.

Perhaps one of Burrell's hardest stunts involved doing absolutely nothing.

KO (*writer / executive producer*): In "American Skyper" [season 6], Phil was out of town for Alex's graduation, so he had to Skype in from an iPad robot for an entire episode. We had to put poor Ty in this little room off in a corner of the stage, where it was him talking into a tiny camera with a sad hotel room set behind him. I'm sure it was torture for him—nobody delights in stage bits more than Ty Burrell.

Overall, he has no regrets.

BURRELL (*Phil Dunphy*): I started the show in my forties, and every week I've had to do something hard physically for the most part. On a selfish level, those are my greatest memories—being given a challenge and then setting out to do it and trying, not always with success, to make it funny. I'm a little bit more intrepid because of it. Not fully intrepid, mind you, but a little more. In a weird way, I think over the last eleven years, it kept me young.

While Bowen's stunts fly a little more under the radar, they end up being just as impressive.

GREENBERG (*casting director*): Julie's become the surprise physical comedy player, and they write to that like crazy.

BOWEN (*Claire Dunphy*): I like those moments. They're really fun. It takes all the onus off having to be attractive in any way.

WRUBEL (*writer / executive producer*): Julie's an athlete, a runner, and fearless. She's funny and comfortable inhabiting someone who's a little bit neurotic played out physically.

LLOYD (*cocreator*): We were shooting at a roller-skating rink. She spent multiple hours over the weekend becoming good at roller skating, a thing that she had never done before.

BOWEN (*Claire Dunphy*): They had this whole crazy, complicated business that Claire worked there as a teenager and could make a Slushee and roll and turn and do all these things. I realized I could barely chew gum and walk in a straight line, so I needed to get comfortable with it.

LLOYD (*cocreator*): She did it flawlessly.*

JON POLLACK (*writer / executive producer*): We did a scene where she has to get to Dylan, and he's locked himself in his van. There's a moonroof, and she has to fall through it. The mat is five feet down and she does it over and over again, and it's fantastic.

> *Both rarely use stunt doubles.*

BOWEN (*Claire Dunphy*): When we had to go to that amusement park on that terrifying ride that makes you pass out. There was no way on God's green earth that I was going to go onto a ride that made you throw up. That was when we used a stunt double.

BURRELL (*Phil Dunphy*): We have a great stunt coordinator, Jimmy Sharp. There have been two or three occasions in the show where I was incapable, and they're really awesome about stepping in if I need it. I really value that.

> *One stunt that illustrates the devotion of Burrell and Bowen together occurs in season 2's "See You Next Fall," in which Phil and Claire move heaven and earth to try to make it on time to Alex's middle school grad-*

---

* Incidentally, Higginbotham points out that in that sweet scene with Bowen, O'Neill's only wearing socks because he didn't want to put on the skates but needed to be able to slide. "If you look at it, it's not nearly the right height," recalls Higginbotham. "He would be so much taller."

uation. The climax involves their falling down a hillside, while dressed up for graduation, and then walking to their seats.

LEVITAN (*cocreator*): We hired two stunt doubles and shot it with them. Then Ty and Julie came over to me and said, "We want to do it."

BOWEN (*Claire Dunphy*): Steve commented that it didn't look like Phil and Claire falling down a hill. It looked like two stuntpeople. They were cartwheeling, flipping, and were amazing. So he was sending them back to do it more real. Ty and I agreed to do it.

ZUKER (*writer / executive producer*): Ty and Julie were looking at it and saying, "That's how we would fall as acrobats, but not as middle-aged parents."

LEVITAN (*cocreator*): The hill's rocky and steep with a lot of brush, sticks, and rocks. It's dangerous, and they're wearing nice clothes with exposed legs. And they said, "We want to do this."

BOWEN (*Claire Dunphy*): Steve said, "It's not a fake hillside. It's a real, dry California hillside covered with gross and thorny little things you find on hillsides." I remember begging Steve. He said, "You can't. You're going to get hurt." I said, "We'll do one take." I could see him giving. I said, "We're not going to do it crazy. It's going to look like us because it is us. We're going to fall and then walk right out onto the football field and sit down in our seats. That's the shot you want, right?"

LLOYD (*cocreator*): It's hard to say no to them, but it's a calculated gamble. It's a dangerous thing.

SAPIENZA (*script supervisor / director*): Julie was in these three-inch heels wearing a dress and tumbling down a hill. They had no idea what to expect—all the bruises they suffered because they wanted it to be funny.

BOWEN (*Claire Dunphy*): Ty and I really feel the exact same way about doing stuff, which is go for it and have the best time. We both have high thresholds for looking like idiots and getting scratched up. As long as you're not breaking stuff, it's fine. What was dumb, but wasn't my fault, was in "Egg Drop."

Season 3's "Egg Drop" included an early scene that served as a single beat in the storyline.

INT. DUNPHY HOUSE—ENTRYWAY—CONTINUOUS

```
Claire walks down the hall. A carton of eggs
falls in front of her. She sees Luke standing at
the top of the stairs.

                    CLAIRE
        Luke, why?
```

MILLER (*assistant prop master*): I was the one dropping the eggs. It was supposed to be one egg, then I was told two, and then I got the call to make it a carton of eggs.

LLOYD (*cocreator*): We're watching on the monitors, which are set up no more than eight feet from where the scene's being shot. The eggs drop in front of Julie, and she slips in it.

BOWEN (*Claire Dunphy*): Both of my feet went out from under me. I fell so hard that it didn't even hurt. My jaw rattled.

LLOYD (*cocreator*): I'm seeing a crimson streak in her cheeks that you can't fake. That only happens because you've been through a shock. Everyone got very still. It's my job to say, "Stop," or "Hold on," or run out and make sure she's okay. I was right on the edge of that because she paused for a microsecond, the way you do when you've hurt yourself.

BOWEN (*Claire Dunphy*): He's right. For a split second, I was sure they were going to go, "Cut. Are you okay?" And when they didn't, it was all

I could do to contain my joy that they were going to keep going. I didn't break my tailbone for nothing. They're going to use it.

WINER (*director / executive producer*): I was so excited that she stayed in it. When you're behind the monitors, you get so caught up in it. You get a little bit ruthless. You want to get that thing on film that's special and fills in the moment. That was one of those moments.

LLOYD (*cocreator*): When we got to the end of the scene, I was prepared for her to either say, "Was anybody going to come out and see if I was okay?" or "God, you let me go through that because I'm sure that that looked as real as real could be because it was real." Fortunately, the second was her reaction.

MILLER (*assistant prop master*): She said, "Thank fucking God you didn't cut, because I wasn't going to be doing that for nothing." That's a real performer's attitude. If I'm going to fall down and get hurt, you'd better get it on-camera.

Stonestreet falling backward on roller skates, crashing down while running with a trash can, flipping over a couch and jettisoning a bowl of chips, falling into Lake Tahoe with Vergara. Ferguson on a crane in a Spider-Man outfit. The list goes on and on. Gould running into a wall.

SPILLER (*director*): In "Earthquake" [season 2], Luke runs smack into a wall and knocks himself out. It was such a believable stunt. Nolan slammed his head right into it. You see it. There's no cut. It's all there.

GOULD (*Luke Dunphy*): Everyone was super concerned for me and asked if I could take it down a notch. They genuinely thought I was going to hurt myself. There were two to three seasons where I had a reckless abandon to try and get laughs. That was all I could think about. I was addicted to entertaining people.

SPILLER (*director*): We put a little foam pad and painted it the same color as the wall, but it's still a standout moment, a tiny little stunt that another child actor might not have done.

In "Travels with Scout" (season 1), the family dog waits for Alex to open the screen door. Claire mentions that all dogs can do that. Then Luke runs by saying he's going to play outside and bursts through the screen door.

GOULD (*Luke Dunphy*): We went through twenty screen doors, and by the end, it was starting to hurt.

Hyland had to push a car. Winter had to pretend to vomit in a diner at the end of "The Last Walt."

WINTER (*Alex Dunphy*): That's me. I remember trying to figure out the physical comedy of that and the sound of throwing up and where I was going to throw up so the camera didn't see I was throwing up.

Anderson-Emmons had to run into a green-screen-padded brick pillar wall ("The Butler's Escape").

AUBREY ANDERSON-EMMONS (*Lily Tucker-Pritchett*): I struggled with it because I didn't want to actually run into the wall.

AMY ANDERSON-EMMONS (*Aubrey's mom*): Your natural inclination is to put up your hands to protect your face, and Steve was like, "Okay, honey, try to really not put up your hands." You're asking her to face this wall, and she did it over and over and over.

Much like the show, for that matter.

Torn Between Two Lovers

In season 9's episode "The Escape," Haley, lying in a hospital bed, has a close encounter with her four long-term ex-boyfriends: Rainer Shine, Arvin Fennerman, Andy Bailey, and Dylan Marshall. The scene gave Hyland pause.

GEERE (*Arvin Fennerman*): She said, "Wow, Haley really doesn't have a type, does she?" The four of us are so massively different, but I thought it was brilliant writing that she could adapt to any one of us.

> *Haley Dunphy, party girl, dated many a boy, man, and boy-man over the course of eleven years. Her first and last boyfriend, high-school crush Dylan Marshall, appeared in the pilot sporting a 1980s "Rick Springfield with a leather jacket" look. They only had planned to use him in the pilot. But like Bebe Neuwirth as Lilith on* Cheers, *a one-off role became an important character.*

EWING (*Dylan Marshall*): When I auditioned for Jeff, I was taking off my leather jacket, and he said, "Don't, it's good for the character."

WRUBEL (*writer / executive producer*): My first reaction was, "He's going to be Judd Nelson in *The Breakfast Club*," but instead Reid had this wide-eyed innocence that made him kind and gentle.

EWING (*Dylan Marshall*): Dylan had that vacant, funny kind of an affect that would drive most parents crazy. I was basically just using my own headspace to do it, maybe standoffish and clueless. To me, he was just perfect.

HYLAND (*Haley Dunphy*): I think Haley's initial attraction was that he was an older guy with a leather jacket and blue eyes. It was that rebellious phase that you have when you're a teenager.

And he played in a band. What more could she want? In that season's fourth episode, he serenaded her and the family with the sweet then raunchy song, "In the Moonlight (Do Me)."

EWING (*Dylan Marshall*): They had the concept that it'll start off beautiful and romantic and then get dirty. I took their lyrics and made my own song based on their concept.

For the writers, Dylan's dimness became his most attractive feature.

O'SHANNON (*writer / executive producer*): A stupid character is catnip to a writing staff. I remember a joke that Brad wrote for Dylan where Haley is talking about meeting the love of her life, and then you pull out and Dylan is there and he says, "And his name is me."

EWING (*Dylan Marshall*): Chris said to me once about writing on *Golden Girls* for Betty White, "We won't make you that stupid." And I thought, "That's funny, but I'm pretty sure you already did."

Dylan's brain may have consisted of a forty-seven-card deck, but as happens with high school crushes and good hair, the life-smart, book-dumb Haley fell under his spell. Their flame burned bright until it didn't, and then it did and then it didn't and did a few more times before he stayed behind in Wyoming.

CORRIGAN (*writer / executive producer*): At the time, we thought dumping Dylan was smart. We didn't know what new wrinkles he would bring and thought it was a funny way to say goodbye. We were thinking of bringing him back having gone to boot camp, and he was now a marine.

That Officer and a Gentleman *moment never happened. Ewing ended up moving back to his home state, Utah, and becoming a certified nursing assistant (CNA).*

EWING (*Dylan Marshall*): Sometimes patients would say, "I saw you on TV. What's going on?" And I would say, "I told you, I was an actor."

In later years, when Ewing returned, they gave Dylan the same occupation.

Meanwhile, Haley played the field, meeting some interesting one-off boyfriends until she landed on her first major relationship with the older and somehow more self-absorbed weatherman, Rainer Shine. To play that role, casting director Greenberg immediately thought: Nathan Fillion.

GREENBERG (*casting director*): He started in comedy on *Two Guys, a Girl and a Pizza Place*. I knew him to be funny. I thought he'd like to do something light. He had just finished *Castle* [2009–2016] when this part came up. He seemed like a weatherman.

NATHAN FILLION (*Rainer Shine*): Most of acting is looking for a job, so when a hit show like *Modern Family* asks, it's such an easy answer. Of course, are you kidding me? Is this for real? How soon?

Fillion's inspiration for his character came from a guest appearance on a local morning show.

FILLION (*Rainer Shine*): I wore my lucky shirt. It's powder blue and has pink flowers on it. It always gets a range of reactions, but in the end people love it. On this particular interview, the weatherman couldn't get beyond it. He kept making comments, and they weren't flattering. I thought for a guy with his teeth that white, skin that tan, with that much makeup on and coiffed hair, if he's got a problem with the color of my shirt, then he's very unaware of himself. I wonder how many people in his life say, "Hey, man, pull back a little bit. Tone it down."

In the story, Phil comes on a local TV show to do a real estate segment. Haley comes along to do his makeup. The weatherman and makeup woman manage to turn away from their own reflections long enough to connect. If you believe that opposites attract, then they never had a chance.

FILLION (*Rainer Shine*): They have the same priorities. They have a lot of shared experiences. They're worried about the same things. I think there's a real comfort in that. To have someone who actually understands what it's like to have to pack an extra hair dryer just in case something happens to the first one, I think that's important.

Shine lasted six episodes before a storm front of differences doomed the lovers.

FILLION (*Rainer Shine*): Haley works a little better in an atmosphere where there's someone who can give instead of just take. She's a good taker. She can't be with a taker as well.

HYLAND (*Haley Dunphy*): Very true. I always found that relationship a little strange. It was like watching a parakeet fall in love with itself in a mirror.

FILLION (*Rainer Shine*): They had so much in common, but there was no heart there. No heart.

HYLAND (*Haley Dunphy*): I agree. No heart; just face.

And what did Haley take from the relationship?

HYLAND (*Haley Dunphy*): I think that relationship really opened Haley's eyes to the sacrifice that she could make for someone if she cared about them. Like him having a stepdaughter. I thought that that was really interesting to watch her go to such great lengths to impress this girl not much younger than herself for the man that she's with. I think that was a really great opportunity for growth. You only regret something if you don't learn from it. And I think she did.

When the writers thought season 10 would be the end, they wanted Haley to get pregnant. Levitan laid the groundwork for Haley to fall in love with one of Alex's professors. Enter erudite professor and two-time Vanderscoff Grant winner for philosophy and math, Arvin Fennerman.

GREENBERG (*casting director*): We read a lot of guys for that part. It was never supposed to be British.

BETH MCINTOSH (*Geere's manager*): I think they didn't really know what they wanted. I think they wanted an opposite to Sarah, someone eccentric. Chris made him a bit more nerdy.

Levitan, a fan of Geere from the series You're the Worst, *only needed to see Geere's audition tape once to know he was the guy.*

ZUKER (*writer / executive producer*): This guy is obnoxiously talented and handsome. You want to say, "Fuck you. You can be funny or handsome. Don't be both. Otherwise, us funny, ugly guys will really get resentful."

Geere worked with Levitan to discover the inner Arvin.

GEERE (*Arvin Fennerman*): Steve said, "Give it more Hugh Grant on one of the takes," and so we messed around with that quite a lot.

Fennerman and Haley meet in a college classroom, in which she interrupts his lecture so Alex, a student in his class, can look over a

writing sample she wrote for her big interview at the lifestyle company
Nerp.

GEERE (*Arvin Fennerman*): The thing he found most attractive was she was the polar opposite of him. He's a scientist. He looks for negatives and positives, things that work well together. If they were too similar, that wouldn't be right. They seemed to be the plus and minus of a relationship.

Shortly thereafter, they meet a second time on a campus bench in which Fennerman declares, "This might sound crazy, but I'm going to marry you."

GEERE (*Arvin Fennerman*): He's a bit of a lovable fool, very smart yet hopelessly romantic. He really loved Haley and genuinely thought they would be together forever. There was a contrast between his views on science and his views on love. I really enjoyed doing that.

HYLAND (*Haley Dunphy*): I agree with Chris on all of that. I really loved Arvin. And I really loved Arvin because I really loved Chris. He's a classically trained actor, performed in the Royal Shakespeare Company with Dame Judi Dench, which, holy fuck, that's amazing. It was one of the first times where an actor was like, "Let's go over the scene to make sure we know the words. Let's break this down."

Time and space ended up separating them, with Fennerman taking a position overseas, dooming his scientific hypothesis of their endless love.

GEERE (*Arvin Fennerman*): To be honest, I'd have liked to see her with Arvin, but you can't have everything. I genuinely think Arvin would have dropped everything for her, whatever she wanted. So I'd love to think of them living together in the countryside with three very nerdy children.

HYLAND (*Haley Dunphy*): I don't think they should have really ended up together, but I could have forced myself to believe that for how amazing of an actor Chris is.

Early in season 5, in the episode "The Help," the writers introduced a new character to the story: the earnest, overzealous male nanny ("manny") Andy Bailey, hired by Gloria to take care of Joe. Levitan, a fan of Workaholics, *thought one of the show's creators and lead actors, Adam Devine, would be perfect for the part. Greenberg contacted his agent.*

ADAM DEVINE (*Andy Bailey*): I said I was busy with *Workaholics,* but what did they have in mind? So we had a meeting. They were going to give me this pretty significant role with a real awesome storyline. I think they wanted to meet me first to find out if I was a psychopath or not, because if you only knew me from *Workaholics,* there's a possibility that I'm a total maniac. Steve asked me, "Can you play sincere and earnest and be a real person?" From what he'd seen, that was a good question. Obviously, I'm not going to say, "Nope, I can't do it." I was confident in my ability.

HYLAND (*Haley Dunphy*): It was the first time I'd ever felt really, really, really overly enthusiastic and excited to go to work because there was someone my age on set, someone on my team. The teenagers at that time, were all doing their teenage things like being really into dating, and I'm like, "Who wants to adopt another dog with me?" It was really fun.

Devine modeled his character on someone from his past.

DEVINE (*Andy Bailey*): I had a friend growing up who was deeply involved in the church. He was such a sweet guy, earnest and real. You couldn't even tell him a dirty joke, because he wouldn't understand what it meant. I took some of his mannerisms. He was always half smiling, even when he was upset; he still had the corner of his mouth curled up because he was trying to look at the bright side of things. That was my basis for the gullible, sweet Andy, who is a really good guy, someone who you might not want to party with, but if you're having a bad day, you might want his shoulder to cry on.

The writers didn't pull any punches with their intentions for Andy and Haley. The audience knew the agenda right away.

DEVINE (*Andy Bailey*): I don't remember anyone spelling it out for me, but it was really apparent in the first few episodes that I'm young Phil and that's why we're having this initial connection.

HYLAND (*Haley Dunphy*): I think it's beautiful because Haley's like young Claire. Every story you hear about Claire is when she was Haley's age, loose and fun, which is what Haley very much was, up until she gave birth to twins.

Audiences ate up the palpable chemistry between Devine and Hyland, not to mention the buildup of their story. Their unrequited love led to social media giving them the moniker Handy *as well as* Anley.

HYLAND (*Haley Dunphy*): I think that Andy's and Haley's "will they, won't they" aspect became today's Ross and Rachel. That was the only aspect the show had really been missing. Everyone else had their life partners set already. There wasn't that drama that comes with young love, something that you can really, really sink your teeth into, invest in, and root for this couple. That's why people loved it so much.

DEVINE (*Andy Bailey*): Steve asked if they wrote more episodes for me would that be something I'd be interested in. No, biggest show on TV, I'm going to go back to my basic cable TV show. I refuse to be more successful.

Devine and Hyland each have their own favorite memories.

HYLAND (*Haley Dunphy*): That run and jump when we're in Phil's showhouse. I leave and then run back in and jump into his arms, and we kiss. I had never filmed anything like that before. There was some teeth hitting involved, but it was worth it. It was really romantic.

DEVINE (*Andy Bailey*): The rain kiss. That was pretty awesome. We really had to crush it because as soon as we were wet, there was no getting dry. And it was very cold.

HYLAND (*Haley Dunphy*): The only reason why the showhouse scene trumps that rain kiss is because it was so cold.

DEVINE (*Andy Bailey*): We had to act like we were so passionate, so in love with each other, and then shivering as soon as they called, "Cut!" and they come running in with big towels and coats.

A variety of factors worked against the young lovers not on-screen but off it. As a result, Devine got written off the show.

HYLAND (*Haley Dunphy*): I saw him at an Emmy party, and I was like, "Oh, hey, movie star, too big to be on *Modern Family* now?" And he said, "What are you talking about? I was contacting them for months to see if they were bringing me back. They said that they couldn't find the funny between Andy and Haley anymore."

HIGGINBOTHAM (*writer / executive producer*): The relationship on-screen could get serious at times, which wasn't as much fun for us to write. We'd be in the romance of it all rather than the comedy.

WALLS (*writer / supervising producer*): Like in any show, there's a struggle when you put two people together, because you're so driven by the pull. Once they're together, there's always trouble in finding what's funny about this.

GREENBERG (*casting director*): Adam's also one of the busiest actors on earth. He had his own show and was making movies. Scheduling him was always the hardest part, but somehow we made it work.

DEVINE (*Andy Bailey*): I shot Tuesday through Friday on *Workaholics,* so I only had Mondays. It was always tough because the time crunch was drastic and it was hard for them to fit everything into my schedule, and to their credit, they bent over backward and did that. I was so thankful, but I think it would have been hard to make me a series regular always knowing they're in second position.

The unfulfilled love arc and the writing off of Andy by merely mentioning him in the premiere of season 6 didn't provide closure or satisfaction for Hyland.

HYLAND (*Haley Dunphy*): Andy went away to Utah to take a job, and they were doing long distance in the season finale. Then in the next season's premiere, Haley says she spent the summer getting over her breakup with Andy. I was devastated. I can't even imagine what the audience felt. I got a lot of personal hate on the internet because everyone thought I wrote the episode. You have this will they / won't they for years. They finally get together, for maybe five or six episodes, and then you throw away their breakup within one sentence? I really wanted Haley to end up with Andy. I will be a Handy fan until the day I die. I will ship that couple until it sinks. That's my *Titanic*.

When the writers designed Haley's pregnancy, they played with many different ideas.

LLOYD (*cocreator*): We weren't always thinking of going back to Dylan. We were actually thinking about a brand-new direction for Haley.

ZUKER (*writer / executive producer*): We did a lot of machinations. "Is there a way we can get Andy back into the mix?" We even went as far as really mapping out how we would do it.

LEVITAN (*cocreator*): But Adam went back to work on another show. It would have become potentially very difficult to try to juggle those two schedules because that shot on the other side of the country. And Andy's such a likable character. It's hard for Claire not to like him. It's hard for Phil not to like him. And it's hard for Haley not to like him. So where does the conflict and comedy come from?

DEVINE (*Andy Bailey*): I wanted more than anything to come back and finish my storyline with Sarah, but unfortunately, that's not how it works sometimes. I was pretty upset when it fell apart. But it's a business. There's a lot of moving parts, and I totally understand. No hard feelings from me. I love my Modern Fam.

They stumbled upon a familiar face almost by accident.

RICHMAN (*writer / executive producer*): I was in Chris's room when Steve came over and said people in the other room came up with Dylan. Immediately, everybody got on board. I mean that minute. It solved the puzzle. It made us laugh, and that was a really liberating thing because we knew Dylan and Haley's relationship would be funny.

EWING (*Dylan Marshall*): Jeff Greenberg called me and said, "We're going to bring you back. And then we're going to have you through the season."

LLOYD (*cocreator*): Once we settled back on Dylan, we thought it was her first love and he has evolved as a character. It's fun to have him and his interaction with Phil and Claire and all the history that I think the audience enjoys.

LEVITAN (*cocreator*): We know some audience members really liked Andy and Haley together, but in our minds we thought Dylan is where we started so it's nice to bring it full circle.

Ewing became a full cast member for the last season, giving the writers their catnip back.

HYLAND (*Haley Dunphy*): He does have this very romantic, sweet, like, teddy-bear type of heart to where he would do anything for Haley. A girl can take advantage of that. But I think it was a give-and-take with them when they were teenagers.

For Ewing, some of the initial pushback stung. People online feel the freedom to post anything from the safety of their own home or device.

EWING (*Dylan Marshall*): Everyone was so mad. I was a little bit hurt at first. It was nonstop posting on the *Modern Family* Instagram account that it should be Andy. I know I am not as mainstream as Adam. I will not be everyone's cup of tea. I would have accepted either way. Now I don't care at all. I'm okay with it. If you're an actor, you signed up for it, so I can't complain.

HYLAND (*Haley Dunphy*): Reid is a very, very kind, very sweet, sensitive soul. He's very much like Dylan. I think America feels like Phil does about Dylan, "Oh yeah, I love that guy."

EWING (*Dylan Marshall*): I don't know how Haley feels about Dylan. I thought that she accidentally had a baby and isn't thrilled about it, but because of circumstances ends up getting married. That's what happened to Phil and Claire. In the end, they ended up being really great with each other. So it's fate. Maybe Haley wasn't going to choose Dylan, but she got pregnant, so here we go.

HYLAND (*Haley Dunphy*): You always hold a special place in your heart for the person you were first in love with. And their relationship was so intermingled in the entire family's life, Dylan was always around, and he was always there. And you know, Phil loved him.

EWING (*Dylan Marshall*): I think that they're the same. They're supposed to be dumb. I think they complement each other like different colors of the rainbow.

HYLAND (*Haley Dunphy*): He'll always be there for her. He always comes back. Dylan may not give her a crazy, beautiful house and life together, but there will always be love there. And he'll always make her laugh.

EWING (*Dylan Marshall*): I think Dylan would sacrifice a lot to be in the family. I think he loves Claire and Phil. He loves everybody.

BOWEN: (*Claire Dunphy*): There's something you get with Reid that you can't buy. He's so genuine. Dylan's a very special character, and they have this weird, funny, odd relationship. Reid is the first to admit he's a bit of a character himself and proudly a fish out of water.

ZUKER (*writer / executive producer*): It was a delightful surprise that rose out of necessity, and Reid really rose to the challenge of it all.

The Last Christmas

Eleven years. In almost any industry, no one stays at a company that long. But here, on this show, the majority have, and because of that, they have shared not just the pleasure of the work but also the courtships, marriages, divorces; the feuds, births, deaths; the everyday and the banal. Walsh captures the passage of time this way: "When the show started, we were all talking about our kids' recitals and first days of elementary school. Now there's a lot of talk about dental surgeries and colonoscopies."

Recently, Hyland, she of the angelic singing voice, performed at the Hollywood Bowl at a Jonas Brothers concert. If you made a drinking game that requires downing a shot every time someone on set raves about her singing, you'd be in detox. Nathan Fillion put it this way: "Some people can carry a tune, and some will make you stop breathing. I could feel my mouth agape. She's a very talented lady."

Backstage at the bowl, some little girls approached her. "They said they've been watching my show their entire life," recalls Hyland. I asked how old they were. "One was twelve, and one was thirteen. I said, 'Oh, wow, you really have been watching this show your entire life.' They don't even remember the pilot because they were in diapers."

This week, the entire cast has gathered to shoot "The Last Christmas," one of those big (and last) all-in-one-room episodes. As the last episode of the front nine, it hints at much of what transpires in the final back nine. Cam, carrying a secret, has put together a large holiday celebration at his and Mitchell's home, thinking it may be the last one for a while.

In place of their living room's standard stage dressing rests a festively decorated, elongated table that fits all thirteen cast members and a stroller with two babies. Because of fire codes, Miller informs me they can only have ten candles on set. It makes me want to count candles on my favorite shows.

During the table read for this episode, Ferguson suddenly got very emotional, foreshadowing what lies ahead for everyone. "I was cold reading the script. When I got to the line in the scene where I say, 'Let's just all enjoy each other while we can,' I stopped halfway. It was embarrassing because it wasn't meant to be a line that garnered tears, but it did. People were crying. I definitely took the air out of the room for a moment. But I think allowing myself to have that moment is what I want to continue to have for the rest of our time together."

Gould takes a more optimistic and youthful perspective. "We know this show's ending. There are moments where we realize this time next year we won't be here. That's sad, but we're so happy to be here and go about our days doing what we love." Burrell likes how the year came together. "It normally feels like your job is being taken away from you, but here we get to say goodbye to the show. We get to have this last hurrah."

It almost didn't happen. Originally, they had planned to go out with Hayley delivering twins at the end of season 10. Levitan certainly wanted it that way. "I make no bones about it," he admits. "I didn't want this season to happen." Lloyd felt differently. "There were valid arguments on the other side. Let's maintain the quality control. Let's go out strong. But my point and others' was we've always had the challenge of not repeating ourselves. There's nothing that says 10 is all anyone could ever do. Bear in mind, this might be the last big hit show any of us is going to work on. Let's not put it to bed before we have to." They ended up with the shortened final season with eighteen episodes.

According to this episode's director, Jason Miller, they will shoot eleven pages today, twice what many other shows by comparison could do. The day will run a little longer than lunchtime, however, prompting cast and crew to break out another verse of the apology tour for me, looking guilty as if they'd accidentally harmed my puppy. This time, not unlike the last, they want me to know that they absolutely, 100 percent swear, hand to God, the show normally operates differently.

Merlin, in one of probably three moments today where she stands still for all of five seconds, grasps the monumental loss the show will represent in her life. "This is one of the best times I've had as an adult. There'll never be another job like this. There'll never be another crew like this. There'll never be another cast like this. It'll be something else, but it'll never be this." She talks about taking a solo road trip after the show ends to decompress. Miller doesn't hold back either. "When this is over and it actually hits us, it's going to be similar to a death. There's going to be that type of grieving process. I can't wrap my head around not seeing these people every day."

No one here fears change; they just mourn loss. Elliott recalls Levitan standing on set a few years ago, looking around and somewhat to himself saying aloud, "I think it's true. Lightning only strikes once."

The babies get prepared for their twenty-minute on-set gig. Taking a page from his years trying to stop the Hiller twins' river of tears, Ferguson holds one while whipping out his go-to song, "A Bushel and a Peck." The baby whisperer returns. Bowen kisses one of Haley's babies during setup and says she loves the smell of baby. Later, the creepy baby dolls, invasion of the body snatchers, will take over.

Bowen will do another of her death-defying stunts soon. Okay, maybe not death-defying, but whiplash-inducing for sure. Claire will flip out a window, in heels, to avoid talking with her dad about working for his dog bed business. "She literally throws herself out a window backward like a scuba diver," says Pollack. "They put a mat for her, but she has to do a backward somersault multiple times and land flat on her stomach so we can't see her." The stunt coordinator tries to convince her to do it a safer way, but Bowen wants to maximize the funny. After rehearsing it four times and then filming it three, she walks away still whole. The next day, she reports back with a sore neck, but doesn't care as long as people laugh.

A little later, a crew member carries in a surprise birthday cake for Gould, who just turned twenty-one. He and Winter and others went to Vegas to celebrate this past weekend. I survived on ramen at that age. They own their own homes.

Over several days, I ask the writers how they would like to see the show end, a date rapidly approaching still without set plans, and their all being writers, they envision different creative conclusions:

ZUKER (*writer / executive producer*): I think we have a great opportunity to honor these characters and explore where this journey on TV ends for this family. I'm interested in giving the audience something to think about, make them interested in the next chapter in all these people's lives.

WALLS (*writer / supervising producer*): If it was up to me, we would end with Ed O'Neill waking up in bed with Katey Sagal, saying he had eaten some bad Japanese food the night before and had the strangest dream. But I'm not in charge of the show.

RICHMAN (*writer / executive producer*): I personally wish for episodes seventeen and eighteen, Chris takes a room and Steve takes a room after it's broken. Half the staff writes one and half the staff writes the second one and then we table it together.

LEVITAN (*cocreator*): I'm a big fan of final shows in which the characters get a chance to voice their feelings toward each other, perhaps some sort of goodbye because there's some sort of change. That leads characters to want to say things that perhaps they wouldn't say in day-to-day life.

During a break onstage, I make my way over to the writers' room to bother them one final time and thank them for letting me be a fly on their wall, one they ultimately didn't swat. Here they prep for the table read of Lloyd and Burditt's episode, which has been pushed off a few days in deference to Fred Willard. The table read wouldn't hit the notes it should if someone reads for him. Willard will never stop being one of the most brilliant improvisational comedians of our or any other generation's list. Having recently turned eighty, he doesn't move quite so fast anymore, but his mind remains as sharp as ever.

You can handle death a thousand different ways on television. Perhaps nothing can top Chuckles the Clown's demise on *The Mary Tyler Moore Show*. As written by Lloyd's father, he dies off-screen in a parade, dressed as Peter Peanut, when a rogue elephant tried to "shell" him, leading to his death. That will always read funny.

Lloyd reports back a week later how the shoot went. "The set was somber but also celebratory," says Lloyd. The scene where Phil offers a toast to his dad was very moving. Ty shed a tear, and it was impossible for everyone else not to at that point. Yes, we were saying goodbye to Frank, but there was also a harbinger of the end of the series in there, too. We will be saying goodbye to each other all too soon . . .

I ask Higginbotham what makes all of this work. "I love these people," reflects Higginbotham. "That's what's so crazy. I've never been on a show this long. We adore each other, and we have our bullshit. I'm not going to paint a perfect picture. That's not real."

Next, I go down to say goodbye to production. They insist that I take *Modern Family* schwag home to my family. Could this be a quid pro quo for a rosier history? Did I just admit to taking a bribe in print? No and no.

I finally have my own "last," as in my last day on set. I can feel the finality myself, knowing opportunities to witness history come few and far between. Years ago, my family went to watch the filming of an episode of *M*A*S*H*. To this day, we wear that as a badge of honor. This to me takes on a deeper meaning, because here, they welcomed me into their world. We broke bread, shot the shit, talked about each other's families, and made jokes not funny enough to print.

When members of the crew say, "See you tomorrow," I inform them that sadly they will not. I could think of a million stories from my time talking with everyone. Some of them, like camera operator Trey Clinesmith, boom operator William Munroe, prop master Rick Ladomade, second-second assistant director Ismael "Cheese" Jimenez, and digital utility dude extraordinaire Sean Kehoe, I never got the chance to interview at length, but had the greater pleasure of talking to. I respect these people for the art they create and the way they treat each other.

I am waiting for a break in shooting to say goodbye to cast members. Kehoe makes that simple. Discovering it's my last day, he escorts me onto the set and notifies me I will be doing the clapper board for this take. At first, I get assigned camera A but, sensing my probable incompetence, get booted to the less stressful camera B. I'm told to announce, "B Mark," and then clap the clapper board. This helps sync camera and sound, but to me, in this moment, to be here with these people, it means something entirely different. I am grateful to, like I said when clapping the clapper board, literally "be Marc."

Fortunately, everything goes off without a hitch. The entire cast gives me a hearty sendoff. I look at everyone and no one in fear of revealing emotion. I must maintain my outer Spock.

Commencement

Bittersweet. When you read about the end of a series, the last frame shot of a film, a closing stage performance, it all comes back to that one word: bittersweet. *Sometime in late February 2020, when Modern Family's family disperses, everyone there will surely leave with a sense of pride, joy, love, and bittersweet loss pouring out of them.*

MILLER (*assistant prop master*): The general consensus is we all know this is the best job we're ever going to have. This is it. This is the watershed. This is the show you work your career to get. We're treated the best. It's the best schedule. It's the closest that I have ever been to a crew.

SEAN KEHOE (*digital utility*): This show gave me more than I could ever ask for. I was given the ability to be around my wife during her pregnancy, be there for the birth of my daughter, and see her take her first steps. Being in this industry twenty years now, I never would have thought that possible. For that, I will forever be grateful. This was truly the best show to have ever worked on.

SAPIENZA (*script supervisor / director*): This is one in a million as far as what we have all gone through and experienced, from the amazing cast to the crew to traveling. The opportunities we've had being on the show are nothing like we will ever encounter again.

MORTON (*executive producer*): Before this show, I think I had only done thirty episodes of a show. I used to joke that after episode seventeen in the first season, it was all gravy. Two hundred and fifty episodes later, here we are. It's all gravy.

ELLIOTT (*on-set dresser*): All the good karma I've given in my life has resulted in three things—my two daughters and *Modern Family*. We have been treated so well over the last decade, since day one. People are still talking to me today about how lucky we are to be here.

KENDALL FOOTE (*set PA*): The community, the camaraderie, the creative work environment with a group of people that supports each other's individuality. That starts at the top. It gives us the freedom to be nice to one another because we don't have people barking down at us. We have a nice flow staying in our own lanes with arms locked as we run around the track again and again and again.

KATHIA "KAT" SANCHEZ-ALDANA (*associate producer*): We're a family, in the whole sense of the concept. We fight, we make up, we hate each other at some point, but at the end of the day, we work it through. Anywhere else it's like, "We're done. We're out. I will see you never." Here, there's legitimate love for one another.

MORTON (*executive producer*): This show has changed every person who worked on it. It changed their life.

The show also changed the career path of many crew members.

KATE RICCIO (*production liaison*): It's been amazing starting on this show as a production assistant and watching all of the production assistants I started with blossom.

ABBY JENKINS (*production coordinator*): I started here as a PA, and now I'm a coordinator.

SAPIENZA (*script supervisor / director*): I've gone from being a script supervisor and had the opportunity to direct.

LLOYD (*cocreator*): We've had ten to twelve people who got their first job directing on the show, and that's something we're proud of.

SANCHEZ-ALDANA (*associate producer*): I started as assistant production coordinator, and I'm leaving as associate producer in a span of five years, which is crazy.

FIELD (*associate producer*): I started as an office production assistant. I kept wanting to write, and Jeff, who's an amazing mentor, said, "I really think you should produce." We made up a title called *production associate,* then I became an associate producer.

MERLIN (*assistant director / key PA*): Anytime we film outside the LA boundaries, Jeff, the producers, the directing team, and Chris and Steve were so kind to upgrade me to assistant director. I got a Director's Guild nomination for the "Las Vegas" episode. That was an amazing thing for my career.

As well as writers . . .

WRUBEL (*writer / executive producer*): I got to work with Chris Lloyd and Steve Levitan, who, for all of their incompatibility, are two of the greatest writers/producers in TV comedy history. I got to write for one of the great ensembles in TV comedy history. Our directors, editors, sound mixers, casting director all won Emmys. So there's the pride of being connected to something that was acknowledged to be of quality. But beyond that— despite their friction—Chris and Steve created a working environment where people were kind to each other and supportive of each other. There was a fundamental decency in those offices and on that stage, and it was because of the two guys at the top. There was a little bit of madness, yes, but it was more often than not a joyful place to spend a decade of my life.

. . . and those in front of the camera . . .

FERGUSON (*Mitchell Pritchett*): When you go through a shared experience like this, the only people who really understand what that is are the other people you've gone through that with. That means the cast and the crew. It's been a very profound eleven years.

WINTER (*Alex Dunphy*): I think I've learned a lot. I've gone through a lot. I've changed a lot. I think that's due to being on the show and the environment I'm in. Twenty years from now, this will be something that I look at very fondly, but also as a learning experience, not in a negative way but in life. This is a big thing to do as a kid and experience and meet all these people. I am so very grateful for that.

HYLAND (*Haley Dunphy*): *Modern Family* has taught me to stand up for myself, that I have a voice and my opinion matters. I can say no to things. It has opened doors for me like nothing did in the past.

VERGARA (*Gloria Delgado-Pritchett*): I'm so grateful. I thought I was going to be on a good show, but never something like *Modern Family*. It never occurred to me that I was going to be able to be part of something so amazing, not with the way I sound. It changed my life. It changed my family's life. I've been able to have so much fun and make so many businesses out of it.

O'NEILL (*Jay Pritchett*): I was never in a show that was accepted by my peers as well as this one. I love how much people like the show. If you're doing that thing, you want that pat on the shoulder, you know?

BURRELL (*Phil Dunphy*): It's been a real blessing and luxury to wake up and come and play a character so well intended and to be around everybody. And it has afforded me family time. I got a late start with my kids, so I feel a real urgency with that. I want to be able to be around them. They're nine and seven, and I'm fifty-two. Not the latest start, but a late-ish start. If I hadn't done this show, I would be out there looking for something and taking what I could get. And that is the reality for every actor. I was here for so long and luckily. I can't believe I won the actor lottery.

A Moving Day

A well-known television sitcom director once told me soundstages exist to have life implanted in them. As each set gets broken down, each prop repurposed or stashed away, another filled with possibility takes its place. A coat of paint here, a newly constructed living room there, and with it the seeds of creation. These soundstages and the pieces they house never lose their history; they only gain more. In that way, with the sadness of loss comes the wonder in knowing that something will fill the void, something different but hopefully as impactful to the new residents of stage 5 as it has been for those departing.

Lloyd likes to recall the words engraved on a plaque outside the soundstage where they taped The Mary Tyler Moore Show *after its conclusion. "On this stage a group of friends came together and created a classic."*

LLOYD (*cocreator*): I thought that was a classy thing they did. A very succinct way to say what a privilege it is to work on a show you care about and people outside care about. If you can create something that people really esteem and have a great time doing it, then you've really licked it.

So after eleven years, what does this show leave behind?

O'NEILL (*Jay Pritchett*): There's only been two shows in the history of television to win five Emmys for best comedy. *Frasier* and us. There's only been one comedy to win four best ensemble awards for comedy from the

Screen Actors Guild: us. That's pretty good. Am I going to tell you it's the best comedy ever made? No, but I think it's right up there. There have been other great shows, *The Mary Tyler Moore Show, All in the Family, Seinfeld, Curb Your Enthusiasm*, but we're in there.

FERGUSON (*Mitchell Pritchett*): I hope that it marks the time but that it doesn't live as a time capsule. I hope that people can continue to watch these stories. I hope they're still relevant and feel as funny and fresh as they were when we first did them. I think about shows that have a certain legacy, like I love rewatching *Friends* and *Carol Burnett*. There are moments in television I feel I can always return to that bring me joy, lift my spirits, and make me feel something. I hope we do that for other people.

CORRIGAN (*writer / executive producer*): For a lot of families, we were a moment where they could all spend time together laughing, having fun, and forgetting what struggles they were going through. It definitely affected me realizing that we were, at the end of the day, not just a funny TV show.

LAMB (*first assistant director / director*): It has changed lives, minds, and hearts. Now people know family that they wouldn't know or talk to people that they wouldn't. They aren't as hateful as they would have been, and there's no way for me to overstate that.

MCPHERSON (*ABC Entertainment president*): When you work in the business for as long as I did, it's surprising that there are only a few projects that you hold dear to your heart. People still ask me about *Modern Family* even today. It was an extraordinary experience, and I'm happy for all those people involved and all the ways it affected so many people's lives. Whether it was the first show they watched with their kids or a special bond with their wife watching it or their father. No matter who you are, it really captured something about family that really spoke to people.

STONESTREET (*Cam Tucker*): The blueprint of the show is being a family show, and families are universal, independent of borders, creed, culture, race, and religion. We are a mirror that holds up. I have nine-year-old fans.

They weren't born when the show started. If the show is resonating with a new flock of nine-year-olds, I think we're good, we're timeless.

VERGARA (*Gloria Delgado-Pritchett*): We were a show that was able to bring people together. One of the most fascinating things for me was meeting people, a grandmother with a grandchild, talking about the same episode. That rarely happens. Men would watch, gay people would watch, young people would watch. I think that's what made it so special. I don't think there are that many shows written that can bring the whole family together.

BURRELL (*Phil Dunphy*): I was in a hotel room, and the guy who was refilling the minibar was explaining that his parents had split up and he had stepbrothers and sisters and they were much younger than him and he didn't know them and the family was estranged, but they were getting to know each other sitting down and watching the show together, starting to feel like they were a whole family. I found that really genuinely touching. It made me cry quite a bit to think that all this ridiculousness amounts to that sometimes.

WINTER (*Alex Dunphy*): It's all reflections of everyone's family in general; everyone can see somebody or something in themselves in our show, which is really special. And I think that's a really great thing that we've been able to do. And so I hope our legacy will continue to show that.

O'SHANNON (*writer / executive producer*): People often say, "It's the end of an era," when a show goes off the air. In this case, it may literally be true. For a sitcom to capture the public's attention the way *Modern Family* did, you need two things: content that appeals to many kinds of people and a platform that reaches those people. In 2009, network television could still galvanize viewers in a way it struggles to now. The public has so many options and the audience is so fragmented, it's increasingly difficult to cast that wide a net. When *Modern Family* goes, it may take with it the way we used to watch sitcoms, starting back when America would obsess over *I Love Lucy* every week.

BOWEN (*Claire Dunphy*): I'm proud to have been on a show that was dedicated to delivering quality entertainment with the minimum amount of cheap humor. Everyone said how network comedy TV was dying. We've now moved to dead. We're the last elephant. I'm proud to have represented, on the elephant's last walk across the Sahara, something respectful that a whole family can watch together. That's important to me, especially now. That we could represent a family in all its interesting and quirky ways and have a good political message, which is a bonus.

LEVITAN (*cocreator*): I'm proud of creating a well-respected show that seems to have brought a lot of people joy. There is so much darkness in the world today and so much content which reflects the negative side of humanity that, as corny as it may sound, I take great pride in contributing a little bit of happiness and laughter into the world.

LLOYD (*cocreator*): We found a way to a show that was a tiny bit wholesome but mostly funny with interesting characters that could make adults laugh and children laugh, too. We made it okay to watch comedy again on TV with your family. For some reason, it appealed across the board. That's meaningful to me because those people, the parents as they become grandparents and the kids as they become adults, will remember having watched *Modern Family* with warmth and hopefully will continue to watch those episodes with that nostalgic attachment that they remember fond times in their household with that show. And if there are people out there with whom the show serves that purpose, then I am very proud of that.

LEVITAN (*cocreator*): Let's face it, goodbyes suck. The only time they don't is when you can't stand the people you're leaving. Unfortunately, I love the people to whom I have to say goodbye; the fictional people who filled our screens for these past eleven seasons and, most of all, the real people who helped make it all happen. Having worked in this business for almost thirty years, I know how rare this experience is. The chance of any of us being part of another *Modern Family,* especially in this new digital age where viewers have endless choices, is smaller than the chance of Phil finally fixing that step.

Modern Family currently airs in more than two hundred countries—places like Italy, Sweden, Israel, and India. Even the Vatican (a TV market unto its own) watches *Modern Family* (I think that would make Mitch and Cam smile). What this tells me is that, no matter where you live, families are families. We may live in different types of buildings or have different forms of government, but at the end of the day, what people want most is to raise their children safely and connect with the ones they love. I will miss so much: the laughter in the writers' room, the crew cracking up hearing a scene for the first time, Jesse's imitations of Ed O'Neill, Ty's delight in doing bits between takes, Sofía's failed attempts at the English language, and so much more. It's a rare thing to realize one's dream, but that's what *Modern Family* has been for me and for so many others—a beautiful dream. We've worked hard, we're so proud of what we've done, so with sadness and with joy, it's time to say, "Goodbye."

Finale: Parts 1 and 2

Early on a February morning, during a frigid LA winter where temperatures can dip below seventy, I find myself back on stage 5. As of today, *Modern Family* has less than two weeks left of production. I can only imagine the emotional state inside. Gail Mancuso, the final episode's director, calls it a funeral march. If so, then I now join the funeral procession to celebrate the life and passing of a piece of television history.

Nearing the stage, I bump into Rico Rodriguez and share a happy "bro hug." Nothing can break this young man's contagious joy, not even his impending unemployment. At base camp, Leslie Merlin greets me with a big, warm hug that has less to do with seeing me and more to do with the march of time that has hit her so hard. "The biggest commitment I made in this life was to this show," she tells me. Over the course of the next week, the much-loved organizer and manager will receive loving support from virtually everyone. "When you go through a shared experience like this the only people who really understand are the ones you've gone through it with," says Jesse Tyler Ferguson.

Ed O'Neill personally feels grateful for this last go-round. "It's a countdown. You ease into it," he says. "I really appreciate that. I never got that with *Married with Children*."

Indeed, he didn't. That long-running series was canceled in the off-season, without a thank-you, a goodbye gift, or a job-well-done. In fact, O'Neill didn't even know the show had received the ax until a newly married couple, in the parking lot of a bed-and-breakfast in his Youngstown hometown, informed him. "She was still in her wedding dress," he recalls. "I took them inside, bought them a little champagne, and wished them well. I'd have rather heard it from fans than executives with another agenda."

Yesterday, cast and crew assembled for the final table read. On everyone's seat, assistants had placed a copy of the script along with a mini-pack of tissues. In retrospect, perhaps they should have left two. With about four pages left, Julie Bowen's voice became the first to crack. And with it the walls started to crumble. When they reached the end, no one knew what to do. O'Neill then stood up and applauded. Everyone quickly followed suit. As the tears flowed, the three Dunphy children, Sarah Hyland, Ariel Winter, and Nolan Gould, embraced in a rib-breaking lock. Executive producer Jeff Morton stared at the ground like a punished child, knowing that if he made eye contact with anyone, he'd bawl like a baby.

Eight-year-old Jeremy Maguire ended up doing exactly that, at his first table read no less. Typically, young children don't participate in readings. Aubrey Anderson-Emmons had started only a few years ago. She, similarly, had an emotional initiation her first time. Somehow she'd accidentally received the wrong script, which proved embarrassing when she couldn't follow along. "I started to cry," recalls Anderson-Emmons. "Jesse asked, 'What's wrong?' and then looked at my script. He gave me another one and then showed me where my line was. That's Jesse." Cocreator Christopher Lloyd comes to Maguire's rescue here, with the most common commodity on set these days, a hug (saying "I love you" places a close second).

Today's morning shoot takes place on location, at a house about a half block west of the Fox lot. Here, Mitchell and Cam are hosting a housewarming party at their new digs. The nursery room for their new baby, Rexford (named after a Beverly Hills street), and their karaoke room, however, remain on set.

Peering inside, I'm instantly accosted by a glaring, six-foot-tall Cabbage Patch doll, a disturbing presence, biding its time here while waiting for Stephen King to write a horror book about him. Seriously, he could pierce souls. Fortunately, he has only a small part to play in this episode as a housewarming gift from Jay. From there he'll retire to the props room, where he'll manage to scare me everytime I enter.

Bowen fortunately scurries me away from Satan's hypnotic trance. After a short conversation, she asks if I'm tired of all the weeping and sobbing like she is. *Not yet*, I think to myself, but I hold the right to be later. Ty Burrell, still the nicest man alive, stops by next. He tells me that he and his family will be moving to Utah soon. At this point in his career, he thankfully no longer has to hustle for work in LA. He gets to choose.

Cocreator Steve Levitan gives direction to the cast. This marks his last episode. The odd-even system he and Lloyd created leaves Lloyd with the finale. While the entire writing staff, including both dads, brainstormed ideas together in one room, they eventually separated into two rooms to build their respective storylines.

Lloyd's half proves particularly challenging, enough so that when cameras begin to roll on the episode, the writers still don't have a completed shooting script. "We wanted to take the curse off of endings," discloses Lloyd. That led to as many as five different versions, such as parties for Manny or Alex's departure, before settling on Mitchell and Cam's big move to Kansas. "You try to generate enthusiasm," Lloyd reveals. "You ask what are the main relationships to focus on? Who deserves a goodbye? You can't do everything to everyone."

They finally settle on a novel idea pitched by Lloyd. What if the big emotional goodbye occurs at the episode's beginning instead of the end? "It's unconventional, starting with something funny and emotional," Lloyd says. "People are used to stories building to an end. But we found a good balance of emotion and comedy."

While the idea captivated Lloyd's room, Levitan felt less beguiled, preferring a more traditional build to an emotional climax. The showrunners divergent and innovative tastes simply don't gibe. But with no control over Lloyd's episode, Levitan has little recourse here, other than sharing his ideas. "I'm still trying to affect what happens next week a little bit," he confesses.

Today, however, he holds the reins as showrunner and director. "I look around and take it all in," he shares. "These people have been such a part of my life and there's going to be a day very, very soon when this doesn't exist and I don't have that place to go to." At the same time, he feels the pressure will be off after Friday. "I won't have anything I need to do other than edit this show. And I won't be thinking of anymore *Modern Family* stories."

In a moment, he'll direct a scene in which Mitchell, making a harmless joke about Cam during a thank-you toast, gets blindsided by a passive-aggressive swipe courtesy of his husband, upset about having to turn down his dream job in Kansas because he thinks Mitchell won't want to go.

                    MITCHELL
     And thank you to my wonderful husband
     who led the charge in making all this
     possible. I couldn't be happier right
     now, and it's all because of him. Now,
     if I could just get him to give up
     hogging the covers—

                    CAMERON
               (sudden outburst)
     'Cause I haven't given up enough for
     you!

The writers have kicked the can on a Kansas plot for years, to the point of labeling it "Modern Farmily." Having seen Cam's mom (Celia Weston), dad (Barry Corbin), and sister (Dana Powell) in multiple episodes, the storyline opens doors, including a potential spinoff with a built-in supporting cast should they ever opt to go that way.*

When Eric Stonestreet perfectly captures Cam's feelings in a few short takes, Levitan levels his enthusiasm with his sense of humor. "That was perfect. Let's do it six more times." Ferguson, meanwhile, gets his own moment in the next scene when Claire congratulates him for announcing to everyone that he'd gladly move to Kansas.

                    MITCHELL
     Everybody was looking at me—what the
     fuck was I supposed to say?

That swear word fits perfectly but will never make it on air of course, meeting the same fate as Lily's swear word in season 3's "Little Bo Bleep."

As the scene concludes, everyone follows the long-standing tradition of applauding a guest star or day player's last scene. Here, longtime stand-in,

---

* Levitan originally wanted Melissa McCarthy to play Cam's sister, Pameron. Stonestreet, well aware that McCarthy's skyrocketing career would make her unavailable for multiple episodes, pushed for his friend Powell.

actor Charlie Trainer, gets the treatment. Next week, it'll be Cousin Pete. Played by hair stylist Kelly Kline, Cousin Pete has popped up in numerous episodes throughout the years as an inside joke, an Alfred Hitchcock cameo.

Back on stage 5, the crew puts the finishing touches on Mitchell and Cam's karaoke room, for a later scene in which the couple will harmonize to Lionel Richie and Diana Ross's *Endless Love*. The room came into existence in mere days. Next week, the crew will construct the body of a plane. Give them a week and they could build a metropolis.

For these last episodes, the show shoots about eight pages a day, without going into overtime. It's impressive stuff. As a result, Levitan requires only a half day on Friday. Because President's Day will cost Lloyd a full day of production next week, he comes in early on Friday to use the other half of Levitan's day.

Mancuso now directs. Having done the most episodes, it only seems fitting. It doesn't hurt that the cast and crew love her, too. "We couldn't think of anyone we'd rather have do it," says script supervisor Iwona Sapienza.

Mancuso's first scenes involve the Dunphy children. In one, Dylan and Haley move into Mitchell and Cam's old condo. In another, Haley and Alex reminisce and conspire to play one last practical joke on their brother. One of the writers calls attention to an Easter egg in the scene—a moving box misspelled "nick nacks." It fits Haley and her husband to a tee, as does Haley informing the family later that they only have one book to move.

Every day, writers pop in and out of video village to watch and suggest ideas. Currently, the multitalented Elaine Ko stands guard. Later Jeffrey Richman stops by. "This cast has elevated everything into the stratosphere," Richman says. "As a writer, you could sit at your computer and go, "This is funny and Julie's going to kill with it or I can't wait for Ed or Eric to say it."

Jay's reflections about family serve as the episode's and series bookends.

```
              JAY (V.O.)
A lot can happen to a family over
the years. New additions . . . New
struggles . . . You don't always mark
the moments because you're too busy
taking care of life. Best you can
```

        do sometimes is remind yourself to
        cherish every single—

As fruitful as the morning proves, the shoot runs long, forcing Levitan to start later than promised. Although irritated, he lets it go because it doesn't matter anymore. Besides, the scene currently on camera, an intimate conversation between Jay and Gloria about their evolving relationship, has proved problematic.

Sofía Vergara finds herself battling the English language, straining to decipher the right words to emphasize. Meanwhile, in mastering Jay's emotion, O'Neill keeps tripping over his lines. Things could quickly go south late on a Friday night, but they don't. Both actors know each other so well and feel so safe performing together that they keep regrouping without incident. "If he wants to do something extra I stay with him and if I want to do something he stays with me," says Vergara.

In some ways, Vergara, with her language barriers, presents a master class in acting. Because she never reads the same line the same way twice, each take plays differently. She can wildly miss a line's meaning once and then nail it in an unexpected fashion the next time.

For Levitan, this last scene doesn't feel like an end. "When I finished with Jesse and Eric yesterday it wasn't like, oh I'm done. All the emotion will be set for next week." In addition, he just learned that Elizabeth Banks has agreed to come in and do a final pickup scene next week as Sal, meaning he'll get to shoot one last scene.

For the actors, next week will mark the end of their relationship with their characters. Winter's already taking auditions. Hyland's producing a pilot loosely based on her life. Ferguson has rehearsals for a Broadway show. Everyone's exploring what comes next.

Writers have started taking meetings, something they'd have done regardless of the show's destiny. Their assistants, like Dan Vallancourt, will try to get their own scripts off the ground. Meanwhile, executive producer Jeff Morton looks for a new show, one in which he can keep the production crew together. He'll take almost anything if it means, as he says, "I can bring 120 of my friends."

Everyone wants set mementos, but prop master Rick Ladomade has been told that Fox wants most of its set decorations back. Really? Even that autographed picture of David Soul? The miniature ceramic Shelley Long and Phil's-osophy book? And what about disturbed Cabbage Patch man? I hope they crate him like they do the Ark of the Covenant in *Raiders of the Lost Ark*.

The last time I see Levitan occurs in the halls of the darkened Dunphy house at day's end. I'm searching for the doorjamb tracing Gould's and Winter's height growth but get lost in the memories of photos taken from the actors' real lives, episodes, and pretend events. Claire Bennett's production design did indeed make this pretend house feel like a home.

Levitan and I by happenstance converge at the doorjamb. He shines his phone so I can take pictures. "I gave it my all," he discloses. "I can say that I was here to the end. That took a lot of discipline and hard work." And he has a lot to show for it.

The following Tuesday, the cast reassembles for the final week. Digital Utility Sean Kehoe shouts a hashtag for the day to Sapienza, part of their own inside joke: #Fourdays. Today, production starts with an emotional punch: the cast goodbye at the episode's head. The ensemble's downcast demeanor suggests that they dread the real emotion of it. No one's bouncing into position. They make little jokes and small talk, but their body language betrays them.

On the one hand, people seem ready to move on. Eleven years at anything takes a toll. But the fear of letting go, well, that's a different story. As cast members rehearse forming a ball of love within an embrace, everyone else whips out their smartphones to capture the moment.

Watching the filming of emotional scenes makes you wonder how actors keep their game elevated take after take. Surely the thrill filters out after hug number seven? Not here, at least not to the naked eye. It makes you wonder, would it be a better world if we all got to practice goodbyes?

"No matter how much you're ready mentally, you're not ready mentally," says boom operator/sound mixer Serge Popovic. To inject humor into the somber moment, Dylan enters at the scene's end, mistaking the gathering as his birthday celebration. This season Reid Ewing became a cast regular, giving him the only security he ever had in the series. After this, he plans to continue acting. If that falls through, he may go back to nursing. As other cast members have said: always have a backup plan.

For casting director Greenberg, watching the finale echoes his memories of *Cheers*' and *Frasier*'s finales, shows he worked on that also lasted eleven seasons. "I'm familiar with this feeling but it doesn't make it easier," he admits. Over the course of 250 episodes, he hired more than 1,350 guest actors for the show, an impressive number that only comes up short when compared to the number of actors who auditioned for the pilot: 1,364. Sometimes the longest journeys start from the largest steps.

After lunch, which I'm told union rules require must last exactly 42 minutes, the cast returns to rehearse goodbye number two, another send-off that will fail to take flight, not that the characters won't try.

```
                   PHIL
      It's going to take me a minute to
      ramp back up to all the emotion.
               (instantly sobbing)
      —I'm there.
```

Every time Burrell does this line, everyone in video village cracks up. "It's been eleven years of comedy school here," says camera operator Trey Clinesmith. "I had to learn how to operate a camera and laugh."

While the crew sets up lighting, the cast chills in the Dunphy's den. Vergara, who always seems to be cold, wears her typical Patagonia down parka. Bowen holds Maguire's arms and lets him run up her legs and flip over. Later, O'Neill tells him that after the last shot on Friday, he can twist the fake wedding ring off of O'Neill's finger, as he likes to do, one final time and then keep it. Maguire squeals with joy. Just don't tell the Fox props department. Stonestreet suggests to Ko that they plan a group dinner for everyone in August, when each season's first table read typically would occur.

To complete the triumvirate of today's pathos, Manny and Luke have a scene in which they express their love in words and then embrace in a bear hug. During rehearsal, surrounded by countless crew members, an eerie silence pervades, as if everyone's embarrassed spying on a private moment. Perhaps in some ways, we are. Cast and crew must feel numb by day's end. I do.

For #ThreeDays, production shuttles to a frozen tundra ice rink in the valley. Vergara's down parka would be great about now, but only Bowen and Ferguson have scenes here. In one, their characters steal back an ice skating trophy from their childhood days as the skating pair "Fire and Nice." Watching them off-screen, you get a palpable sense of the loss the actors feel. It reminds me of one of Bowen and Ferguson's filmed hugs yesterday in which Ferguson put his hands lovingly on Bowen's cheeks at the take's end. It felt bigger than the scene.

On the ice, filming concludes with a reenactment of one of their childhood duets. Crawling across the ice toward each other looks and sounds wrong, which the characters come to realize themselves.

                    MITCHELL
          This is more sexual than I remember.

Claire spins him around then bends him
over and HOWLS.

                    CLAIRE
          Yeah, I'm starting to think we might
          have won for the wrong reasons.

Looking at people like second assistant director Ceci Mak and unit production manager Matt Baker, I wonder what must be going through their minds. "We'll all be different hereafter, forever different," says Lloyd. That sentiment applies to the show and their own lives. "It's a celebration and a funeral with people you cherish, that make you laugh, but it's also a cause for bereavement."

This afternoon, Burrell and Bowen have a final scene with their pretend children, who zip in and out, each in a state of flux before disappearing and leaving an empty nest behind, for the show as well as for production. "The family as a unit saying goodbye to the family as a unit," says Lloyd. "It's sad to feel the change but exciting for the new journey." Here, during one of the takes, dammit all if Bowen's voice doesn't crack again, just enough in that distinctive rasp of hers, to make your heart cry.

                    CLAIRE
          They're really leaving. What do we
          do?

                    PHIL
What people have always done—leave
the porch light on. They come back.

Lloyd likes how the episode implies what comes next, without defining the details of change. "What didn't feel right was THE END," he says. "I'd rather leave it open-ended. Let the audience take over writing and imagining what will happen."

So what will happen? On the show, the characters will remain forever a family, spread out but connected and loved. While their past will live on in reruns, their future will come from fans' hopes and dreams.

Finally on Friday, when the end arrives, everyone joins in the funeral procession. Cast and crew, emotionally exhausted by week's end, break out in unison, singing Green Day's "Time of Your Life." Later, they gather outside stage 5 for a group photograph and drone video. To commemorate their accomplishment, they hold parties the next two nights. And then as fast as it began, it ends.

Rather than try to sum up this experience for them, I leave the show's final say to Jay, and to everyone who created the laughter and tears for eleven years.

                  JAY (V.O.)
Life is full of change: some big,
some small. I learned a long time
ago, you can fight it, or you can
try to make the best of it. And
that's all a lot easier if you've
got people who love you helping you
face whatever life throws at you. At
least that's what helps me sleep at
night.

EXT. JAY & GLORIA'S HOUSE - NIGHT

All the household lights turn off.

EXT. MITCHELL & CAMERON'S DUPLEX - NIGHT

All the household lights turn off.

EXT. DUNPHY HOUSE - NIGHT

All the household lights turn off. A beat.
The porch light turns back on.

                    END OF SERIES

Acknowledgments

This book represents the collaborative efforts of myself, friends, family, peers, mentors, people I admire, people I've never met, people I'd rather avoid, and people no longer here.

First, this book would not be a book—nor I an author—without Josh Karp. Josh put the bug in my ear to stretch beyond myself and do the writing I wanted to do versus what I had been paid to do all my life. He made the inconceivable seem not only possible but inevitable. For that, I will be eternally grateful, as I tell him ad nauseam and will continue to for years to come.

I want to thank my agent, Jonathan Lyons, for believing in me and helping me make the leap from journalist to author. Years ago, a writing teacher told me, "There are no stupid questions, except for the ones never asked." I've tested Jonathan to try to prove that wrong, and to his credit, he has hung in there. His advice has been priceless. To Marc Resnick and St. Martin's Press, for taking on my passion and mishmash of words, and helping guide me toward my north star. For a first book, I couldn't have asked for a better editor, collaborator, and publisher.

Special thanks to some of television's legendary comedy writers and performers—whose shows I grew up with and whose work inspired me in ways that exceed words: James Brooks, Glen and Les Charles, Mike Farrell, Joe Keenan, David Lee, Ken Levine, Bob Newhart, and Dan Wilcox. Special thanks to Michael Elias, whose counsel I'm so happy to have, and Martin Lewis, who has mentored me for years.

To David Isaacs, for spending time with me and starting me on an amazing journey to *Modern Family* by introducing me to Peter Casey; and to Mr. Casey, for his kindness and friendship, which led me to the *Frasier* family, and in particular Chris Lloyd.

When I first broached the idea of this book to Chris, he emailed, "I imagine you would encounter a very cooperative writing staff / cast / crew on the project." That statement epitomizes Chris as a writer to me, in that he can take the simplest of responses and transform them into these seamless, erudite, poetic, and often humorous statements. I couldn't ask for a better foreword, not to mention the doors he opened for me with cast and crew, the countless hours and effort he gave in support of this project, and his friendship. To share bound pages is more than a feather in my cap, it's the whole bird.

Steve Levitan, meanwhile, didn't know me from Adam, Isaac, or Jacob, but he entrusted me to try to recount the history of eleven years of his life, giving me invaluable unlimited access, source material, and time. I was told early on by writers on the show that he saves everything, and apparently he does. Without his participation, I could not have told the story and wouldn't have enjoyed telling it as much as I did.

Jeff Greenberg is an elite casting director, but to me he was an adviser, sounding board, connector, and open book. I'm glad I got to share some of his contributions here for everyone to read. I hope to pay forward one day what he did for me.

To the *Modern Family* cast, for their talents, reflections, and most important, for being themselves, thank you. Without their honesty and humor, this project would not have happened. I will thank them personally and in depth privately, but for now, let me give an alphabetic shout-out to Aubrey Anderson-Emmons, Julie Bowen, Ty Burrell, Reid Ewing, Jesse Tyler Ferguson, Nolan Gould, Sarah Hyland, Jeremy Maguire, Ed O'Neill, Rico Rodriguez, Eric Stonestreet, Sofía Vergara, and Ariel Winter. I can't wait to see what they each achieve next in life.

To everyone from the *Modern Family* writers' room who helped me with logistics and who shared their fascinating processes, memories, embarrassments, and inspirations: Jack Burditt, Natalie Campbell, Bianca Chan, Vali Chandrasekaran, Cindy Chupack, Jerry Collins, Paul Corrigan, Sameer Gardezi, Daisy Gardner, Andy Gordon, Abraham Higginbotham, Elaine Ko, Stephen Lloyd, Clint McCray, Morgan Murphy, Dan O'Shannon, Matt Plonsker, Jon Pollack, Jessica Poter, Jeffrey Richman,

Christy Stratton-Mann, Brad Walsh, Ryan Walls, Bill Wrubel, and Danny Zuker.

To Jeff Morton, who helped produce this book, much like the show, in many ways by pointing me in certain directions and sharing his razor-sharp memory. So many people I spoke with singled him out for their gratitude and careers. And to Jason Winer, so important to establishing the look, rhythm, and style of the series and who offered me whatever I needed for however long I needed it. I ended up needing a lot, and he delivered.

To the amazing production team, unsung heroes all, so instrumental to the show's and this book's success: James "Baggs" Bagdonas, Michael Bagdonas, Noah Bagdonas, Claire Bennett, Richard Berg, Stephen Brenes, Andrew Brooks, Ryan Case, Jesse Cervantes, Trey Clinesmith, Josh Elliott, Rachael Field, Kendall Foote, Joel Gelman, Allen Hooper, Abby Jenkins, Ismael "Cheese" Jimenez, Sean Kehoe (thanks for the clapper board experience), Jason Kemp, Rick Ladomade, Helena Lamb, Ceci Mak, Gabriel Mann, Leslie Merlin, Steve Miller, William Munroe, Srdjan "Serge" Popovic, Kate Riccio, Sharon Sacks, Kathia Sanchez-Aldana, Iwona Sapienza, Lisa Statman, Toby Tucker, Dan Vallancourt, Kyle Weber, and Sally Young, as well as Shawn Ryan, Shine Studio, and Michael Riley. Anyone associated with the show accidentally omitted here due to my own incompetence, I apologize.

Thank you to series guest stars who shared their experiences: Elizabeth Banks, Christian Barillas, Benjamin Bratt, Matthew Broderick, Adam Devine, Nathan Fillion, Josh Gad, Chris Geere, Peri Gilpin (xoxo), Nathan Lane, Peyton Manning, Stephen Merchant, Patton Oswalt, Chazz Palminteri, Rob Riggle, and Fred Willard. That cast would make one hell of a movie. Even better if directed by the amazing Gail Mancuso, Beth McCarthy-Miller, and Michael Spiller, who walked me through their episodes and memories.

Also, special thanks to the super kind Stephen McPherson, Samie Kim Falvey, and Claudia Lyon for providing invaluable memories from the network side.

To my friends Sam Kaplan and Luanne Brown, both über-talented writers who create on a higher plane and deeper level than myself. Without their guidance and input, this book would have resembled a junior-high journalism project with pretty pictures. That leads me to photographer Mike Larsen. How he keeps managing to exceed expectations with his camera's eye decade after decade is beyond me. He took so many good pictures of the show, making my life difficult to choose the best. That's a good problem to have. Thank you.

To friends old and new, I'm happy to write your names in print and appreciate and love each of you for your support here and through the years: Ray Cecire and Katherine Culleton, David Friedman, Brenda Robb Jenike, Mitchell Klein, Lori Little, Jeff Maxwell, Zia Munshi, Eric Piel, Jared Smith, and Traci Smolen. And to another brilliant writer, Andy Munsey, for decades of support and friendship.

To my parents, thank you for having faith in me, and to my siblings, thank you, too. In particular my sister, Joanne, known to the immediate world as Yale professor Joanne Freeman, but known to me as *sis*. She talked me through this whole book's *mishegas* and gave me some great ideas I'd have never thought of myself.

And to my wife, Joanne, and daughter, Olivia. Under this roof, I place a distant third in creative talent, which I state out of admiration. Jojo, what would any of this mean without you prodding, poking, and encouraging? You're a sounding board, muse, friend, and partner, each equally important in their own way. And to Olivia, dear sweet Boo, as your father, I am proud of who you are and can't wait to continue to see who you will become. I apologize for the late writing nights and thank you for your ideas. Your hugs are the best currency, and our daddy-and-daughter adventures are some of the best times. Life can be challenging, but that makes it more worthwhile. Love to both of you.

The Family

Creators

Steve Levitan
Chris Lloyd

Cast

Ed O'Neill: Jay Pritchett
Sofía Vergara: Gloria Delgado-Pritchett
Rico Rodriguez: Manny Delgado
Jeremy Maguire: Joe Pritchett

Jesse Tyler Ferguson: Mitchell Pritchett
Eric Stonestreet: Cameron Tucker
Aubrey Anderson-Emmons: Lily Tucker-Pritchett

Ty Burrell: Phil Dunphy
Julie Bowen: Claire Dunphy
Sarah Hyland: Haley Dunphy
Reid Ewing: Dylan Marshall
Ariel Winter: Alex Dunphy

Nolan Gould: Luke Dunphy

Producers

Jeffrey Morton: Executive producer
Andrew Brooks: Associate producer
Rachael Field: Associate producer
Kathia Sanchez-Aldana: Associate producer
Kyle Weber: Associate producer
Sally Young: Production manager / producer

Directors

Jason Winer: Pilot director / director / executive producer
Gail Mancuso: Director
Beth McCarthy-Miller: Director
Michael Spiller: Director

Casting

Jeff Greenberg: Casting director
Allen Hooper: Casting associate

Writers' Room

Jack Burditt: Writer / executive producer
Bianca Chan: Writers' assistant
Vali Chandrasekaran: Writer / executive producer
Cindy Chupack: Writer / coexecutive producer
Jerry Collins: Writer
Paul Corrigan: Writer / executive producer
Sameer Gardezi: Writer

Daisy Gardner: Writer
Andy Gordon: Writer / coexecutive producer
Abraham Higginbotham: Writer / executive producer
Elaine Ko: Writer / executive producer
Stephen Lloyd: Writer / executive producer
Clint McCray: Script coordinator
Morgan Murphy: Writer / coexecutive producer
Dan O'Shannon: Writer / executive producer
Matt Plonsker: Writers' assistant
Jon Pollack: Writer / executive producer
Jessica Poter: Writer
Jeffrey Richman: Writer / executive producer
Christy Stratton: Writer / consulting producer
Ryan Walls: Writer / supervising producer
Brad Walsh: Writer / executive producer
Bill Wrubel: Writer / executive producer
Danny Zuker: Writer / executive producer

Production Crew

James Bagdonas: Director of photography / director
Claire Bennett: Production designer / art director
Richard Berg: Production designer
Ryan Case: Editor/director
Trey Clinesmith: Camera operator
Josh Elliott: On-set dresser
Kendall Foote: Set PA
Jim Hensz: Director / assistant director
Abby Jenkins: Production coordinator
Ismael "Cheese" Jimenez: Second-second assistant director
Sean Kehoe: Digital utility
Jason Kemp: First assistant director
Rick Ladomade: Prop master
Helena Lamb: First assistant director / director
Gabriel Mann: Musician/composer

LESLIE MERLIN: Assistant director / key PA
STEVE MILLER: Assistant prop master
WILLIAM MUNROE: Boom operator / utility sound
SERGE POPOVIC: Boom operator
KATE RICCIO: Production liaison
MICHAEL RILEY: Shine Studio
SHARON SACKS: Studio teacher
IWONA SAPIENZA: Script supervisor / director
ALISA STATMAN: Director / assistant director
TOBY TUCKER: Camera operator

Episodes

Season 1

1. Pilot
2. The Bicycle Thief
3. Come Fly with Me
4. The Incident
5. Coal Digger
6. Run for Your Wife
7. En Garde
8. Great Expectations
9. Fizbo
10. Undeck the Halls
11. Up All Night
12. Not in My House
13. Fifteen Percent
14. Moon Landing
15. My Funky Valentine
16. Fears
17. Truth Be Told
18. Starry Night
19. Game Changer
20. Benched
21. Travels with Scout
22. Airport 2010
23. Hawaii
24. Family Portrait

Season 2

25. 1. The Old Wagon
26. 2. The Kiss
27. 3. Earthquake
28. 4. Strangers on a Treadmill
29. 5. Unplugged
30. 6. Halloween
31. 7. Chirp
32. 8. Manny Get Your Gun
33. 9. Mother Tucker
34. 10. Dance Dance Revelation
35. 11. Slow Down Your Neighbors
36. 12. Our Children, Ourselves
37. 13. Caught in the Act
38. 14. Bixby's Back

39. 15. Princess Party
40. 16. Regrets Only
41. 17. Two Monkeys and a Panda
42. 18. Boys' Night
43. 19. The Musical Man

44. 20. Someone to Watch Over Lily
45. 21. Mother's Day
46. 22. Good Cop Bad Dog
47. 23. See You Next Fall
48. 24. The One That Got Away

Season 3

49. 1. Dude Ranch
50. 2. When Good Kids Go Bad
51. 3. Phil on Wire
52. 4. Door to Door
53. 5. Hit and Run
54. 6. Go Bullfrogs!
55. 7. Treehouse
56. 8. After the Fire
57. 9. Punkin Chunkin
58. 10. Express Christmas
59. 11. Lifetime Supply
60. 12. Egg Drop

61. 13. Little Bo Bleep
62. 14. Me? Jealous?
63. 15. Aunt Mommy
64. 16. Virgin Territory
65. 17. Leap Day
66. 18. Send Out the Clowns
67. 19. Election Day
68. 20. The Last Walt
69. 21. Planes, Trains, and Cars
70. 22. Disneyland
71. 23. Tableau Vivant
72. 24. Baby on Board

Season 4

73. 1. Bringing Up Baby
74. 2. Schooled
75. 3. Snip
76. 4. The Butler's Escape
77. 5. Open House of Horrors
78. 6. Yard Sale
79. 7. Arrested
80. 8. Mistery Date
81. 9. When a Tree Falls
82. 10. Diamond in the Rough
83. 11. New Year's Eve
84. 12. Party Crasher

85. 13. Fulgencio
86. 14. A Slight at the Opera
87. 15. Heart Broken
88. 16. Bad Hair Day
89. 17. Best Men
90. 18. The Wow Factor
91. 19. The Future Dunphys
92. 20. Flip-Flop
93. 21. Career Day
94. 22. My Hero
95. 23. Games People Play
96. 24. Goodnight Gracie

Season 5

97. 1. Suddenly, Last Summer
98. 2. First Days
99. 3. Larry's Wife
100. 4. Farm Strong
101. 5. The Late Show
102. 6. The Help
103. 7. A Fair to Remember
104. 8. ClosetCon '13
105. 9. The Big Game
106. 10. The Old Man & the Tree
107. 11. And One to Grow On
108. 12. Under Pressure
109. 13. Three Dinners
110. 14. iSpy
111. 15. The Feud
112. 16. Spring-A-Ding-Fling
113. 17. Other People's Children
114. 18. Las Vegas
115. 19. A Hard Jay's Night
116. 20. Australia
117. 21. Sleeper
118. 22. Message Received
119. 23. The Wedding, Part 1
120. 24. The Wedding, Part 2

Season 6

121. 1. The Long Honeymoon
122. 2. Do Not Push
123. 3. The Cold
124. 4. Marco Polo
125. 5. Won't You Be Our Neighbor
126. 6. Halloween 3: AwesomeLand
127. 7. Queer Eyes, Full Hearts
128. 8. Three Turkeys
129. 9. Strangers in the Night
130. 10. Haley's 21st Birthday
131. 11. The Day We Almost Died
132. 12. The Big Guns
134. 13. Rash Decisions
134. 14. Valentine's Day 4: Twisted Sister
135. 15. Fight or Flight
136. 16. Connection Lost
137. 17. Closet? You'll Love It!
138. 18. Spring Break
139. 19. Grill, Interrupted
140. 20. Knock 'Em Down
141. 21. Integrity
142. 22. Patriot Games
143. 23. Crying Out Loud
144. 24. American Skyper

Season 7

145. 1. Summer Lovin'
146. 2. The Day Alex Left for College
147. 3. The Closet Case
148. 4. She Crazy

149. 5. The Verdict
150. 6. The More You Ignore Me
151. 7. Phil's Sexy, Sexy House
152. 8. Clean Out Your Junk Drawer
153. 9. White Christmas
154. 10. Playdates
155. 11. Spread Your Wings
156. 12. Clean for a Day
157. 13. Thunk in the Trunk
158. 14. The Storm

159. 15. I Don't Know How She Does It
160. 16. The Cover-Up
161. 17. Express Yourself
162. 18. The Party
163. 19. Man Shouldn't Lie
164. 20. Promposal
165. 21. Crazy Train
166. 22. Double Click

Season 8

167. 1. A Tale of Three Cities
168. 2. A Stereotypical Day
169. 3. Blindsided
170. 4. Weathering Heights
171. 5. Halloween 4: The Revenge of Rod Skyhook
172. 6. Grab It
173. 7. Thanksgiving Jamboree
174. 8. The Alliance
175. 9. Snow Ball
176. 10. Ringmaster Keifth
177. 11. Sarge & Pea

178. 12. Do You Believe in Magic
179. 13. Do It Yourself
180. 14. Heavy Is the Head
181. 15. Finding Fizbo
182. 16. Basketball
183. 17. Pig Moon Rising
184. 18. Five Minutes
185. 19. Frank's Wedding
186. 20. All Things Being Equal
187. 21. Alone Time
188. 22. The Graduates

Season 9

189. 1. Lake Life
190. 2. The Long Goodbye
191. 3. Catch of the Day
192. 4. Sex, Lies & Kickball
193. 5. It's the Great Pumpkin, Phil Dunphy

194. 6. Ten Years Later
195. 7. Winner Winner Turkey Dinner
196. 8. Brushes with Celebrity
197. 9. Tough Love
198. 10. No Small Feet

199. 11. He Said, She Shed
200. 12. Dear Beloved Family
201. 13. In Your Head
202. 14. Written in the Stars
203. 15. Spanks for the Memories
204. 16. Wine Weekend

205. 17. Royal Visit
206. 18. Daddy Issues
207. 19. CHiPs and Salsa
208. 20. Mother!
209. 21. The Escape
210. 22. Clash of Swords

Season 10

211. 1. I Love a Parade
212. 2. Kiss and Tell
213. 3. A Sketchy Area
214. 4. Torn Between Two Lovers
215. 5. Good Grief
216. 6. On the Same Paige
217. 7. Did the Chicken Cross the Road?
218. 8. Kids These Days
219. 9. Putting Down Roots
220. 10. Stuck in a Moment
221. 11. A Moving Day

222. 12. Blasts from the Past
223. 13. Whanex?
224. 14. We Need to Talk About Lily
225. 15. SuperShowerBabyBowl
226. 16. Red Alert
227. 17. The Wild
228. 18. Stand by Your Man
229. 19. Yes-Woman
230. 20. Can't Elope
231. 21. Commencement
232. 22. A Year of Birthdays

Season 11

233. 1. New Kids on the Block
234. 2. Snapped
235. 3. Perfect Pairs
236. 4. Pool Party
237. 5. The Last Halloween
238. 6. A Game of Chicken
239. 7. The Last Thanksgiving
240. 8. Tree's a Crowd
241. 9. The Last Christmas

242. 10. The Prescott
243. 11. Legacy
244. 12. Dead on a Rival
245. 13. Paris
246. 14. Spuds
247. 15. Baby Steps
248. 16. I'm Going to Miss This
249. 17. Finale Part 1
250. 18. Finale Part 2

Index